Cultures of Staff Wel
Mental Health in Schools

Cultures of Staff Wellbeing and Mental Health in Schools

Reflecting on Positive Case Studies

Edited by Stephen Waters

With a foreword by Professor Dame Alison Peacock, CEO, Chartered College of Teaching

 Open University Press

Open University Press
McGraw Hill
8th Floor, 338 Euston Road
London
England
NW1 3BH

email: enquiries@openup.co.uk
world wide web: www.openup.co.uk

First edition published 2021

A catalogue record of this book is available from the British Library

ISBN-13: 9780335248896
ISBN-10: 0335248896
eISBN: 9780335248902

Library of Congress Cataloging-in-Publication Data
CIP data applied for

Typeset by Transforma Pvt. Ltd., Chennai, India

Praise page

This book provides readers with a comparative for their context, their school setting. It allows them to be informed and reassured, with conviction about what actions are needed. Colleagues who desire to do more for staff wellbeing, now have a guidebook to proceed. Stephen Waters has cleverly captured the stories so that readers can assimilate the ones that resonate with them the most. This book exemplifies good practice and will hopefully inspire others to follow its case study leads.
David Gumbrell, Founder of *The Resilience Project*

This book is exemplary. For too long now, the profession has witnessed good teachers and leaders leaving well before their time. Most often due to a disregard shown towards mental health and a lack of attention for teacher wellbeing. I am so impressed with the work of the head teachers and schools in this book, who are evidently leading the way. The leaders referenced within this book inspire others with their compassion, humility and commitment towards staff wellbeing. This book is an outstanding reference guide for all school leaders who wish to implement a culture of wellbeing based on evidence and success. A must read!
Suneta Bagri (FCCT), Former Head teacher, Founder of
The Every Teacher Matters Project &
Cultivate Coaching & Consultancy

This book shines a spotlight on the benefits of creating a culture of staff mental health & wellbeing. The editor not only encourages the reader to engage & empower all staff to see and own their own wellbeing, but also for leaders to model self-care & the promotion of sustainable wellbeing behaviour. The all phases and key stages case studies provide ample examples of the benefits and impact of this approach and prioritisation of staff mental health and wellbeing as an antidote to the everyday stresses of life in school and any prevailing toxic leadership!
Patrick Ottley-O'Connor, Executive Headteacher

There has never been a more apposite time to highlight the role leaders have in creating and sustaining a culture of wellbeing, underpinning good mental health, in schools. This book covers a diverse range of case studies where this has been engendered, challenging thinking about how it may be achieved.
Dr Victoria Carr, Headteacher at the Woodlands Primary School, UK

A must read for any school wanting to strengthen the wellbeing of their school community. There are many books highlighting teacher stress and burnout, most of which focus on personal wellbeing strategies for individuals including self-care plans. In this book however, each case study goes deeper to suggest practical and realistic ways school leaders can improve the system and processes which may be causing teacher stress. How wonderful it is it hear 'there is another way', one of hope and possibility where teachers feel valued and empowered.

Daniela Falecki, Founder and Director Teacher Wellbeing Pty Ltd, Sydney Australia

Contents

x Contents

Foreword

It is a genuine privilege to write a foreword for this important book. My role as chief executive of the Chartered College of Teaching is to support, connect and celebrate teachers as we seek to raise the status of our profession. We need confident, kind school leaders who are able to work with their staff to create schools where academic and vocational standards are exemplary, and every individual is understood and valued in a culture of mutual respect. We need schools such as the ones you will read about here where teachers work together in a mutual collective that enables others to thrive. Schools where professional learning for colleagues is understood as what Jeremy Hannay from Three Bridges School describes as a 'nutrient', encouraging intellectual growth.

This book offers a combination of research-informed practical advice alongside powerful stories of schools where leaders have the courage and wisdom to see that wellbeing is a fundamental part of any successful school. We hear from a range of inspirational school leaders about the practical actions they have taken within their own settings. What draws all of these case studies together so importantly, is that each and every school has to 'find a way through' against the overall tide of anxiety related to system-level performance pressure. Staff wellbeing and mental health will never be helped through surface-level actions such as placing flowers in the staffroom – but a relentless leadership focus that thinks deeply about what it is like to teach, learn, lead and play within each individual school community *is* likely to bring about change for the better.

Stephen Waters' research into levels of teachers' mental ill-health illustrates an alarming backdrop of Burnout and exhaustion. Of particular concern are the numbers of teachers leaving the profession, many teachers early in their career. He begins by discussing how school leaders need to identify what colleagues are feeling in order to begin tackling issues such as workload, and also considers what could be put in place to support students in their own wellbeing. Parallels are drawn between staff experiences and those of students to situations such as bullying and harassment. What we are learning is that the culture of a school applies to every person within it. When this is a safe, positive culture, everyone benefits. Where teachers know they are valued as professionals, trusted to prioritise, and to respond to what they feel really matters, workload feels much more manageable.

Jonathan Glazzard, from the Carnegie School of Education, Leeds Beckett University, presents his research linking teacher wellbeing to pupil progress. Through interviews with teachers and students we see clearly how poor mental health impacts the atmosphere within the classroom and detracts from a shared ethos of collective purpose, becoming instead one of keeping your head down, trying not to make things worse.

The stories of leadership practice are drawn from primary, secondary and special schools and colleges. Although individual settings, context and circumstance are different, the strategies put in place are often very similar. The importance of genuinely listening is shown. Leaders who truly listen show us the importance of really understanding what is happening in order that improvements can be made. The need to offer collective leadership and to support colleagues as a team when issues arise related to behaviour is also explored. Throughout, we are treated to examples of policies, staff surveys and action plans where clear evidence of impact is described. We hear about the importance of coaching, mentoring and mutual support. Actions such as minimising stressful encounters, reducing email traffic and listening to staff about triggers that could be avoided are all presented within the context of school leaders tackling the leadership challenge of swimming against the tide of hyper-accountability. Opportunities to celebrate talent within performance reviews as opposed to 'management' are shown. There is so much that lies within the gift of the school leadership team and governing body, so many ways of making school a better place for everyone.

High-stakes accountability has undoubtedly impacted on the wellbeing of teachers. This book illustrates an alternative approach that is similar to the one in the school where I was fortunate enough to be headteacher. Removing lesson monitoring and book scrutiny and replacing them with collaborative research lesson study is an important example of removing judgement in favour of shared problem-solving to support learning. Schools that offer trust, focus on professionalism and development of talent see their results improve.

This book provides an alternative narrative about what it is possible to achieve when the leadership focuses on the health and flourishing of every individual student and member of staff within a school. Ultimately, although there is much to unsettle us and to cause us to ask important questions, within this book we have a narrative of hope. We hear from schools with the courage and vision to put their people first – the outcomes speak for themselves.

I recommend this book to you and would advise that, as you grow your career, you spend time subtly interviewing the team who will be leading you whenever you change school – you may not be lucky enough to join one of the headteachers featured here, but choosing leaders who value and care for everyone in their team makes a world of difference to a teacher's life. The job of being a teacher can be all-consuming, but it does not have to feel unmanageable or unworkable. We all deserve to be valued and to have an opportunity to contribute meaningfully within our workplace. As you will see again and again in this book, when teachers know they are respected as professionals, they are able to work together to transform. When teachers flourish, so do the children. What can possibly be a more compelling argument for change?

Professor Dame Alison Peacock
Chief Executive, Chartered College of Teaching

Acknowledgements

I owe an immense debt of gratitude and thanks to the teachers, headteachers and principals in the 32 primary, secondary and alternative provision schools who gave so generously of their time in writing a case study for this book. Many did so between March and July when the Covid-19 pandemic changed our lives immeasurably. Schools remained open for vulnerable children and children of key workers, such as hospital staff, paramedics, the police and maintenance workers and delivery teams who, usually unseen, keep our lights on and stock our supermarkets. Almost overnight, teachers moved to offering lessons online for pupils who were in lockdown at home. In these exceptional times, the authors of the case studies made space to share their experiences of developing staff wellbeing and mental health. In doing so, they have helped to create an invaluable resource of good practice in implementing a culture of staff wellbeing and mental health in schools. In every sense, this is their book.

Part 1 would not be as authoritative without the inclusion of Jonathan Glazzard's research in Chapters 4 and 5 while at the Carnegie School of Education, Leeds Beckett University. Especially ground-breaking, and of great significance to teachers, is his research connecting teacher wellbeing to pupil progress. Particularly compelling are Jonathan's interviews with children who show an awareness of the state of mind of their teachers and how it affects them during their work in class. I look forward to continuing to collaborate with Jonathan in the future and wish him well as he takes up a new post as Head of Children, Education and Communities at Edge Hill University.

A special thanks to Suneta Bagri, founder of Cultivate Coaching and the Every Teacher Matters Project, my business partner and friend, for her encouragement and support and her belief that the book would be published, when it looked as if Covid-19 might derail it.

Thanks also to those colleagues who, before a word was written, approved of the book as a concept. A special mention for David Gumbrell, author and Founder of The Resilience Project, who not only read my proposal to Open University Press/McGraw-Hill but also provided invaluable feedback on the structure of the book in the final stages. David's advice brought a coherence to the final edit, which has undoubtedly made it a better book than it would otherwise have been.

I am also grateful to Professor Dame Alison Peacock, Chief Executive of the Chartered College of Teaching, for her thoughtful and supportive foreword which captures the content spirit and purpose of the book.

Finally, my thanks to Beth Summers, editorial assistant at Open University Press/McGraw-Hill, for her support and belief in the book and in me as the editor. I lost count of the number of times she agreed to move the deadline for the final manuscript so that I could continue to search for willing chapter writers during the Covid-19 lockdown. I am grateful, also, to Eleanor Christie, executive editor, whose oversight undoubtedly improved the book's structure, without ever intruding on the writing process.

Preface: Setting the scene

Stephen Waters

In September 2019, I interviewed Jeremy Hannay, headteacher of Three Bridges Primary School in Southall, West London. Chapter 7 is a summary of that interview. I had been inspired by a talk that Jeremy gave at an event in London the year before where I had also been invited to speak on staff wellbeing. His talk was radical and came from the heart. He spoke of the damage high-stakes accountability was doing to staff in schools in the UK [Jeremy is originally from Canada] and how we needed to trust teachers and give them back control of their own professional development. By interviewing Jeremy, I hoped to find out more about his approach, its impact on staff and pupil progress and attainment. I wasn't disappointed!

If anything, Jeremy's interview was even more inspirational than his talk. I began to consider whether a book of case studies would provide a resource to schools that were considering developing staff wellbeing and mental health. I began to contact other schools that I knew were committed to staff wellbeing to ask if, in principle, they would be willing to write a chapter for a book on the wellbeing strategies they used and the impact on their own school or college. I received sufficient interest from a number of schools to encourage me to send a proposal to Open University Press/McGraw-Hill in early 2019. It was accepted and so the book was born. Little did I know how challenging Covid-19 would make it for schools to submit their contributions. Offers to write chapters reduced; schools had more important challenges to face. They were faced in school with the challenge of educating vulnerable pupils and the children of key workers – such as doctors, nurses and members of the emergency services – who continued to attend school, while offering online classes to children and young people at home.

In May 2019, chapter submissions came to a halt and the book stalled. I needed more schools to contribute. From March to July schools remained open, despite varying stages of lockdown in the UK. Through my company, the Teach Well Alliance, I had launched an accreditation, the 'Teach Well School Gold Award: Covid-19 Pandemic', to recognise schools that had gone the extra mile to take care of staff during the Covid-19 outbreak. By July 2020, 135 schools had gained the Award. It was to these schools I turned to ask for further chapters, as I knew from the testimonials from staff who submitted the nomination forms that the care their schools were taking of staff was exceptional. In May 2020, I had a total of seven schools that had submitted chapters. By July, I had a total of 32.

I am so grateful to everyone who has contributed. Each chapter tells a compelling story of how the school promoted staff wellbeing and its impact on staff morale and results. Many of the schools are in areas of high deprivation and/or were struggling with pupil attainment. Some had received an Office for Standards in Education (Ofsted) judgement of 'Requires Improvement' at their last inspection. By focusing on staff wellbeing, all made progress. Some schools were completely turned around when a new headteacher introduced a focus on improving morale and staff were recognised for their achievements and commitment.

Taken as a whole, the case studies provide a powerful and unique resource of good practice. Some strategies used in the primary phase or alternative provision schools are transferable to secondary schools and vice versa. Of course, not every strategy will work in your school or will need to be adapted to your context. You know your school best. As Dylan Wiliam, Emeritus Professor at UCL Institute of Education said, 'Everything works somewhere; nothing works everywhere' (2018).

The composition of the schools is as follows:

Primary schools

- There are 15 primary schools; 10 schools are described as having higher than average numbers of pupils eligible for Pupil Premium.
- 8 schools are maintained by the local authority.
- 4 schools are academies.
- 2 schools are voluntary-controlled.
- 1 school is voluntary-aided.

Secondary schools

- There are 13 secondary schools; 4 schools are described as having higher than average numbers of pupils eligible for Pupil Premium.
- 5 schools are academies.
- 2 schools are maintained by the local authority.
- 2 schools are voluntary-aided; 1 of the schools is non-denominational.
- 1 school is a selective boys' grammar school.
- 1 school is a free school.
- 1 school is a private girls' school in the United Arab Emirates.
- There is 1 Academy Trust.

Alternative provision schools

- 1 school is a pupil referral unit (PRU).
- 1 school is an independent special school for pupils with autism spectrum conditions/disorders.
- 1 school is an academy for pupils who struggle with mainstream education.
- 1 school is a free school for pupils with social, emotional and mental health difficulties, and autism spectrum conditions/disorders.

How to navigate the book

In this section, I explain how you can find content in the book related to your own school phase and circumstances. Before you begin your search, I urge you to read the first case study in Chapter 7: 'There is another way', by Jeremy Hannay, headteacher of Three Bridges Primary School. If ever there was a rallying call to change how we deliver education and treat our teachers in the UK, this is it. It also sets the scene for replacing high-stakes accountability with a caring, trusting staff culture, an approach which many of the schools featured in the book have taken to a lesser or greater degree.

At first sight, this book might look daunting. You might have taken an interest in it because you are looking for ways to implement staff wellbeing and mental health. Perhaps you need to understand why teachers are leaving your school or the profession and how you can reverse the trend. Or you have made good progress in focusing on staff wellbeing but want to add to the strategies you have put in place. Or maybe you want to read some research into the impact of teacher wellbeing on schools in general and on pupil progress in particular.

To help you find what you are looking for, here is an explanation of how this book is structured. Once you know how to navigate it, you can go straight to the section that interests you. You can, of course, read the book from cover to cover, but this might not be the best way of approaching the content. If you are a reader who simply must read the whole book from beginning to end (I used to be like this, so I understand!), I suggest that you do so after dipping in and out of the contents to get an overview of how the book is put together.

The structure of the book

There are four parts to the book, as follows:

Part 1, Chapters 1–6: Teacher Wellbeing and Mental Health: Whole-School Strategies and Impact on Pupil Progress

Part 1 is primarily research-based and provides a framework for understanding the impact of high-stakes accountability on teachers' wellbeing. In Chapter 1, I draw on the work of Christina Maslach on workplace Burnout and explain how it relates to teachers in schools. Jonathan Glazzard's research sits alongside Chapters 2 and 3, where I report on the findings from two surveys on teacher wellbeing and mental health which I conducted with my company, the Teach Well Alliance, and which emphasise the importance of staff wellbeing as an organisational responsibility. [Ed: The Teach Well Alliance works in partnership with schools to develop a culture of staff wellbeing and mental health.] In Chapter 4, Jonathan reports on primary school research into the connection between teacher wellbeing and pupil progress which he carried out when he was Professor of Inclusion at the Carnegie School of Education at Leeds Beckett University. The theme of the importance of a whole-school approach to staff wellbeing and mental health runs throughout the research covered in Chapters 2–4. The potential positive impact of an organisation implementing a culture of staff wellbeing and mental health is comprehensively explored by

Jonathan in Chapter 5, 'A whole-school approach to wellbeing'. He suggests that such an approach would significantly improve recruitment and retention, including in the teaching profession as a whole. Chapter 6, 'Buffer leadership and staff wellbeing', considers the largely unexplored demanding role that school leaders play in protecting their staff from external pressures.

Part 2, Chapters 7–21: Primary School Case Studies

Part 2 contains 15 case studies of primary schools that have successfully implemented a culture of staff wellbeing and mental health, written by a member of staff. Each school has its own chapter. At the beginning of each chapter, there is a **quotation** which captures the spirit, the vision or ethos of the school. This is followed by an **overview** of how the school implemented a culture of staff wellbeing and mental health. Then, under the heading **'Context'**, there is a summary of the demographic and social circumstances of the school. Here is an example from Chapter 7: Three Bridges Primary School:

'There is no pupil wellbeing, there's no pupil achievement, there's no pupil collaboration, there's no pupil collective responsibility, there's no pupil anything, until the adults experience it first ... it's quite a simple equation – if we're not putting our adults in a soil that is nutrient rich – that will allow them to flourish into whoever they want to be as an educator, they have no chance of doing that effectively and sustainably in a classroom of children. Because sometimes, very often as a child, you have to watch somebody love something before you can learn to love yourself. That is a nutrient that gets overlooked in many schools – that we need to make sure as leaders that we take care of the people who take care of our pupils.'

Overview

Jeremy Hannay, headteacher of Three Bridges Primary School, is a frank and outspoken critic of high-stakes accountability leadership of schools and the Ofsted inspection process by which schools are judged. In this forthright interview with the book's author and editor, Stephen Waters, he describes how he has rejected the model that, in order to raise standards and improve results, teachers must be scrutinised, monitored, and controlled. By restoring trust and professional respect and supporting teacher-led professional development, Jeremy explains how teacher agency leads to teacher mental wellbeing.

Context

Three Bridges Primary School is in Southall, West London. It is a larger than average two-form entry community school, with over 400 pupils, a nursery class, and two reception classes. Over 40% of the children are identified as

Pupil Premium (PP). Ninety-six per cent of the children are Black, Asian, and Minority Ethnic (BAME); 75–80% come from a wide range of heritages and have English as an additional language (EAL). A small number of children are at the early stages of speaking English. The proportion of disadvantaged children is well above average, as is the proportion of pupils receiving Special Educational Needs and Disability (SEND) support at 25%. Transience is also high, with 35% of the children leaving or joining the school before they reach Year 6, and the proportion of pupils joining the school after the early years is higher than the national average. One of the catchment estates is in the second percentile for crime and violence, and Three Bridges Primary School is one of 75 primary schools with the most disadvantaged communities in the country. Results are excellent, with the school in the top 3% in the UK in terms of progress over the last 7 years.

Three Bridges is an outward-facing school offering training and support and development for schools, teachers, and school leaders. Between 2016 and 2020, the school supported and trained over 300 schools, and more than 2000 teachers and school leaders, locally, nationally, and internationally.

The **overview** and **context** provide you with sufficient information to decide whether the school is on a similar journey to your own and if its case study could provide insights that you might consider applying in your own school. At the end of each chapter is a bulleted list of key strategies each school has used in implementing a culture of staff wellbeing and mental health. As an example, here are the strategies Jeremy Hannay used at Three Bridges:

Key strategies

- No high-stakes accountability. No: hierarchical observations, book scrutinies, marking policy, learning walks, performance management, display board rules.
- Creative and inspirational environment, including displaying pupils' work in progress.
- Belief that there is no pupil wellbeing without staff wellbeing.
- Culture of enabling staff to grow and develop.
- Staff are encouraged to take risks, without fear of failure.
- Learning and Study Lessons.
- Teacher Research Groups.
- Open lessons.
- No 'one way' of teaching and learning: instruction integrated with creativity.
- No onerous data drops.
- Rejection of the belief that monitoring teachers and inspecting schools are the only way to raise standards and get results.

Part 3, Chapters 22–34: Secondary School Case Studies

Part 3 focuses on secondary schools and follows the same structure as Section 2, with a chapter for each school.

Part 4, Chapters 35–38: Alternative Provision

Section 4 contains accounts from four specialist schools: a pupil referral unit; an alternative provision academy; a school for pupils on the autism spectrum; and an independent free school for children with social, emotional and mental health difficulties, and autism spectrum disorder.

Part 5, Chapter 39

The final chapter reflects on the challenges that schools faced from Covid-19, how the case-study schools responded, how the pandemic prompted discussions on social media about the purpose of education, and the importance of a culture of wellbeing and mental health in coping with additional workload, stress and anxiety.

There is also a **Glossary** of key educational terms, a **Reference List** and an **Index** that will help you to find a staff wellbeing and mental health strategy that has been commonly adopted by different schools.

Part 1

Teacher Wellbeing and Mental Health: Whole-School Strategies and Impact on Pupil Progress

1 Teacher Burnout, Ofsted, wellbeing and mental health

Stephen Waters

Overview

This chapter sets the scene for considering the importance of staff wellbeing and mental health. It describes the negative impact of poor staff wellbeing by exploring the meaning of '*Burnout*', as defined by Christina Maslach of the University of California, Berkeley, a world authority on workplace Burnout. I connect the six factors Maslach identifies as the causes of Burnout to the work that teachers do. I suggest that school leaders need to find out to what extent each of the six factors applies to their staff, and implement strategies to counteract them and to promote staff wellbeing. I introduce an evaluation tool that I have created to enable teachers and schools to evaluate Burnout both in themselves and within the organisation. The tool, 'The Waters Index of Teacher Burnout', adapts Freudenberger's 12 Stages of Burnout (in Kraft, 2006) to the work of teachers and enables individual teachers to assess their personal level of Burnout.

I then turn my attention to the Ofsted Inspection Framework, as published in the *School Inspection Handbook* (Ofsted, 2019c). Since September 2019, leaders have been expected to address staff workload, wellbeing and bullying as laid out in the 'Leadership and Management' criteria for 'Good' and 'Outstanding'. I explain how I devised two further evaluation tools to assess how a school is likely to fare when assessed by the Ofsted criteria: 'The Waters Index of Leadership Support for School Staff Wellbeing and Mental Health' and 'The Waters Matrix: Impact of the Relationship between School and Individual Responsibility for Staff Wellbeing and Mental Health'. I suggest that, while Ofsted is not the only – or even the most important – reason to implement a culture of staff wellbeing, it nevertheless will inevitably influence the school's approach and could also be useful when seeking support from school governors for staff wellbeing resources.

Burnout

What is Burnout?

The term *'Burnout'* has found its way into our everyday language to describe a range of debilitating responses to an unsustainable workload. Whereas the generic term 'breakdown' can be applied to any context in which we suffer from mental ill-health, the concept of Burnout is applicable only to the workplace. Burnout is not regarded as a mental illness by doctors or psychiatrists and therefore cannot be proposed as a diagnosis for the purposes of sick leave or sickness benefit. General practitioners (GPs), therefore, often describe mental ill-health resulting from Burnout as the reason for absence from work: most commonly, anxiety, stress, and depression. In this respect, Burnout is similar to post-traumatic stress disorder (PTSD), which was not formally recognised as a mental illness until the 1960s, despite having been seen in soldiers traumatised during the First and Second World Wars. In time, perhaps, Burnout will be classified as a form of mental ill-health, but we seem to be still some way off that day. In this book, the initial letter of Burnout has been capitalised to emphasise the seriousness of the condition and how it impacts on teachers' mental and physical health in schools.

The following definitions cover the range of mental illnesses caused by Burnout:

> 'Burnout is a syndrome conceptualized as resulting from chronic workplace stress that has not been successfully managed. It is characterized by three dimensions: feelings of energy depletion or exhaustion; increased mental distance from one's job, or feelings of negativism or cynicism related to one's job; and reduced professional efficacy. Burn-out refers specifically to phenomena in the occupational context and should not be applied to describe experiences in other areas of life' (WHO, 2019).

> 'Burnout occurs when passionate, committed people become deeply disillusioned with a job or career from which they have previously derived much of their identity and meaning. It comes as the things that inspire passion and enthusiasm are stripped away, and tedious or unpleasant things crowd in' (Mind Tools, 2020).

> 'Burnout occurs when the balance of deadlines, demands, working hours and other stressors, outstrips rewards, recognition, and relaxation' (Michel, 2016).

The term 'Burnout syndrome' was introduced in 1974 by Herbert J. Freudenberger, a New York psychoanalyst. Freudenberger had become aware that his own job, which was once so rewarding, had come to leave him feeling fatigued and frustrated. He noticed that many of the physicians around him had, over time, turned into depressive cynics. Together with his colleague, Gill North, Freudenberger devised a 12-stage model of Burnout, beginning with relatively mild symptoms and culminating in total breakdown (in Kraft, 2006).

Figure 1.1 Waters Index of Teacher Burnout V3 (based on Freudenberger's 12 stages)

The Waters Index of Teacher Burnout V3

(Based on Freudenberger's 12 Stages)

Stage	My behaviour and emotions	Tick statement that best describes your behaviour and emotions
1	I must prove myself and show my headteacher and leaders that I am a good teacher and can do what I was appointed to do. I like giving myself challenges and achieving them. Perhaps I should aim higher.	
2	I must set myself high standards and can't afford to say 'No' in case people think I'm not committed. I find it difficult to take time off and to have a good work-life balance. I want to get ahead of deadlines and find it difficult to prioritise tasks.	
3	I am not looking after myself properly, but preparation and marking must come first. I know I shouldn't work as late as I do. I wish I could have more time off at weekends. I am making mistakes I didn't use to make.	
4	I feel resentful of my friends who leave work behind when they go home. I feel a bit empty and I am often exhausted. I've noticed I'm getting headaches and aches and pains and sometimes feel sick. I'm worried about school. I am forgetting to do things.	
5	I feel as if I'm on autopilot and emotionally spaced-out. My whole life is taken up by work. I'm neglecting family and friends.	
6	I prefer to be on my own. I often feel angry and I lose my temper with pupils and sometimes staff. I know it's due to workload and setting myself high standards. I've had a few days off recently.	
7	I feel isolated and retreat to my classroom. That one drink I have to relax in the evening has increased to two or three. I sometimes self-medicate to get through the day. I have a hangover sometimes which makes teaching so hard in the morning.	
8	I've changed so much since I first qualified. I used to be outgoing, but I think staff are avoiding me. I've had to go to see my GP and she has put me on anti-depressants. I look stressed and drawn and worn out.	
9	What's the point of teaching if it is destroying me? I keep going but I don't enjoy it like I used to. The medication is helping but I feel tired all day. I can't think beyond the next lesson. I'm find it difficult to plan and to look ahead.	
10	I feel empty and lost. I am eating too much to comfort myself. I feel that there is no one to help me.	
11	I am so depressed. I am lonely. I can't see any light at the end of the tunnel. Even when I sleep, I get up exhausted. I feel so guilty that I'm doing such a bad job and letting the children down. I don't enjoy anything. I don't know how much longer I can take it. Perhaps I'd be better off out of it.	
12	I can't face going in . I can hardly get out of bed. I'm losing weight . I feel anxious and guilty. I can't face it any more. I am wondering if I have the courage to put an end to my life.	

© S Waters: Teach Well Alliance 2021

Stages 1–3: Opportunity to reduce impact via self-help or accepting help from others. 4-6: Need to seek professional help, such as counselling, to prevent further decline of health. 7–9: Urgent professional help a necessity. 10–12: Emergency help needed, especially at Stage 12 where there is a threat to life.

I applied Freudenberger's stages to teachers' workload and devised the 'Waters Index of Teacher Burnout' (Figure 1.1). This self-measurement tool is designed to alert the user to what extent they are in danger of being overwhelmed by their job, and suggests what self-help action they should take to avoid Burnout worsening and becoming seriously physically and mentally debilitating.

Christina Maslach and burnout

Christina Maslach is Professor of Psychology and a researcher at the Healthy Workplaces Center at the University of California, Berkeley, and has been researching Burnout since the 1970s. She is regarded as a world expert on Burnout and her Maslach Burnout Inventory™ is used to identify the level of risk of employee Burnout. Her work is not well known in the UK outside of academic circles, but I believe that it offers considerable insight into the conditions in schools which cause Burnout and, conversely, how Burnout can be avoided by developing a whole-school approach to staff wellbeing and mental health.

The six causes of burnout

Maslach identified six causes of Burnout. She countered the belief that work overload was synonymous with stress and argued that workload, by itself, was insufficient to cause Burnout.

> 'It is a common belief that there is just one dimension to job stress – work overload. Indeed, work overload is often considered to be a synonym for stress. But in our Burnout model, overload is only one of six mismatches in the workplace' (Maslach and Leiter, 2000).

Maslach's approach sheds light on a finding in the author's own unpublished research (see Chapters 2 and 3) that workload is frequently cited by staff in schools as the most significant causative factor in their lack of morale, exhaustion, and disillusionment with teaching. However, in surveys where teachers identify workload as a cause of stress, there are typically a range of other negative factors at play, such as high-stakes accountability, micromanagement, and a lack of appreciation and trust. In the worst cases, the workplace is toxic and there is bullying, usually from the headteacher and/or the executive headteacher – who has oversight of several schools in an Academy Trust – or the chief executive officer (CEO) of the Trust. Governing bodies or Trust boards can also bully their headteachers. In common with the identification of bullying as an outcome of a dysfunctional relationship where there is a target of the bullying and a perpetrator, bullying can occur wherever there is a power imbalance between two individuals. This is more frequently seen in a hierarchical relationship where the perpetrator has line responsibility for the target of the bullying. Bullying can also occur between teachers who are not formally responsible for one another – for example, two or more colleagues of equal standing professionally and hierarchically – but this is less common. In extreme examples, a school can become a bullying institution, where bullying behaviour at different levels of the organisation is either ignored or condoned. This is one – and perhaps the most important – characteristic of toxic schools.

Where teachers are trusted and respected as professionals, they report workload as less of a concern. Teaching is a demanding job and teachers expect to have to work hard, but it is when Maslach's five other factors are present that it becomes intolerable. Of course, in schools where leaders, in the words of Ofsted, are realistic and constructive in the way they manage staff, including their workload, the reverse is true – that leadership's concern for workload is accompanied by strategies that often address each of the other factors that lead to Burnout, irrespective of whether they are aware of Maslach's identification of these factors.

The six factors that Maslach identified as causing Burnout are (in no particular order):

1 **Work overload:** Maslach and Leiter (2000) define workload in terms of the quantity of work exceeding the amount of time available, or when the job is simply too difficult with the resources an employee is given to do it.
2 **Lack of control:** Other people make decisions about your work: for example, how you should teach; what resources you can have and should use; the structure of the curriculum; how testing is to be carried out; what data you should collect and when; and how you should mark.
3 **Lack of reward:** While pay is important, it is rarely the only factor or even the main factor. Social recognition, acknowledgement for a job well done, and praise are more important. The strategies that are effective in motivating children are also effective in motivating staff, as gaining social recognition and being appreciated are fundamental human needs.
4 **Lack of community:** 'People thrive in community and function best when they share praise, comfort, happiness, and humor with people they like and respect. In addition to emotional exchange and instrumental assistance, this kind of social support reaffirms a person's membership in a group with shared values' (Maslach et al., 2001: 415).
5 **Lack of fairness:** The perception of unfairness is as important as the actions that cause it. In organisations where trust in leadership is poor, there tends to be a greater perception of a lack of fairness. Promotions are seen as biased or 'rigged', leaders are seen to have favourites, and the favoured few are considered to be more appreciated and rewarded.
6 **Conflict of values:** Your values as a teacher – the reason you entered teaching in the first place – do not coincide with those of the school. This is most often seen in schools which place high value on achieving results at any cost and where there is an unshakeable belief that the children must come first, even if this is at the expense of the staff. Self-evidently, teachers join the profession because they enjoy teaching and working with children. However, if, by putting children first, a school puts teachers last, the likelihood

of Burnout is high. And teachers who are suffering from Burnout are unable to put children first. You can't have pupil wellbeing without staff wellbeing. They are two sides of the same coin.

Maslach devised the Maslach Burnout Inventory™ (MBI) to assess whether someone was suffering from Burnout. Recognised as a leading measure of Burnout, the MBI has been validated by the extensive research that has been conducted since its initial publication in 1981.

Maslach produced a version of the MBI for educators, the 'MBI: Educators Survey' (MBI-ES: Maslach et al., 1986). The MBI-ES can be used with teachers, administrators, other staff members, and volunteers working in any educational setting. It includes three sub-scales:

1 **Emotional exhaustion** measures feelings of being emotionally overextended and exhausted by one's work. This can include irritability, permanent tiredness, nausea, stomach pains, and an inability to focus.
2 **Personal accomplishment** measures feelings of competence and successful achievement in one's work. Lack of accomplishment can lead to self-blame, lack of confidence, feeling a failure, not doing a good job.
3 **Depersonalisation** measures an unfeeling and impersonal response towards others. Depersonalisation can include cynicism; isolation; distancing from work, colleagues and pupils; and blame and negativity directed towards pupils and/or colleagues.

In a blog post, 'A message from the Maslach Burnout Inventory Authors', on Mind Garden in March 2019, its authors make the important point that Burnout is not an individual response to being unable to cope:

'Conventional wisdom holds that Burnout is primarily a problem of the individual. That is, people burn out because of the flaws in their character, behavior, or productivity. From this perspective, the individual is the problem and the solution lies in changing the person.

'But Burnout is experienced in response to the social and work environment … The Burnout of individual workers often says more about the workplace conditions than it does about the person. It is not the person but the relationship of the organisation with people that needs to change' (Mind Garden, 2019).

This important clarification clearly shifts responsibility for Burnout from the individual to the workplace. In toxic schools, in common with other toxic workplaces, staff are often regarded as weak if they are unable to cope, whereas it is the school itself that is making them ill. While anxiety or depression, for example, can be individual responses to a range of individual physical and mental factors, Burnout is located firmly in the workplace. Burnout often does include depression and anxiety, but these mental ill-health conditions are part of the collection of adverse responses caused by the school as an organisation and not individual responses. In toxic schools, as in other toxic workplaces:

Figure 1.2 Pattern of Maslach Burnout Inventory (MBI) subscales across profiles (adapted from Mind Garden, 2019)

Profile	Emotional Exhaustion	Depersonalization	Personal Accomplishment
Engaged	Low	Low	High
Ineffective			Low
Overextended	High		
Disengaged		High	
Burnout	High	High	

'… the individual with a Burnout profile may report a wide range of worklife issues, including work overload, autonomy, collegiality, justice, and value conflicts with the organization. This combination differs substantially from just beginning the workday feeling tired and it presents more serious challenge for action' (Mind Garden, 2019).

The chart in Figure 1.2 clearly shows the impact of a teacher's condition or state of mind (their 'profile') on Maslach's three dimensions of Emotional Exhaustion, Depersonalisation, and Personal Accomplishment, and how personal accomplishment cannot be achieved unless emotional exhaustion and depersonalisation are low. A lack of personal accomplishment gives rise to low morale and a lack of self-confidence, as it frequently stems from a school culture in which staff are not praised, appreciated, or recognised for the work they do.

Now let's take a look at how Ofsted fits into the school wellbeing picture.

Ofsted

The Ofsted Framework (September 2020 onwards)

In May 2019, Ofsted published an update to its Inspection Framework, which had taken effect in September 2019. For the first time, there were explicit statements about staff wellbeing, workload, and bullying. Below are extracts from the *School Inspection Handbook*: from the 'Good' and 'Outstanding' criteria on

Leadership and Management in Sections 277 and 278 (Ofsted, 2019c). The statements that relate specifically to wellbeing have been italicised.

'Grade descriptors for leadership and management

277. In order for the leadership and management of a school to be judged outstanding, it must meet all of the good criteria securely and consistently, and it must also meet the additional outstanding criteria.

Outstanding (1)

- The school meets all the criteria for good in leadership and management securely and consistently.
- Leadership and management are exceptional.

In addition, the following apply:

- Leaders ensure that teachers receive focused and highly effective professional development. Teachers' subject, pedagogical and pedagogical content knowledge consistently build and develop over time. This consistently translates into improvements in the teaching of the curriculum.
- Leaders ensure that *highly effective and meaningful engagement takes place with staff at all levels and that issues are identified. When issues are identified, in particular about workload, they are consistently dealt with appropriately and quickly.*
- *Staff consistently report high levels of support for wellbeing issues.*

278. In order to judge whether a school is good or requires improvement, inspectors will use a 'best fit' approach, relying on the professional judgement of the inspection team.

Good (2)

- Leaders engage effectively with pupils and others in their community, including, when relevant, parents, employers and local services. Engagement opportunities are focused and have purpose.
- *Leaders engage with their staff and are aware and take account of the main pressures on them. They are realistic and constructive in the way they manage staff, including their workload.*
- *Leaders protect staff from bullying and harassment.*'

What do the Ofsted criteria for 'Good' and 'Outstanding' mean in relation to how leadership and management promote and support teachers' wellbeing and mental health?

I have set out below the questions I believe leadership and management should address to ensure that the school is judged to be 'Good' in supporting staff wellbeing. Phrases taken from the *School Inspection Handbook* (Ofsted, 2019c) are in italics.

1 **How do *leaders engage with their staff*?** What mechanisms are in place to positively engage staff? Anonymous surveys? Focus groups? Suggested

strategies from Middle Leaders' meetings? Supportive line management meetings? 'Door always open' policy?

2 **How do leaders *take account of the main pressures on staff*?** How does leadership know the pressures staff face? How much of this pressure is caused by external forces and how much by internal leadership and management? What does leadership do to reduce the pressures?

3 **How do leaders show that they are both *realistic and constructive* in how they manage staff and their workload?** Do leaders know how many hours staff are working per week? Do they encourage and support a work–life balance? Are they aware of circumstances beyond the school gates which affect the extent to which individual teachers are able to manage their workload?

4 **Leaders *protect staff from bullying and harassment.*** Sadly, there are too many teachers reporting incidents of bullying and harassment on social media. It is unacceptable, as well as illegal. There are some schools where leaders regard ruling with fear and putting pressure on teachers to perform better, work harder, or even to leave their schools so they can replace them, as legitimate leadership behaviours. There are headteachers who believe that, unless their staff are exhausted, they are not working hard enough. Bullying can cause long-term mental ill-health. Some teachers are leaving the profession scarred and demoralised because they have been bullied, often never to return. The bold Ofsted statement that leaders must protect their staff from this kind of treatment places the responsibility for addressing bullying and harassment squarely on the shoulders of staff, especially CEOs, executive headteachers, headteachers, and senior leadership, as well as governing bodies or boards, but also at every level where a teacher has a line management responsibility for other members of staff.

How does your school ensure that all staff (not just teaching staff) are protected from bullying and harassment? What mechanisms are in place for staff to report incidents? Does your school have a staff anti-bullying and harassment policy that includes how they should report incidents and the actions that will be taken? Is there a whistleblowing policy? If so, how are whistleblowers protected? Are the governors involved in more serious cases? If so, how? What happens to the bullies? Is there a different reaction when pupils are being bullied? If so, why? Are the teaching unions and non-teaching unions involved? Where there is no union representation, has the school taken account of the unions' position on staff bullying and harassment in drawing up its own policy?

What do the criteria for 'Outstanding' mean in practice for wellbeing and staff mental health?

1 **How does leadership identify 'issues' that need to be addressed?** Can issues be reported anonymously, or does reporting them rely too heavily on whistleblowing? When issues of workload are raised, does leadership deal with them consistently, appropriately, and quickly?

2 **What processes are in place to enable staff to evaluate the support that the school provides for their wellbeing?** Is there a commonly understood definition of what 'wellbeing' means? How does your definition relate to the context of your school? Does wellbeing include the headteacher and senior leadership team? Is there an ethos of the school as a community and 'we are in this together'? Are some teachers leaving because they are suffering from mental ill-health? What is the school doing about this? The Ofsted criteria can only be met if your school is implementing a culture of staff wellbeing which permeates the school as one mutually supportive community at all levels.

As a result of my research for this book and the introduction of the Ofsted criteria on staff wellbeing, workload, and bullying, I created the 'Waters Index of Leadership Support for Teachers' Wellbeing and Mental Health V6' (Figure 1.3). Although the Index itself is copyright and therefore cannot be altered, teachers and school leaders have my permission to use it in their own schools.

In collecting the school case studies for this book, I saw a pattern: because their schools were taking care of them, staff were taking better individual care of themselves. I realised that I needed a way of mapping school care against self-care. A third matrix was created to accompany the Waters Index of Leadership Support for Teachers' Wellbeing and Mental Health (Figure 1.4).

Teaching and the company workplace

The novelist and cultural activist Wendell Berry said in a conference speech entitled 'Health is Membership', that a healthy community isn't merely human, but also 'its soil, its water, its air' (Berry, 1994). In the last five years, there has been a shift in how company owners and employers view wellbeing and mental health. Businesses are moving slowly away from placing sole responsibility for wellbeing on the individual employee to recognising that working conditions, including workload, have a major part to play in creating a healthy environment. Wellbeing is not only about the physical conditions of our work but how we relate to others in our work community and how that community functions as a whole to support us.

Mental wellbeing and Covid-19

The Covid-19 pandemic has shown us that it is healthy to share how we feel mentally. Whether we are able to do this is heavily influenced by the people around us or the extent to which we feel cut off from them. If you are unable to talk about your mental health at school, it is important to ask yourself why. The answer is likely to reveal that your school views wellbeing as your concern and is not taking the responsibility it should for your mental health. If the headteacher

Figure 1.3 Waters Index of Leadership Support for Teachers' Wellbeing and Mental Health V6 (July 2020)

Waters Index of Leadership Support for Teachers' Wellbeing and Mental Health (V6) ©

To calculate your school's score, choose which column best describes your school. Use a 'best fit' picture, rather than focusing on individual statements.

(This index is Part of the Teach Well Toolkit, the Teach Well Alliance programme for developing a whole-school culture of staff wellbeing and mental health)

Negative impact: Toxic -2 or -1	Low Support 1	Medium Support 2	High Support 3	Flourishing 4
No positive action. **No support** – solve your own problems. **High accountability** – results are everything and failure each teacher's fault. **Excessive workload.** **Lack** of empathy with staff. **School and children come first.** **Leave home and family at door.** **High rates of absence.** **High turnover.** **High recruitment costs.** **High cover costs.** **Mental ill-health regarded as weakness.** **Bullying** of staff is a daily occurrence. Most staff who leave have mental ill-health and have lost confidence. **There is a culture of fear.** **No responsibility taken by leadership that their actions are causing teachers' mental and physical ill-health.** **Happiness is fluffy** – it's got nothing to do with results. **'If you can't cope, leave'** – teachers are dispensable. **Maternity/paternity leave regarded as inconvenience.** **Looking** after sick relatives, including children, leads to payback: time or salary. **Flexible/part-time working refused.**	**Some** positive actions but mainly peripheral or token gestures e.g. exercise class, cakes on Friday. **Some support:** listening without offering solutions. **Accountability** overrides concern. **Family** time acknowledged but little or no work-life balance. **Staff** absences of concern. **Turnover** of concern. **Cover** costs of concern **Recruitment** costs of concern. **Mental** ill-health often judged as being unable to control class or cope with workload or demands of teaching. **Leadership** shows some understanding of teachers' mental ill-health but blames government for it. **'We want you to be happy, but happiness is your personal responsibility.'** **'We appreciate that teaching is stressful. Perhaps you should consider taking some steps to look after yourself better.'**	**Positive** actions include some whole-school strategies but lack coherence e.g. limits in use of email, together with peripheral or token gestures. **Support** depends on line-manager providing it. **Family** time promoted verbally but limited attempt to create a work-life balance. **Turnover** erratic and subject to variations. **Cover** costs are variable and show some evidence of falling. **Recruitment** costs are variable and show some evidence of falling. **Mental** health is acknowledged verbally, and staff are encouraged to seek support. Provision depends on line manager. **Leadership** has a good understanding of its responsibility to support teachers with mental ill-health, but response lacks systematic strategy. **'We** appreciate that the pressure in teaching sometimes leads to mental ill-health. Come and see us and we will support you.'	**School** is on a journey to take positive action with evidence of whole-school strategies in place, together with a staff wellbeing policy. **Staff** wellbeing policy includes advice on what staff should do if they have mental ill-health and how line managers should respond. **Work**-life balance is actively promoted. **Turnover** is low. **Cover** costs are low. **Recruitment** costs are low. **Mental** health is discussed both informally and formally in Inset/Staff meetings. **Leadership** has a very good understanding of its responsibility to support teachers with mental ill-health. Its response is improving, and self-improvement is in place in this respect. **'We** want you to be happy and are open to suggestions about how we can improve our support and response if you are mentally unwell.' **'We** are determined to reduce pressure on staff. You know how we will support you if you have mental ill-health.'	**Whole-school** approach to support mental health. **All** strategies and policies examined to strip back any actions which do not contribute to teaching and learning. **Family** comes first. School covers teachers when family emergency. **School** examines its own actions when teacher is suffering from mental ill-health. **School** has Staff Wellbeing Policy, reviewed yearly. **'Talking School'** where staff encouraged to talk about problems without judgement. **Low** absence rate. **Low** cover costs. **Low** turnover – staff don't want to leave: they love their school. **Mental** health regarded as important as physical health. **Leadership** transparent about their own stresses and difficulties. **'We're** all in this together. Come and talk. We're listening and will act'. We value you as a person and as a teacher - you are a precious resource.' **Happiness** is fundamental to good teaching and learning.

© Steve Waters Teach Well Alliance (July 2020)

Figure 1.4 Waters Matrix: Impact of Relationship between School and Individual Responsibility for School Staff Wellbeing and Mental Health V2

Waters Matrix: Impact of Relationship between School and Individual Responsibility for School Staff Wellbeing and Mental Health (V2)

(Mapped against 'Waters Index of Leadership Support for School Staff Wellbeing and Mental Health')

	High support for wellbeing and mental health of staff	Low/no support for wellbeing and mental health of staff
Staff take care of their own wellbeing and mental health	**Good** school community wellbeing and mental health. **Good** individual wellbeing and mental health. **Staff** support one another. **High** retention. **Low** cover needs for teachers absent through stress. **Supportive** culture: staff support one another, including support for headteacher and SLT. **Staff** able to model resilience and self-care to pupils. **Teaching** and learning are strong **Low** monitoring – staff trusted to do their jobs. **Score = 3/4 Flourishing**	**Poor** community wellbeing and mental health. **Staff** struggle to maintain wellbeing and mental health. **Staff** support one another to overcome lack of school support. **Retention** under pressure – some teachers can't cope and leave school and/or the profession. **Cover** under pressure – increases during school year. **Staff** struggle to model resilience and self-care to pupils. **Teaching** and learning are variable and dependent on teachers' energy levels and state of mind. **Monitoring** and micromanagement are high. **Score = 1 Low**
Staff don't take care of their own wellbeing and mental health	**Good** community support for wellbeing and mental health. **Poor** individual wellbeing and mental health - teachers don't take advantage of support available. **Staff** hide their lack of wellbeing and mental health. **Retention** is good but presenteeism (coming to work when ill) is high. **Cover** is under pressure and increases during school year. **Staff** model self-sacrifice to pupils but unable to effectively model resilience and self-care. **Teaching** and learning are variable and dependent on staff's energy levels and state of mind **Score = 2 Medium**	**Poor** school community wellbeing and mental health. **Poor** individual wellbeing and mental health. **Staff** often work in isolation. **Low** retention. **High** cover needs for teachers absent through stress, increasing during the year. **Staff** unable to model resilience and self-care to pupils. **High** presenteeism. **Teaching** and learning are weak. Excessive, negative monitoring increases poor mental health. **Score = –2 or –1 (Toxic)**

Note: This is a 'best-fit' model. Statements are not intended to be evaluated separately

Teach Well Alliance ©

does not share their own vulnerability and humanity, it is less likely that the staff will do so. The Covid-19 pandemic has drawn our attention to the need for schools to support teachers when someone in their family is physically ill. This is as important, if not more so, when teachers or their families become mentally unwell. Leaders that do not invest time and money in their teachers and who regard them as expendable, create instability and low allegiance to the school. The 'If you don't like it, there's the door' or 'The job is the job' or 'Leave your problems at the school gates' style of leadership causes high rates of teacher absence through physical and/or mental illness, low morale, disengaged staff, and low outcomes for pupils.

One-off school strategies to improve teacher wellbeing are ineffective. So, a fitness class once a week will have little or no impact unless it is part of a whole-school cultural commitment to teacher wellbeing. We all need to take better care of ourselves, to eat more healthily, to exercise more – perhaps even more so because of Covid-19. But it should not be because your work as a teacher is causing you to be ill. Apart from it being the right thing to do, schools have a 'duty of care' under the Health and Safety at Work Act (1974) to look after their staff physically and mentally, just as school staff have a duty of care for their pupils. With school budgets further stretched by the impact of Covid-19, it also does not make financial sense to have teachers absent because your school has made them ill.

As the case-study schools featured in this book show (Parts 2–4), looking after staff wellbeing and mental health is not only morally and legally the right thing to do, it produces a positive, motivating environment for the pupils – and reduces spending on supply staff and recruitment, as fewer staff are absent through illness or leave the school.

The role of line manager

The most important person in any teacher's school is their line manager. Their head of department, or head of subject, or head of year, or, if they are a member of the senior leadership team, their headteacher, influences their day-to-day teaching, their happiness, and the environment and context in which they teach. Despite the responsibility of the role, neither the National Professional Qualification for Middle Leadership (NPQML) nor the equivalent for Senior Leadership (NPQSL) includes promoting and managing wellbeing and mental health as part of the line manager's job description. This is a gap which, for now, schools can learn how to fill by including training for their line managers on mental health, for example, by enrolling them on a First Aid for Mental Health course. Creating a working group to advise the school on lessons learned from training can also be very powerful, as long as the advice is acted upon.

We return to the theme of the impact of staff stress and Burnout on pupils in Chapter 4. Professor Jonathan Glazzard, Head of Children, Education and Communities at Edge Hill University, presents his research findings on the link between teacher wellbeing and pupil progress from studies undertaken when he was Professor of Inclusive Education at the Carnegie School of Education, Leeds Beckett University. Jonathan's research sits alongside Chapters 2 and 3, where I present two research studies into staff wellbeing and mental health which I carried out between 2017 and 2019, and which emphasise the importance of staff wellbeing as an organisational responsibility. The theme of the importance of a whole-school approach to staff wellbeing and mental health runs throughout the research covered in Chapters 2–4 and is comprehensively explored by Jonathan in Chapter 5: 'A whole-school approach to wellbeing'.

Let us now look at the research findings from a small-scale survey I conducted into teachers' wellbeing and mental health from May 2017 to June 2019 under the name of the Teach Well Alliance.

2 Findings from a small-scale survey of teacher wellbeing and mental health conducted by the Teach Well Alliance

Stephen Waters

A Teacher Wellbeing Survey was created in Google Forms and posted on Twitter, Facebook, and LinkedIn, as well as on the Teach Well Alliance website (www. teachwellalliance.com) on 21 May 2017. A link to the online survey was embedded in the website. Invitations to complete the survey were also posted on Twitter, Facebook, and LinkedIn. A typical post on social media inviting teachers to contribute was:

'The govt/DfE keeps data on the numbers of teachers in post but not about their mental health. Complete our anonymised survey on the Teach Well Alliance resources website …'

The survey was conducted between 21 May 2017 and 12 June 2019. The Executive Summary, including recommendations, was published online via a link and on my website as a download. This is what it said.

1. Rank order of scores of factors affecting respondents' mental health

Mental health is affected by the following factors in rank order, determined by respondents' individual replies. As can be seen, the overall category of workload has the most impact, followed by specific tasks that make up workload: admin tasks, lack of time to prepare classes, preparing for Ofsted, and following up learners for failure to submit homework were all within 2 percentage points of one another, with marking only 6 percentage points behind in terms of impact on teachers' mental health. This suggests that these factors have a similarly high impact on teachers' wellbeing. Learners' behaviour and class size, although of relatively lower impact, are still significant factors. Only 'Duties' falls below 50% in the rank order.

- Workload: 92%
- Admin tasks: 77.8%
- Lack of time to prepare classes: 77.7%
- Preparing for Ofsted: 75.8%
- Following up learners for failure to submit homework: 75.8%
- Marking: 71.8%
- Learners' behaviour: 63.3%
- Class size: 61.4%
- Duties, e.g. corridor, playground: 46.1%

2. Rank order of the extent to which teachers felt professionally valued and their personal lives were taken into account

- Professional expertise 43.5%
- Level of concern from organisation when respondent is ill: 20.8%
- Work–life balance: 18.8%
- Level of concern from organisation when a member of respondent's family is ill: 18.8%
- Level of concern from organisation when a member of the respondent's family has problems which affect the respondent at work: 15.9%

Unlike the factors that adversely affect teachers' mental health, where only one of the factors was below 50% in terms of impact, none of the scores identifying the extent to which respondents felt valued was above 50%. In other words, the factors contributing to mental ill-health far outweigh the factors contributing to wellbeing.

Recommendations for leadership

Recommendation 1: Reduce admin

- Reduce teachers' workload by addressing each of the areas in turn, according to the extent to which they impact negatively on teacher wellbeing, i.e. reduce admin tasks first, followed by increasing the amount of time that teachers have to prepare classes, and so on.
- Create time by reducing tasks that have little or no impact on pupil emotional wellbeing or academic progress.

Recommendation 2: Take positive action to improve teachers' mental health

The rank order of actions that teachers believe could be taken by the school to improve their mental health were as follows:

- Tell me when I have done a good job: 19.8%
- Show that you value my professional expertise: 18.3%
- Reduce admin tasks: 13.9%
- Less marking: 8.9%
- Smaller class sizes: 8.4%
- Higher salary: 6.9%
- Fewer duties: 6.9%
- Wellbeing group: 5%.
- Other: 6.4%

The top two priorities teachers identified for improving their mental health are appreciation for doing a good job and the school demonstrating that it values their professional expertise (see also Recommendation 3 below). These priorities are well above higher salary in the rank order. There is very low support for a wellbeing group. This may have been because a 'nice-to-have' approach to wellbeing was implemented in some schools, with limited impact on whole-school staff and wellbeing and mental health. It may also have been because the role of the wellbeing group was poorly understood. This is an area that is worthy of further investigation, as a number of case-study schools in Parts 2–4 of this book report the positive impact of a staff wellbeing group.

Recommendation 3: Acknowledge the work that teachers do

- Ensure that teachers are complimented for doing a good job.
- Ensure that teachers' expertise and professionalism are respected both personally, with a comment, and publicly – e.g. as a number of case-study schools recommend, with a 'shout-out' during a staff briefing or with an award voted for by the staff.
- As in Recommendation 1 above, remove or decrease admin tasks that have no impact on pupils' emotional development or academic progress.

Recommendation 4: Support teachers who are ill and improve work–life balance

Valuing teachers is linked to the extent to which the school supports them when they are ill and supports their work–life balance and family lives:

- Introduce strategies that show the school's concern when someone is ill for more than a week.

- In combination with the strategies in Recommendation 1, support teachers to achieve a work–life balance, including an email policy that restricts the sending of and replying to emails to weekdays and during a specified time period.
- Get to know teachers' family circumstances and make adjustments, especially when a family member is ill and/or a teacher has problems at home that are affecting them at work. Avoid the 'leave family problems at the school gate' approach. Considering the family circumstances of staff became very important when the Covid-19 pandemic hit schools in March 2020, when some staff and relatives with health conditions had to 'shield' from the virus at home.

We will now consider the results of a much larger survey into school staff wellbeing and mental health which the Teach Well Alliance ran between 22 November 2019 and 22 December 2019.

'Teachers' Lack of Wellbeing and Mental Ill-Health in Schools': A survey conducted by the Teach Well Alliance

Stephen Waters

This report provides an analysis of factors, self-reported in a survey by 1000 teachers and support staff, that contributed to a lack of wellbeing and mental health as a result of working in schools between 22 November and 22 December 2019. At the time of the survey, an expert group had been formed by the Department for Education (DfE) to consider teacher wellbeing. The results of the survey were forwarded to this group by one of its members. As with the smaller survey described in Chapter 2, invitations to complete the survey were posted on 22 November 2019 on the Teach Well Alliance website (www.teach-wellalliance.com) and on Twitter, Facebook, and LinkedIn.

Data was collected from an online survey produced on the survey/form creation platform Typeform. Responses to closed questions were automatically counted. Open questions were analysed using content analysis to count the frequency of words and groups of words to identify the relative importance of recurring themes. Final results for each question were presented in tabular form and illustrated by representative quotations.

The following key findings emerged from answers to the open questions.

Key findings

Adverse mental and physical impact of working in a school

- The greatest adverse mental impact of working in a school is stress (43.4%), followed by anxiety (27.7%), pressure (18.8%), and sleep disturbances (10.1%).
- The main factors causing stress are workload (141.2%: the word 'work' or derivations of it occurred more than once in many responses), expectations (49.4%), meetings (14.1%), Ofsted (14%), change (13.2%), cutbacks (10.4%), and lack of funding (10.3%).

- The greatest adverse physical impact of working in schools is exhaustion (11.3%), followed by crying (2.3%) and headache/migraine (2.1%).

Consequences of adverse impact of working in a school

- The most significant adverse consequences of working in schools are: mental ill-health (12.8 per cent); own family time lost (8%); signed off (5.2%); resigned or about to resign (2.5%); and overwhelmed (2.5%). Three teachers reported considering committing suicide; another had considered 'going missing'.

What the school does or did to help

- Respondents reported the following: talk through situation (6.8%); school counsellor (5.4%); staff support one another (4.2%); and external services available (3.7%).

No help offered by the school

- Alarmingly, 21.5% of respondents were offered no help while 3.1% stated that their wellbeing was acknowledged as important, but no action was taken by the school.

Negative perceptions of staff mental health at school

- The most negative perceptions of staff mental health were as follows: school can't do anything about it – pressures from government/DfE (10%); Ofsted to blame (1.9%); didn't ask for help (1.9%); and budget restricts what can be done (18%).

What the DfE Expert Group on Teachers' wellbeing should consider

- Reduce workload (54.4%); reduce pressure from, change or remove Ofsted (39.2%); create more time including downtime (37.1%); reduce general pressure (20.1%); fund schools adequately (19.3%); reduce expectations (17.7%); reduce admin (13.9%); reduce stress (7%); and more support for dealing with parents (6.1%).

Limitations of the report

While the survey produced wide-ranging results from its open questions, it was unable to address *to what extent* the catch-all term 'workload' included factors that respondents identified elsewhere, such as lack of time, or pressure from Ofsted. It may be worth considering research conducted with online focus groups to identify the main contributory factors to work overload and to explore their interrelationships in more depth. This is especially important for understanding and identifying those factors which, if reduced or removed, would have the most impact on workload reduction.

Overview

Content analysis is very effective in identifying key issues and themes from open responses. What it is unable to do as effectively is to get a sense of the voices behind the responses and the tone of the contributions. In the same way that analysing a work of literature by collating groups of words to explore themes without reading the whole text would lead to an incomplete understanding, the same is true of the outcomes from content analysis. Despite the shortcomings of content analysis, by reading through the responses and counting their frequency, it was possible to identify the following emotional impact of the answers to the open questions:

- There is a worrying tone of low morale, hopelessness, and scepticism that things will change.
- Every teacher who commented on their own family life had a sense that their partners and children or relatives who depend on them are suffering because they are unable to spend time with them.
- Many teachers in this survey dislike or even hate how being a teacher is making them feel.
- Many teachers reported that their love of working with children and young people was being destroyed by their role becoming compromised by workload and never-ending tasks.
- There is very little comment that it is the classroom that is causing the workload. Some teachers reported that it is the least pressurised part of their work. Other teachers stated that admin tasks prevented them planning and/or delivering lessons effectively.
- Headteachers are under pressure to be strong for their staff but often have no-one to turn to for support.
- Governors can be a source of support, but many are not adequately trained or prepared for their role.
- Sadly, in some schools, bullying of staff is the norm. Some schools are abdicating responsibility for taking care of their staff and leaving teachers to care for themselves. Other schools are making token gestures towards promoting wellbeing. A number of schools are doing what they can but are limited by a lack of funding or a lack of understanding or knowledge about wellbeing and mental health.
- The survey clearly revealed that, even in schools that are doing what they can to support their staff, the external pressures from the DfE and government become internal pressures which neither the individual school nor the individual teacher has the financial resources or capacity to manage alone.

Teachers identified an urgent need to reduce external pressure and increase funding, at the same time as exploring strategies at an individual school level to reduce internal pressures. This requires an understanding of the impact of both workload and the discharging of responsibilities at every level, from governing bodies to support staff, and the creation of school communities where each person supports the wellbeing and mental health of its members, including the school's leaders.

- Sadly, and worryingly, three teachers were so depressed that they were suicidal. In order to protect their identities, their responses are not included in the representative quotations.

- As the most recent Ofsted framework was implemented in September 2019 and inspections were suspended during the Covid-19 pandemic from March 2020, there has been insufficient time to assess the impact on school leadership of the statements in the *School Inspection Handbook* (Ofsted, 2019c) on teacher wellbeing, bullying, and harassment, which were included for the first time under Leadership and Management. Several teachers also referred to this point in their responses.

The consequences of staff in schools experiencing mental ill-health are felt, seen, and heard most of all by their pupils in the classroom. While they often literally 'put a brave face on' for their pupils, even young children recognise when their teachers are unhappy and stressed. In Chapter 4, Jonathan Glazzard, Head of Inclusion at the Carnegie School of Education at Leeds Beckett University, reports a research study in which he found a link between teacher wellbeing and pupil progress.

4 Teacher wellbeing and pupil progress

Jonathan Glazzard

Introduction

The World Health Organization (WHO) defines mental health as:

> '... a state of wellbeing in which every individual realizes his or her own potential, can cope with the normal stresses of life, can work productively and fruitfully, and is able to make a contribution to her or his community. Health is a state of complete physical, mental and social wellbeing and not merely the absence of disease or infirmity' (WHO, 2014).

The problem of teacher stress is pervasive. It is evident across all sectors of education and across countries (Gray et al., 2017) and results in Burnout and lower job satisfaction. Teachers are consistently reported to experience an increased risk of developing mental ill-health (Stansfeld et al., 2011; Kidger et al., 2016). Research demonstrates that multiple factors impact on teacher wellbeing, including school climate (Gray et al., 2017). A negative school climate can lead to high rates of teacher absenteeism and staff turnover (Grayson and Alvarez, 2008).

However, many teachers continue to work even when they are ill because they do not want to let their students or colleagues down. They may also be worried about how their absence will be viewed by senior leaders. Research indicates that teachers who demonstrate 'presenteeism' find it more difficult to manage their classrooms effectively (Jennings and Greenberg, 2009) and are less likely to develop positive classroom and behaviour management strategies (Harding et al., 2019). Presenteeism is evident when teachers with poor wellbeing and mental health continue to work. The quality of their work is reduced, and this affects relationships with their students (Jennings and Greenberg, 2009), student wellbeing (Harding et al., 2019), and overall teacher performance (Beck et al., 2011; Jain et al., 2013).

Research study

In September 2018, the Carnegie School of Education at Leeds Beckett University (LBU) conducted a short piece of exploratory research into the effect of.

teacher wellbeing and mental health on pupil progress. The study was based around the following three research questions:

1 What factors affect teacher wellbeing and mental health?
2 How do teacher wellbeing and mental health impact on the progress of students?
3 What resilience strategies are used by highly effective teachers with poor mental health to ensure that their students thrive?

Teachers, headteachers (HTs), and pupils were interviewed in 10 primary schools (the abbreviation 'CS' represents case-study schools). We interviewed teachers with poor mental health (TPHM) and teachers with good mental health (TGMH). Sixty-four primary school pupils were interviewed, representing all year groups. The following sections present an overview of the findings.

Triggers

Teachers reported a number of factors that might trigger feelings of anxiety and stress, some of which were directly related to their professional lives, some to their personal lives, and some that concerned both. Work-related stress triggers included:

- busy times of the year, for example, assessment periods;
- extracurricular activities;
- unexpected and unplanned events.

Interview comments included:

'Keeping up with the pace of change and growing demands and changes in school leadership. It's never about the same thing. It can be about preparing for registration week, or complaints, it changes. Things change, they can pile on and pile on. Nothing is ever piled off. Things keep on being added' (TPMH, CS1).

'I think, for me, I'm good at hiding it, but occasionally you just reach your limit. You're tired, you might have had loads of things to do, the work pressure is piling up, things like Christmas nativities, and fates [sic] and singing carols and things like that ... we are not robots. I think people like to think that we are' (TGMH, CS2).

'Just that there are times when it is so busy and there is so much to do, so much work to do outside of school, as well as inside of school, I think that can have an effect because there isn't enough time to do everything' (TPMH, CS8).

'We get more and more asked of us but no one taking it away and the days aren't any longer' (TPMH, CS4).

'I've had a few personal relationship issues. You can't say it doesn't affect your work, because it does. It's hard to balance a new relationship and a teaching career. They all impact on each other and being a teacher does take more of your time than you think' (TGMH, CS4).

'I think there have been times in this job when it has affected my mental health because I think it is the balance between work life and home life. I think that's what becomes the difficulty, especially when you're having troubles at home it's hard to separate yourself, that becomes hard sometimes' (TPMH, CS8).

Impact of teacher mental health on teaching

Teachers and headteachers identified the negative impact of poor mental health on their pupils:

'When I had poor mental health, I was not able to focus on my teaching. I found it difficult to concentrate on my planning and I struggled to teach with a clear mind. However hard I tried, the other things going on in my life were still there. I couldn't forget about them just because I had walked into school. They were always on my mind' (TPMH, CS4).

'I think as with any walk of life, if you're not performing to the best of your ability, then that will have a knock-on effect on your performance. So, a teacher who is happy, settled, and has a strong sense of wellbeing will perform better than a teacher who's not. And obviously if you teach well, the children make good progress. And if you don't teach so well, they don't' (TGMH, CS6).

'The children's progress isn't going to be the same as with that one consistent member of staff that knows them really well. Their behaviour will go so that all impacts on learning. It takes so long for each individual to build a relationship with those children, then get prepared and sorted out. All that time they're not learning as much as they would have done with their teacher that would have been with them. It will undoubtedly have an impact' (TPMH, CS7).

'I think the children pick up on how the teacher is feeling and then in turn they are not being given that quality teaching experience, so in the short term they are not making the progress that you would expect' (HT, CS8).

'I do think it has an impact, it has an impact on them themselves and how they then want to interact with the teacher or not. So, I think learning is impeded in that way because I wonder if sometimes if they don't like to ask a question again just in case they might get a snappier answer. Or they might get the retort that perhaps you should have been listening' (TGMH, CS8).

'The class that had a long-term supply teacher made less progress during that time. I cannot give you numbers, but they definitely made less progress' (HT, CS9).

Some teachers felt that performance and delivery in the classroom were below par at times of poor mental health, with one commenting: 'teachers who are not in a good state of mind cannot teach effectively' (TGMH, CS6). Some senior leaders reported that a teacher's confidence might suffer or that pupil behaviour in the classroom might deteriorate. The general consensus was that to be fully effective, teachers need to be in good mental health:

'I had realised that the children were suffering, and that progress wasn't brilliant, they weren't getting what they needed from me. You tell yourself to just get on with it as such, which some people would do and some people can't' (TGMH – previously poor, CS3).

'I tried my best to put the children first when I was in school. But my mind was elsewhere. I struggled for a couple of weeks. Then the headteacher pulled me aside and said: 'You're not alright, are you?' I said no and it was the first time that I actually cried. Then I took some time off' (TPMH, CS4).

Coping strategies

There were two types of strategies in place that helped teachers cope with their mental health. Coping strategies included:

- accessing counselling;
- avoiding social media, especially during non-school times;
- listening to music;
- prioritising tasks;
- reducing hours;
- limiting the amount of work they do at home;
- putting time aside for hobbies.

Comments included:

'I've got to that stage in teaching now where I can think, I can organise myself. I can prioritise my workload. A lot of the little things you do when you are an NQT like, classroom displays, etc., I leave that now to the TAs [teaching assistants] or classroom assistants or volunteers. I focus on what is important. It's about delegation, but also knowing that this can wait. It's just prioritising workload and making time for yourself and thinking I'm going home now, I need to put my mind at rest, when I feel like getting back to it I will get some work done without feeling guilty' (TPMH, CS1).

'Making lists, I'm very good at making lists and prioritising. That way I can see that all the things I'm stressing about can actually be achievable and put into some sort of logical order. Sometimes you think I've got this to do and that to do, when am I going to do this and when you actually start and write it down you think, it's not actually that bad' (TPMH, CS2).

'Your job list is never done. You have to find peace with it' (TPMH, CS4).

'It's the realisation that you can't do everything 100%. I think I came into the job eight/nine years ago, thinking, right, I'm going to do everything, 200%, fire it out all of the time, but then it takes over your life so you have to say right, what's the priority?' (TPMH, CS8).

'I used to think that if I didn't get things done people would think badly of me but now I think, actually tonight I'm absolutely exhausted so I'm not going doing anything. If I choose not to plan one night but I have an idea, it's not the end of the world. I'm much better at prioritising' (TPMH, CS10).

Impact on pupils

The majority of children who took part in the pupil discussion groups were familiar with terms such as mental health, stress, and anxiety, even where their school was only at the beginning of their wellbeing journey. They were less likely to have heard of 'depression'; some schools used different terminology calling it 'having a grump on' or being 'in a blue mood':

'Mental health is something that you can't see but that you have. You feel like you are stuck in a wall' (Pupil, CS5).

'It's like, not checking your heartbeat or anything like that; it's like checking your mind' (Pupil, CS8).

'Anxious – when you're very, very scared' (Pupil, CS4).

'Depression – it means you're very upset about something and you can't get it off your mind and it's causing you different problems' (Pupil, CS7).

Children were most familiar with the term 'stress' and many could recall a time when they had felt stressed, either at home or at school. Some Year 6 pupils were feeling stressed by their impending SATs and some were anxious about which school they would be going to next year. Most pupils were feeling happy on the day they were interviewed. All pupils agreed that it was normal to feel a range of different emotions at different times and that adults experience these emotions just as much as they do:

'Sometimes when you're doing something wrong, they get angry. Their facial expressions. You can see from their face if they are angry or happy' (Pupil, CS2).

'When she can't find the rubber, "Where's the rubber?, I can't find the rubber." When people take her white rubber. Sometimes she starts to shout when she is stressed' (Pupil, CS4).

Teachers who were stressed reportedly became short-tempered with their pupils and uncharacteristically irritable when things did not go according to plan. This could be anything from the technology not working properly, to the pupils not understanding the work they were given. Sometimes pupils said the teacher may forget what they had asked the class to do:

'If the teacher is feeling really grumpy, the teacher is like "Urrrh"' (Pupil, CS4).

'Our teacher gets pretty mad when someone can't understand a really easy maths question' (Pupil, CS6).

'Sometimes they start telling people off more frequently because they are having a hard time, so some of the kids get a hard time' (Pupil, CS7).

'When they are happy, they will shout in a good way like when we win or something like, "Yesssss, we did it" [hands up in the air – victory shout]. When they are stressed, it is more of a "What are you doing?" shout' (Pupil, CS6).

'At the start of the year they are really energetic, but when it gets later on in the year they get less [energetic]. Towards test times for KS1 and KS2, they get stressed' (Pupil, CS7).

Pupils reported that when a teacher is stressed, classroom behaviour deteriorates:

'They try to talk but everyone talks over them' (Pupil, CS5).

'When she's like frustrated, in the morning I can tell because she's normally really happy. She's frustrated because she is trying to hide it. But because I've been with her for nearly two years, I can sense it. I'm just like, I know it's not going to be a good day' (Pupil, CS8).

Pupils proved to be quite attuned to the mood of their teacher. Some children tried to help them to be happier by:

- asking the teacher questions she/he can help them with;
- behaving well;
- cheering them up by doing something nice for the teacher and being kind to them;
- giving the teacher some time to get things done;
- keeping quiet or not talking so much in class;
- not upsetting the teacher further or making it worse;
- trying to get others to stop talking;
- trying harder.

Some pupils felt an obligation to try and make things better for the teacher, their classmates, and themselves: 'When our teacher is having a bad day, we just try to help them. We don't want to make it worse so we just get on with our work' (Pupil, CS9).

Some children spoke to the headteacher when they had concerns about their teachers:

'The children in this school tend to seek me out as the person to talk to and they will do that sometimes rather than talking to their own teacher. To me, that says something. And two children from the class where the teacher's mental health, I would say is probably not as healthy as it should be, there are two children that will come and speak to me, or have spoken to me, and have said, "We don't know what to do. We feel that things are not quite right"' (HT, CS8).

When their teachers are happy and in a good mood, pupils said their lessons were more creative, fun, relaxed, and they were given more interesting work to do. Children were keen to impress their teacher and work hard for them. They all felt they made more progress. However, when their teacher was in a bad mood and stressed, children felt it had a detrimental effect on their learning. Children reported that, at such times, they often worked in silence and they tried not to upset their teacher further. Their learning 'slowed down', they found it difficult to concentrate, and the quality of their work was not as good as usual. This was because they tried to finish their work quickly:

'It makes me rush. So that I don't get told off for not finishing it' (Pupil, CS8).

'When the teacher was stressed, some children were left not knowing what they were supposed to be doing, they became confused or got a bit muddled' (Pupil, CS4).

CS1: Extract from pupil discussion group interview:

Researcher: So, when your teacher is sad or stressed, how does that make you feel in the lesson?
Boy 1: The class is silent, there is no talking.
Girl 1: It makes you feel down. You feel stressed as well.
Girl 2: When the teacher's upset, it makes everyone else silent and makes everyone really unhappy.
Boy 2: She gives us more work and we have to work in silence.

CS2: Extract from pupil discussion group interview:

Researcher: How does it make you feel when your teacher is sad?
Girl 1: It makes me want to prove that they don't need to be angry at me. That I can actually do this.
Girl 2: It's not you particularly; they've got too many things going on.

Children in the study had all experienced having a cover teacher stand in for their regular classroom teacher (but not necessarily as a result of the teacher being off through poor mental health) at some time during their school life.

Their views varied on how much it impacted on their learning. Often it was directly correlated to how often, and for how long, the cover was required. For those where it was minimal or where the cover teacher belonged to the school, it did not present too much of an issue. However, for others where cover had been longer-term or involved multiple teachers, it was more problematic. Here, pupils agreed that it had affected their learning and progress. Some pupils found it confusing, reporting that they often got different messages from different teachers and different styles of teaching. The only time they worked harder for a cover teacher was when it was the headteacher.

CS2: Extract from pupil discussion group

Girl 1: When we were in Year 4. I think it may have happened that we had loads of teachers. When we had our first teacher, we learnt quite good stuff, but when we had the second teacher, we had to start all over again. We started over and over and over again.

Boy 1: It's hard to concentrate with them, because you have a new teacher.

Girl 1: They have new ways of how they do it.

Boy 1: This teacher taught us a different way to do it and then another tells you different way.

CS9: Extract from pupil discussion group

Boy 1: The cover teachers don't know us. They don't know where we are up to in our learning, so the work might be too easy or too difficult for us. They might think we have covered things that we haven't yet covered.

Boy 2: They are not as strict as our usual teacher, so we don't work as hard for them.

Teachers, especially headteachers, were keenly aware that having cover teachers can be disruptive for pupils:

'When one of my teachers was off long-term, we had a supply teacher, and the marking and feedback and the consistency following school policy that we had worked hard on as a staff, weren't there ... For children it was that insecurity. You've got your teacher in and you're happy with that person and then a supply comes in for some time, it can knock their confidence. They were upset. You'd started to build a relationship and you have started to see that you have brought children along in their confidence, and then that rug gets pulled out from underneath them, and it does have a negative impact' (HT, CS7).

Conclusion

This small-scale exploratory research into the effects of teacher mental health and wellbeing on pupil progress in primary schools provides a valuable snapshot of some of the current issues facing teachers and their potential impact on pupils in the classroom. The study highlights examples where pupil learning has been affected by their teacher's mood, to a lesser or greater degree, and that pupils are often aware of how their teacher is feeling – no matter how hard the teacher tries to hide it. Pupils reported that they were more productive and learnt more when their teachers were happy, and teaching was consistent. The relationship that develops between pupil and teacher is also key to a primary child's ability to thrive. Some teachers acknowledged that their poor mental health had a detrimental impact on the quality of their teaching and the progress of their pupils. Pupils were very knowledgeable about mental health and were able to articulate strategies for managing their own mental health. They felt that the use of cover teachers for absent teachers had a detrimental impact on both their ability to learn and on their progress. As one teacher said:

'Having the right teacher in the class who is in the right mental health is fundamental to the child's success. The best classes are the ones that have the most stable teachers. The class feed off that. They know that you're a consistent, strong personality in that classroom, every day. And they know that you don't get phased by anything. Then they aspire to that, they want to be like that' (TGMH, CS6).

5 A whole-school approach to wellbeing

Jonathan Glazzard

Introduction

Findings from Education Support (2019), the charity which supports the wellbeing of education professionals, suggested that levels of stress are increasing. The Teacher Wellbeing Index found that:

- 72% of all educational professionals described themselves as stressed (84% of senior leaders).
- 74% of education professionals considered the inability to switch off and relax to be the major contributing factor to a negative work–life balance.
- 57% of all education professionals have considered leaving the sector over the past two years due to pressures on their health and wellbeing.
- 78% of all education professionals have experienced behavioural, psychological, or physical symptoms due to their work.
- 71% of education professionals cited workload as the main reason for considering leaving their jobs.
- 49% of all education professionals considered their organisational culture had a negative effect on their mental health and wellbeing.

(Education Support, 2019)

School culture plays a crucial role in many of these issues. Positive school cultures can mitigate the effects of stress. This chapter outlines the aspects of a whole-school approach to wellbeing for staff and pupils.

The role of the school leadership team

The leadership team is responsible for creating the school culture which influences wellbeing for staff and pupils. It also oversees the development of policies and initiatives which support wellbeing. Before new policies are introduced, it seems sensible for leaders to consider their impact on staff. Policies which result in unnecessary workload for staff are likely to have a detrimental impact on staff wellbeing. Policies which restrict access to the full curriculum or result in punitive behaviour management approaches are likely to have a negative impact on pupils' wellbeing. Including 'wellbeing' as a standard discussion item during senior leadership meetings ensures that it always remains a focus. Ensuring that wellbeing is part of the school improvement plan demonstrates to stakeholders that it is a strategic priority. Developing a policy to support a whole-school approach to mental health is an effective way of demonstrating a strategic commitment to mental health and wellbeing. Allocating a member of staff to take strategic responsibility for the leadership and management of the whole-school approach to mental health and wellbeing is an important step in demonstrating the school's commitment.

The role of governors

Governors play an important strategic role in holding school leaders to account and in monitoring progress towards school improvement targets. Allocating a named governor to take responsibility for monitoring mental health and wellbeing demonstrates a strategic commitment to both staff and pupils. Governing body meetings should address mental health and wellbeing for staff and pupils as a standing agenda item.

School culture

Teacher wellbeing is influenced by factors such as life satisfaction and personal happiness (hedonic perspective) and positive psychological functioning. Teachers demonstrate positive psychological functioning when they are able to form good interpersonal relationships with others, have a sense of autonomy and competence, and when they have opportunities for personal growth (Harding et al., 2019). School culture influences teachers' daily experiences in school. It is shaped by the school ethos which is established by the senior leadership team. Limiting teacher agency can result in diminished teacher wellbeing, which has a detrimental impact on teacher performance (Beck et al., 2011). A negative school climate can lead to high rates of teacher absenteeism and staff turnover (Grayson and Alvarez, 2008). Evidence also suggests that there is an association between school climate and teacher and student wellbeing (Gray et al., 2017). Additionally, research indicates that a positive school climate increases student academic achievement (MacNeil et al., 2009). This might be because a positive school climate results in better teacher engagement, higher levels of commitment, and increased staff and student self-esteem and wellbeing (Gray et al, 2017). Research even suggests that a positive school climate can mitigate the negative effects of the school's socio-economic context on students' academic success (Thapa et al, 2013). [Ed: This is exemplified in many of the case-study schools.] It would appear that a negative school climate detrimentally impacts on the wellbeing of both teachers and students and has a negative impact on student attainment.

Positive teacher–student relationships support children and young people to be mentally healthy (Kidger et al., 2012; Plenty et al., 2014). These relationships help students to feel more connected to their school (Harding et al., 2019) and improve student wellbeing (Aldridge and McChesney, 2018) through fostering a sense of belonging. Research demonstrates that teachers with poor mental health may find it more difficult to develop and model positive relationships with their students (Jennings and Greenberg, 2009; Kidger et al., 2010). In addition, higher rates of teacher absence can impact on the quality of teacher–student relationships (Jamal et al., 2013). This is because relationships are fostered through human connection.

Resilience

Resilience is not fixed, innate, or unified. It changes according to context and is supported by the nested systems which surround individuals. Therefore, resilience is relational. This conceptualisation of resilience suggests that access to social support from peers, supportive colleagues, and personal relationships can increase an individual's resilience. Access to supportive workplace environments plays a crucial role in supporting resilience. Policy and legislative contexts also influence resilience positively or negatively depending on the extent to which they are supportive.

Greenfield's (2015) model of teacher resilience offers a useful conceptual framework because the model describes a more insightful perspective of resilience compared to existing models which simply offer lists of personal and protective factors (Figure 5.1). It demonstrates how teacher resilience is situated within an ecological framework and is influenced by a variety of factors. These factors are outlined below:

- **Capacity to take action:** engaging in professional development, stress relief, reflection, and reframing can enhance resilience.
- **Challenges:** the nature of the challenges that teachers are exposed to influence their resilience.
- **Context:** the broader policy context influences resilience in teachers. The emphasis on performance-related indicators of success in recent years can have a detrimental impact on resilience.

The link between teacher wellbeing and pupil progress

This section reports more findings from the research study that was introduced in Chapter 4. Across the ten case-study schools, we explored a range of strategies that schools had established to support staff wellbeing.

Figure 5.1 Proposed model of teacher resilience (Greenfield, 2015)

Most of the schools had, or were about to put into place, strategies to help staff cope with issues of mental health and wellbeing. Some were whole-school strategies that included pupils as well as all staff. Some were practical, work-based strategies, whilst others were more about giving emotional support or boosting morale.

Common strategies included the following:

- At least one school had a wellbeing policy in place.
- An afternoon off during the term for staff to do with as they please.
- Being more aware of how decisions taken by senior management affect staff.
- Implementing a buddy system – where everyone is paired up with someone (in a different year group) they can talk to when they are feeling stressed. 'Sometimes you don't want to go to the senior managers or the HT if you have a problem. You just want to have a more relaxed chat with your buddy' (TPMH, CS2).
- Having an open culture throughout the school, driven by the headteacher and the senior leadership team.

- Headteachers being more visible in the classroom to support staff.
- Including wellbeing in performance targets.
- Inviting staff to form a wellbeing group.
- Managing or reducing workloads; for example, one school (CS4) had returned to planning lessons in handwritten form instead of what was described as 'beautiful schemes of work, typed up in loads of detail' that are just not necessary.
- Reducing unnecessary planning and marking, and reducing assessment.
- Phased returns for staff who have been absent.
- Random acts of kindness, with one school having an impromptu 'happiness fairy' where staff anonymously left each other gifts.
- Rationalisation of initiatives, ensuring they are joined-up and there is no duplication.
- Staff training around mental health and wellbeing, of both children and adults.
- Subscribing to an external wellbeing service which provided packages of support.
- Treating staff well and with respect.

One teacher rewarded himself by coming to school later on a Friday, not arriving in school until 'bang-on' 8:15 a.m. He commented: 'I prepare the night before but don't come in until 8:15 a.m. I go to McDonald's for breakfast and a coffee. It's my treat, because every other morning I'm here from 7/7:15. So Friday morning is my treat morning.'

Some members of staff were encouraged to leave at 3:45 p.m. As part of their mental health target, they were encouraged to go home and recharge. Several schools had proactive strategies in place that were driven by the head-teacher and the senior leadership team. These mainly centred around senior leaders (SLs) being more aware of staff moods – much easier to do in a small primary school – and having an open culture that encouraged staff to talk and keep the lines of communication open:

'We have a senior management meeting each week and one of the standard items is staffing. We talk about any staff that we are concerned about, because we want them to be ok. It's not that we are concerned about the job that they are doing, that's completely different. It's more the personal side of things. That's not just myself, it's my assistant head and my deputy head as well because they'll get different vibes from their position that I get from where I am' (HT, CS4).

'It's about being flexible and staff understanding that they don't always have to stick to the timetable. It's trusting people' (HT, CS7).

'It is almost knowing their personalities, and with it being a small school, you're working very, very closely with people and you get to know them on a closer level, if you like. So, you are aware of what may work well with them or some of the ways to deal with them. It's that emotional intelligence; that is what I'm getting at' (HT, CS8).

'It's about picking things up as a team. We have moved away from "this is your class; these are your pupils". If one teacher is feeling that they are struggling, they will take on that responsibility together, talk about it, and have collective responsibility for progress … They know what's coming up and when. It's that clarity of communication between us all' (SL, CS10).

A senior leader at CS2 summed up the general direction in which many of the case-study schools were moving:

'As a leadership team we just started to become more aware of how our decisions, how our practices, affect our staff. We can't take the stress away; we can't make it a school that has no stress, or no pressure, that's just not reasonable. The job is high stress, high pressure because it comes with accountability. And with any accountability comes stress. So, we can't remove the stress, but what we can do is be aware of it and try and put measures in place to reduce it and manage it so that it is reasonable' (SL, CS2).

However, some schools missed the fact that their teachers were stressed and, as a result, failed in their duty of care. As one teacher with poor mental health highlighted:

'I feel like the teachers in my old schools should have noticed that I wasn't coping. I was staying in school until 10 p.m. every night and they should have questioned that to see if everything was alright at home. They didn't question it and I didn't go home because I was experiencing domestic violence by my partner. So, I stayed in school and worked and worked and they let me. In fact, they just piled on more work' (TPMH, CS3).

Reducing planning

There is no DfE requirement for teachers to produce lengthy lesson plans. Reducing time spent planning lessons will support teachers' wellbeing. Teachers can use commercially produced lesson plans and annotate these to meet the needs of their classes. There is no need to rewrite them. Commercially produced schemes of work with accompanying resources also help to save time. Collaborative planning with other colleagues reduces the burden of planning.

Reducing marking

School marking policies need to take into account the impact that they will have on staff workload. Many schools have now moved away from policies which require teachers to mark every single piece of work. Ways to reduce marking include:

- providing children with verbal feedback during lessons;
- marking work with pupils during lessons;
- book sampling – marking a selection rather than a whole-class set of books to identify pupils' strengths and weaknesses; misconceptions are addressed in the next lesson;
- marking with the pupils in class, for example, by marking work on a visualiser;
- using more pupil self- and peer-assessment during lessons;
- planning lessons so that pupils work practically and do not record work in their books, or finding alternative ways of documenting learning rather than through writing;
- marking one piece of work in-depth every half-term and using 'quick' marking the rest of the time.

Making assessment manageable

Reducing the number of assessment points will support staff wellbeing. [Ed: In the research by Waters, covered in Chapter 3, inputting or providing data was one of the factors that led to stress.] A typical comment was:

'Stop making teaching such an impossible job; the pressure on teachers and management is unreal and unnecessary: the data, evidence, assessments, observations, book scrutinies, pupil progress meetings, targets, planning, the list goes on. Give teachers and the profession the care and respect it deserves. Value good teachers and treat them well to hang on to them, stop the mentality of teachers not being good enough and always throughout every term having to prove themselves and justify their pay, etc.'

Supporting pupil and staff wellbeing

Pupil and staff wellbeing are supported by a whole-school approach to mental health which is driven by the leadership team. The model shown in Figure 5.2 includes the following key aspects of building a whole-school culture of wellbeing and mental health:

- **Leadership and management:** mental health and wellbeing should be driven by the school leadership team, included in the School Improvement Plan (SIP), and documented in a policy which outlines how the different facets of wellbeing will be addressed.

Figure 5.2 Eight principles to promoting a whole-school and -college approach to emotional health and wellbeing (Public Health England, 2015)

- **School culture:** leaders should create a positive school culture which allows staff and pupils to experience a sense of belonging.
- **Curriculum, teaching, and learning:** pupils should be given a broad curriculum which enables them to develop their knowledge and skills. All pupils should have a mental health curriculum which develops their mental health literacy and their wellbeing.
- **Schools should develop a range of approaches to support mental health and wellbeing in partnership with pupils:** for example, by developing peer mentoring schemes or mental health ambassador schemes.
- **Staff:** all staff require training to equip them to identify the signs and symptoms of mental ill-health. In addition, whole-school approaches to staff wellbeing enable staff to thrive.
- **Identification of need:** schools should develop approaches to identify mental ill-health. These approaches should go beyond being reactive, i.e. identifying children with visible signs of mental ill-health. Some children

(and staff) develop mental ill-health but do not demonstrate visible signs. Approaches to universal screening and ongoing monitoring and tracking of mental health and wellbeing ensure that needs are quickly identified and targeted.

- **Interventions:** different levels of interventions are required for all pupils (universal offer), groups of pupils, and individual pupils who require highly personalised interventions. Clinical interventions are not suitable for all children and therefore schools should develop a range of educational interventions to support wellbeing and monitor the impact of interventions.
- **Working in partnership with parents:** schools should provide guidance to parents on how they can support children's mental health needs at home. In addition, schools should also consider how to support parents with mental ill-health – for example, by signposting them to services in the community, or by providing parental workshops.
- **Referral:** schools should develop clear policies for referral for children who have persistent and serious mental ill-health. Schools should work in partnership with health and social care services to ensure that the needs of children with mental ill-health are met.

Conclusion

Most teachers knew where to go to for support should they need it. Many felt comfortable approaching their headteacher or a member of their senior leadership team. CS2 had recently conducted a psychologically safe staff survey which found that all staff felt comfortable going to an identified person to talk about their mental health should they need to. One teacher stated: 'Professionally, my first port of call would be my headteacher, because I respect his opinion. And I think he will actually think about my wellbeing and the wellbeing of the children' (TGMH, CS6). However, this was not the case in all schools. One of the teachers with poor mental health at CS1 clearly felt their current headteacher was not as open or approachable as they could be, commenting:

> In terms of leadership, I don't think anyone dare go and knock on the door and say it is all a bit too much. You need to hear it from the leaders. Just someone that says: "We know you are human." The previous head organised Wellbeing Team fun activities. Especially on the first day back. We went to the seaside once. Socialising made us really happy and relaxed. We did ballroom dancing. It just reminded you that we are human and can have fun. Now you walk in and no-one says good morning, you go and make yourself a drink, sit yourself down with the laptop, and at 9 o'clock your children come in and that's when you leave that table. And the same happens at night (TPMH, CS1).

Most teachers agreed that a teacher's wellbeing affects their performance as an education professional, especially their ability to deliver in the classroom.

Teachers' wellbeing is finely balanced; the challenge is not necessarily increased workloads, as is commonly assumed. It can often be a crisis in their personal life – especially relationship difficulties, family bereavement, illness, or childcare issues – which tips them over the edge. Teachers reported a number of work-related stress triggers, including busy times of the year, such as assessment periods; the pressure of extracurricular activities; the unexpected; keeping up with the pace of change; and changes in school leadership. Many teachers who experienced poor wellbeing professed to wanting to stay in control and were striving to do everything to perfection all of the time; realising this is not always possible appeared to be a large part of their recovery. [Ed: A lack of control is one of the six factors identified by Maslach as contributing to Burnout; see Chapter 1.]

Being organised and the ability to prioritise are two essential skills teachers need to maintain good wellbeing. Key coping strategies included talking to family and friends and putting a time limit on the amount of schoolwork they did at home. Most case-study schools had a number of strategies in place to help staff with their wellbeing and mental health; some were formal, some were informal in nature. Several revolved around reducing workloads and sharing responsibility. At least one school now includes wellbeing and mental health in each teacher's annual performance targets. All schools in the study were striving to be more open about wellbeing and mental health.

6 Buffer leadership and staff wellbeing

Stephen Waters

Overview

This chapter considers what I have called 'buffer' leadership, where head-teachers and school leaders place themselves as a cushion between the DfE, the government, Ofsted, and the governing body/trust board and their school, protecting staff as far as possible from the pressures and stresses of external accountability. Discussion focuses on how leaders can become emotionally drained by adopting this role, if they do not ask for support and help from the staff.

What is 'buffer' leadership?

In schools where there is high staff motivation and good morale, senior leadership acts as what I have called a 'buffer' between government policy, Ofsted, and the staff. While this is not always an explicit or conscious strategy, its impact can be seen in some of the case-study schools featured in this book.

'Buffer' leadership can be defined as leadership which seeks to protect the staff from the adverse consequences of government policy and Ofsted inspection requirements. It can include reducing high-stakes accountability strategies or replacing them with approaches that develop trust and support professional development. In schools where buffer leadership is evident, staff are also invited to take risks, without being afraid that they will fail. Mistakes are regarded as learning opportunities.

Buffer leadership is characterised by some or all of the following strategies:

- Replacing hierarchical and judgement-based teaching observations with teacher-led professional development strategies, such as Lesson Study. This is typically where two or more teachers work together to observe and feed back to one another, usually after self-identifying a specific focus when they are being observed. The focus is either an aspect of teaching and learning that they would like their colleague to see because it is successful or, alternatively, because it is not going as well as expected and they would like feedback to improve it.

- Replacing book scrutiny with sampling work across a number of classes to identify misconceptions or to identify examples of excellence, followed by collaborative discussion.
- Marking: replacing micromanaged marking policies where a certain number of books or exercises must be marked each day – and, in some cases, in a specific manner or with different coloured pens – with verbal feedback in the classroom. At the time of writing (2020), methods of verbal feedback were still evolving. One method is to give the whole class verbal feedback on a task that they have handed in; another is to give individual pupils feedback on what is successful in their work and what they need to improve; a third is for pupils to assess each other's work by giving verbal feedback to their peers, with the teacher providing the criteria for the assessment. In these examples, pupils can also be asked to add comments to their own work or that of a peer.
- Reducing meetings or the length of meetings.
- Setting a daily deadline when emails can be sent and/or received.
- Removing the requirement that staff stay until a certain time at the end of each school day (excluding 20 minutes directed time for supervision of the site to ensure the safety of the pupils).
- Removing specific, and often unnecessarily prescriptive, 'non-negotiables' (a phrase loaded with implications). An example mentioned by staff often on social media is how displays should be mounted in classrooms, including being triple backed, staples facing in the same direction, lamination requirements, use of specific colours, use of specific designs of borders, size of lettering, and so on. (All of these 'rules' were reported by teachers.)

Buffer leadership can never remove the stress of staff workload completely – teaching is a demanding profession – but it can go a long way to reducing its impact by addressing its worst excesses and promoting wellbeing, not only in individual teachers, but in the school community as a whole.

Covid-19 and teacher wellbeing

At the time the script for this book was sent to the publisher – September 2020 – schools in England had just returned after the summer break. From March to July schools had been open to vulnerable children and children of key workers, such as doctors, paramedics, and nurses, because of the Covid-19 pandemic. Teachers had also had to adapt to teaching children who were not in school online, via platforms such as Zoom or Microsoft Teams.

From anecdotal evidence gathered from teachers on Twitter, Facebook, and LinkedIn, many teachers were very concerned about their wellbeing when schools reopened to all children. Some of their major concerns were:

- The contradictory DfE advice about wearing masks. Masks were obligatory at the time on public transport and in shops but the DfE guidance stated that staff did not need to wear masks in schools because the risk of infection among children was low. If the headteacher believed it was necessary, masks were advised for pupils in corridors and other confined spaces where footfall was high or in schools in a high-risk area where a local lockdown had been imposed for a period of time to reduce transmission of infection. At the time of writing, more than 600 schools in England had sent pupils and staff home from their 'bubble' (a group of children and/or their teacher(s) who spent most of their time in school together) to self-isolate because a case of Covid-19 had been confirmed. There had been no mention by the DfE and government ministers of the increased stress and anxiety that staff were experiencing in reopening schools fully.

- A number of teachers were worried about their own risk of catching Covid-19 because they had family at home who were vulnerable.
- The government concluded that the risk of pupils catching the virus was small and that, if they became infectious, most would recover quickly. However, facts about children and young people being carriers, and therefore able to pass on Covid-19, were limited.
- Some teachers were concerned about a perception held by some members of the public that they are being dictated to by the teaching unions and were creating problems where there were none.
- There was a tension between schools returning in full and the need to sustain the economy. Some teachers felt that their wellbeing was being put at risk so that people could go back to work.
- There was a concern that some children would have 'fallen behind'. This is an argument that the government used repeatedly to justify an urgent need to reopen schools fully.

Headteachers and wellbeing

It is clear from the schools' accounts in this book that their headteachers look after the staff and pupils by providing buffer leadership, often at the risk of their own wellbeing. This is seen in the way that:

- Headteachers work long hours, including at weekends, and were never 'off duty'.
- They put the needs of their staff first and their own needs last.
- They seek to maintain morale by remaining cheerful in the face of challenge and adversity.
- They are self-effacing about their own role in motivating staff, saying that they have a wonderful set of teachers, non-teaching staff, and support staff.
- They publicly acknowledge and praise the work of staff, both individually and as a group.

- They go the extra mile if staff need support at school or if they are ill and on sick leave.
- They create a strong sense of school community where staff are encouraged to ask for help and support one another.

You will recall (see p. 7) that Maslach identified a lack of community as one of the six causes of Burnout. Conversely, as reported by the case-study schools, a school community reinforces wellbeing. In schools where a sense of community is all-pervasive, rather than the headteacher adopting buffer leadership and protecting the staff from external pressures, the school community acts as a protector of all staff, including the headteacher. The characteristics of such schools are:

- Anyone, including senior leadership and the headteacher, can ask for support from anyone else. So the headteacher can, for example, ask an early career teacher for help.
- There is a strong tendency towards a flat management structure where relationships are more important than the formal hierarchical structure created by job roles.
- Authenticity, honesty, and transparency are valued highly. The headteacher sets an example of these values in practice by being prepared to admit when they are struggling and need support. An example might be that the headteacher is concerned about the length of time they are spending in school after the pupils have gone home. They might ask their staff to remind them about maintaining a work–life balance if they are still in their office after a certain time at the end of the day. A school-based example might be a request to the staff from the headteacher to remind them to take a break from a daily duty if they seem to be stressed or looking tired. By setting an example of asking the school community for support, the headteacher creates a climate where staff feel able to approach their colleagues in a similar manner and reinforces a sense that 'we're all in this together'.

In schools, then, where a culture of staff wellbeing and mental health has replaced high-stakes accountability and takes priority over formal relationships defined by line responsibilities and role definitions, the school community looks after its staff and the staff look after one another. To achieve this self-supporting culture of staff wellbeing, trust and respect have to be built over a period of time. Once attained, however, the benefits are considerable, not least that teachers are more able to withstand the considerable challenges presented by the wonderful, but challenging, work of being a teacher.

Part **2**

Primary School Case Studies

7

Three Bridges Primary School, Southall, Ealing, London

'There is Another Way'

Jeremy Hannay, Headteacher, with Stephen Waters

'There is no pupil wellbeing, there's no pupil achievement, there's no pupil collaboration, there's no pupil collective responsibility, there's no pupil anything, until the adults experience it first ... it's quite a simple equation – if we're not putting our adults in a soil that is nutrient rich – that will allow them to flourish into whoever they want to be as an educator, they have no chance of doing that effectively and sustainably in a classroom of children. Because sometimes, very often as a child, you have to watch somebody love something before you can learn to love yourself. That is a nutrient that gets overlooked in many schools – that we need to make sure as leaders that we take care of the people who take care of our pupils.'

Overview

Jeremy Hannay, headteacher of Three Bridges Primary School, is a frank and outspoken critic of high-stakes accountability leadership of schools and the Ofsted inspection process by which schools are judged. In this forthright interview with the book's author and editor, Stephen Waters, he describes how he has rejected the model that, in order to raise standards and improve results, teachers must be scrutinised, monitored, and controlled. By restoring trust and professional respect and supporting teacher-led professional development, Jeremy explains how teacher agency leads to teacher mental wellbeing.

Context

Three Bridges Primary School is in Southall, West London. It is a larger than average two-form entry community school, with over 400 pupils, a nursery class, and two reception classes. Over 40% of the children are identified as Pupil Premium (PP). Ninety-six per cent of the children are Black, Asian, and

Minority Ethnic (BAME); 75–80% come from a wide range of heritages and have English as an additional language (EAL). A small number of children are at the early stages of speaking English. The proportion of disadvantaged children is well above average, as is the proportion of pupils receiving Special Educational Needs and Disability (SEND) support at 25%. Transience is also high, with 35% of the children leaving or joining the school before they reach Year 6, and the proportion of pupils joining the school after the early years is higher than the national average. One of the catchment estates is in the second percentile for crime and violence, and Three Bridges Primary School is one of 75 primary schools with the most disadvantaged communities in the country. Results are excellent, with the school in the top 3% in the UK in terms of progress over the last 7 years.

Three Bridges is an outward-facing school offering training and support and development for schools, teachers, and school leaders. Between 2016 and 2020, the school supported and trained over 300 schools, and more than 2000 teachers and school leaders, locally, nationally, and internationally.

In January 2020, John Dutaut, CEO of Elemental Learning and Skills, interviewed Jeremy for *Schools Week*. Jeremy emigrated to the UK with his partner, also a teacher, from Ontario, Canada in 2012. He joined Three Bridges while a supply teacher. At the time, the school was 'Outstanding' but Jeremy explained how 'he found an accountability culture he hadn't imagined possible'. He subsequently took up post as assistant headteacher in another 'good' school but, in a matter of weeks, it went into 'Special Measures'. Jeremy returned to Three Bridges as a teacher and team leader and, within a year, the school narrowly avoided a judgement of 'Requires Improvement', saved only by its previous results. As Key Stage 2 lead, Jeremy took a completely different approach to achieving results and they improved. He then became assistant head and deputy head before becoming headteacher designate and then substantive headteacher of Three Bridges in 2017. From the start of his headship, Jeremy's focus was on teamwork and trust, two qualities that he had learned from his time as the Regional Director of Athlete Development in Ontario for the sport of volleyball. In September 2020, Jeremy began his ninth year in the school.

His catchphrase, 'There is Another Way', has become synonymous with a growing number of headteachers, teachers, and educators who believe that high-stakes accountability is affecting teachers' wellbeing and mental health, driving them out of the profession and contributing to the challenges of recruiting staff (see www.the-otherway.com).

My interview with Jeremy Hannay

This chapter is based on a video-recorded and transcribed interview I conducted with Jeremy one late afternoon in September 2019. I had become aware of Jeremy's approach to staff wellbeing and mental health via Twitter conversations and his blogs on teacher accountability. His views coincided with my reason for creating the Teach Well Alliance: in order for teachers to engage pupils in their learning and to take care of them, the wellbeing and mental health of teachers must come first. I wanted to explore Jeremy's approach further and he kindly agreed to be interviewed. He allowed me unrestricted use of the content.

Before the interview, Jeremy took me on a tour of the school. Even without children in the building, the environment was inspirational. Creativity, freedom of expression, joy, wonder, and pride oozed from every pore of the building. Life-size papier-mâché figures, built by the children, stood in the corridors. Jack was climbing up his beanstalk in the stairwell between the ground and first floor. Displays celebrated children's work or presented a theme or topic which the children were exploring. Jeremy explained that all the displays and figures had been created by the children, supported by their teachers. There were no 'rules' about how displays should look, no insistence on having the same borders of the same width or of the same colour, no rules about which direction the staples should point. The quality of each new display was influenced by previous displays.

Classrooms are inspiring places of learning, with ongoing work or projects hung from washing lines across classrooms. Evidence of teachers' lessons from the day is work in progress, rather than sanitised for other eyes. Enjoyment in teaching and engagement in learning was evident in every room I visited. I remarked that there are similarities between layout and displays in classrooms. Jeremy explained that this is embryonic, that it had evolved from teachers visiting each other's classrooms and using ideas from one another. There are no top-down rules about how teachers should design or present their rooms.

We returned to Jeremy's office to video the interview. I began by asking him how he would describe Three Bridges:

'I probably wouldn't describe it any differently than most headteachers describe their schools ... it's academically rich. I think that our children come away from our school, you know, being able do the core skills – reading, writing and solving problems quite strongly, but I would also say that there is a much larger part to what we do here. A big part of our curriculum is around adventure; the children here are not just learning to read, write and solve problems – they are canoeing and kayaking, learning teamwork and resilience and self-direction. They're learning to build fires and use chemical tools ...

'... I can tell you that we're the happiest school on earth ... there is a really heavy focus on ensuring that the adults in the building are well-taken care of ... I think some of my colleagues are saying you've got to put pupils first. Put the children first, that's going to be the centre of all decision-making and I don't want anyone to think that what I'm suggesting is counter to that message.

'I guess it's simply put like this: There is no pupil wellbeing, there's no pupil achievement, there's no pupil collaboration, there's no pupil collective responsibility, there's no pupil anything until the adults experience it first. I think to me it's quite a simple equation – if we're not putting our adults in a soil that is nutrient rich – that will allow them to flourish into whoever they want to be as an educator, they have no chance of doing that effectively and sustainably in a classroom of children. Because sometimes, very often as a child, you have to watch somebody love something before you can learn to love yourself. That is a nutrient that gets overlooked in many schools – that we need to make sure as leaders that we take care of the people who take care of our pupils. It's a crucial element.'

Staff wellbeing and mental health

I asked Jeremy what he did to improve staff wellbeing and mental health when he took up the post as headteacher:

'I've been at Three Bridges for eight years. I've been here quite a long time and I have had a number of different roles in the school and the work … building a culture around the development of staff, the support of staff, the wellbeing of staff started before I was the headteacher here. And it really meant interrogating all of the pieces of the school that we had always done … There's a poster somewhere, somewhere in my office here that … the most dangerous phrase in our language is "We've always done it that way".

'So, it was really about asking why. Why are we marking for four hours a night … for children sometimes who can't read what it is you're writing and is that the most effective way of communicating? Is that the best way to give feedback?

'And we looked at … collective responsibility and collaborative design, so taking care of the instructional programme. When I started at Three Bridges … the achievement of the children was not great, was poor … there wasn't a lot of consistency or rigour around the instructional programme. It hadn't been clearly disseminated or collaboratively decided, so it was really about taking, taking the bits and pieces I thought would get the monkeys off our back and dealing with those things first. So, we redesigned as a collaborative our instructional programmes … what I mean by that is I think this school was used to someone coming in saying "we're going to do this and I'll be in next week to check that you're doing it, and then I'm going to take a look at your books and your planning to make sure it's to the standard … that's how I'm going to know you're doing it". And I grew up in a system [in Ontario, Canada] that does not behave that way and understands that if you want long-term sustainable impact you can't treat people that way.'

Leadership and management

'So, I guess those were the first … those were the first changes … about interrogating how it was we were going to change. Was it going to be through management practices or was it going to be through leadership? And ... that's something that has become a real challenge in our system in the last decade ... that we are dressing up management as leadership and it's not. So, monitoring and scrutinising and holding people to account and observing lessons and rating things, scrutinising books, scrutinising planning in advance ... those are management practices and I'm not suggesting that there is no place for management in schools ... management helps systems run effectively, organisations run smoothly. But we can't dress it up as leadership because it's not ... it's a part of effective leadership but it is not the whole, it is not the whole piece.

'And so, I think what I tried to do was build our social capital. Really put teachers in situations where they were talking effectively and directly about learners and learning, so that it wasn't just meaningless meetings ... they were purposeful and that the decisions that they were making in those meetings about instruction, they were immediately putting into practice and then they have an opportunity to come back and say whether or not it was working and so that's how we constructed our instructional programmes ... not I'm telling you what to do and I'm going to make sure you're doing it, but let's look at what research says is high-quality instruction, let's go give it a try, let's go away and have a play. Let's come back and analyse what works in our school in our context and what's not working and when things are not working, let's support each other making those things better ... those were the initial seeds planted to help Three Bridges grow into the collaborative success perhaps it is today.'

In June 2019, a month before I interviewed Jeremy, he had been interviewed by the magazine *Teach Primary* and had said this about the culture of professionalism he encourages at Three Bridges, which is integral to teacher wellbeing:

'The teachers know that they are afforded the capacity and professionalism of disagreeing. They don't do things because I want them to do it. No one in this building is afraid to tell me if they think something isn't right. But they also know they're part of the solution. They can say "This isn't working, so why don't we try it this way?"'

'There is Another Way'

In following Jeremy on Twitter and reading his blog posts, I had seen his phrase 'There is Another Way' recurring in the context of school leadership. I asked Jeremy to explain what he meant by it.

'... over time, I've eliminated virtually every overt invasive, interrogative management practice and replaced it with leadership and that's at every level, not just from me. I would say actually today very rarely from me ... the purpose of doing a lot of this was to create a self-sustaining school, to be a leader who's uncovering a leader who's uncovering a leader. You know, the hero leader paradigm is one that's been proven as a failure over and over again.

'So, what is the "other way"? I think the other way is looking at why … what it is we're doing and why we're doing it and then moving those practices as far away from us as possible and replacing them with things like lesson and learning study, with teacher research groups, with collective responsibility … with decisional capital, giving teachers the opportunity not only to study learners and learning but enact decisions that make a difference in the lives of their children.

'I think it's really been about also identifying what management practices are requisite. What is it that we need to do to ensure that the organisation runs smoothly, and things are improving and how is it that we're gauging those things, but enacting … the decisions, the determinations from those management practices in the most humane and the most ethical way possible?

'So, observation is a common one … we hear of schools where teachers are being observed … six times a year. They're being given a feedback sheet; it's coming from someone who is hierarchically above them and when you ask why that is, why is it you're observing teachers, often people say "well, it's about consistency" or "it's about practice". I make sure that the practice is good enough or it's about compliance, making sure they're doing what we said is best practice in our school and I don't think anybody would argue that there's a problem with having consistencies in a school. I think most teachers say that that's a positive thing. I don't think that there would be teachers who would say high-quality practice is something that's a bad thing, I think all teachers inherently want to be their very, very best …

'… leadership, I think at its heart is influence. So, if what we want are consistencies or we want high-quality practice or we want professional people who are growing to be better professionals than they were last week or last month or last year, then it's really about asking under what conditions can we facilitate that happening without putting them under pressure, without making it high-stakes, without making them feel like there's a gun to their head. How can we put them in the right soil? So, at Three Bridges those are the kinds of questions that we ask ourselves. What are the conditions that are necessary for professional people to take responsibility for their own learning – teacher-led learning – and what happens when you pull away the observation and you input something like micro-research or lines of inquiry for professional growth? You see development take off because … someone once said to me "you can mandate mediocrity, but you can only unleash greatness" and that's what's happened here.

'As a leader I want the teachers in the school to be a better teacher than I was. I want them one day to be a better leader than I am. It's like, you know, being a parent, you want your children to have better opportunities and a better life than you have. Well, as a leader you should wish the same thing for your staff. I want the teachers here to be the very, very best they can be. The teachers in this school today are better teachers than I was. That's why I know I'm doing the right thing. They're self-regulating, they're inquisitive, they never ever settle – they always want to be better – a healthy dose of self-improvement but it's because they're leading it on things that they're passionate about. They're able to reflect now without pressure and say, "I'm struggling here, and

I've heard you're doing some cool stuff with that. Can you help?" And it's a culture now of self-referral. When someone's struggling or someone's uncertain, it's a culture of collaborative development, so the reception teacher is working with the Year 3 teacher to improve. It's about collective responsibility. Nobody refers to themselves as a classroom teacher, they're schoolteachers. We here are the stewards of all of our children. There's no sense at Three Bridges being a great teacher if the teacher down the hall is struggling.'

In his interview for *Schools Week*, Jeremy had referred to how staff planned series of lessons collaboratively and took collective responsibility if learning did not happen as they intended. Teachers were only too willing to examine what had gone wrong and to work as a team to put it right. He described this approach as being located in a 'professional coaching culture'.

At the heart of improving teaching and learning were three collaborative processes which Jeremy identified in a series of blog posts, 'No Ordinary Classroom', in July 2019:

1 Learning and Lesson Study
2 Teacher Research Groups
3 Open lessons

Learning and Lesson Study

Learning and Lesson Study originated in Japan. A group of three teachers collaborate on a series of lessons that involve research questions related to teaching and learning. Learners are placed at the centre of the enquiry as the teacher identifies pupils who will report back to the teacher on the lesson. After the lesson, the pupils are interviewed and the group of teachers discuss the lesson, the pupils' feedback, what was successful and what might need further development.

Teacher Research Groups

As in Learning and Lesson Study, a Teacher Research Group (TRG) is often a group of teachers from different schools who collaborate to explore an aspect of pedagogy over an extended period of time, usually 12 months. A facilitator, knowledgeable about the aspect of teaching to be investigated, supports each member of the group to conduct research on the agreed topic in their own setting, organises debriefings and a group conversation to discuss the findings. The facilitator also sets 'gap tasks' between meetings which take place every two months. The aim of the TRG is to encourage reflective practice and to influence teaching approaches by sharing and creating good practice.

Open lessons

An open lesson shares characteristics with the Teacher Research Group but is a single lesson and is an alternative to judgemental hierarchical lesson observations. As with the TRG, a facilitator discusses the focus of the lesson with one or more observers. The lesson is observed live or through a video link or recording. The teacher who has taught the lesson shares their view of the lesson with the observers; the intention is to open up a learning conversation, rather than arriving at a judgement.

At the time of my interview with Jeremy, a polarisation was emerging on Twitter, on educational forums, and in educational magazines and journals, between traditional and progressive education, with a resurgence of interest in Rosenshine's work on instruction (EdCentral Team, undated). As Jeremy had referred to 'instruction' earlier in the interview, I wanted to know what his views were on this apparent dichotomy and the relevance of it to his views on leadership.

Traditional or progressive?

'... I guess my view is that there is a time and a place for virtually everything ... I mean, in our school when we teach phonics it is direct instruction. There's a scripted lesson. There is no fluff or bells and whistles. It is a very, very direct instruction, a scripted programme and it is incredible ... until I find something that is more incredible than that, this will be what we do. There is nothing better in my mind. I have never seen children learn to read as joyfully and quickly as they do with the way we teach phonics. But we don't teach maths that way ... and I think that that's where people ... struggle. They get hung up on one way. You know, this is the way that it should always be done ... always should be teacher telling, showing, working with the children and then they produce on their own ... I guess I have the joy of not feeling hamstrung to any particular ... traditional belief or progressive belief. My belief is ... based on the children in the context of the subject, the people, those are factors that you need to consider. Are there times when sitting in rows is really effective? Absolutely there are. Are there times when having a conversation at a table ... that perhaps has a Kagan model ...? Absolutely there is, but I think here what I try and do as a leader is to be far less prescriptive.'

Is workload to blame for a lack of teacher wellbeing?

'You know, teachers aren't haemorrhaging out of our profession because of ... what we're calling workload, you know marking, planning, admin, they're not haemorrhaging out because they're marking too much or planning too much ... what I try and do here is give people the opportunity to develop, to reflect, to research, to be critical of their own practice and be involved in coaching conversations that further that, but I give them the agency and the autonomy to make decisions that affect their own practice ...

'... we don't have a marking policy here. There's no proforma that they need to complete, or codes they need to use. They get to choose. If they think that ... writing a paragraph in a pupil's book is going to be right for that child in that day and that lesson, then they do it and if they don't, then they won't ... I think that's why people are haemorrhaging out of this profession because we've taken a group of university graduates who are inspired and passionate, intelligent and budding professionals and put them in an environment where we're telling them what to do at every single turn. You need to mark this way. You need to plan this way. You need to teach this way. The kids need to sit this way ... we've over-engineered schools. We've over-managed them and I think that's where I go back to this piece about leadership. Our job as leaders is to influence change and that's by putting teachers in the conditions under which change and teaching about learning are possible. So, it's not teachers get to make random decisions whenever they want about anything – the teachers here are researchers, they're collaborators, they're studiers, they're put in an environment where they are able to make decisions that are right for them and for learners ... it's not a free-for-all but they get to choose because they're put in the environment where they want to make the very best choices.'

In the summer term of 2019, before my interview with Jeremy, Three Bridges had been inspected and had received 'Outstanding' in every category. I wanted to know what Jeremy thought about the judgement and how the school had achieved it.

Ofsted

'... Ofsted ... that's a tricky one ... Ofsted is the root of all things evil in this country and the worst ... the worst bit is that they don't know it and ... it is it is one of the most challenging things for me personally, but the badge that they have given me and this school will be the badge that I use to dismantle them.

'The challenging bit is having to acknowledge that they gave me the badge because, if I'm honest, I don't recognise it. I don't recognise it as any indicator of success whatsoever ... but I'm very aware that many people do. That's parents, that's governors, that's other headteachers – and I am able to sleep at night knowing that I end up having to talk about Ofsted now and again because I know that it's a platform that some people can connect to that I would otherwise be unable to reach ... I've been speaking about this approach to leadership and this approach to leading a school for years and there are always people in the room who are going, "Well, we hear what you say. We like where you're going with this but you're only Good. Right? Your school's only good." And ... at the time our school has been outstanding. We've had an incredible school for years. I've known it. The staff here know it. The community has known it ...

'... speaking to other headteachers, speaking to colleagues, the badge that they've given me that I don't recognise, other people do, and [I'm] using it now

as a platform to be able to speak to a wider audience ... While it's slightly con-
flicting, I think it serves the greater good.

'How do I think that we got that badge? Well, I think ... I think it probably is
a number of factors ... our results are good, they're very good, and they're very
good in a very disadvantaged community. So ... 40–50% [of pupils are] Pupil
Premium. Eighty-five per cent [have] English as an Additional Language.
Thirty-five per cent of our children between Years 1 and 6 turn over ... You know,
one of the estates across the road is in the second percentile for crime and
violence. We're one of the 75 primary schools with the most disadvantaged ...
the children in this school come from some serious challenges so I think that
the ... first way we got that badge is through results but the way that we got the
results, I think, is the important bit and that's ... to me that's the joke of Ofsted.

'Getting results, building a curriculum even, can be done in a million and one
ways. Right? I mean you can drill and kill kids, you can teach to the test, make
sure they can do that, and you get the grades and [Ofsted] come in and things
are good. I know schools that ... have not done a fantastic job with their children through the school. They get to Year 6 ... a ton of teachers are poured into
Year 6, they're teaching them the test for the whole year, only maths and English
are happening in that school. The kids do well in the test, forget a bunch of it
after they've done that, and they get the fancy badge too. So, am I in incredible
company with the outstanding badge? No. No different company that I was in
before, but I think ... that's one of the flaws. One of the flaws is that there are a
million and one ways to get a result and Ofsted doesn't have the capacity to
unpick that. Was that done a good way, the right way, a sustainable way in the
long term? Right? How many staff left in the last four years since we were here?
How much turnover do you have? None of those things are measured. Right?
It's just the headline figures.

'... the results were ... the first thing they were probably looking at but the
way we got those results, I think, is the important thing and I think that when
they got here that's what they saw. They saw a staff that had been reprofession-
alised. They saw a staff that were, you know, inquisitive, collaborative, connected. They saw a staff that were deeply invested in moving learners and
learning forward and doing whatever it took to be the very best they could be
in front of those children, working on pedagogy, working on practice, seeing
content as important but also seeing themselves as educators, as part of the
hidden curriculum. I think that there are a number of factors like that ... after
the first ten minutes of them being in the building they saw straightaway and
that can only be good.'

Accountability

I asked Jeremy whether the 'Outstanding' judgement enables him to challenge
the narrative that, in order to get outstanding, you need to have a high accountability culture in a school and whether his slogan 'There is Another Way' is part
of that narrative.

'... I think that that is at the heart of exactly what I'm talking about ... So, I think that's exactly it. The badge that they've now given our school, very rightfully, so very well deserved, this staff is incredible, nobody's working harder than the people here, that badge is the same badge I will use to dismantle the view that the only way you can have an outstanding school is high-stakes scrutiny, monitoring, observation ... that, that is a lie. It's not the truth. It is what as a headteacher you're told ... if you speak to a local authority, you speak to an HMI, you speak to a consultant, if you're a new headteacher, if you're a headteacher that's experienced in a school that's "Good", they're telling you this is how you gain an "Outstanding" rating. You monitor more, you scrutinise more, you hold people to a higher account. That is a flawed narrative. It is the narrative that is destroying our schools and our teachers and ultimately our children, and that is the narrative that I'm going to dismantle.'

In April 2019, Jeremy had written an article in *The Guardian*, 'Teachers are miserable because they're being held at gunpoint for meaningless data', in which he had referred to the mess in education which was leading to a third of teachers leaving teaching within the first five years. He described how schools, teachers, and leaders were under pressure to force their pupils through a series of narrow tests. He argued that while high-stakes accountability and using control and coercion to achieve results might work in the short term, it causes long-term damage to the wellbeing and mental health of teachers. He goes on to criticise Ofsted inspections as a blunt instrument of judgement rather than a supportive force for sharing good practice between the schools it inspects.

Jeremy continued in our interview to explain how, on arriving in England from Canada, he was told that holding teachers at gunpoint was the only way to ensure results:

'... it started when I first came to this country ... as an immigrant ... from Canada ... and what I was told in the very first part of my time here was, "Listen Jeremy, if you don't like the way we do things here, jog on back to Canada." Whoa! And then the narrative shifts to, "Listen, you can have one of two types of schools, Jeremy. You can have a happy school. You know, you can treat your staff well. Give them freedom, be a little bit lax with them, you're never going to get the results, you need to monitor. You need to scrutinise ... that's what's going to tip them over the edge. Or you can run a tight ship – monitor, scrutinise, push, pull, you can hold everybody to a high account. Pupil progress means every six weeks observations, every six weeks constant feedback, that's how they grow, that's how you get an Outstanding school. So, you can run a happy school but it's not going to be Ofsted successful or you can run a school like this and you will get the badge you need and life will be good for you" ... not only is it completely untrue, the reverse is true that, while you may get recognised with a badge from Ofsted because you behaved that way, I guess what people are not seeing – because it's very challenging to see, because it has been this way for so long – is the opportunity cost.

'What we're not seeing is who our professionals can become when they're not constantly monitored, measured, and scrutinised. When people have a gun to their heads they behave strangely, they make rash decisions, they panic, they're filled with anxiety, stress, fear. You're not making the decisions … you're not flourishing, you're not growing, it's not the very best version of yourself. You're definitely not helping other people do that, and so what I'm suggesting is that there is a better way, that you can get the fancy badge if that matters to you, but you can actually grow better teachers, better leaders, and ultimately you might have a much stronger experience for the children. And I think as a school now, you know, that's what we're talking about. We're talking about curriculum and we have been for a number of years, but it comes in many forms. I think what happens is in schools that are very compliance oriented, very militaristic, very much of a scrutiny observation, curriculum to them is content …'.

In another interview for the education blog 'A Head of Our Time' in June 2017, when Jeremy was headteacher designate at Three Bridges, one of the topics that John Bishop covered was teacher observations. Jeremy commented that they were 'the most overrated idea in British education' and 'stifle at least 90% of the workforce'. As described earlier, he made clear that the form of observation he believed in was reflective practice of the kind encouraged in Learning and Lesson Study, Teacher Research Groups, and open lessons.

The curriculum

'What is it they are specifically teaching and when, and that is a part of curriculum building but there's a much bigger piece to it than that and that is about the hidden curriculum. And when I say hidden curriculum, I mean a number of things but the things that I think are important right now are, what is the pedagogy and how does the pedagogy align with your curriculum? Because in our school we're talking about global citizenship. We're talking about sustainable development, social justice and equity, power and governance – themes that are bold, propelling our children into the twenty-first century. But if your pedagogy is "I'm the fount of all knowledge at the front of the classroom and you are receptacles to be filled", how is that aligned with equality, how does that align with social justice? … if in school we want children collaborating, we want children connecting, we want children enquiring, we want them to see the relationship between themselves and the professional in the presence of knowledge, as one that is not hierarchical but horizontal, where that exchange is learners learning and learners teaching and teachers learning and teachers teaching … if that's we're trying to do, surely our adults have to be in same environment first, they must be exposed to those same principles, those same practices, that same leadership pedagogy as we want the children to experience, and you cannot have that in a system that is very, very much compliance oriented. You can't. It's not possible.'

Advice to new headteachers?

I asked Jeremy what advice he would give a headteacher taking up post for the first time:

'Disrupt. Be a positive disrupter. I wish I'd made that up, that's Jaz Ampaw-Farr! [Ed: Jaz Ampaw-Farr is a keynote speaker, author, coach, storyteller and workshop facilitator] ... be somebody who is looking for solutions that aren't immediately apparent. Dig more deeply. Think about the wider picture. Think about the long look. But disrupt.'

My final question was to ask Jeremy where he thought Three Bridges would be in three years' time:

'I would like Three Bridges to be a beacon of hope and I want Three Bridges to be – along with some other really, really incredible schools – leading the revolution in schools in this country ... not that ... we should be kind of colonial and copy ... this is Three Bridges because of a number of factors. This community is incredible, the people here are amazing, the staff here are unique and developed in their own ways. You could never recreate Three Bridges anywhere else, but that doesn't mean that there isn't a piece of music here that can be played somewhere else ...

'I think that ... is why I stay. I mean it would be easy to go back to Ontario, be the principal of a school about the same size as this, in the Ontario system where there's no Ofsted, there's no SATs, there's no high-stakes accountability, there's no nonsense. Professionals are respected and paid well, cost of living is lower ... your pension is earlier, there's a lot of factors to draw you back but this is why I stay, because I believe that Three Bridges has found a number of steps in the right direction and ... we're learning all the time from other schools as well about more steps in that direction, but Three Bridges is going to lead a revolution.

'It is going to be the school that we're going to look back on in twenty, thirty years and say that's one of the places where this started. You know, the environment that we have in schools today is as a result of the work that was going on twenty-five years ago at Three Bridges when they said there was "Another way" and that's not about ego, it's not about money, it's not about power, it's not about control, it's about harmony, it's about the future of this nation, it's about an entire profession of people.'

Jeremy's vision of Three Bridges as a pioneer school in putting teachers' well-being, mental health, and growth at the centre of the school was summarised in his final comment in the *Schools Week* interview when he said that his ambition was to create a network of schools with the beliefs and values of Three Bridges and where high-stakes accountability was replaced with trust and respect for teachers as professionals. His aspiration is to bring about social change by giving schools like Three Bridges a collective voice.

And that is a perfect summary of what Jeremy Hannay means by 'There is Another Way'.

Key strategies

- No high-stakes accountability. No: hierarchical observations, book scrutinies, marking policy, learning walks, performance management, display board rules.
- Creative and inspirational environment, including displaying pupils' work in progress.
- Belief that there is no pupil wellbeing without staff wellbeing.
- Culture of enabling staff to grow and develop.
- Staff are encouraged to take risks, without fear of failure.
- Learning and Lesson Study.
- Teacher Research Groups.
- Open lessons.
- No 'one way' of teaching and learning: instruction integrated with creativity.
- No onerous data drops.
- Rejection of the belief that monitoring teachers and inspecting schools are the only way to raise standards and get results.

8 Kingham Primary School, Kingham, Chipping Norton, Oxfordshire

Staff emotional health

Bretta Townend-Jowitt, Headteacher

'Staff wellbeing and emotional health are a right, as is ensuring everyone is personally and professionally satisfied in their job and career.'

Overview

By creating a improved staff room on taking up her appointment as headteacher in 2016, Bretta Townend-Jowitt signalled her intention to give staff wellbeing the highest priority. This was followed closely by the creation of the Emotional Health and Wellbeing Policy and Action Plan, which set out Bretta's commitment to the mental health of her staff, as well as their physical health. A range of workload reduction strategies were aligned with continuing development, replacing judgement with the professional sharing of good practice.

Context

Kingham Primary School is a maintained one-form entry school in rural west Oxfordshire. The school has 201 pupils aged 4–11 years and a nursery class with 26 places (full-time equivalent). The school is located in a village and serves other small surrounding villages, all within an area of low deprivation. As such, the school has few pupils eligible for Pupil Premium (PP) funding (3.5%), which places us in the lowest 20% of all schools for free school meals. Our pupils are predominantly White British at 94%. We have one looked-after and three previously looked-after children. We have eight full-time class teachers, a part-time special educational needs coordinator, a part-time planning, preparation and assessment cover teacher, three part-time office staff, a part-time school business manager, three full-time and 11 part-time teaching assistants.

I became headteacher of the school in September 2016. Whilst staff wellbeing and emotional health seemed fine, I believed it could have been even better. Both workload and accountability were onerous; for example, there were too many meetings each week, an unreasonable marking policy, regular graded lesson observations and work scrutiny. Four data drops each year also added to workload and levels of stress and were having an adverse impact on staff emotional health. Staff did not always prioritise their own mental health. Cars could be seen in the car park at unreasonable hours – before and after school as well as during school holidays. Staff were taking piles of exercise books home to mark and were spending hours at home each evening and over the weekend planning. Something had to give, or our staff would experience Burnout or, worse still, leave the profession.

Emotional health and wellbeing in the school community

We work towards positive emotional health and wellbeing in the whole of our school community – for adults, as well as children. We believe that the aims and objectives of our school can only be achieved if children and staff have good emotional health.

There is no doubt teaching is a stressful job. But, by implementing a culture of staff wellbeing and emotional health, I aimed to ensure that staff wanted to remain working at Kingham Primary School, had a reasonable workload, and would know when 'good' is 'good enough'.

I aimed to decrease staff workload to ensure everyone had a healthy work–life balance, increase recruitment and retention by supporting their wellbeing, and improve professional development to ensure it met the needs of all staff rather than being a one-size-fits-all model. I wanted to ensure staff were able to cope, felt motivated and engaged and were able to bounce back from challenges.

Teaching staff give their all during term-time and can sometimes be their own worst enemy. We all know staff who continue to come to school even when ill, giving everything they have for the pupils in their care – often to the detriment of their own health – and ending up being more ill during school holidays. By having a school focus on wellbeing and mental health and reducing workload, I believed we could reduce staff illness and Burnout. For those times when staff are ill and shouldn't be in school, or life outside school throws them a challenge, I wanted them to be able to come and say they needed help and support or time off – my door is always open. I wanted them to stop being the martyrs many of us in education so often are and 'put their own oxygen mask on first'.

The school environment

Our first step was to improve the physical environment, increase opportunities for staff to have time away from their classrooms, and to interact with each other socially. Our staff room is in an old part of our building and was used for lunch, break, meetings with parents, interventions with children, and also housed the photocopier and resources. It was not a dedicated space for staff to relax and take time out from their busy schedules and the four walls of their classrooms. During the summer holidays of 2018, the photocopier and other resources were moved out and a breakfast bar fitted for staff to eat lunch (rather than on their laps). The room became a staff-only space and was not used for pupil interventions or meetings with other professionals or parents. We added cushions, provided snacks – sometimes treats, sometimes healthy – herbal teas and other drinks, ensured it was a space staff could go, relax and unwind, making it much more comfortable, although it still needs some improvement As a consequence of these improvements, teaching staff frequent the space more often at lunchtime and it has led to us having a little more time to chat and get to know each other better.

We have utilised a space in school that wasn't used to its potential to rehouse the photocopier and laminator and provide a desk for staff to work during non-contact time, adding screens to ensure it is as quiet a space as we can make it.

The Emotional Health and Wellbeing Policy and Action Plan

After the success of this seemingly small step, we wrote an Emotional Health and Wellbeing Policy and Action Plan for both pupils and staff and added it as a key objective to our school development plan. We also reviewed and updated policies and procedures around wellbeing.

The objectives of the Emotional Health and Wellbeing Action Plan are:

- to decrease workload for teaching staff to ensure a healthy work–life balance;
- to strengthen recruitment and retention of staff through improved health and wellbeing;
- to develop continuing professional development in school to ensure it meets the needs of all staff;
- to support the health and wellbeing of pupils;
- to build stronger links with the local community to support the health and wellbeing of staff, pupils and parents.

The reason for writing an Emotional Health and Wellbeing Policy, based on practice and an action plan as part of the school development plan, was to ensure it remained a focus for everyone: support staff, teaching staff, senior leaders and governors – everyone who has a remit to ensure staff wellbeing and mental health.

Quick wins from the action plan include:

- removing gradings for lesson observations;
- reducing the length and volume of staff meetings;
- rationalising staff communication by creating a whole-school calendar on Outlook; and
- removing first aid duty at break and lunchtime for teaching staff.

Accountability

Accountability is important but is becoming unmanageable and stressful, due to external pressures. If we know a teacher is good and is producing good results, why are we putting them under undue stress by constantly monitoring everything they do and grading what we already know about them? Nor is it possible to provide an accurate grading from just one lesson. Ofsted does not require schools to undertake a specific number of lesson observations, as their expectations are about the action school leaders take to improve the quality of teaching. We have embraced drop-ins, learning walks and staff discussions to replace formal lesson observations and are working towards a coaching approach. We decided collaboratively to implement personal professional development rather than continuing professional development by ensuring we are able to spend time in each other's classrooms, learn from each other and support one another in a manageable way. This was introduced to teaching staff initially after I took up post as headteacher on the first training day in September 2016. The staff were enthusiastic and looked forward to this approach to professional development. We decided to disaggregate several in-service training (INSET) days to provide staff with time in lieu for conversations or planning, after spending time in each other's classrooms. Staff were expected to take more responsibility for their own professional development and for improving their own practice.

The new approach to staff development started well, with a number of staff willingly volunteering to open their classroom doors, and other teachers leaving their classes for 20 minutes with their teaching assistants to observe the practice of their colleagues. However, not all staff bought into the project with the enthusiasm that was evident on the INSET day and, without the prompts and facilitation of senior leaders, it soon diminished. I still advocate that all staff should see each other teach and learn from one another. Why should only senior leaders observe great practice when they teach the least? My challenge is to find a way to promote and facilitate the project, whilst handing it back to staff so that they understand that seeing each other teach is a way to improve practice across the school.

Feedback, not marking

Our next major project was to improve marking and feedback, as our marking policy was out of date and there were different codes, rules and expectations of

Key Stage 1 and Key Stage 2. Key Stage 1 was very prescriptive, as staff were using green and pink pens to highlight strengths and areas to develop, as well as writing a positive comment and a comment for improvement. In addition, they were using marking codes for grammar and punctuation such as finger spaces, capital letters and full stops. Key Stage 2 teachers used a variety of stamps with written comments, such as positive comments, areas to improve and targets or next steps. Pupils were expected to respond to teachers' marking. For Key Stage 1 and pupils who struggled to read, this meant that additional time was needed by teachers and teaching assistants in class to ensure they could access the feedback given. Staff marked *all* pieces of work and provided feedback comments, next steps or action points/targets. This had a major impact on staff workload and, as a school, we lacked consistency.

In her foreword to 'Eliminating Unnecessary Workload Around Marking' – the DfE report of the Independent Teacher Workload Review Group – Dawn Copping, the chair, wrote:

> 'What was very clear from the start was the shared view that marking had become a burden that simply must be addressed, not only for those currently in the profession but for those about to enter it. Our job was to discover how we ended up here and how we could make the long overdue change needed to help restore the work-life balance, passion and energy of teachers in this country ...' (Copping, 2016: 3).

As I was responsible for staff workload and their wellbeing, I carried out research around marking and feedback. I wanted what I was saying to the staff to be accurate and not based on hearsay or new 'fads'.

As a staff, we discussed the research report during a staff meeting and unpicked the myths around marking. Our discussion was both animated and robust. Most staff had mistaken beliefs about what Ofsted would want to see, such as: the volume of marking, frequency of marking, written feedback, pupils responding to feedback, every piece of work being marked, verbal feedback needing to be recorded, and the required depth of marking – all of which contributed to an excessive workload. We asked ourselves who were we marking for? Was it for: Ofsted? Senior leaders? Subject leaders? Parents? Pupils?

Our response was to create a new policy – not a marking policy but a feedback policy – and to start trialling the ideas in June and July ready for the start of the new term in September 2017. It meant we would do much less written marking and increase our live feedback to pupils as they were working. The policy developed over the next few weeks and staff eventually challenged me to create a policy that eradicated the word 'marking' altogether. It was a bold move, but one we managed and a move I am very glad we made.

It has had the greatest impact on staff workload and wellbeing at Kingham Primary, demonstrated by the fact that staff take fewer books home now than they used to. After a year of implementation, we are also able to demonstrate that it has not had a detrimental effect on pupil progress. I am proud of the positive impact this has had and will continue to advocate a move to feedback rather than marking in all schools whenever I can.

You can find the feedback policy in my pinned tweet (@headspiration). Twitter analytics show that it has been liked over 150 times, has been seen 24,000 times and has had more than 1800 interactions. I am happy for anyone to access and use it in their own school. Our feedback policy can also be downloaded from Google Drive at https://drive.google.com/file/d/1vX6BEy03WogB7I--83rNl8m0I3mTxOVe/view.

'Out of the box' wellbeing initiatives

We are constantly trying to think of 'out of the box' ways to thank staff and to introduce more wellbeing initiatives. We have:

- reduced the number of data captures;
- provided lunch on INSET days;
- completed mental health and wellbeing professional development;
- introduced staff social and wellbeing events;
- provided wellbeing bags at the start of the school year;
- completed wellbeing conversations with staff shortly after the start of the school year;
- introduced open requests for part-time and flexible teaching and we accommodate as many as possible;
- created a feedback box where staff can share improvements;
- provided staff with food during parents' consultation evenings and built in breaks for them to eat, unwind and relax together;
- introduced subject leader release time (as well as planning, preparation and assessment);
- ensured effective and regular communication about changes and initiatives;
- offered stress and resilience workshops;
- provided time in lieu for evening or weekend training events attended;
- held mindfulness workshops; and
- provided staff with a wellbeing voucher to use at any time during the school year for a family event or even a duvet day!

We have low staff absence rates and retention is high. In the last three years, only two of the staff have moved on: one teacher moved to a new post in a school nearer to home to reduce travelling time; the other relocated due to their partner being in the armed forces.

Staff wellbeing and emotional health are never complete. Internal and external pressures from accountability and standards mean that they should always be at the forefront of every decision we make as a school, and they will remain a key objective on the school development plan.

The action plan will be reviewed, and a new wellbeing lead sought from the staff team. A wellbeing working party will also be established.

Future developments

Future developments will include:

- Dedicated staff time for pupil progress meetings and data inputs.
- Review of annual reports to parents.
- Production of a staff bulletin to reduce staff meeting time further and improve communication for part-time staff.
- Consideration of the timing of school events so that they are spread as equally as possible through the school year.
- Review of the school behaviour policy.
- Removal of the expectations that emails will be answered after 5.00 pm or at the weekend. Staff will be able to send emails at these times, but a reply will not be expected.

Staff wellbeing and emotional health are a right, as is ensuring everyone is personally and professionally satisfied in their job and career.

Key strategies

- Improving physical environment for staff.
- Reducing high-stakes accountability.
- Reduction in staff workload.
- Giving staff more control over their professional development.
- Moving from marking to verbal feedback.
- Restructuring judgemental lesson observations.
- Implementation of Emotional Health and Wellbeing Policy and Action Plan.
- 'Out of the box' wellbeing initiatives, including wellbeing bags and feedback box.

9 Brimsdown Primary School, Enfield, North London

Staff: The most important school resource

Dani Lang, Headteacher

Overview

Dani Lang, headteacher of Brimsdown Primary School, explains how she worked closely with the staff to move the school from 'Requires Improvement' to 'Good'. Improving morale by acknowledging both staff needs and successes was crucial in realising school improvement. The creation of a staff wellbeing group, a survey to identify issues, improving pupil behaviour, introducing 'fun' rewards, reducing workload, and introducing a new continuing professional development programme – all enabled the school to be confirmed 'Good' with outstanding features in its Ofsted section 5 monitoring report in January 2019.

Context

Brimsdown Primary School is in a deprived area in Enfield, North London. It has 630 pupils, including a nursery, with an equal number of boys and girls. Thirty-nine per cent of its pupils are Pupil Premium (PP) and 56% have English as an additional language (EAL). Nineteen per cent of pupils are receiving Special Educational Needs and Disability (SEND) support, including 4% with an Education, Health and Care Plan (EHCP) – double the national average. The staff comprise: 32 teachers, including school leaders; five newly qualified teachers and three trainee teachers; 36 support staff, including teaching assistants, a graduate teaching assistant, communication support workers and early years workers; and 17 other staff, including office staff, a site manager, lunchtime and breakfast club staff.

I began my secondment in December 2014 as associate headteacher at Brimsdown Primary during a troubling time for the school. It had received two

'Requires Improvement' Ofsted inspections and was judged to be in the lowest 10% in the country for Year 6 reading progress. Morale was low and there were high levels of staff absence. It was clear that in order for the school to improve, we would need to make a lot of changes.

We introduced a new English and phonics scheme and revised our behaviour policy and staff procedures which had a positive effect on the school. However, as with any period of major change, it was initially unsettling for staff and budget constraints led to some redundancies.

Milestone 1: Staff wellbeing team

In order to support staff through these changes and improve morale and wellbeing, I introduced a staff wellbeing team in 2015. Wellbeing of staff was not something that had been considered previously.

In April 2016, I became a permanent member of staff and, in September 2017, I was appointed as the headteacher. Wellbeing and mental health continue to be a key focus and priority for me and for the school.

My main aims were to create a culture of kindness and understanding and to ensure that staff were supported and on-board with the changes that would need to be made. I also wanted to improve staff attendance to reduce supply cover and minimise the associated costs. However, creating our school wellbeing team has done so much more than this. Staff are much happier at work, they have ownership of their roles and responsibilities, an improved manageable workload, a good relationship with school leaders, and the school has a family feel to it.

We started by initiating an open discussion with staff. My first meeting with the wellbeing team included some hard truths for me to accept as a leader. Each member of the team was encouraged to be honest and open about how they felt about a range of issues in a safe and non-judgemental space. It was clear that the changes I had initially implemented, although for the benefit of the school, had caused stress, but staff were still keen to engage with further training and development.

While I was part of the problem, I also wanted to be part of the solution. We created a staff wellbeing survey and introduced an open-door policy, encouraging people to approach the wellbeing team if they had any issues or concerns. The team then used the results of this survey and any feedback we received to focus on different areas over the coming year.

There had also been issues historically around fairness and consistency in terms of staff hours and overtime, behaviour expectations for children, and the level of support for staff from line managers. The new policies and procedures introduced, such as the behaviour policy, went some way towards addressing this. For example, within the support staff restructure, the new contracts included one hour of continuing professional development (CPD) each week. It was clear, however, that more work was needed.

Milestone 2: Wellbeing survey

As a team, we devised a set of questions to ask staff about their wellbeing and workload. We wanted everyone to have the opportunity to be open and honest and to express any concerns. We also needed a baseline to identify the areas we needed to discuss and to create ideas and solutions. We distributed the questions via an anonymous online survey and encouraged staff to talk to us if they had any issues. The wellbeing team helped staff to approach a member of the senior leadership team (SLT) if they had a problem so that we could work on being solution-focused. The results of the survey were analysed and we began to consider possible solutions. This was done as a team and also involved the SLT so that we could make practical changes.

Acquiring a second photocopier, employing an intern to help with laminating each week, and setting time aside during in-service training days to prepare resources – all helped with problems associated with workload, particularly on an administrative level. Other solutions focused on fun activities and events – both free and paid for by staff; considering how the school ran staff meetings and training; ensuring staff had ownership of their job role; and reviewing and reorganising line managers and staff teams.

Milestone 3: Fun and small initiatives

We introduced small, fun initiatives. The wellbeing team's plans started small. We added a wellbeing board to the staffroom and displayed motivational posters in the staff toilets. Messages such as 'Make today ridiculously amazing' and 'Potential: We have the tools for greatness within us' provided a lift throughout the day. A bookshelf was added to the staff room so that there could be a book and DVD swap.

We started to 'mug' people – leaving mugs filled with treats, sweets and stationery for a member of staff. There were no criteria for picking staff to be mugged, as every member of staff was encouraged to take part, so people chose their friends and team members. The wellbeing team focused on people who looked like they needed a pick-me-up and, in my office, I had a variety of sweets they could use to mug staff if they wanted. Mugging each other proved particularly popular and made staff smile.

Milestone 4: Addressing workload

Something that was clearly an issue for all staff was getting their work–life balance in check. A wellbeing survey was an excellent tool to identify where there were issues around staff workload – not just teachers, but all staff at the school. As well as a new photocopier and help with laminating, we ran training sessions for the school's new English and phonics schemes. A member of the

SLT would go to the year group planning, preparation and assessment (PPA) sessions and offer support, working alongside teachers.

The teaching assistants, many of whom taught phonics groups, had their own weekly PPA session to prepare resources, share good practice and ask the phonics lead teacher questions. An appraisal system was put into place for all support staff and the feedback form included the question: 'How could your role be made efficient? You know the job best. How can you improve it?'

In September 2016, we introduced a no-marking policy across the school, a change we were nervous about, but which has had an immeasurable impact on our staff. Children mark their own work and all feedback is given verbally, which has reduced staff workload and encouraged the children to take pride in their work. All staff had initial training on this and continue to have follow-up training.

Workload was continually reviewed, and staff were encouraged to speak to their line manager, a member of the SLT or the wellbeing team if they had any ideas. The survey was carried out again after nine months and there are still questions from it that we use today when asking staff to complete our annual feedback survey.

Milestone 5: Continuing professional development

Weekly CPD was reviewed. Rather than teachers and support staff attending the same meeting each week, there were two different meetings and staff decided which was the most relevant for their professional development, therefore giving them ownership. They were also allowed a free pass once a term so that they could decide to use the time for something they felt they needed to do for the children they supported, such as make resources, organise their book corner, and so on. Feedback was requested about the new system, and ideas for possible training shared by staff with the SLT.

The wellbeing team held regular staff meetings to talk about ways to manage workloads effectively, to work smart and how to relax. Sharing resources between different teams has been an effective approach, as well as writing weekly priority lists and practising mindfulness activities.

The impact of ensuring that staff wellbeing and mental health come first has improved many areas of the school. Staff feel overwhelmingly that they belong to the community of Brimsdown. They are happy in their roles, support one another and morale is high. They feel respected by the school and tell us that the wellbeing team makes them feel valued. They feel well supported by leaders and there is a family feel to the school.

The staff now feel that their feelings are respected by all. This was confirmed by the results of our latest staff survey in November 2019. One example of the comments we received: 'The SLT and Headteacher's open door policy lead staff to feel supported by the school.' In our Ofsted report, in December 2019, inspectors wrote: 'Staff appreciate the way leaders consider their workload and wellbeing.'

Staff enjoy rewards linked to their good attendance and are supportive of each other when there is long-term absence. Staff absence rates have decreased by just over 2% and exceed national expectation. Staff pull together when members of their team are absent to ensure that the children still receive the best education. The school has a good level of retention, not only for teachers but for all staff across the school. Teachers see that there are career progression opportunities and all staff enjoy the pick-and-mix CPD. There are no issues recruiting new staff, as the school receives many strong applications.

It makes me truly proud as headteacher to work in such 'a happy and caring school' (Ofsted, December 2019), with such a dedicated and supportive staff team. The school is currently part of the Sandwell Wellbeing Charter Mark, a project to promote a whole-school approach to wellbeing. We have created an action plan from all stakeholders' feedback. This action plan ran until December 2020 and the staff survey from summer 2020 was used by the wellbeing team to make further adjustments. The team will continue to meet at least monthly to discuss staff wellbeing and workload, and to create fun and exciting initiatives which promote staff wellbeing and happiness.

Key strategies

- Staff wellbeing team.
- Staff wellbeing survey.
- Fun, small initiatives.
- Addressing workload, including admin support.
- Professional development, with choice built in.

10 St. Peter's C of E Primary School, Farnworth, Bolton, Greater Manchester

Flexible working arrangements allow staff and pupils to walk down Progress Avenue

Lynn Williams, Headteacher

'My belief in the extensive power of collaboration and collegiality can be demonstrated by the fact that my initial headship at St. Peter's in 2006, was, at the time, a rare role – that of co-headship ... In working in partnership, co-heads can and do stand alone as effective leaders and managers, but also act as catalysts to one another's creativity, solving problems through stimulating discussion, questioning each other openly and frankly. Whilst flexible, we also became inseparable, continually holding each other to account for the work we did and the outcomes of the school. Neither was prepared to let the other down and our united front became quite a force. As Isaac Newton said in 1675, "If I can see further, it is by standing on the shoulders of giants." By working together as co-heads, we used each other's shoulders not only for extended vision, but also for vital support.'

Overview

Headteacher Lynn Williams explains how co-headship laid the foundations of collaboration and teamwork that underpin a culture of staff wellbeing and mental health at St. Peter's. This is captured in the naming of corridors as achievement 'Avenues'. In walking along the corridors, staff and pupils are reminded of the goals that lead to success.

Context

St. Peter's is a larger than average Church of England voluntary aided primary school in Bolton, Lancashire. The school recently underwent a significant expansion programme, converting the old single-form entry Victorian building into a modern two-form entry school with 420 children on roll. The school serves one of the most deprived communities in the borough. The deprivation statistics are high and rising. In January 2020, over 90% of pupils on roll at St. Peter's lived in a Layer Super Output Area (LSOA) in Bolton – among the most deprived 30% of LSOAs in England. [Ed: A LSOA is a geospatial statistical unit used in England and Wales to facilitate the reporting of small area statistics. They are part of the coding system created by the Office for National Statistics. They have a minimum population of 1000 with a mean size of 1500.]

The catchment of the school is in the highest quintile for deprivation and, in some classes, over 50% of the pupils are considered to be disadvantaged. The percentage of boys outweighs that of girls (53.8% vs. 46.2%) and over 90% of the pupils are classified as White British. It is, however, a highly inclusive school. Currently, 10.4% of pupils are registered as receiving Special Educational Needs and Disability (SEND) support (slightly below the national average of quintile 4). However, 3.1% of pupils have an Education, Health and Care Plan (EHCP), which places the school above the national average of 1.6% (quintile 1 – highest 20%).

Given other contextual factors, the school's low SEND figure may seem surprising. This is attributed to the rigour in ensuring only those children for whom additional support – beyond that which the school will ordinarily provide – are registered with a special educational need. The extensive knowledge of the staff, the internal expenditure on specialist in-school provision – learning mentors, speech therapy, Every Child a Reader (ECAR) and Every Child a Talker (ECAT) – mean that many reasonable adjustments are made, thus avoiding the need for a pupil to be registered as SEND. The school's thorough, considered, well-developed, graduated response ensures that many such reasonable adjustments are made across school, and increased provision is put in place as necessary to ensure SEND needs are met.

'Learn, Sparkle & Shine'

In February 2016, the school was rated 'Outstanding' by Ofsted and, in June 2016, was also judged to be 'Outstanding' by the Manchester Diocese Board of Education, thus making us one of only 8% of schools in our demographic judged to be outstanding.

Our logo, 'Learn, Sparkle & Shine', reflects our ethos and is a highly visible motto for the children. The logo is brought to life across school and is fully reflected in our mission. Each day we aim to:

- Develop learners who recognise their own learning goals, aspirations and the role they play in determining their own destiny (Learn).
- Provide a curriculum that allows for a wide range of opportunities to be promoted and excellent outcomes achieved, across a wide range of areas (Sparkle).
- Promote a community of kind, respectful learners, with an underlying value of hope for their own future and that of the wider extended community, underpinned by Christian and British values (Shine).

School culture and staff wellbeing

The culture of the school is based on two pillars, both of which contribute significantly to the wellbeing and thus effective productivity of the staff:

1 Effective teamwork through shared responsibilities, cooperation and collaborative working.
2 A fundamental belief that success is achievable by all and is not dependent upon inherited talents or traits. This belief is characterised in school by the metaphor 'Progress Avenue', which is also the name of a physical corridor that children walk along.

Co-headship: Effective teamwork, cooperation and collaboration

My belief in the extensive power of collaboration and collegiality can be demonstrated by the fact that my initial headship at St. Peter's in 2006, was, at the time, a rare role – that of co-headship. Throughout its tenure, the co-headship structure brought many advantages as a direct consequence of a collegiate way of working that directly impacted on a highly positive wellbeing culture in the school – starting at the top with the two headteachers.

The co-headship structure provided a strong, secure leadership base, combining leadership skills to ensure that the highly challenging circumstances of the school did not divert leaders from the core purpose of ensuring the maximum flourishing of all children. Over the years of co-headship, numerous adaptations were made, both practically and logistically, but the interrelationship between the headteachers themselves, and the headteachers' relationship with the school, remained successful. While each was capable of standing alone, their combined minds led to the extension of thoughts and ideas. Each was able to contribute something unique to the partnership, yet both worked to the same end, thriving on the dynamic discussion that collaboration provides.

Together, we demonstrated that an effective partnership is able to have two people with views that are often similar, yet often different, each representing a different perspective, thus leading to a new dimension being given to each other's thoughts. These 'balanced discussions' lead to more effective leadership. A united approach was ultimately derived from an evolved shared vision, arrived at through discussion and open communication.

In an effective team, each member brings skills and talents into the partnership, which may contrast with or complement the skills of the others. While no single individual is perfect, the combined talents of individuals can create a highly effective unit. Co-headship offered the school a wider knowledge and skills base, with two pairs of eyes focusing on the same issues, but each seeing things from a different perspective.

In working in partnership, co-heads can and do stand alone as effective leaders and managers, but also act as catalysts to one another's creativity, solving problems through stimulating discussion and questioning each other openly and frankly. While flexible, we also became inseparable, continually holding each other to account for the work we did and the outcomes of the school. Neither was prepared to let the other down and our united front became quite a force. As Isaac Newton said in 1675, 'If I can see further, it is by standing on the shoulders of giants.' By working together as co-heads, we used each other's shoulders not only for extended vision, but also for vital support.

This way of working created a strong ethos of staff wellbeing and established a culture that now openly supports flexible working arrangements. As co-headteachers, we proved that collaborative working has substantial mutual benefits across the entire organisation, not least on the removal of feelings of isolation and the exceptional performance benefits that a highly effective team can generate; all of which contribute to strong emotional and mental health and wellbeing.

From two headteachers to one

In 2015, the original head retired from post and I now lead the school as the substantive head. The transition was seamless. The stakeholders already had trust and confidence in the leadership team and the governors simply extended my contract to a full-time post.

I have since become a National Leader in Education and the school is a National Support School, reflecting the success of the co-headship model under which I served my apprenticeship.

I am now in a strong position to invest time in supporting others. As Tom Peters said, 'Great leaders do not create followers; they create more leaders' (Peters, in Van Vliet, 2010). I am a coach for participants on the National Professional Qualification for Headship (NPQH – C of E schools) and I am a strong advocate for the Women in Leadership collaborative, coaching women into leadership roles and speaking at women leaders' events.

Flexible working requests are actively supported and seen as beneficial to the organisation. Many of the teaching staff have 0.6 or 0.8 full-time equivalent contracts, bringing a diverse range of skills and competencies into the workforce, while managing their own commitments beyond directed time, creating a balance between the school and home life wellbeing.

Progress Avenue, Cooperation Alley and Achievement Road

All schools share ambitions about wanting the very best for their pupils, students and staff. A cursory look at the motto, ethos, values or vision and mission statements of schools will readily confirm this. St. Peter's C of E Primary School is no exception. As described earlier, we have made our purpose explicit via our school motto: 'Learn, Sparkle & Shine'.

As staff and pupils walk through the school entrance doors and step into St. Peter's, they are asked to imagine themselves taking daily steps down Progress Avenue, a name we have chosen to adopt as our mantra. As our last Ofsted report said,

'Each corridor is labelled to reinforce a value or an ambition and emphasises the aspirational ethos which pervades the school. Pupils regularly walk up Progress Avenue, Cooperation Alley or Achievement Road on their way to lessons, assembly or out to play.'

The vision continually reinforced to our children is that Progress Avenue is endless. It does not seek to limit someone to a predetermined potential:

- It does not assume a natural talent or predisposition.
- It recognises that hard work and effort will lead to greater outcomes and achievement.
- It starts with you and takes you as far as you want to go.

This philosophy has helped our staff to open their minds to the meaning of inclusion and avoid limiting beliefs, both for themselves and the pupils. By building a belief that anything is possible, you can take the first step towards achieving it. The school community shares the motivational belief that its members have the power to determine their own destiny.

Underpinning much of the work we do at St. Peter's, therefore, are two basic assumptions:

1 The premise of the universal potential for high intelligence for all.
2 If you want to get better at something, you have to practise it and purposefully work towards it, be that knowledge of multiplication facts, phonetical interpretation of graphemes, reading musical notation, kicking a ball, or being a highly effective teacher or teaching assistant.

The concept of Progress Avenue defines our school's purpose – staff and pupils come to learn and practise, and each day to be slightly further on that journey to success than they were the day before. We need to provide our communities with the belief that intelligence is malleable, that the things we are able to learn are limitless, that school is a place where learning is offered and, by engaging in the learning process, the knowledge they can acquire is limitless.

By physically labelling our corridors with street signs that are metaphors for learning progress, we continually offer a reminder to our community that, when they walk through our doors, they are entering an environment where learning will be promoted and excuses that detract from our ability to make progress and improve will be challenged.

The poster in Figure 10.1, displayed on our doors and windows, indicates the type of environment you are entering: 'Come to St. Peter's if you want to work hard to achieve success'.

Figure 10.1

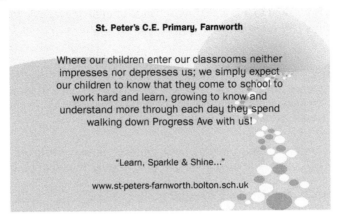

St. Peter's C.E. Primary, Farnworth

Where our children enter our classrooms neither impresses nor depresses us; we simply expect our children to know that they come to school to work hard and learn, growing to know and understand more through each day they spend walking down Progress Ave with us!

"Learn, Sparkle & Shine..."

www.st-peters-farnworth.bolton.sch.uk

Progress Avenue is a metaphor for the belief that at St. Peter's barriers to success are hurdles along the route; they will be identified and removed, and excuses will be given a 'so what' response, so that chances to 'Learn, Sparkle & Shine' are maximised.

Nationally, disadvantaged pupils are achieving lower outcomes than their non-disadvantaged peers. As head of a school in a disadvantaged area, I strongly argue the case that high attainment is possible for all; but hard work, focused and determined effort, and strong teaching are the key to success. Working in an environment where cultural advantage is significantly limited, we have to strongly propose the view that intelligence is accessible universally, not just to those who inherit it.

For staff to flourish, they need to feel they are on a learning journey, a journey of success, a journey taking them beyond where they are currently. A journey where ideas will be grasped and developed, in a place where they will be nurtured and helped to become more skilled and effective in their role. Schools that wish for their children to succeed must invest in their staff too, so they feel valued. Without highly effective staff, operating at their best, children will not succeed. At St. Peter's the concept of Progress Avenue is an embedded ethos, a cultural metaphor for the 'way we do things around here', open to both pupils and staff.

A culture of success and staff wellbeing

This culture of success for all also carries significant advantages for staff development and therefore their wellbeing. Staff are strongly encouraged to develop their skills, extend their knowledge, and develop their role and contribution to the school.

Three of my senior leadership team have secured the role of specialist leader of education (SLE), which entails them working alongside colleagues in other schools to support and develop their provision. One of the staff is an evidence leader in education (ELE), working with schools to explore research-based evidence to develop their practice.

The leadership team have been supported to follow leadership courses, with six members of staff now holding nationally recognised qualifications: Master of Education (MEd); National Professional Qualifications in Middle and Senior Leadership (NPQML and NPQSL); and the National Professional Qualification in Early Years Foundation Stage (NPQ EYFS).

The school applied for, and was awarded, the Best Practice with Teaching Assistants Award (BPTAA) in recognition of the support offered to teaching assistants. In 2018, the school was shortlisted for one of the highly acclaimed TES awards in the 'Employer of the Year' category, in recognition of the time dedicated to maximising the opportunities for staff at the school.

The impact of supporting staff

At St. Peter's, the leadership team are relentless in their drive to innovate and improve, in order to ensure that all pupils succeed, regardless of their socio-economic background. To achieve this vision, we support our staff to ensure that they are highly effective, aligned to the vision, well-trained and determined to ensure our children succeed, regardless of their starting point.

Investing in staff wellbeing plays a crucial role in ensuring our vision is realised. The school employs over 70 staff and is in the highest 10% of similar schools for its expenditure on teaching assistants. This significant investment in human resources reaps high rewards.

Since achieving our outstanding judgement, the school has gone from strength to strength. Key Stage 2 outcomes data for the period since our last inspection (three-year combined data 2017–2019) shows that the progress made by our pupils is significantly above the national average (data taken from the Fischer Family Trust).

Staff turnover is very low and, as recorded in our last Inspection Data Summary Report (IDSR), 0.4 days on average were lost to teacher sickness absence, compared with a national average of 4.0.

Staff enjoy working at St. Peter's, as summarised in these quotes from members of staff when speaking to the Investors in People assessor:

'I love it – it doesn't feel like a job. I love the school, the children and the staff. The staff are very friendly and approachable, and we all get on. It's not luck – it's been planned that way. It's a nice, happy place to be.'

'A breath of fresh air! I love coming to work. I feel I am trusted to teach but support is there for me. I am not left to flounder. If I need help, I could go to so many people for help.'

Key strategies

- The impact of our school motto 'Learn, Sparkle & Shine'.
- Co-headship and teamwork.
- Progress Avenue – a metaphor for walking towards success.
- Staff development, including teaching assistants.
- School is promoted as a place where staff learning takes place alongside pupil learning.
- Flexible working arrangements.
- Intelligence can be acquired and developed.

11 Cleadon Church of England Academy, Cleadon, Sunderland, Tyne and Wear

Workload, wellbeing and the workforce

Jayn Gray, Principal, with Stephen Waters

Overview

Jayn Gray, Principal of Cleadon Church of England Academy, describes how Christian values permeated the school's approach to Covid-19. From the beginning of the academic year 2019/20, there was a sharper focus on staff wellbeing and workload, with the Department for Education's 'School Workload Reduction Kit' (2018) acting as a guidance document. Following an anonymised survey, plans were implemented to address staff workload issues. Actions were interlinked with the Academy's approach to Covid-19 during the period between March and July 2020 when schools remained open for vulnerable children and the children of key workers.

Context

Cleadon Church of England Academy is a larger than average two-form entry school with 482 pupils aged 3–11 years. There are 14 classes and a 78-place Nursery. The school converted to academy status in June 2014 and is part of the All Saints' Multi-Academy Trust. The Academy is very popular and is currently full. It is regularly over-subscribed, and stability is high. The local area is mainly residential, and the majority of property is privately owned, with several new housing developments planned on the outskirts of the village. Between 45–50% of the children live outside of the village and travel to school from the surrounding area. The percentages of pupils from minority ethnic groups, those entitled to free school meals, and children identified as receiving Special Educational Needs and Disability (SEND) support, are all below the national average. Unemployment levels are comparatively low in the village.

There are 66 members of staff. Three classes are job share, where teachers work 2½ days each. The Academy has employed two additional teachers for one year to help support a catch-up programme following the lockdown period during the Covid-19 pandemic between March and July 2020. In common with all schools, the Academy was open for vulnerable children and the children of key workers. The Academy also has two teaching students and two teaching assistant apprentices. Staff mobility is very low; a wellbeing audit showed that staff enjoy working as part of a supportive team and that strategies employed in school allow them to have a healthy work–life balance.

A very positive Christian ethos underpins the work of the school and ensures the distinctiveness of the Academy as a church school. There are strong parish links with All Saints Church. This ensures a secure three-way partnership between school, home and church. The children develop Christian and British values such as compassion, forgiveness and respect. This helps to prepare them fully for their future. Children also learn about other major world faiths.

In February 2017, the Academy had a Statutory Inspection of Anglican and Methodist Schools (SIAMs) inspection and, as previously, was graded 'Outstanding'. The inspector commented on the way in which, 'The Principal, staff and Directors place Christian values and ethos at the heart of this school and encourage the whole school community to support them in this endeavour.' The current Ofsted rating of the school is 'Outstanding'.

The Academy is a strategic partner in The Prince Bishop Teaching Alliance. It works closely with partner primary schools to offer specialised training for senior and middle leaders, as well as teachers and staff across the North-East region.

The school has achieved a number of nationally accredited awards, including: Active Mark Award; Information and Communication Technology (ICT) Mark; Rights Respecting Schools; Fairtrade School; Green Trees Woodland Trust Award; Rainbow Flag Award; School Games Award; Modeshift Stars; Gold status in the All Together Against Bullying programme, and Healthy School status. It achieved the Teach Well Alliance Teach Well School Gold Award: Covid-19 Pandemic in Summer Term 2020 for looking after staff wellbeing during Covid-19. The school is continually looking to achieve further awards and is currently working on its application for the Religious Education (RE) Quality Mark.

The Academy remained open throughout lockdown, including all holidays and bank holidays. The number of children of key workers rose steadily. By July, every child in every year group whose parents wished them to return had done so, with the exception of Nursery.

Staff wellbeing and workload

Staff wellbeing and workload were identified in the Academy's 2019/20 School Improvement Plan (SIP) and remain a priority in the 2020/21 Plan. Teacher wellbeing is directly linked to workload. A stressed teacher cannot be an effective teacher; it is in everyone's interests to care for staff wellbeing and to monitor workload.

From the start of the present academic year (2019/20), the Academy dedicated two staff meetings to Staff Wellbeing and Workload and used the Department for Education's 'School Workload Reduction Kit' (2018) as a guidance document to inform our process of consultation and taking action. The steps involved were as follows:

- Gathering information.
- Setting targets to reduce workload.
- Reviewing the impact of the changes made.

Addressing workload and wellbeing

On 5 January 2020, over two months before lockdown due to the Covid-19 pandemic, a staff meeting was held to address workload and to improve wellbeing. The meeting was supported by the Department for Education's 'School Workload Reduction Kit' (2018), which was updated in October 2019. Staff had a structured conversation about workload in small groups and then completed an initial anonymised workload questionnaire. The staff questionnaire and results appear below (see Tables 11.1 and 11.2).

Staff questionnaire

'We would be very grateful if you could complete this short survey about your workload. We will use the responses to review processes in the school and discuss resulting actions to reduce your workload with you. We will also use responses over time to review progress. The survey does not include any information that could identify you so your answers will all be anonymous. We expect it will take no more than 10 minutes to complete. If you have any questions about the survey, please contact ....'.

1 Consider how long you spent on the following activities other than teaching in your most recent full working week, including activities that took place during weekends, evenings or other out of classroom hours. Was the time spent on each activity too little, about right or too much when considering the impact it had on pupil outcomes?
2 To what extent do you agree or disagree with the following statements about your working hours?

The areas where a significant proportion of staff felt they spent too much time were:

1 General administrative work (including communication, paperwork, work emails and other clerical duties.

Table 11.1 Cleadon Church of England Academy: Results of survey on weekly staff activities other than teaching

	Too little	About right	Too much	N/A
Individual planning or preparation of lessons either at school or out of school	13	3	2	
Teamwork and dialogue with colleagues within school	4		16	
Marking/correcting pupils' work		14	1	1
Pupil counselling (including career guidance and virtual counselling)	4	6	6	3
Pupil supervision and tuition outside of timetabled lessons (including lunch supervision)	3	6	2	6
Pupil discipline, including detentions		8	1	7
Participation in school management		8		9
General administrative work (including communication, paperwork, work emails and other clerical duties you undertake in your job)		7	10	1
Communication and cooperation with parents or guardians		12	5	
Engaging in extracurricular activities (e.g. sport and cultural activities after school)		7	1	9
Cover for absent colleagues		2	3	12
Appraising, monitoring, coaching, mentoring and training other staff	3	10	1	3
Contact with people or organisations outside of school, other than parents		13	3	2
Organising resources and premises, setting up displays, setting up/tidying classrooms	4	9	3	1
Staff meetings		17	1	
School policy development and financial planning		9	2	4
Recording, inputting, monitoring and analysing data in relation to pupil performance and for other purposes		5		
Planning, administering and reporting on pupil assessments		6	9	
Other activities (you may wish to specify)				1

Table 11.2 Cleadon Church of England Academy: Results of survey on workload and work–life balance

	Strongly disagree	Tend to disagree	Neither agree nor disagree	Tend to agree	Strongly agree
I have an acceptable workload	5	2		8	1
Overall, I achieve a good balance between my work life and my private life	7	2		6	1

2 Recording, inputting, monitoring and analysing data in relation to pupil performance and for other purposes.

3 Planning, administering and reporting on pupil assessments.

Ideas to reduce and streamline workload

The following ideas were discussed at the staff meeting. First, staff were reminded of the protocol relating to the sending and receipt of emails from parents, which was written in 2019 as part of the workload reduction initiative:

'**Emails**
- All emails should be directed to the office email address, not to individual staff emails.
- Receipt of an email will be acknowledged within 48 hours during term-time, but not at weekends.
- Responses to emails will be provided by email, telephone or in writing within 5 working days. (Unless longer is required to provide a full response. In this case, staff will indicate a time frame in which a response may be expected.)
- If a staff member is unable to deal with the email directly, then they will pass it on to the most appropriate person, informing the sender they have done so.
- Staff are not expected to monitor or respond to emails out of their normal working hours, including weekends and published holidays.
- If a member of staff receives an email which is of an aggressive tone, sets unreasonable demands or could otherwise be interpreted as harassing, they will refer this to a senior leader, who will decide on any further action.'

I suggested having a time restriction on sending and replying to emails, and discussion followed. The staff felt that everyone had different working patterns;

for example, staff with young children often work after the children have gone to bed. We all accept these different patterns and understand if someone does not respond immediately.

Some staff would have found an imposed 'curfew' very frustrating, defeating the point of improving wellbeing!

- Printer breakdown issues. A new printer was purchased and every Hub in the school was also provided with their own printer, enabling staff to print off work and small photocopy jobs.
- Phone calls to staff during lessons. To prevent staff being disturbed with notifications by the classroom telephone, MSN Messenger was suggested as an alternative way to send staff messages.
- The Academy has reduced the number of Classroom Monitor Targets and also streamlined the reporting systems. Classroom Monitor is the monitoring and tracking system used by the Academy. The system was updated, reducing the number of curricular targets staff were expected to track, greatly reducing workload without diminishing the data provided. The Assessment Lead looked at streamlining the reports staff were required to submit at data capture points across the year. These had already been greatly reduced, but further adjustments were made to utilise some of the features Classroom Monitor provided
- These actions were revisited at the end of the summer term to review the impact of the changes made. Due to Covid-19 lockdown, workload issues had altered, and the Academy was unable to revisit many of the actions. The School Improvement Plan carried actions forward to be implemented in 2020/21 when schools fully re-opened in September.

Wellbeing partners

It is important that all staff feel that they can 'offload' with someone who will listen and be non-judgemental. Sometimes we encounter stressful situations with young people who have difficult behaviour or emotional issues. When we respond to their needs, it can be stressful and emotionally draining. The 'wellbeing partner' is someone we can talk to at such times. By sharing our experience, we can offload some of our emotional needs.

Our wellbeing partner can reassure us about decisions or actions we have taken or can offer friendly advice or practical support.

Staff wellbeing

Staff were asked to update their health information and to identify support they might need at the staff meeting in January 2020. Staff completed a confidential form which was shared with the principal and the school business manager, who is responsible for HR within the Academy. Any significant issues highlighted were discussed with individuals and required adjustments made. Most staff were happy for the information to be shared with others when necessary. For example, one member of staff who has a phobia regarding needles will not be asked to administer to diabetic children; his was a particularly helpful piece of information, as it meant we could always make sure trained staff were available. Information from this meeting was collated and used to inform the next stage of the Reducing Workload project. The main actions were identified and working parties established. These actions were fed back to staff at a staff meeting in October.

The following actions to improve staff wellbeing were agreed once information from staff questionnaires had been analysed and discussed.

Actions to improve workload/wellbeing

- Written annual reports to parents were streamlined/condensed. This had been planned and was agreed during the lockdown period.
- Classroom Monitor [software program for monitoring progress against subject targets] was 'simplified', with the number of targets for core subjects reduced.
- Analysis of data was simplified and reduced to three times a year – the frequency recommended by the Department for Education (DfE).
- Marking was reduced.
- Parent meetings – consultation sheets were streamlined. It was also agreed that staff should make clear how long a meeting would last: 15 minutes for parent consultations; 30 minutes for multi-agency meetings; and 5 minutes for phone calls.
- Written homework was reduced.
- Planning of lessons was generally agreed to be less than in past years, e.g. with the use of Inspire Maths. [Inspire Maths is a whole-school primary maths programme that supports a mastery approach to teaching and learning mathematics, so that pupils can aim to meet the higher expectations of the National Curriculum.] However, whole-school topics, while engaging for the children, entailed new planning and resourcing and were therefore reduced.
- Staff had regular opportunities to participate in social activities (e.g. Christmas meal, Escape Room, Bongo's Bingo).
- Staff had an outside area equipped with tables and chairs to use at lunchtimes.
- Staff had access to Maggie, the school dog, who arrived in November 2019.
- It was planned that staff would have access to mental health support through a mental health practitioner, employed one day each week. Due to lockdown, she has not been able to attend school, but has kept in regular contact. She will return when it is safe to do so.

Workload reduction ideas from other schools

We discussed ideas from other schools that would reduce workload, including the prevention of 'pinch points' during the year, where there is a clash of events happening at the same time (e.g. class worship/parents' night). A slide deck of activities and events in 2020/21 was shown to the staff who were asked to suggest how the calendar could be reorganised to avoid clashes.

Staff self-care strategies

Staff were provided with a list of self-care tips and strategies, including self-care mindfulness, breathing and visualisation exercises:

Relaxation and mindfulness activities

Rainbow Breath: On chair/standing – deep breathing, stretching and relaxation: https://www.youtube.com/watch?v=O29e4rRMrV4

Let's Unwind: Behind chair/standing – stretching and releasing tension: https://www.youtube.com/watch?v=k4gkvyZYxb0

Bring it Down: Sitting in chair – visualisation to relax; best with eyes closed: https://www.youtube.com/watch?v=bRkILioT_NA

On & Off: Sitting on chair and eyes closed – tensing and relaxing activity; calms you down: https://www.youtube.com/watch?v=1ZP-TMr984s

Victorious: Standing behind chair – stretching and deep breathing activity to release tension and to calm: https://www.youtube.com/watch?v=rC0m_-HQcRU

Think About It: Guided short visualisation – to aid relaxation: https://www.youtube.com/watch?v=bYlRFIzI4WA

Strengthen Your Focus: Standing behind chair – standing yoga and balancing; increases focus and calm: https://www.youtube.com/watch?v=0vuaCHEAs-4

3 Minutes Body Scan: Relaxation: https://www.youtube.com/watch?v=i-hwcw_ofuME

5 Minutes Body Scan: Relaxation: https://www.youtube.com/watch?v=9AOS54yAgEg

2 Minutes Relaxation: Walking part – just walk feet on ground whilst sitting: https://www.youtube.com/watch?v=i3OoBoY3Sek

Relaxing music

Calm piano and guitar music with birdsong: https://www.youtube.com/watch?v=9ulk_91GQYI

Beautiful piano music with birdsong: https://www.youtube.com/watch?v=-F7IGIKkgCrU

Tips for good mental health at work

Staff were also made aware of the free self-care support available from the mental health charity Mind and the following link shared with them: https://www.mind.org.uk/workplace/mental-health-at-work/taking-care-of-yourself/tips-for-employees/

Caring for staff wellbeing during the pandemic

During lockdown, the Academy implemented a range of strategies and organised a number of events to support the wellbeing of the staff. They were submitted to the Teach Well Alliance as part of the Academy's successful application to be one of 135 schools to be awarded the Teach Well School Gold Award: Covid-19 Pandemic.

- Zoom social nights.
- Supportive phone calls.
- Open door policy for staff to voice concerns.
- Mindfulness/yoga/relaxation training.
- Links to mental health and wellbeing resources online were signposted regularly to staff.
- Support for staff working from home, including use of Zoom meetings, to ensure that staff were not isolated.
- Birthday greetings during lockdown – ensuring staff with birthdays have greetings sent, via WhatsApp.
- Staff WhatsApp groups were used to share social information and to keep in touch with the whole staff.
- Staff team meetings – Key Stage 1 have a weekly 'Cuppa and Chat' catch up on Zoom. This enabled staff at home and staff at school to keep in touch, to understand one another's challenges and successes, and to support one another.
- For staff who are churchgoers – church online services and resources have been shared, to support staff spiritually in their faith.
- For staff working at school, throughout the pandemic, free school lunches were provided, which were well received!
- The Mental Health Champions emailed all staff to say that they are available for a 'listening ear', if anyone needed someone to talk to confidentially.
- The special educational needs coordinator and vice-principal completed online training as adult mental health first aiders during the pandemic, giving them greater knowledge about staff mental health and how to offer support.

Summer term 2020: Better Health at Work Award

The Academy continued to prepare for submitting the Better Health at Work Award, which entailed identifying targets for wellbeing for all staff [Ed: North

East Better Health at Work Award is a partnership project unique to the North-East to take health and wellbeing into the workplace. The partnership is led by the twelve local authorities, the National Health Service and the Northern Trades Union Congress.] This built on the wellbeing actions already in place and described earlier, such as staff social events, regular 'treats in the staffroom', and the encouragement of staff to develop wellbeing partners with an identified colleague.

Returning to full re-opening in September 2020

Curriculum delivery and content

In preparation for the wider re-opening in September 2020, a Recovery Curriculum was planned and agreed in line with DfE recommendations.

The Recovery Curriculum was designed around three key priorities:

- Pupil and staff wellbeing
- Daily activity and outdoor learning
- Repairing learning gaps

The curriculum was compatible with the key requirements of the National Curriculum:

'**Priority One:** Pupil and Staff Wellbeing

'Ensure a positive and safe learning culture committed to supporting pupils' and staff wellbeing and one which directly engages with feelings of loss, uncertainty and anxiety associated with the current Covid-19 response.'

The following actions were taken in relation to staff wellbeing (Table 11.3).

Teacher wellbeing

Teacher workload was high on full re-opening, due to teaching both in school and remotely. In order to alleviate pressure:

- No formal assessment/key task assessments were required during the phased return.
- Formative assessment, during lessons and of pupil work, allowed for verbal, rather than written, responsive teaching.
- There was continued use of quizzes and tasks, which could be self-assessed, using online teaching programs which could be accessed at home.
- Brief planning summaries replaced formal planning.

Clarity of communication was key to reducing anxiety around change – our expectations regarding planning, delivering and assessing were clearly communicated.

Table 11.3 Cleadon Church of England Academy: Staff wellbeing actions

Area	Staff wellbeing actions
Workload	Work collaboratively within school to minimise teacher workload. Make sure that within your year group team, staff have responsibilities for different curricular areas and resources for that area **for both classes** across the year group
	Prioritise the areas of work that are of **most importance and have the greatest impact on pupil wellbeing and academic progress** (the senior management team will offer support by leading this and identifying priorities for workload)
Working hours	Set **realistic work hours and stick to them**! Don't fall into the pattern of working too late every night as, both physically and emotionally, you will be unable to sustain this in the long term, in the current stressful situation [the Covid-19 pandemic]
Break times	Try to **take your breaks**. Use the **school grounds**, wherever possible, as fresh air and natural light are good for your wellbeing
Eat well	Make sure you are **eating regularly** and not skipping lunch to work – take time out to eat!
Exercise	Try to build in some **exercise** during your day at work, or straight after. Use the school grounds
Wellbeing partners	Your year partner and support staff for your Bubble are your '**wellbeing partners**' during the pandemic. Please take time to talk to them and share any worries you have, several times a week
Adult mental health	Where you have a **concern for yourself, or another member of staff**, regarding wellbeing and mental/emotional health, please contact XXXXX, XXXXX or XXXXX, and we will do our best to offer support

The Recovery Phased Action Plan

The Recovery Phased Action Plan was detailed and comprehensive. The document set out our key priorities, the intended impact of the key priorities, and the strategies to be implemented in order to be successful. It also pinpointed the typical behaviours we would expect from our children. The following sections related specifically to staff (Tables 11.4, 11.5 and 11.6).

Table 11.4 Cleadon Church of England Academy: Recovery Phased Action Plan 1 (for school re-opening in September 2020)

To support the wellbeing of pupils, staff members and community members and be mindful of the policies and strategies that we adopt, ensuring a continuous flow of support and dialogue is taking place between the senior management team (SMT), staff and children.

Support systems put in place during school closure ensure that all members of the school community feel supported throughout and beyond the period of closure, so that staff and students return to school mentally and physically healthy.

- Communication groups have been set up for staff to stay in touch and support one another as required. In addition, individuals are contacted privately.
- To offer additional support, again as required.
- Children continue to receive existing support through Microsoft Teams meetings and telephone conversations.
- SMT will contact vulnerable families regularly to identify how they can be further supported.
- SMT contact children, each week, to celebrate those who have achieved well.
- A weekly evaluation form is completed by staff and returned to the principal. This enables staff to share their thoughts confidentially.
- The SEND pupils at KS2 have their Cool Learner Group, which the SENCO leads. As well as academic activities, wellbeing activities are planned on a regular basis.
- Throughout home schooling, the SENCO has ensured that wellbeing/mental health resources and guidance are emailed to all parents so that the strategies can be applied at home.
- Mental health resources and links are also regularly sent to staff.
- Mental health training is also allocated to all staff on a weekly basis, with some staff being identified for training as mental health first aiders, for children and adult support.
- The Value of the Week is sent to parents each week, with the newsletter. This ensures that parents continue to focus on wellbeing and implementation of Christian values at home.
- The SENCO has also worked closely with XXXXX to further develop the resources on the Academy website for mental health, ensuring that all new resources are posted as soon as possible.
- A list of bereaved persons has been started to ensure that their families are offered advice, and an email with suggested bereavement resources is sent to those identified.
- A bereavement page on the Academy website pinpoints useful resources and links.
- Risk assessments have been completed for all EHCP pupils (5 in school) and submitted to the local authority.
- A contact chart regarding contact with families of all vulnerable children is kept up to date by XXXXX.
- Risk assessments for return to school, regarding emotional and SEND vulnerability, are being compiled.
- All children at home to receive a telephone call from their class teacher.

Table 11.5 Cleadon Church of England Academy: Recovery Phased Action Plan 2 (for school re-opening in September 2020)

Issues	Actions	Success criteria
The Academy has remained open for vulnerable children and children of key workers #	Staff meeting agendas will include a focus on the wellbeing of staff # Expectations beyond the school day will be removed in the initial stages #	After the first half-term, staff are fully back in the swing of things # Staff felt well supported during the return period and feel more confident about leaving vulnerable family members #
Staff have continued to work, alternating between home and school. This included the Easter and half-term holidays #	Staff will be encouraged to focus on their family members when at home # Teachers' workload will be a key consideration; the assessment of academic subjects will not be expected in the initial stages #	Normal after-school arrangements have been re-established after the first half-term #
Some staff have been providing home learning tasks while home-schooling their own children #	Staff will assess children's wellbeing and social and mental health, and accommodate as necessary # SMT will discuss the curriculum with staff and what subjects need greater emphasis #	Staff are better equipped to continue to assess children's social and mental health #
Some staff could be coming back both physically and mentally tired #	SMT will make time for all staff to talk to senior leaders about their personal situation # Risk assessments put in place to support staff who feel less confident #	Normal timetable arrangements have been re-established after the first half-term #
Many may have had additional worries (and may continue to do so) about members of their family and friends	Staff will be reminded of any internal support plan system that is in place # Staff wellbeing activities to be regularly built into school, e.g. encouraging staff to exercise in school grounds	Staff have valued time to talk about their particular issues

Table 11.6 Cleadon Church of England Academy: Recovery Phased Action Plan 3 (for school re-opening in September 2020)

Issues	Actions	Success criteria
The Academy is very keen to support staff, including those who will have suffered loss or trauma	LACs will need to focus on the wellbeing of all staff in the first half-term back	Lacs have played a significant role in supporting staff as they return to 'normal' routines
#	#	#
Some staff have been in school while others have worked almost exclusively at home	LACs will accept that data will not be accurate until at least the end of the Autumn term	LACs and senior leaders accept that checking data is not the priority and have not pressured staff to provide information related to academic progress
#	#	#
We need to allow time to rebuild the school community	Rather than spending time monitoring learning or writing subject-specific reports, staff instead will identify key concepts to be covered in subjects to minimise the long-term impact of lost learning	SMT and staff will have a clear overview of where the children are working academically to ascertain starting points
#	#	#
The principal has had to make some very difficult decisions and has had to respond to a range of government guidance	A key focus will be on assessing children's wellbeing and creating a healthy environment to enable children to be ready for learning	Staff will have mostly focused on children's wellbeing and have not felt pressured into providing reports or monitoring progress
#	#	#
Staff need to be aware of the stress that the principal has faced and need to be considerate	LACs will accept that, when children return, this will be a new situation for everybody, and nobody has a blueprint of what it should look like	There has been a strong focus on creating a healthy environment
#	#	#
The Local Academy Councillors (LACs) have a role to play to support all staff [Ed: LACs are the equivalent of school governors]	There will be a little of 'feeling our way'	Children have made excellent adjustments and are rapidly back into the swing of things
		#
		There has been an acceptance that certain routines have had to be changed for the sake of children and staff
		#
		The 'feeling our way' approach has been eradicated and routines established

Home Learning Rationale

As with the Recovery Phased Action Plan, the Home Learning Rationale was wide-ranging and considered the needs of everyone in the school community, including staff. It was drawn up after lockdown and a final version was agreed by staff at the beginning of April. The following sections are those most relevant to staff wellbeing and are taken largely verbatim from the school's documentation:

'In order to ensure a smooth, effective and high-quality system, which enables evolution in line with the ever-changing situation, we adopted a three-phase approach to home learning:

- Initial phase covers the time period pre-Easter (2020).
- Adjustment phase relates to the time period post-Easter (2020). (Many of our key priorities cover the first two phases.)
- Recovery will occur when the return to school period begins.'

The detailed approach we took to supporting staff wellbeing and mental health during the Covid-19 pandemic was an extension of our care for staff before it. We try to ensure that there is a culture of care for both staff and pupils which permeates the school, ensuring supportive actions are embedded into its DNA, rather than being tokenistic and tick-box. At Cleadon Academy, our aim is that children and adults belong to a caring organisation which reaches beyond the school gates to the community beyond.

Key strategies

- Addressing staff wellbeing and workload, including voluntary self-reporting of concerns.
- Staff questionnaire.
- Staff meetings devoted to teacher wellbeing.
- Wellbeing partners.
- Staff wellbeing, including voluntary self-reporting.
- Counsellor employed one day each week.
- Self-care strategies circulated, including mindfulness, breathing and music.
- Caring for staff wellbeing during the pandemic.
- Better Health at Work Award.
- Workload reduction ideas from other schools, e.g. reducing 'pinch points'.
- Link to free support on Mind website.
- Returning to full re-opening in September 2020, including staff wellbeing, and the Phased Recovery Action Plan.

12 North Walsall Primary Academy, Walsall, West Midlands

The North Walsall Way

Natalie Hawkins, Principal

'As communication, staff recognition and thanks were celebrated, these motivational practices were now becoming positive, powerful habits. This enabled me to begin to tackle some of the deeper-rooted, harder to change barriers I faced, when considering staff mental health and wellbeing. Staff could see I cared and that I was at least trying to make positive changes. They started to believe not just in me but in one another. I felt supported because they felt supported and valued.'

Overview

Principal Natalie Hawkins describes how staff wellbeing and mental health were the key to building staff trust and relationships on taking over the leadership of North Walsall Primary Academy. She explains how working closely and collaboratively with the executive principal gave her the support and impetus to improve staff morale. Natalie emphasises the importance of beginning the development of a culture of staff wellbeing and mental health by asking staff to complete a survey to identify the key issues standing in the way of a collective positive mindset. Consistency of approach to pupil behaviour and encouraging distributed leadership were both instrumental in the school's transformation.

Context

North Walsall Primary Academy (NWPA) is based in the borough of Walsall in the West Midlands and is part of the Academy Transformation Trust. The 2020 census data recorded that the school had 242 pupils on roll, including the Nursery, 47.9% girls and 52.1% boys. The Income Deprivation Affecting Children Index (IDACI) 2019 quintile band E shows that the school is in the one of the most deprived areas in England.

Table 12.1 Breakdown of 2019/20 intake at North Walsall Primary Academy compared with the national January 2019 census

Number	Total (%)	National average (%)	(%)
Number of SEND children	43 children 17.6	SEND	14.6
Number of EHCP children	7 children 2.86	EHCP (all-form entry)	2.8
Children who are PP + SEND	20 children 46.5	PP + SEND	13.7
Children who are EAL + SEND	29 children 67.4	EAL + SEND	21.2
% of PP	43, not inc. EYFS	PP	23

Abbreviations: PP = Pupil Premium, EHCP = Education and Health Care Plan, EAL = English as an additional language, EYFS = Early Years Foundation Stage.

Table 12.1 shows a breakdown of our 2019/20 intake against the national January 2019 census. Table 12.1 does not include children who present with social-emotional needs but are not identified as requiring Special Educational Needs and Disability (SEND) support.

We are a one-form entry school consisting of 37 staff: five members of the senior leadership team (SLT), four of whom teach; nine class teachers; 15 class-based support staff; and eight other support staff, including admin, site and lunchtime staff.

I joined NWPA from a different Multi-Academy Trust (MAT) in September 2017 as the vice-principal. I was then internally promoted to head of school in September 2018, prior to taking on the role of principal in June 2019. As a newly appointed head of school in September 2018, it was clear to me that the culture of staff well-being needed to change, and quickly, for the sake of my staff and any future development of the school. In my role as vice-principal, I had been acutely aware of areas of improvement required from an SLT point of view but had a limited understanding of how staff really felt until the results of a staff survey in September 2018 were published. In all schools, staff workload is an issue but information from the survey helped me to identify a number of root causes of staff discontent.

The survey asked staff to name two things they thought the school needed to improve. The most common responses were:

- Appreciation of staff and their achievements.
- Staff mental health and wellbeing.
- Staff workload/work–life balance.
- Communication.
- Distributed leadership – linked to work–life balance.
- Support with behaviour from SLT.

Some of the open comments were powerful and spelt out my task loud and clear (my emphasis):

- Support staff *mostly* a friendly team.
- *Most* staff work hard.
- Leadership model *unrealistic*, with *unrealistic* expectations.
- Staff mental health and wellbeing *need to be improved*.
- *Lack of appreciation* of staff and their achievements.
- Communication on a *daily basis*, not just via email.
- *Some* teachers are *rude* to support staff.

I had had negative experiences throughout my career that affected my own mental health and wellbeing and I was eager not to create the same environment as a newly appointed head. I wanted to have a positive impact on the lives of my staff. I wanted to be a headteacher my staff could be proud of and to create an environment staff wanted to work in.

I began work on implementing cultural change as soon as I was appointed, as I could see not only the implications for staff wellbeing, but also the impact on whole-school improvement. These improvements hinged on a much-needed shift in direction of how staff felt about the school and their place within it.

I was extremely fortunate to have an executive head appointed alongside me. We shared the same vision for the school, and she came from a school very similar to NWPA. She had also inherited her school in a similar way. The bond we forged as a duo exemplified the kind of bond and symbiotic relationship I wanted for all the staff. I knew this would improve wellbeing, which, in turn, would lead to greater levels of whole-school improvement. I had a vision of what we needed to begin our journey.

In 2018, we didn't have anyone leading on staff wellbeing and mental health. I had an unhappy workforce, not to mention an impending Ofsted. Having already worked at the school for 12 months prior to the publication of the survey, I too had contributed to its findings. I shared some of the opinions in this summary of teacher comments or was at least aware of them. Staff wellbeing was seldom talked about prior to September 2018 and it was clear that there was a disparity between how staff treated one another and how they wished to be treated. There was also the issue of the two completely separate groups of staff: the teachers and the teaching assistants.

We hold the Inclusion Quality Mark (IQM) award as a centre of excellence for our inclusion provision; the quality mark recognises how well we provide for our children. By implementing a culture change that put staff wellbeing and mental health at its forefront, I hoped to create a metaphorical 'centre of excellence' for the staff at NWPA.

'We are what we repeatedly do. Excellence, then, is not an act, but a habit.'
Aristotle – Greek philosopher (384 BC–322 BC)

With this in mind, we had 'habits' to break if we were to create a happy workforce, with a warm inviting environment: one with a shared vision for the school and shared appreciation of each other, one devoid of hierarchical stature that impeded the giving and receiving of recognition.

Change is hard and takes time. It's even more difficult with a newly-formed SLT team and a staff body with a history of embedded detrimental practices (habits) that had led to a less than happy workforce, 'habits' not conducive with the vision I was aiming to achieve. I needed staff to be a part of the changes willingly, with open minds and a sense of self-fulfilment, stemming from the knowledge that the changes made came from their voices and the knowledge that they had been heard and valued.

I wanted to tackle and overcome the identified barriers from the 2018 staff voice survey, as I felt this would be a better starting point than any other, namely:

- Lack of appreciation of staff and their achievements.
- Staff mental health and wellbeing.
- Staff workload/work–life balance.
- Communication.
- Distributed leadership – linked to work–life balance.
- Support with managing pupil behaviour from SLT.

I had also identified other areas that were causing undue pressure and anxiety for staff. I knew that from previous experience and research that, once addressed, these areas would have a hugely positive impact on mental health and wellbeing.

- The school's physical environment (climate for learning).
- Diet and nutrition (healthy lifestyle).
- Positive parental engagement – supported and upheld by a strong SLT.

Finally, I needed to address how staff viewed themselves and one another. There was very much a 'them and us' attitude between teachers and teaching assistants and no-one seemed to value their own expertise and what they had to offer, not just to the children but to each other. Staff continuing personal development (CPD) needed to become a whole-school priority.

Knowing where to begin was the key, so I started by tackling issues from the list of areas identified in a staff voice survey that would have the greatest impact with the least effort in the shortest amount of time (quick wins). I chose to initially focus on improved communication and improved staff appreciation. I began by surveying staff on their preferred methods of communication and frequency. From this, I then embedded three key forms of communication:

1   The Monday morning staff briefing.
2   The fortnightly communication board.
3   The Friday email.

The purpose of these methods of communication is for staff to be informed of what is happening in school, have a platform to have their voice heard, and to give thanks.

We begin the week with an 8:00 a.m. Monday morning briefing; this allows for key messages for the coming week to be communicated and for voices to be heard in a shared environment.

This is supported by a staff notice board outlining key events and messages for the following two weeks. This allows staff to sync diaries, provides staff with a visual reminder of meetings and events, and uses the board as a space where they can write me silly messages, such as: 'Can we please have chocolates not fruit!'

Finally, every Friday, I send a 'Happy Friday' email, thanking staff and recognising individual and collective successes. I begin with congratulating everyone for making it successfully through another week (including a humorous GIF). I then identify shared excellence across the school, usually accompanied by a funny quote from a child such as:

Teacher: 'What do we call an animal that only eats plants, etc.?'
Year 6 child: 'A herbivegan!' …

… just in case we needed reminding why we do what we do!

I then give explicit praise and thanks to individuals, such as 'This week's big shout-outs go to **** for facilitating our Teach Well Alliance Gold Award for Staff Well Being, and **** for speaking to every parent in the school to confirm visits – no small task.' I end by wishing everyone a happy weekend, accompanied again by a humorous GIF. Staff then reply to the thread with lovely comments, thanks, and appreciation for each other. I enjoy sending these emails and staff enjoy receiving them. It makes us happy.

To further embed staff recognition and thanks we introduced the North Walsall Fairy. She visits once a week (providing she isn't too busy or doesn't forget). She takes recommendations from a staff recognition box. Staff are asked to nominate their colleagues for their 'excellence' such as '**** works tirelessly on school displays and always supports me with mine'. The fairy then gathers the recognitions and chooses one well-deserving person to visit. She leaves a small gift for the person along with a note and shares an email with all staff, recognising their excellence and thanking the whole school, thus allowing everyone the opportunity to share in the collective happiness.

This was just the beginning. As communication, staff recognition and thanks are now celebrated, these motivational practices have become positive, powerful habits. This has enabled me to begin to tackle some of the deeper-rooted, harder-to-change barriers I faced, when considering staff mental health and wellbeing. Staff could see I cared and that I was at least trying to make positive changes. They started to believe not just in me but in one another. I felt supported because they felt supported and valued.

Along the way there have been what I would call 'big game changers' that have really turned the tide for positive mental health and wellbeing. The first of these game changers came in September 2018, with the implementation of a new behaviour policy for children and a code of conduct for parents. A key issue the school faced at the time was embedded bad habits when it came to tackling children's behaviour in school, subsequently followed by less than supportive parental communication. Over time, the school had developed a culture of inconsistent approaches to managing behaviour. This resulted in some less than happy parents, who behaved in an unacceptable way towards staff. Parents were frustrated and staff felt unsupported.

I appointed a new behaviour lead and implemented a new behaviour policy. I also listened to my staff, who said they had felt unsupported by the SLT in the past when parents had verbally abused them and even threatened them. The new behaviour policy was shared with parents, and staff were fully trained on how to implement it with consistency. The SLT were placed front and centre when it came to dealing with difficult parents. A Parent Code of Conduct was shared with all families and wider stakeholders, and a clear appointment system was implemented for parents to discuss issues with a senior member of the team. Sounds simple but, as you can imagine, it was less than plain sailing – new habits take time to embed and old ones take even longer to break.

The policy was not always followed with consistency, which led to slow short-term progress. Staff needed ongoing CPD on behaviour strategies. Children were being held to higher account with greater rigour and a zero-tolerance approach, which, of course, they found difficult. Parents could not understand why their child was now being rebuked for negative behaviours they had been allowed to get away with previously, so they too found it difficult to adjust. In the short term (Autumn 1 + Autumn 2 2018), fixed-term exclusions, detentions and in-school isolations increased while children adjusted to the new rigorous practices (habits). To be clear – behaviour had not deteriorated; we were just doing a better job of identifying it, recording it and managing it. Early on, unfortunately, we had to issue site bans to parents and even called the police when parents were verbally aggressive and made threats towards staff. The first term and a half were difficult, as staff, children and parents slowly broke their bad habits and forged new positive ones. I am pleased to say that we now have a new lease of life when it comes to how we manage behaviour. In the academic year of 2019/20, we issued no fixed-term exclusions or parental site bans. Most importantly, staff stated in the 2020 staff voice survey that they felt supported when they had a problem with a pupil's behaviour: 22% strongly agreed and 74% agreed.

The second 'big game changer' came from distributed leadership. This began in 2018 but culminated in the appointment of a new assistant principal in September 2019. Staff workload factored highly on the 2018 staff voice survey, from teachers to members of the SLT team. The consensus across the school was that some staff worked harder than others – or at least there was a perception that this was the case – and that some staff were valued more than others and held in much higher regard. Common phrases I heard bandied around were, 'Well I'm just the teaching assistant'; 'I'm only a teacher, you're SLT'; 'Teaching assistants don't need to stay for after school training (PDM).' No-one seemed to value themselves or each other and it was each person for themselves.

I began by mapping out termly CPD which all staff were to attend, as it focused on our core business of 'teaching and learning' and that was everyone's job. All staff needed to understand that, regardless of our role, we were all in the business of teaching and learning and we all need ongoing CPD to improve. I talent mapped our cumulative expertise and appointed a head and a deputy lead for every subject in the school, based on skillset and passion (passion is so important). I then broke the proverbial mould and appointed teaching assistants where appropriate to subject leads, not just as deputies. I did this because they were the best persons for the job. In a number of cases, the teaching assistants hold subject degrees that teachers do not, and they have a real passion for what they do. This really made people stand back and question the value of one another and of themselves.

Each subject now has a teacher and a teaching assistant in either a lead or deputy role and they work together to drive their subject forward. The symbiotic relationship I mentioned at the beginning of this chapter between myself and the executive head is now becoming a reality for my team. In the early stages, I forced staff to recognise one another's skillsets and expertise and to give mutual respect at all times. Now my team bask in each other's wealth of knowledge, and they seek each other's support and guidance. No-one thinks twice about the title they hold when it comes to who is the best person for the job. I am proud to say we now have two members of support staff on the National Professional Qualification for Middle Leadership (NPQML) training, officially recognising their skillset and the part they play in the team. Staff are happier because they value themselves and each other. Shared distributed leadership is also leading to reduced workload.

It took me two years, but I now have a complete SLT team who complement each other well. I believe I chose wisely (if I do say so myself), making sure I appointed people who had all the skills I lack. When I was appointed head of school in 2018, the SLT team were nothing more than a group of teachers with a title. I started from scratch, keeping two members of the existing team, the SENCO and the EYFS lead. I knew what I was lacking – a teaching and learning lead and someone with an operational/financial background.

Creating the perfect SLT team is a difficult task and for distributed leadership to be implemented fully, the right staff needed to be appointed. In June 2019, I appointed the SENCO as assistant principal in charge of inclusion and safeguarding. In September 2019, I appointed a new assistant principal in charge of teaching and learning. Finally, in July 2020 the office manager joined the SLT team to offer much-needed logistical and financial guidance in the running of the school. The SLT need distributed leadership just as much as the staff when it comes to managing workload.

As I embark upon my third year leading NWPA, I can honestly say we are a different school in every sense of the word. I began this transformational journey in September 2018 and, of the staff who began the journey with me, 84% of them remain by my side. Of those who parted ways, I am pleased to say and can say with all honesty, the majority left through natural career progression choices. We still have a way to go in terms of 'work–life balance' but show me a school that has really cracked that nut!

The journey itself began with us receiving 'The Call' in October 2018. [Ed: A colloquial term used by schools, referring to the telephone call from Ofsted to inform the school that it will be inspected on the following day.] We pulled together and dug in deep and we came out victorious with a 'Good' rating. This was it – this was the beginning of our collective belief. We had weathered the storm. We now knew we could do it and we believed this was our fresh start. I tackled each issue identified in the 2018 staff voice survey, including my own observations, one at a time, over the course of two years. The approaches were gradual in many respects. They had to be, as 'habits' embed over time, not over-night. Improvements can be seen in many ways: staff absence reduced; staff retention stabilised; staff–parent communication improved; and recorded behaviour incidents diminished. All of these issues were indicators of improved staff wellbeing and mental health. The two staff voice surveys taken in 2019 and 2020 outline our progress and success, and indicate our next steps clearly. I am proud of what we as a team have achieved and the 'North Walsall Way' has changed our culture and ethos for the better.

Excerpt from 2019 staff voice survey

Name two things you are proud of in your school (words in *italics* indicate next steps):

> 'Support from other staff, we are a close-knit team, the way *support staff* go above and beyond.'
>
> 'Working environment and colleagues.'
>
> 'The hard work and the executive head and principal since they took over.'
>
> 'The appreciation you receive from certain staff.'
>
> 'The principal and the SLT team are approachable, and care what I think.'

From these comments and key words, I could see the SLT team were now valued and appreciated by staff, but this shared value of the SLT did not yet extend fully to one another as colleagues. Next steps were clear.

Excerpt from the 2020 staff voice survey

- The school is better than it was a year ago?
  48% strongly agree; 48% agree; 4% can't say
- The school works hard to promote a reasonable work–life balance?
  22% strongly agree; 59% agree; 15% can't say; 4% disagree
- Staff morale is generally good?
  22% strongly agree, 78% agree

- The leadership of the school is at least good?
  52% strongly agree; 48% agree
- I am well supported if I have a problem with a pupil's behaviour?
  22% strongly agree; 74% agree; 4% can't say
- I am praised and recognised for the work I do?
  41% strongly agree; 56% agree; 4% can't say
- The views of staff are taken into consideration when decisions are made?
  15% strongly agree; 74% agree; 7% can't say; 4% disagree
- Staff are well informed about what is happening in the school.
  37% strongly agree, 63% agree

As you can see, we are not perfect, but we are a million miles away from where we were back in 2018.

Our school is improving daily, we are finally 'pulling as one'. We support each other and, more importantly, we value each other. I want our school to be a centre of excellence when it comes to staff mental health and wellbeing. My immediate goal is for our staff to remain happy and continue to feel supported every day, and to know that they are appreciated in everything they do. I unpick the findings of a survey if staff can't articulate their views: Why is this? What can I do to help facilitate staff expressing their feelings? How can I tip the balance in all areas to 'strongly agree'?

We also want our improvements to be formally recognised by Ofsted during our next inspection. When we had our last Ofsted in October 2018, we were graded as a 'Good' school. Since then, the Ofsted Education Inspection Framework (EIF) has changed. Staff wellbeing now forms part of the leadership and management judgement:

'Leaders engage with their staff and are aware and take account of the main pressures on them. They are realistic and constructive in the way that they manage staff, including their workload' (Ofsted, 2019c: 74).

Ofsted recommends leaders:

'Develop staff well-being by creating a positive and collegial working environment in which staff feel supported, valued and listened to and have an appropriate level of autonomy ... a positive working environment is a predictor of staff well-being. Creating such an environment is one of the main ways in which we can improve wellbeing and enhance retention' (Ofsted, 2019a).

I feel we have created such an environment at NWPA and we would like our Leadership and Management to be graded as a '1: Outstanding' during our next inspection.

Additionally, a Teacher Wellbeing Research Report found that '[p]oor behaviour is a considerable source of low occupational well-being, and teachers do not always feel supported by senior leaders and parents with managing it' (Ofsted, 2019a). This is another area that we have worked extremely hard to improve over the past two years and staff now tell me that they feel fully supported in this area and that positive behaviour is a strength of our school. We feel confident as a school that we meet the criteria in Behaviour and Attitudes of a '1: Outstanding'.

These are our medium-term recognition aspirations for our school. Watch this space!

Key strategies

- Staff surveys to highlight key issues of staff wellbeing and mental health.
- Cultural change, not isolated strategies.
- Close working relationship with executive head.
- Tackling divide between teaching staff and teaching assistants/support staff.
- Introducing Monday morning briefing.
- Communication board.
- Friday email recognising staff, including humour.
- 'Walsall Fairy' visits staff recognition box and rewards someone.
- New behaviour policy and appointment of behaviour lead.
- Revised Parent Code of Conduct.
- Distributed leadership.
- CPD linked to teaching and learning.
- Teaching assistants appointed as subject leads based on merit and qualifications.

13 Elsley Primary School, Wembley, London

Staff wellbeing and mental health during the Covid-19 pandemic

Alice Codner, Class Teacher and Outdoor Learning Leader

Headteacher: Raphael Mossi

'The most visible sign of the school valuing wellbeing is the staffroom, which has received considerable investment, making it lush and comfortable to spend time in. There are sofas, soft chairs and a long table that can seat many staff members. This has encouraged a culture in which the norm is for staff to take a break together at lunchtime, which in turn affords them the opportunity to share experiences, to give and receive support, and to enjoy each other's company, building up trust and leading to strong relationships between colleagues. Friendly advice, informally exchanged around the table on a daily basis, essentially amounts to bespoke "on-demand" CPD, creating just one of the ways in which care for staff wellbeing positively contributes towards Elsley's pupil progress and attainment. The cumulative effect of time spent in the staffroom is that, when a crisis does happen, staff are already acquainted with each other's home situations, and it is normal to be looking out for each other informally.'

Overview

The Covid-19 pandemic, which impacted schools from March 2020 and hit the area around Elsley in North-West London badly, presented a set of challenges which were unique and without precedence. While schools remained open for vulnerable children and the children of key workers, teachers had to provide online lessons for children at home within days of lockdown. Alice Codner explains how the headteacher regarded Elsley Primary School as a 'family' and acted immediately to protect vulnerable and ill teachers by advising them to remain at home and isolate or shield. The strong support system for staff and the sharing of expertise not only further strengthened staff wellbeing but also provided targeted professional development, enabling staff to use Google Classroom for online learning.

Context

Elsley is a four-form entry school with a very wide range of ability and socio-emotional needs and an above average number of children with Special Educational Needs and Disabilities (SEND). A third of our pupils join the school after the start of Reception. Many are new arrivals in the country, often with no English, and sometimes with no prior school experience. Over 85% of our pupils have English as an additional language (EAL), and it is common to have 10 languages spoken in one individual class. We are a referral agency for a food bank and, throughout the Covid-19 pandemic, we set up our own food bank at school to support children and families in need.

Although only a small number of our children are eligible for free school meals, this is often because they do not qualify, as their families are new arrivals in the country, or are working full-time on a minimal wage, or do not have the necessary paperwork. This also means that our low number of Pupil Premium (PP) children is not reflective of the true levels of deprivation, which sees children frequently living in temporary accommodation and in over-crowded living conditions.

We have 70 members of staff: the senior leadership team (SLT), comprising the headteacher, two deputy headteachers and four assistant headteachers; 33 teachers; 22 support staff, including teaching assistants and learning support assistants; and eight admin site and school support staff.

Background to Elsley Primary's response to the pandemic

The phrase 'Elsley Family' appeared more frequently than usual in the last few weeks of June 2020. It wasn't a new phrase, but it now had the sense of belonging that comes from staff feeling genuinely cared for.

This sense of family is irrelevant to the position a staff member holds. One teacher commented that, 'There is no feeling of hierarchy; every staff member is as valued as the next.' A teaching assistant pointed out, 'Whether you are his deputy or a teaching assistant, [the head] listens to what you have to say, and he values it.'

This sense of being listened to is especially important when staff home situations develop, such as needing to pick up a sick child from school or go to a funeral. The leadership team has an open-door policy, allowing staff to speak with them whenever they need. One staff member described making use of this policy, saying: 'I felt I was able to be totally honest about a situation that was hard for me to talk about, and there was no judgement.' The policy meant that, when the pandemic hit, staff were already confident that their home lives were valued by the school. A level of trust between the leadership and other staff members was already in place, enabling the support offered during the pandemic to be effective.

Not only are the individual needs of staff prioritised, but the contributions of the staff are also regularly celebrated through half-termly staff breakfasts, Christmas dinners and Secret Santa events, end-of-term socials and special mentions in the morning briefing. At the end of each Summer term, the SLT arrange a special afternoon for a staff social, putting a lot of effort into food, dressing-up themes and games. Everyone is given an individual, personal note of thanks from the SLT and a small gift. These afternoons are fun and silly, designed to bring everyone together, reinforcing the sense of family and celebrating the shared sense of achievement.

The most visible sign of the school valuing wellbeing is the staffroom, which has received considerable investment, making it lush and comfortable to spend time in. There are sofas, soft chairs and a long table that can seat many staff members. This has encouraged a culture in which it is the norm for staff to take a break together at lunchtime, which in turn affords them the opportunity to share experiences, to give and receive support, and to enjoy each other's company, building up trust and leading to strong relationships between colleagues. Friendly advice, informally exchanged around the table on a daily basis, essentially amounts to bespoke 'on-demand' CPD, creating just one of the ways in which care for staff wellbeing positively contributes towards Elsley's pupil progress and attainment. The cumulative effect of time spent in the staffroom is, that when a crisis does happen, staff are already acquainted with each other's home situations, and it is normal to be looking out for each other informally.

Staff safety at the forefront of all decision-making

As soon as the pandemic appeared on the horizon, the headteacher reassured staff that, should schools need to close, their pay would be protected and their safety, along with that of the children and their families, would be at the forefront of all decision-making processes. Well before the lockdown was officially announced, staff with underlying health conditions and those living with vulnerable adults were encouraged to stay at home. All staff members were then given a choice as to whether or not they were comfortable with being on the rota to open the school for vulnerable children and the children of key workers. Each individual was supported in making their decision, taking into account their personal situation and their travel arrangements on getting to school, ensuring that they could avoid public transport. Communication was clear before the pandemic reached the UK, ensuring that when the lockdown started in March 2020, any potential anxiety connected with work was minimised.

Support for staff and family illness

Throughout the lockdown, staff were encouraged to keep the leadership team updated about their situation and to stay in touch. The leadership team emphasised that this was both to keep them informed about staff availability and also to take care of the staff. They then texted, messaged and regularly phoned staff who needed support, especially those who experienced bereavements, illness (either themselves or family members), or issues around where to quarantine.

The message that staff wellbeing came first was given loud and clear, and was deeply appreciated by staff, two of whom commented:

'They put my wellbeing first and helped me to make tough decisions about where would be best for me to isolate, even when it meant I would be unable to come into school for the rota.'

'All of them understood my situation and made clear that I was not expected to return to work until I was fully recovered and let me know that the most important thing was me and my recovery.'

Bereavement

The area in which the school is situated was particularly badly affected by Covid-19, with both children and staff members experiencing bereavement. It is clear from staff comments that the headteacher, the leadership team and individual members of staff members, all supported each other through the pain that people experienced, both practically and emotionally:

'The phase leaders have been really supportive during the bereavement we had in our family and I got lovely messages from my year group staff along with a beautiful bouquet of flowers.'

'During self-isolation … it was so heart-warming for [the SLT] to check up on me and to even get a direct message from Raphael [head], offering support with home deliveries.'

'When I lost a family member due to Covid, [the head] sent me a personal message of condolence and another message of support on the day of the "Zoom" funeral.'

Light relief during lockdown

During the lockdown, leaders ran Zoom quizzes for their teams to give everyone some light relief when it was much needed and to make sure that no-one felt isolated. The computing specialist teacher also gave the staff opportunities to join in with fun activities that brought everyone together, making a music video in which everyone who wanted to take part could feature. There were also informal times on Zoom for the staff to connect with one another before staff meetings began.

Setting up Google Classroom

Google Classroom was set up in a measured way, ensuring that staff workload was always manageable. It was trialled for two weeks with one year group to iron out the main challenges before training was given to the rest of the staff. The training was clear, with video tutorials available to remind staff of how to use certain features, and an 'expert' staff member assigned to support each year group in learning to use it, led by the computing specialist teacher. Online learning was rolled out slowly, starting with simple quizzes to help the staff gain confidence, ensuring that the work was never overwhelming. For staff with children, their own family's needs were always prioritised by the SLT.

Leaders consulted with all staff about the key decisions, including how much work to set children online, how to help the children with no online access, and how and when to re-open the school. All staff completed a detailed survey to communicate their feelings on re-opening and felt that they were listened to and were not put under pressure. One member of staff commented:

'I have trust in the school, not only because they have strategically planned it out but because they discuss that plan with us and, together, we are able to also input and share our feedback.'

As another staff member succinctly put it, 'At no point have I felt that I would have to choose between my health and my job.'

Delaying full re-opening

Staff were overwhelmingly comforted by the decision not to 're-open' the school on 1 June 2020, appreciating that their safety and wellbeing were clearly being prioritised. This was especially important for the many staff from a Black, Asian or Minority Ethnic background:

'He [the head] has shown great understanding and empathy with the Black members of staff and students, who are more likely to contract/die from the virus and has not forced us to return to work before he feels it is safe.'

It is clear that the decision to ensure staff felt listened to was made deliberately. As the headteacher wrote in a blog post:

'Now, more than ever, staff need my empathy, need me to know their anxieties and their context, need to be able to challenge my views, and need me to have a clear rationale for what we're doing and why we're doing it. It wouldn't be good leadership to dictate and not listen. This will take time. It will take me longer to get my school up and running again than leaders with a different approach. But I believe that this way will have a greater long-term benefit. What we may lose by opening a few days (or even weeks) later, we will make up for through the enormous goodwill of staff, children and parents' (https://headshipintheuk.edublogs.org/2020/05/20/taking-back-control/).

It is clear from the recurring word 'proud' in staff comments that the head's approach paid off:

'I think everyone in Elsley has really come together in their own way to support each other and I couldn't be prouder to work in such a school where wellbeing comes first.'

'I cannot be prouder to belong to a school which is always looking after the wellbeing of not just pupils and families, but everyone in there.'

Throughout the pandemic, from the attitude and efforts of the senior leaders as well as from the kindness of the staff members, staff felt that there was always someone looking out for them, and that they were part of a caring family.

The wellbeing team

Finally, Elsley has an official wellbeing team, which finds new ways to support staff. At the end of Summer 2019, the wellbeing team sent out a survey to seek the opinions of staff members regarding what they appreciated and what they would like to change. The results of this survey were taken seriously, and an immediate change in the management of resources was put into effect, since this had been highlighted as a challenging area. The team have also arranged work socials, fitness classes such as zumba and yoga for staff, and little things like moisturiser in the toilets for staff to use.

In caring for the physical and mental health and wellbeing of staff, Elsley's response to the pandemic has been exceptional. However, this has not taken place in a vacuum. Elsley has a long-standing history of staff who have cared about each other over the years, building the base for a culture that has proved itself robust, surviving changing leadership teams as well as the development of the school from two-form to four-form entry. The ongoing nature of such a culture is by no means automatic but is nurtured every time it is taken into consideration, both in the large decisions and the small choices made on a continual, day-to-day basis.

Key strategies

- Staff safety first.
- Support for staff and family illness.
- Support for bereavement.
- Light relief during lockdown.
- Setting up Google Classroom.
- Delaying full re-opening.
- Background to Elsley Primary's response to the lockdown: a long track record of staff wellbeing.

14 St. John's Church of England Primary School, Canterbury, Kent

One size doesn't fit all

Jo Williamson, Headteacher

'*I believe that leading a team in a school is about knowing your staff individually, just as a good teacher knows their pupils well, and therefore planning is individual to their needs. This takes time. I have learnt that it doesn't mean lowering your expectations of the team; it's rather a balance of ensuring high expectations whilst supporting staff wellbeing and mental health.*'

Overview

Jo Williamson, headteacher, describes how she and her staff implemented strategies to improve staff wellbeing and mental health. She believes that a culture of staff wellbeing is a balance between whole-staff implementation and allowing individual flexibility when accessing the strategies available. Jo reflects on how she came to appreciate that wellbeing events were part of the school's culture, rather than creating the culture.

Context

St. John's Church of England Primary School is a two-form entry primary school, with a maintained Nursery taking children from two years pf age. Our current roll is 395. Our school is situated in the Northgate Ward of Canterbury. St. John's is a larger than average sized primary school. The number of pupils with English as an additional language (EAL) has increased over the last four years from 16% to 27.1%, with 24 different languages spoken in the school. The most common languages are Romanian, Urdu, Chinese and Albanian. The school supports 31% Special Educational Needs and Disability (SEND) pupils, significantly higher than nationally. The proportion of disadvantaged pupils entitled to Pupil Premium (PP) funding is also above the national average at 50%. Pupil stability across the school is significantly lower than nationally. Our school team consists of 52 members of staff, including teachers, teaching support staff, the leadership team and other support staff.

Wellbeing takes time

We did not take a sudden decision to focus on staff wellbeing and mental health; strategies have increased over time. I believe that leading a team in a school is about knowing your staff individually, just as a good teacher knows their pupils well, and therefore planning is individual to their needs. This takes time. I have learnt that it doesn't mean lowering your expectations of the team; it's rather a balance of ensuring high expectations whilst supporting staff wellbeing and mental health.

My personal view of leading is that people need to know and trust you. St. John's Primary School is my first headship and the post was the result of the amalgamation of two schools. After eight years of leading the school, I have built a team of extremely dedicated staff. We believe in our joint vision and that, in order for staff to invest in our community, they must be both physically and mentally healthy. For this to be achieved, we must support staff wellbeing. We first trialled a wellbeing day; we quickly realised that staff wellbeing and mental health were about a culture, not a day off!

By implementing a culture of staff wellbeing, we aimed for a happy and healthy staff, which would have a positive impact on the children they were teaching. We looked for staff attendance to improve and to reduce turnover. Our staff turnover at St. John's is very low. We even have staff who have left and then returned!

Slowly, over the years, we have introduced practical ways to support staff wellbeing and mental health. On our journey, we have realised that wellbeing is very individual; some strategies would help some staff but cause more stress for others. For example, we tried to have an early finish once a week to encourage people to leave site on time and to see family or friends; for some, this added more stress. We learned that giving staff more flexibility and then equipping them to control this flexibility themselves are more effective.

One size doesn't fit all

As part of her Masters, a member of staff surveyed our school team to find out where staff believed the challenges were in their work–life balance and what caused additional stress in the workplace. The results were fascinating, as no trends were identified. This highlighted that supporting wellbeing was not about a 'one size fits all' approach. We set up ways to support staff and allowed people to choose what worked for them:

- We have a staff wellbeing breakfast once a term. Instead of a briefing, we catch up and have breakfast together.
- On the first day back in September, we focus on mindfulness and how to take care of ourselves. Staff create a personal plan which they refer to throughout the year.
- Planning, preparation and assessment (PPA) time can be taken off site, if that works best for the member of staff. Some staff leave early, collect their

own children and then work in the evening. Others go to the local coffee shop to plan, while others simply enjoy working from their own home.

- We have a staff counsellor in school once a week and a designated member of staff to coordinate appointments. Staff have used counselling support in many ways, ranging from personal issues to how to manage their time effectively in school. As headteacher, this is something which I do not get involved in, as counselling is private to the individual.

- We created a school planner which has enabled us to think about periods when time could be pressurised, and staff discuss this in advance. Staff are involved in designing the school plan for the year and we highlight the need to reduce stress in some areas if pressure in others are increasing. For example, during parent consultation weeks, we encourage staff to plan lessons that do not require marking. We also provide staff with a 'goodie bag' for the week. Our gesture shows that we recognise the additional work that parent consultations create.

- We have 'shout-outs' at our weekly briefing when staff can celebrate a colleague for their work or an initiative or the way they have supported a colleague during the week. Celebrations come from the staff. It is, therefore, not only what leadership has seen; those small moments can be missed by leaders and could be the moments which should be most celebrated.

As a leadership team, we look to protect our staff so that they can be the best they can be for our children. At times, this can be to the detriment of the leaders' own wellbeing, so we have to ensure that we are not just moving a problem from a member of staff to leadership, but actually diminishing it. We look to what will have the best impact on the children rather than 'ticking a box'. If staff see wellbeing as 'box ticking', it has a negative impact, exactly the opposite of what we are trying to achieve.

Two significant milestones

Milestone 1: March 2016 – The St. John's Way!

As the school made its journey from 'Requires Improvement' to 'Good', the key change was that we had a defined 'St. John's Way' that was well supported by our governors. We found that the different ideas, strategies and initiatives to improve our school were causing a great deal of stress. What we needed was to find a method which worked for our children and staff and to ensure this was consistent across the school. This didn't mean individual staff could not develop their own strategies – it was more that there was a clear starting point. Staff like structure and routine and changing constantly was causing additional stress.

Milestone 2: September 2019 – Culture is not an event

We had tried the previous year to introduce a wellbeing day voucher. A day for your wellbeing! But we soon learnt that this needed to be a change in culture rather than a day off. As much as staff enjoyed their day, we didn't see a change in school life. We wanted things to be different in our 'being'. This was the point where we introduced a range of strategies. Although not every idea suited everyone, there was a variety of strategies to choose from.

We have music playing in the corridors, sometimes upbeat and, at other times, calm and relaxing. We have our own 'tea lady (or man)' delivering a hot drink (in safety cups) to classrooms mid-morning for staff to sit and enjoy with their class as they have snack-and-chat time. We try to make sure that we don't have more than one meeting a week for any member of staff. We alternate staff meetings and leadership meetings for full-time teachers who are also leaders. Most importantly, we look out for each other and, if someone is struggling, another member of staff steps in. Our year group partnerships are strong, which has been key in transforming our culture. Wellbeing and mental health have to be valued from the 'top' but they have to be put into action by everyone.

Staff morale is good, and retention is strong, often recognised when people visit the school. Staff stress levels are low and, if staff reach a point of crisis or, better still, can identify it coming, we listen and agree action. We haven't yet seen the impact of this strategy on staff attendance and we need to explore this further. For St. John's, next year is about 'time'. Following the period of time in lockdown due to Covid-19 between March and July 2020, many staff have shared how much they have enjoyed cooking, exercising, spending time with family or just slowing down. During lockdown we also found that many of our staff wanted to connect with the families they were missing so we created a video that you can view at: https://www.youtube.com/watch?v=VPTPv7fcPdg

I believe staff wellbeing and mental health are about a culture. Our culture has changed but it will always be a 'work in progress'. Listening before acting, communicating, taking time to observe what is working and recognising where change is necessary are all important.

We must ensure we continue to value ourselves and each other. We have a great team at St. John's, and they are a privilege to lead.

Key strategies

- Steady increase in strategies over time to support staff wellbeing and mental health, not a one-off event.
- Building trust in leadership.
- One size does not fit all: choice in wellbeing strategies is important.
- Joint vision created with the staff.
- Termly staff wellbeing breakfast.
- First day of term: mindfulness is part of self-care.
- Planning, preparation and assessment time can be taken off-site.
- Staff counsellor.
- Staff involved in planning school year to avoid pressure points.
- 'Shout-outs' to celebrate staff.
- Reducing change and ensuring a clear structure.
- Valuing time with family.

15 Fatfield Academy, Washington, Sunderland, Tyne and Wear

Embedding a culture of staff wellbeing

Nicky Dowdle, Deputy Headteacher and Designated Safeguarding Lead

Headteacher: Tracey Pizl

'When the current headteacher, Tracey Pizl, was appointed in 2017, we agreed that improving staff wellbeing needed to be our first priority. It was crucial that we created a stable group of staff. This would enable leaders to work with staff strategically to promote their individual skills in the classroom and to develop them as curriculum leaders. This would also improve parents' perception of the school and create consistency for the children.'

Overview

Nicky Dowdle, deputy headteacher, describes how Tracey Pizl made staff wellbeing her priority when she was appointed as headteacher in 2017. She implemented distributed leadership to give staff more responsibility and to recognise that they too could be leaders. There was also a focus on work–life balance and a reduction in workload. Staff wellbeing was included in the School Improvement Plan (SIP). Staff were praised and recognised for the work they were doing. Joining the Inspire Multi-Academy Trust enabled the school to share good practice and consolidate its culture of staff wellbeing and mental health.

Context

Fatfield Academy is a smaller than average primary school in Washington, Tyne and Wear and is part of the Inspire Multi-Academy Trust, together with four other primary schools. It converted to an academy in 2016. The large majority of pupils are of White British heritage, with 216 pupils on roll. There is no attainment gap between boys and girls. The numbers of Pupil Premium

(PP) children and children identified as requiring Special Educational Needs and Disability (SEND) support are both below the national average: 21% of pupils are identified as PP and 16% as SEND. Early years provision is full-time in both the Nursery and Reception classes. The school provides a breakfast club and an after-school club each day.

I joined Fatfield Academy (then Fatfield Primary School) as deputy head-teacher in September 2014, shortly after the school had been given its second 'Requires Improvement' judgement from Ofsted (Office for Standards in Education) and was then overseen by Her Majesty's Inspector.

The long-serving headteacher retired in December 2014. Two headteachers were drafted in by the local authority to support the school in the Spring and Summer terms of 2015. A substantive headteacher was appointed in September 2015 and remained in post until 2017. Consequently, there was a great deal of instability in the senior leadership team (SLT).

A commitment to raising standards and bringing about swift improvement meant that there were a number of whole-school structural changes that were required to improve attainment, as well as to provide security and certainty for the staff. During this period of substantial change, several other long-serving staff members left the school and took up posts elsewhere. Staff morale was very low. When the current headteacher, Tracey Pizl, was appointed in 2017, we agreed that improving staff wellbeing needed to be our first priority.

It was crucial that we created a stable group of staff. This would enable leaders to work with staff strategically to promote their individual skills in the classroom and to develop them as curriculum leaders. This would also improve parents' perception of the school and create consistency for the children. We implemented the following strategies to achieve our goals:

- We built a distributed leadership model, with staff at all levels becoming a collaborative driving force to bring about school improvement. We harnessed the passions of members of staff and gave them ownership of aspects of school life so that their passions were passed onto the children.
- We improved staff work–life balance by balancing reasonable expectations and high standards.
- Staff were supported to ensure that they achieved their performance management targets.
- We embedded a whole-school culture of wellbeing with staff, parents and pupils.

Staff wellbeing

- Staff wellbeing was embedded into our School Improvement Plan (SIP) and was my key performance management target as the only deputy head-teacher in 2018/19 and 2019/2020.

- We invested in staff training on wellbeing. Whole-Trust in-service training (INSET) was led by our educational psychologist. External training on wellbeing was advertised to all staff, with individuals taking part in aspects of wellbeing which interested them.
- An open-door policy was created, ensuring clear methods of communication, with all leaders giving a consistent message.
- We used questionnaires and open forum staff meetings to hear the voices of the staff. Changes that were made as a result of staff voice were communicated clearly so that staff knew that their voices were valued. If it was not possible to implement a request, we explained to staff why certain policies and practices could not be changed so that they understood why.
- We reduced workload by purchasing subscriptions to pre-prepared resources to reduce planning time. Additional planning, preparation and assessment time was given to staff during the last day of each half-term to do the jobs that staff would normally do over the holidays. We also reduced meeting times and ensured that meetings were conducted effectively.
- We embedded an ethos of positive improvement. Weekly monitoring became an opportunity to praise staff and acknowledge their hard work. Areas for improvement identified were accompanied by an offer of support to enable staff to develop further.
- Teaching assistants were given areas of responsibility and time to manage them. They have fortnightly meetings with me to ensure that their voices are heard and that they feel valued.

Impact of staff wellbeing strategies

In May 2016, the Academy received a 'Good' judgement from Ofsted, recognising the hard work that had taken place, including improving staff wellbeing. Parental perception started to change. Staff became confident that what they were doing was having an impact. They started to believe in themselves as good practitioners. Confidence in the SLT increased, as staff could see that the changes that had been made were producing results.

In September 2017, the school – then Fatfield Primary School – joined the Inspire Multi-Academy Trust and became Fatfield Academy. The SLT was strengthened by being supported and developed by other experienced SLT members within the Trust. Good practice was now regularly shared, as staff had confidence that their strategies were making a difference. Staff were partnered with a teacher in the same year group in another school in the Trust, and groups of five teachers in the same year group across the Trust now meet regularly to share strategies. This also reduced workloads. There were more opportunities for staff development at every level, both for postholders and staff who were seeking more responsibility and/or promotion.

In September 2019, the school made a commitment to work towards the Sunderland Mental Health Charter Mark. Wellbeing was integrated into my performance management as deputy headteacher to raise its profile. This ensured a strategic approach to monitoring wellbeing and evaluating impact. The whole school community was clear that this was a priority.

A full complement of teaching staff was retained for the second year running, which increased opportunities to share good practice. The staff became a united body and supported one another, and a stable environment was created for the children. There was a clear signal to the wider community that Fatfield Academy was a happy school and that staff and children were proud to belong to it.

The school achieved the Teach Well Alliance Teach Well School Gold Award: Covid-19 Pandemic in June 2020, demonstrating that, through unprecedented times, staff wellbeing remained a priority for the SLT.

Impact of wellbeing strategies

- Staff retention rose significantly, with few members of staff wanting to leave the school.
- Staff absence through illness reduced.
- There is two-way communication with the SLT and between members of staff.
- Staff are empowered to lead whole-school improvement in their areas of responsibility.
- Staff believe in themselves and are confident in supporting staff from other schools.
- Staff are prepared to take more risks and, when things go wrong, they regard it as a learning opportunity, rather than a failure.
- Staff have worked towards awards for the school in their areas, such as the Arts Award, School Games Award and Anti-Bullying Award.
- Staff have been supported to achieve additional qualifications; for example, in setting up a Coastal School and Forest School or a special educational needs coordinator (SENCO) qualification.
- A member of staff works as part of the local authority School Improvement Team.
- More staff attend social events and enjoy spending time together and celebrating one another's achievements.
- There is a happy school community – often commented on by external visitors.

The impact of the Covid-19 pandemic (March 2020 onwards)

Prior to the pandemic, our plan was to focus on wellbeing of parents and the wider school community while continuing with staff initiatives. Since partial opening, we feel that staff wellbeing needs to remain a focus. It is vital that we have a clear understanding of everyone's personal circumstance on returning to work. Individual risk assessments have been written and will be regularly evaluated for staff with medical conditions. This may include seeking support from external agencies. It is also important that we speak to staff regularly about whole-school risk assessments and safety measures that are in place to check they feel safe and comfortable within school. We need to ensure that our open-door policy is maintained so that members of the SLT are aware of the wellbeing of staff at all times.

The physical and mental wellbeing of staff have never been as important as they are now. By continuing to implement staff wellbeing strategies that took the Academy from 'Requires Improvement' to 'Good', we intend to support our staff during the Covid-19 pandemic and ensure that their wellbeing remains our highest priority.

Key strategies

- Distributed leadership.
- Work–life balance.
- Staff supported to achieve their performance management targets.
- A whole-school culture of wellbeing with staff, parents and pupils.
- Staff wellbeing embedded in School Improvement Plan.
- Staff training on wellbeing.
- Open-door 'listening' policy.
- Workload reduction.
- Praise.
- Teaching assistants given more responsibility.
- Staff partnered with a teacher in another school in the Trust.
- Achievement of Sunderland Mental Health Charter Mark and Teach Well Alliance Teach Well School Gold Award: Covid-19 Pandemic.

16 Crowcombe Church of England Voluntary Aided Primary School and Stogumber Church of England Voluntary Controlled Primary School, Taunton, Somerset

The elephant outside the room: The connection between staff wellbeing and pupil progress

Julie Norman, Executive Headteacher

Context

Crowcombe Church of England Voluntary Aided Primary School and Stogumber Church of England Voluntary Controlled Primary School are much smaller than the average size school. There is one executive headteacher and one governing body. Subject leadership is shared across the two schools. Reception and Key Stage 1 pupils from both schools are taught in two mixed-age classes at Stogumber Primary School. Key Stage 2 pupils from both schools are taught in two mixed-age classes at Crowcombe Primary School.

There is a Nursery, which is managed by the governing body. Nursery children are registered at Stogumber Primary School. The Nursery is based at Stogumber Primary School.

There are fewer than 15 reception-aged children registered at Stogumber Primary School. The majority of pupils are of White British origin. The proportion of pupils eligible for the Pupil Premium (PP) is well below the national average at 18%. Only 2% of pupils speak English as an additional language

(EAL). The proportion of pupils who receive support for Special Educational Needs and Disability (SEND) ranged between 27% and 30% during 2019/20. Two pupils have an Education, Health and Care Plan (EHCP). A breakfast club and an after-school club are held at Crowcombe Primary School and attended by pupils from both schools. A minibus is used to transport pupils to and from each school.

I am the executive headteacher for two small rural schools in West Somerset, with only 104 children at full capacity. Some would argue that the staff have little to worry about or get stressed about, but they would be wrong. Some teachers have three year groups in their class, 30% of our children are designated as SEND, and many in the farming community believe the children will run the farm when they leave school and therefore an education is unnecessary! As well as teaching, the staff run the school, serve lunch, clean toilets, and do all the play and lunch duties, with the school secretary often taking care of sick children and toileting issues. The staff do it all with a smile. All staff work as one team, so everyone does everything.

Look after the staff – they will look after the children

I have always firmly believed that if you look after your staff, they will look after your customer. My customer is not Ofsted, but our children. The children come to us and rightly expect to be educated well, so that they have the same opportunities as other children worldwide. That is a huge responsibility for any group of teachers and, in order for them to cope — or dare I say, enjoy the responsibility – I must support them in every way possible. The staff should only have one thing on their minds – the children! If they are going home worrying about being behind with paperwork, exhausted, unable to focus on home life due to workload, concerned about not marking enough, not having planning to hand into the headteacher, or just the politics seeping down from above, then they are not fully focused on the children and their learning. If the teacher is not focused, the children see this and that causes them stress and worry, as well as instilling a lack of security and being valued. In order for our children to throw themselves into their learning with gusto, excitement, curiosity, collaboration and drive, they must have nothing else to concern themselves with. A tired and worried teacher will be a barrier to the children's happiness and progress. In order to create a happy, progressive and productive school, I need to focus on the staff.

I have been working on reducing teacher workload and improving staff mental health for four years. I joined the two schools in 2014 as executive headteacher and we needed to improve the children's outcomes. We raised standards during the next two years, but I found there was a ceiling. I believe any child can learn and should be working to their full potential, but I knew this was not happening, despite our assessments showing great progress. I discovered four years ago that the only way to break through that ceiling was to take the pressure and workload away from the teachers and support staff so they could focus entirely on the children – our customers.

I had previously been a deputy headteacher in a large school when I decided to become a headteacher. I was fed up with watching headteachers spending time on pushing teachers to the brink of a breakdown in order to be 'Ofsted ready', believing that the odd token gesture of wellbeing would make up for it all, such as the odd half-hour out of assembly or the odd staff meeting cancelled – or a mug of chocolate delivered to their desk once a year! If teachers did not work miracles, the headteacher would ask me to 'drive them out' through the appraisal process. The more this happened, the worse their performance became! It was a no-brainer. The simple fact is: if you support a teacher to rise up, they work miracles. I wanted to work in a school where I could prove this was the case.

When I arrived at Crowcombe and Stogumber Primary Schools Federation, the staff seemed happy in their work but led themselves. They worked well as a team but with no vision or direction. Their only concern was to have happy, lively children. This was a superb basis to work from. I wanted them to use this strength to drive up standards. The teaching staff worked hard on teaching and planning, marking and enrichment. In order to raise standards, I needed to remove paperwork from them which I deemed unnecessary, such as marking, monthly testing, filling in forms and planning documents, and instead to give them support, structure and time.

What does this look like? First, I asked teachers to stop planning. Planning should be done with the children so that they have ownership of their learning. Staff were asked to offer verbal feedback wherever possible or to use SeeSaw to record the children's feedback and evaluations. [Ed: Seesaw is a platform designed to increase student engagement. Students use creative tools to take pictures, draw, record videos and more to capture learning in a portfolio.] The teachers needed to stop 'teaching' and to start facilitating the learning by asking questions. A teacher only needs to ask a good question and the child will continue to drive forward with learning. Lessons were structured using Bloom's Taxonomy and were derived from the loops of learning created with the children. 'Loops of learning' is a process usually carried out with the children at the beginning of term. The teacher plans the celebration of learning with the children, including what you want to achieve together to celebrate. You then build the learning needed in order to achieve your goals. One way of doing this is by creating a pack of paper circles (Figure 16.1). On one circle is a goal such as 'the best story ever'. It is agreed that is the end goal. With their teacher, the children fill in all the other circles with what they feel they need to achieve this goal, such as support to improve their sentence structure, help to write better paragraphs, read lots of brilliant stories to identify the competition, improve spelling, and so on. Together, the teacher mounts the circles on the wall putting

Figure 16.1 Crowcombe and Stogumber Primary Schools: An example of a 'loop of learning' on slavery

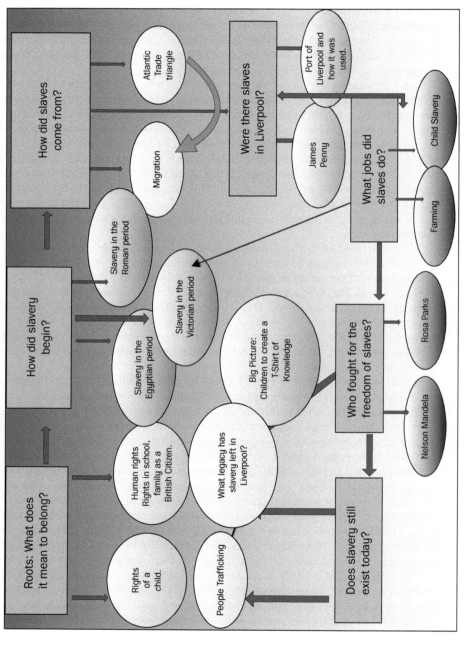

them in the order which best fits a sequence of learning, with the goal at the end. In simple terms, a loop of learning is an aid for children to plan their goals, listing all the things they need to be successful, and allowing the teacher to facilitate the process with their agreement.

Children write feedback and behaviour policies

The children wrote the school's feedback and behaviour policies so they could design the best support and facilitation they wanted from their teachers. The children were clear that they wanted just highlights/symbols or, preferably, verbal feedback. They wanted learning to be meaningful, purposeful and progressive, allowing them to create change in the world. They wanted to value themselves, others and the world around them. They wanted a behaviour policy that allowed them to learn. When a child does something unacceptable, they receive a polite warning with an explanation and offer of support. They appreciate this respectful way to remind them when they forget where they are, and the expectations that they had identified for themselves. If they continue to behave in an inappropriate way, the 'punishment' is to put it right. Go to the person you upset, make it better and change how people perceive you. Restorative justice is combined with forgiveness. The children rightfully wanted behaviour to be part of their learning.

Removal of subject-based learning

We needed to address the incomprehensible way schools teach in this country – subject-based, with few links between a constantly changing day. We no longer teach subjects. We identified three areas of learning: 'Sense of self', 'Sense of others' and 'Sense of the world'. Our children learn what it means to be themselves, what it is to understand others, and how to be a valued member of a local, national and global society. They learn about belonging, relationships and change.

Half-termly staff meetings on staff wellbeing

We dedicated one staff meeting every six weeks to staff wellbeing, where we talked about our relationship with our own mental health, self-care, care of each other and, of course, dinner in the local pub! All staff were trained in how to care for themselves, such as meditation, speaking out when concerned, and how to spot stress in one another. We made a pact to care for each other. We introduced a counselling service, Care First, provided by the local authority which we pay into as a school, created time to talk and emphasised the importance of an annual holiday. All staff have freedom to book a term-time holiday at low cost. External staff were brought in to deliver yoga, music – to teach children how to play musical instruments – PE and assembly sessions, allowing a regular time slot during which the teacher could take a break. We ensured that there was time away from class most days and hugs, lots of hugs!

Caring children – caring schools

With little or no marking, no planning, children who loved coming to school, children who policed their new behaviour policy and invigorated staff, the two schools became calm, happy and caring places to be for everyone. Children in our schools are kind, caring, thoughtful, ambitious and have the kind of relationships with staff and each other that any headteacher would wish for. The children are protective of the staff and tell me if their teacher looks tired, is upset or lacking in energy. They remind the staff not to 'spend all day Sunday marking my book that I won't read' and to spend time with family instead. We create time to talk about how we feel, how to feel better and how to support each other.

Behaviour issues disappeared. Of course, we have children who bicker at times over a game, much like healthy siblings, but such incidents are always easily resolved and quickly forgiven. As headteacher, I have not dealt with a child's poor behaviour for 18 months, and I haven't had to deal with a child not working in class. They plan the learning, so they love the learning. Each term they get to change the world, how they think, how others think, and encourage others to care for the world as they do.

Pupils plan the learning

In order for the children to love learning, I knew that they had to see why they were learning. It had to be meaningful. In order for them to fully understand and immerse themselves in their learning, they had to be part of the planning. Children who are valued, listened to, supported and their ideas facilitated into fruition are driven, resilient, ambitious, happy, focused and, above all, confident. Confidence enables children to speak up and to share their feelings and thoughts. They are, therefore, less likely to suffer mental health issues. They also see that, by owning these characteristics, they begin to make more progress, see purpose in learning and know that they are important enough to change the world for the better. This is the environment my teachers deserve to work in, the kind of children they deserve to work with, and an ethos and culture we all deserve to enjoy every day.

Last year, we asked the children what they wanted to focus on (we normally choose an issue that is relevant that term) and they chose climate change. Why? Because they were not sure what all the fuss was about and wanted to know more. They had some ideas of their own, but they were extremely misinformed ideas and led to the children becoming confused, causing them to lack confidence, feel insecure and to avoid participating in wider conversations.

The children created a 'loops for learning' plan for the term and identified that their desired outcome was to know enough to educate the world. The plan was set. They decided they needed to read a lot about the subject, carry out extensive research, follow Greta Thunberg, the Swedish environmental activist, and ensure that they heard all sides of the argument. They then needed to look at the science behind it all and evaluate what information was important and what was not.

Teachers cleverly wove into the plan the learning objectives for that year group: such as geography, history, science, literacy, reading comprehension and maths skills, as well as foundation subjects. The children found that single-use plastic was a huge problem and began a local campaign to educate the surrounding villages about waste. They were interviewed on radio, wrote to businesses and shops, used science to support their argument, worked with local charities and ended their campaign with a play for the community, which they wrote themselves. It gave the audience information about the effects of climate change, the damage single-use plastics do and how it can be overcome. They gave tips for change, supported by data designed to shock. They also wrote the songs they sang in the play. The community loved it, learned a lot and the children facilitated sustainable change in their community. The staff were praised publicly on radio and television, and recognised for awards such as the Public Health Lifestyle award, Public Health Relationships award, and Public Health Belonging award.

The children were admired through the media attention, received great feedback and felt they had done something wonderful. In that term, the children met almost half of the year's objectives for their year. They also made another year's progress to exceed that achieved last year, creating a five-year upward trend. This led to the children being happy, confident, focused and becoming little people filled with humility and care. There were no behaviour issues that term, no child not making progress. All of the PP children made the expected progress or more and all SEND children made more than expected progress. Happy, confident children learn. In turn, happy, confident teachers love coming to work.

Academic progress was just one of the outcomes of focusing on staff wellbeing, staff having a voice and being able to focus on their expertise – teaching. All members of our community benefited, because we looked at the cause of teacher stress and workload and changed it.

The journey towards staff wellbeing

To begin this long journey, I carried out a vision workshop with the staff and governors to ensure we all wanted the same thing. I then had to convince the staff to reduce their working hours, do less to achieve more, to trust me when I asked them not to mark, plan or teach subjects. It frightened them. Thankfully, after some time, they began to trust me, and I had 100% of the staff on board. I grouped them into curriculum area teams rather than subjects, such as 'Knowledge of the World', which incorporated Science, Geography and History. This helped them to see that subjects could be a barrier to learning. It didn't matter what we called our areas of learning in order to teach the objectives and we could do this as a team rather than putting the onus on one person – the 'subject specialist'. The more they shared, the less stressed staff became.

I then introduced structure. Staff meetings were timetabled and given a focus, including wellbeing. Staff appreciated this, as they saw purpose and reason for the staff meetings and looked forward to them, as they led them together. I also removed some structure – no teaching timetable. The transition to open learning was difficult for staff to make. Some jumped in feet first and some just dipped their toe in for a while. That was okay. They soon realised they had been doing 80% of the work and the children 20%, and that change was needed. I trained the staff in how to question effectively so the children would feel part of the learning and, at times, drive it. Good quality questioning was essential to allow the teachers to facilitate learning as opposed to teach, thus switching the children-to-teacher ratio to 80:20, where the children are doing most of the thinking and most of the work.

I organised mental health training for the staff, not just to spot stress in ourselves but also in each other. We planned activities to support one another, such as going for a walk and deep breathing at lunchtime, yoga, not taking books home to mark, and leaving work at a reasonable time and switching off at home.

Once we arrived at a place of calm, happy staff, who were working less, children doing far more and everyone empowered, I changed the curriculum teams into a Character Curriculum. This meant teaching no subjects, other than RE/PE and maths/literacy skills, and focusing mainly on the project as a vehicle for learning. Staff were able to seamlessly move over to this model and we pooled all the objectives for each year group into three key priority areas as described earlier: Sense of self, Sense of others and Sense of the World. All that we do and learn must focus on how we see ourselves. We must have a good understanding of who we are, why we are who we are, how we learn, what we care about, how we change, how we gain character and what we want to be. We must also understand how we see other people and treat them with tolerance, care and humility, embracing other faiths, ethnicity and cultures, appreciating that we are all different but equal. We must develop an understanding of where we fit in to our world: what is our responsibility, what is the world, what is it made of, and how can we make it even better? We found that every single objective from Year R to Year 6 fitted beautifully into these three areas and there are many objectives which cross over.

Our children have a good understanding of who they are, what makes them happy, what makes them sad and how they can help themselves and others, as well as the world they live in. They are empowered and given a voice and relish taking on new responsibility. They are confident, highly ambitious and the most caring little humans I have ever worked with. Teachers want to come to work; they want to be with our little people, and they know they are highly valued.

Suggestions for your own journey

So, what are the key areas I suggest you focus on if you want to improve staff wellbeing and mental health?

1. Help staff to feel valued, cared for and trusted. This will have positive outcomes for the children and school as a whole. The biggest milestone was for staff to see that they were working too hard and that their workload could be reduced without affecting the children's learning. They also needed to allow the children to take control – 'loosening the reins'. This began in September 2014, my first term.

2. I began with a vision workshop and lots of staff meetings to get to know each other and to share our ideas. I created time with each member of staff by giving them personal coaching to see how much they worked in the classroom and at home, compared to how much the children did in class. The staff needed to see that every time they had a 'wow' lesson, where the children learned much more and there was a buzz in the room, was the time when the teacher moved away from the lesson plan and allowed the children to take some direction. We spent a term trying that in class and sharing those 'wow' moments in staff meetings. This encouraged everyone to loosen the reins.

Age-related expectations went from 20% to 70% in the first year. The challenges were that some staff needed to really see it to believe it and therefore took longer to accept this style of teaching. Everyone was on their own journey. Their personal coaching with me encouraged them to keep trying for more 'wow' moments, and I had to show them that they could trust me. If it went all wrong, that was okay. The more they witnessed this and the more they tried, the better things became. Ask yourself – if a child calls out in class, 'Miss, there is an elephant outside going past the window!', how would you respond? Would you say, 'Don't be silly and listen to me. Look this way and stop interrupting', or would you say, 'Oh wow, that's amazing, let's go and have a look'? Sometimes you go outside, and the elephant has gone. That's okay and it was worth the try. Sometimes you go outside, and the elephant is there and you all stare in awe, take in the moment and never forget it. That's the wow lesson! It's a risk but, when it works and you let a child lead the direction, it can be amazing, rewarding and unforgettable.

3. Give everyone time. Time to talk. Time to share their thoughts. Time to share their feelings. Set time aside in staff meetings, after school, create a WhatsApp wellbeing group to share funny stories. Give the children time to chat, mull over ideas and thoughts. It may not seem important, but it builds confidence, empowers them and creates an ethos of value and care.

In June 2015, I gave staff, children and parents questionnaires to offer ideas to make the school great. I suggest you do the same. I followed it up with 'You said – We did' and ensured feedback was swift. Give each member of staff time to chat with you – the paperwork can wait. The time you spend chatting and getting to know each other is so valuable. The children too. Spend time in class and, at times, ask groups of them for advice such as, 'If you were the head, what is the first thing you would do?' Then follow through as many ideas as you can, as quickly as possible. At first, staff and children say what they think you want to hear, but soon trust takes over and you get the good stuff – the truth. Parents also feel heard and part of their child's success. Build that community.

4. Look at what everyone else does. Ask why? Why do we do that? Why do we do it this way? Why have we not done it another way? Go back to the beginning and ask – what do we want for our children? Build the curriculum and ethos as though it is a new school. The chances are you will change such a lot, as we tend to follow procedures and systems just because we always have. But the teachers have been suffering with mental ill-health, work–life imbalance and exhaustion for many years, so it needs to change from the roots up. It was a milestone to get to a place where everyone was asking the WHY question about everything.

By 2016, we decided what we were doing had no relation to what we wanted to achieve. Who knew? We wanted children who are thinkers, independent learners, open-minded, globalised, full of character, ready for the future, and excited to create and build their dreams. Through teaching in subjects, having timetables, unnecessary rules, ineffective and laborious marking, strict planning and creating stressed teachers did none of these things.

5. Staff need to realise they are a team – not one teacher in one classroom – but a team of teachers looking after all the children to achieve the same outcomes. Staff had to find out about each other's strengths, weaknesses, likes, dislikes, quirks and funny ways. They needed to really get to know each other and respect all the attributes each person brought to the team. This change had to be meaningful, such as team planning and sharing resources, enrichment days, staff time, and allowing the children to share their ideas and thoughts across year groups. The children are also a team and so had to go through the same journey. Collectively, we are members of a community team, with different roles to play in our mission to learn, change the world and be the school every child wishes they attended. This is not a one-off staff meeting or assembly. This is every single day, an ethos, a way of life.

6. The biggest milestone was during 2015 when staff said they trusted me, governors said they trusted me, and parents wanted their children to attend my schools. When I arrived, there were only 67 children and within months there were 104. Trust takes time. It comes from sharing, listening and talking. The more we know about each other, the more we care about each other, the more we want for each other. That is the true meaning of love. The whole school needed to learn how to love each other, listen and care. This was the biggest milestone and the most precious.

The impact of such small but important changes can be measured in many ways. Quantitative measures, for example, showed in the children's progress: from 20% to 70% age-related expectations (ARE) in 2015. By 2019, 85% of children were reaching ARE and in foundation subjects they were 96–98% ARE. Over 20% were at working at 'greater depth'. More and more children were earning scholarships to independent schools for sports and music, as well as academic subjects. The children took part in 12 sports tournaments a term; two choirs were booked out during the year; 100% of PP children were making expected or greater progress; SEND children were making expected progress or more; many SEND children in Key Stage 2 gained two years extra progress before Year 6 and attendance rose from 92% to 98%. We have also narrowed the gap considerably between boys and girls this year from 20% to 8%.

Recently, during the Covid-19 lockdown, we had 100% of children engaging in online learning between 8.30 a.m. to 3.30 p.m. Monday to Friday. The children would clock in with a 'Good morning' to the teacher and stay all day, engaged, happy, upbeat, and setting challenges and questions for each other. Wellbeing is at the heart of what we do but from wellbeing comes resilience to focus on learning too.

We had 100% attendance regularly for swimming, music lessons, singing lessons, yoga morning and Forest School during the first couple of years, then 98% attendance overall. Children came to school at first because they enjoyed those particular curricular and extracurricular areas, but soon realised they just loved coming to school. Absences of 2% in the last three years are due to some parents taking holidays during term time and our 48-hour policy on sickness: if a child has vomiting or diarrhoea, they have to stay home for the next two days whether they feel okay or not. This is to prevent other children becoming infected. These are two reasons for absence which the children could not control.

7. Behaviour. The low-level disruptive behaviour that was evident every day had, by the second year, dropped to just a few a term. By 2018, all behaviour issues directed to the headteacher or senior teacher had stopped. Children learned how to care for each other and show tolerance and love. They enjoyed school and knew their strengths and weaknesses, as well as those of others. This made for a harmonious but productive and shared responsibility culture. Ofsted remarked last year, 'Your children know the true meaning of love. They actually love each other; they really care for each other. I know you don't teach subjects and don't have a lot of tests or extensive writing tasks but, talking to your children, I was really surprised how knowledgeable they are.'

Our emotional literacy support assistant (ELSA) was originally employed four days per week and now only works two days per week; her focus is now building the self-esteem of our looked-after children, as well as working with children who are struggling with family situations.

I no longer needed to belong to a supply agency or have a list of supply teachers, as there was little or no absence from staff by the second year. By 2018, the only supply teacher left who covered training sessions was employed by the school. Staff support and cover for each other, as they are mainly part-time and will work the extra day to cover a training day. All support staff opt to attend staff meetings, as they feel included and valued. Each support staff member took on a responsibility in the learning teams and reviewed school development plans with teaching staff. They had a voice and shared their opinions, which I always followed up. Yearly appraisals focused only on two things:

1 Discuss and record everything staff achieved during the last year and how they have helped to move the school forward in our vision; and
2 What they want to improve next year, learn, enjoy and embrace.

From 2018, there were no more exclusions, temporary or permanent. No support was needed from this time from the SEND team in the local authority, as the environment allowed the SEND children to flourish. We went from 20% to 30% SEND, with some children transferring after struggling in other schools. We believe if a child cannot settle, then change the environment – true inclusion. Happy children = happy staff!

A couple of the qualitative 'measures' we received:

- I recently received a note from one of my teachers (2020) saying, 'Julie, you're hands down the best Head I've worked with in my 20 years. Trust, respect and an insane amount of belief in me have allowed me to soar free, both as a class teacher and now in my work–life balance.' Once the reins were taken off this teacher, he became 'Outstanding' in his practice. This was the greatest reward I could receive.
- A note from a child leaving to go to secondary school (2020) said, 'Thank you for constantly encouraging me every step of my way through Primary School. You inspire me to be a better person, with everything you did for us was full of love. It's the little things that count, such as treating us like we were your children, treating us all the same.'

Where are we on our journey?

So where are we now? Children plan their own learning projects. They cover basic maths and basic literacy skills required for their project, as the need arises. The children do not learn subjects, as these are barriers to learning, but they learn how to be citizens who are empowered to change what is not working well and celebrate what is. They learn how to adopt new characteristics and celebrate those who achieve them. They learn how to think, share their thinking and learn from other's thoughts. The children make excellent progress and outcomes improve year-on-year. The children now do better in foundation subjects than English and Mathematics, showing how much they develop in all areas and in the depth of their learning.

This year, we earned the Gold Arts Mark Award; Gold Sports Award; the Teach Well Alliance Teach Well School Gold Award: Covid-19 Pandemic; Public Health/Somerset County Relationships Award; Public Health/Somerset County

Lifestyle Award; and Public Health/Somerset County Belonging Award. The school has families waiting to move their children to the school as soon as places become available. In 2007, both schools were under threat of closure due to a lack of children attending and federated to work together to help them survive. We are now well known in the county for our excellent practice.

I am often booked as a keynote speaker about how we engage our children, build relationships with them, and encourage health and wellbeing alongside character building and learning. I receive invites from the National Association of Headteachers (NAHT) to offer talks to local cluster groups of headteachers and also consultants from Devon, Wilshire and Gloucester, saying they have heard of our schools and want to visit. I also receive regular visits from trainees, headteachers and teachers from all over the country. The children enjoy these visits, as they know this is their school, their policies, their learning plans and their work that is shared on TV, radio and through our award collecting. They are proud, as are the staff; they are encouraged, invigorated, ambitious and excited about the future and the part they play in it. When one teacher was asked by a visiting CEO what it was like to work at the school she cried and said, 'I never thought it would ever be this good.'

My dream is to enable all teachers and children to achieve their wellbeing goals, their academic goals and flourish. It really is the small things that make it happen and it is all achievable.

The future

Over the coming months, the school will continue in its drive to keep wellbeing at the heart of all it achieves. Sport, music, yoga and mindfulness will continue on a weekly basis. The governing board have a Safeguarding, Health and Wellbeing Committee which will see that all staff have the opportunity to go on holiday in term-time for a week during the academic year, just as parents do. We value the life experience and shared learning which will come from it. The governors will ensure the staff continue to enjoy counselling; wellbeing staff meetings; one-to-one meetings with their link governor to see how they are; and appraisals that celebrate the year and contribute to the enjoyment of working at the school the following year. The staff will enjoy wellbeing sessions to focus on their self-care and their care of each other. The Health and Wellbeing Audit I created and share is heavily monitored by governors and rightly so.

During the next academic year (2020/21), the school will continue to do the following:

- Continue to teach without subjects.
- Literacy and maths achievements will continue to mirror those of foundation subjects at 90–100% ARE or more. The school will aim to improve 'Working at greater depth' to well above national average across all areas of learning. The school will use Bloom's Taxonomy to structure all project

planning: key concepts remembered, understanding shared; new learning applied; learning analysed; its importance evaluated – thus being able to create innovative ideas to find ways to improve our world.

- Embed the Children's University and online additional learning opportunities to allow all children of all backgrounds to continue their good work, projects and research outside school hours, earning them their degree. Children have been issued with a Chromebook if they did not have one at home, so they all have access to home learning. There is a learning platform where staff upload activities, guidance, support, feedback and discussion, making learning a way of life, not just in school.
- Continue to direct the schools' charitable nature towards needy and relevant causes, as well as ensuring the school continues to work with local, national and global charities each term.
- Ensure the audit and reporting tool we buy into from School Omega Solutions is fully embedded to allow the headteacher to stop writing reports from scratch for various stakeholders.
- Enable governors to know the school inside and out, with support and challenge having real practical application.
- The headteacher will continue to focus on the wellbeing of the staff. This is a lifestyle, not a new initiative.
- Ensure every stakeholder has a valued voice, is focused on the customers (our children) and their future.
- Without ensuring that the staff are cared for and appreciated, they are unable to focus on the customer. Wellbeing of staff and children are two sides of the same coin. Simple!

Key strategies

- Look after the staff; they will look after the children.
- Reduce paperwork, marking, lesson planning.
- Improve staff work–life balance and enable them to spend more time with their own families.
- Stop teaching in subjects. Create project-based learning, informed by Bloom's Taxonomy, and teach thematically.
- Involve the children in creating the curriculum, behaviour and feedback policies.
- Support staff with counselling service.
- Hold a staff meeting on wellbeing once each half-term.
- Train staff in how to take care of themselves.
- Each member of staff is part of a team. The team looks after all the children.
- Ask yourself, 'Why?' 'Is it because that's the way it's always been or because other people say so?'
- Train the staff to ask questions which lead the children into learning.

Preston Primary School, Eaglescliffe, Stockton-on-Tees, County Durham

Wellbeing – or a way of life?

Sue Richardson, Headteacher

'[We have] developed a culture where staff are happy to take risks. Sometimes they work, sometimes they fall flat on their face. Both are fine, and then we reflect. It is as important to know why something worked, as why something didn't. Sometimes, I make mistakes that some would rather curl up and die than admit. I always share these with staff. Why? It shows I walk the walk as well as talk the talk.'

Overview

Headteacher Sue Richardson describes her approach to staff wellbeing at Preston Primary School. She makes the point that wellbeing is not a policy but a culture. By allowing staff to make mistakes and regarding them as learning opportunities, rather than failures, she encourages risk-taking in a supportive environment. Sue emphasises the importance of listening to staff, of getting to know their individual wellbeing needs, and treating staff with respect. She makes it clear that she must show an example as a leader and be prepared to do whatever she is asking her staff to do. Sue refers to the importance of recognising the signs of fatigue and acting quickly to tackle it.

Context

Preston Primary School is a maintained primary school in the borough of Stockton-on-Tees, on the outskirts of Eaglescliffe in the North-East of England. We have a diverse catchment, with children from the highest decile ranking and the lowest according to the Income Deprivation Affecting Children Index (IDACI). In introducing or changing anything, we are always aware of this diversity and ensure that nothing we do disadvantages children from either end of the spectrum. In total, we have 217 pupils aged 3–11 years, including children from our hearing and visual impaired base. We have a greater than average proportion of special needs children within the school, in addition to our base children.

We have 41 staff (some from companies that work within the school) that we call our own. We have 17 teachers, many of whom are on part-time contracts. We have a higher-level teaching assistant (HLTA), eleven teaching assistants, and the rest are employees who do not work in class, such as lunchtime staff, cleaners and caretakers.

The content of this chapter is my own view of staff wellbeing. It may be controversial, or not aligned with everyone's thinking. It is what I believe is right for my little school.

Wellbeing – a culture, not a policy

When I was asked to write this chapter [Ed: by the editor Stephen Waters], he offered to write the chapter from my wellbeing policy and school documentation, if I did not have time to write it myself. I actually laughed aloud. I remember, some years ago, a good friend of mine worked with the Department for Education (DfE) on workload and wellbeing. After the DfE report was published, schools across the country included wellbeing as an action point in their development plans. I did not. When asked by an external visitor if they could see my policy on wellbeing, I said I didn't have one. I still don't. For me, wellbeing isn't an 'in-thing' like community cohesion, cultural capitalism or whatever buzz words are current. It's a way of life, a way of working, and of treating one another. It runs deep, as part of the moral 'veins' that supply the lifeblood of our school. It may be impossible to articulate, but I am going to give it a try!

Looking back at my career, I have worked with people who inspired me and people who did the opposite. There were roles I bounded out of bed on a morning for and some that I had a sinking feeling in the pit of my stomach driving to. My productivity and results were directly impacted by the way I felt about being in the building, and how I felt was directly impacted by the people and leaders I worked for. As a newly qualified teacher, I had a slogan across the top of my rolling blackboard:

If you believe you are Superman, eventually you will fly.

There is an awful lot of scaffolding between becoming a teacher and then a leader and we all need people to help us grow the wings to get there. It is my fundamental belief that even the most talented person will never get to achieve their potential if they don't have someone that believes in them and if they don't believe in themselves. This is deep-rooted and stems from my own school experiences. I was told I wouldn't amount to much. I remember my first day as a supply teacher having just qualified, seeing one of my previous teachers who was disgusted to learn I was a teacher, and who walked off saying, 'What has this profession come to?'

In the schools where I have been part of leadership, I have always ensured that we look after each other and sow and cultivate the seeds of wellbeing.

I became head of Preston Primary School in September 2014. When I looked around the school and chatted to the deputy head, I had an immediate sense that we were on the same page, with our moral purpose and ideologies aligned. The school and the community had been through two years of turmoil. The much loved and respected head had left for the summer break in July 2012 and became ill, never to return. The deputy head had acted as the interim head for two years but wanted to remain in the classroom more than a headteacher role allowed. Staff looked out for each other in their own classrooms and within teams. However, staff wellbeing needed to be developed from a whole-school perspective rather than from separate silos.

I didn't write a wellbeing policy. Why? Because, for me, wellbeing is personal. What one person finds useful for their wellbeing, another might find stressful. I chuckle sometimes when I see schools' staff meeting time being given over to yoga or 'wellbeing colouring'. I would have been the naughty one in yoga class, giggling at the back, while the poor PE coordinator was trying his or her best to keep me in line! As for colouring in, only now at 41 years old am I managing to stay within the lines! My idea of wellbeing isn't forced upon people. It is a menu of choice, with the ability to opt in or opt out, with no judgements attached. When I was a single mum to a new-born and a toddler, wellbeing was not having any marking to take home or having an adult conversation at lunchtime. Now, as a mum to teenagers, wellbeing is a night off the 'taxi' runs and spending time with colleagues with whom I can offload. What I hope I have achieved is an individual approach to staff wellbeing in my five years at Preston Primary School. This is our journey.

The path to wellbeing: Listening

The first thing I did was to listen. Each member of staff from the deputy, to the cleaners, to the kitchen staff (who aren't *my* staff, and told me so) came to spend some time with me. I asked them three questions: (1) Tell me about yourself; (2) What is good about this school?; and (3) What could be better? This gave me insight into people's personal circumstances and what they loved. It was also a chance to 'sound off' and, boy, some really did. I began to paint a picture of what people were feeling and what they needed for their own wellbeing.

Creating a staffroom

I spotted straight away that the staffroom was way too small. I kid you not, on my first day, I saw one teacher sitting on the floor trying to eat soup and, yes, they did spill it! The teachers had no space to work. On their designated planning, preparation and assessment (PPA) day, they moved around the school looking for somewhere to work, dismantling and setting up their workspace every 45 minutes. I rolled up my sleeves and repurposed some rooms. We have a 1970s prefab building that was an eyesore but was accessible from the yard – this became the library. What was previously the library became a staffroom and designated PPA space. It cost around £1000 to put in a mini kitchen but, in terms of productivity for staff, it was priceless. Creating a proper staffroom planted the seed with the staff that I valued them, that they deserved a space which recognised their needs and that I was going to look out for their well-being as well as that of the children.

Restructuring timetables to enable a weekly staff meeting

I inherited staff who worked at different times of the week. This meant that all staff were *never* in the same room, not even for staff meetings or professional development days. Weekly diaries were emailed, and notes handed out after staff meetings. It felt remote and distant. I found some money that went into a pot for overtime. To ensure that we were all in the same room weekly, I changed the staff meeting to the middle of the week, tweaked contracts, and gave the part-time teachers PPA. I felt it was crucial to hear messages first-hand. We now had a format to be able to do this. It also meant that, when staff requested part-time working, they knew that this was the holy grail – that staff meetings are part of the working week.

This proved to be worth its weight in gold during Covid-19. When things started going wrong in February 2020 [Ed: Covid-19 was spreading throughout the UK], we scheduled daily briefing meetings. Sometimes, they were 'nothing to report'; at other times, staff were handed a sheet with issues or events that they needed to remember – let's be honest, nothing sticks in a state of heightened emotions! Throughout Covid-19 lockdown, we continued with weekly staff meetings, not because I wanted training to continue, but because I wanted staff to see one another and to have a feeling of normality throughout this strange time. I sent weekly updates to them and shared my faux pas with them to make them chuckle. I set up a WhatsApp group for them to keep in contact with each other. Sometimes they received up to 100 notifications per day. The rationale behind these strategies was to facilitate dialogue across teams, between teams and across job roles. This also increased the feeling of being part of a team. Our coaching partnerships are across key stages; continuing professional development is in mixed-stage teams and therefore our whole-school team continues to thrive. It has also made moving between key stages to teach easier for staff, as they already have relationships with colleagues outside of their own key stages.

Although asked to include five key milestones in my chapter, I feel our well-being culture is more ethos-driven than specific actions-driven.

1. Mistakes are not failures

It is alright to make mistakes. This shows you are outside of your comfort zone; we learn from them and move on.

This has developed a culture where staff are happy to take risks. Sometimes they work, sometimes they fall flat on their face. Both are fine, and then we reflect. It is as important to know why something worked, as why something didn't. Sometimes, I make mistakes that some would rather curl up and die than admit. I always share these with staff. Why? It shows I walk the walk as well as talk the talk. An example of this is a letter I wrote to parents during lockdown. It also links with number two of my wellbeing beliefs (see below). At the time, there was lots in the media about lazy teachers, extra time off, doing nothing – my blood was boiling. Whilst I did not think our community would think that of us, I wanted to make sure they knew what staff were doing. I wanted to praise the staff to the parents. Figure 17.1 is a snapshot of what I sent!

Figure 17.1

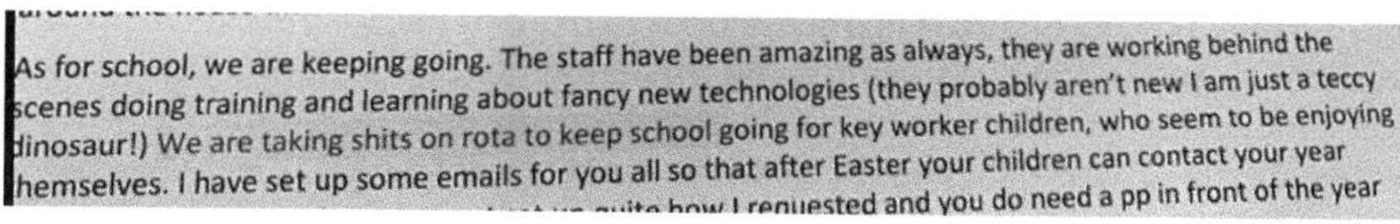

As for school, we are keeping going. The staff have been amazing as always, they are working behind the scenes doing training and learning about fancy new technologies (they probably aren't new I am just a teccy dinosaur!) We are taking shits on rota to keep school going for key worker children, who seem to be enjoying hemselves. I have set up some emails for you all so that after Easter your children can contact your year

I could quite easily have not shared, but I did. They laughed. I laughed and cried! Parents emailed me back. I learnt from it!

2. Praise and feedback

Praise in public, pan in private.

Everyone that comes anywhere near me will hear me wax lyrical about how amazing the staff, children, governors and parents of the school are. This doesn't mean that we don't face challenges, have difficult conversations and sometimes need to up our game, but all of these things are done behind closed doors. All of the wondrous applause is done in the most public forum. I am without doubt the luckiest person to lead such an amazing school. But a leader without avo followers is just someone going for a walk. People have to believe in what you say and the message you give, and, in my opinion, this starts with mutual respect. If I have an issue with someone or something they have done, they will be the first to know about it. You won't find me moaning in corridors or grumbling about staff to other people. I wouldn't want it done to me, so I don't do it to them. This also works both ways. If I am doing something that people don't believe in, I actively encourage them to tell me. Let's talk this out! Let's deal with the issue. No grudges. Move on. This applies to all staff: teaching staff, support staff, ancillary staff, site staff. It generates a culture of conversation. Shout about the good things in public, write them on our staff shout-out board and say thank you – lots. When we have an issue, we deal with it in a fair manner and then we move on, all together, in the same direction with the same common purpose – for the children and families we serve.

3. Leading by example

Lead by example. Don't ask anyone to do something that you wouldn't do yourself.

It astounds me the number of times people ask me, 'Why are you doing that? Haven't you got more important things to do?' To me, that depends on the definition of 'important things'. Important things to me are the children, the staff and the community. I do lunch duties, break duties, story times, assemblies, clean up, displays – the list is endless. We all have important 'stuff' to do and who am I to tell someone that my version of important should be placed higher on their job list than their own? Clear expectations and deadlines mean everyone knows what needs doing and by when. But if I suddenly decide I want a set of shelves painting bright and beautiful colours a week before the summer holidays, then I need to do them myself! If I am the first person a child finds when they feel sick and then they promptly throw up on the floor in front of me, why should someone else clean it up? Walking past something is accepting it. If I see something on the floor, I pick it up and find its home. If I hold a door open for someone, people see this and subconsciously begin to do the same. I always say, 'Good morning'. Guess what? So do the staff and children. When a child says thank you, I reply, 'You're welcome.' Now most of my children and staff do the same. If you want to read more about this approach, it's called 'Nudge Theory'. I just call it, 'Treat and respect people the way you would like to be treated and respected.'

4. Gratitude for a job well done

Show thanks for the 'normal' stuff, as well as the additional jobs people do.

Saying 'Thank you' costs nothing. It is so simple, but we all know how it makes us feel when someone acknowledges what we do. We grow a little. What we have done is recognised and appreciated and is shown to have had a positive effect. So, we repeat the behaviour again! Staff will find 'treats' in the staffroom on 'Fat Friday', normally of the chocolate variety, and, when I can, home-baked. During lockdown, when staff came in for their first shift, their pigeon-holes contained a Star Bar. The name said it all. It wasn't about liking the chocolate. To me, they are stars. They were putting our community before the health and wellbeing of their families. There are other points in the year I always try and acknowledge, such as an Easter egg, or a chocolate heart on Valentine's Day. I can honestly say I roll with the mood in school and, when a lift is needed, I try and do something about it. To be honest, these gestures are the icing on the cake. Wellbeing isn't about cakes in the staff room. The cakes are about saying thanks for the daily, weekly, monthly commitment and going above and beyond. If the underlying foundations of staff wellbeing are not built, they are just token gestures.

5. Listen ... listen ... listen

Listen, listen and listen some more.

I don't just use my ears to listen. As much as I try not to be in charge, ultimately my name is above the door and, whilst I ask people to be honest and tell me what's going on, some people are just not there – yet. I do, however, have ears everywhere. I have people who I trust who will tell me when things are going on that I should know about, especially with regard to wellbeing. If I find out someone is struggling, I do what I can to help them. This may be support from a colleague, extra time out of class – it depends on what is needed and what the underlying issue is. This is where my view on wellbeing is individualised. Every week, I ask for feedback from the different teams and this continued in lockdown. I want to hear the good, the bad and the ugly, as only then I can help to deal with it. Sometimes our emotional intelligence just tells us that something isn't right with someone and then we need to dig to find out why. Staff trust that I will do what I can to help and, if I haven't the tools to do it, I will find someone who does. It is no good listening if we do not hear what is being said. If things aren't going right, unless we know about it we can't reassess and change our course or slow things down. During lockdown, I did shopping for someone too afraid to leave the house. This would never have been in a policy. After attending a course about behaviour, we, like many others, started 'Hot Chocolate Friday' for the children. It got back to me that staff were wondering if they would be invited at any point. The next week I brought in my slow cookers, made two huge batches of the stuff – but hid it. At break time I put the first clue in the staffroom and the staff had to follow the clues to find their 'pots of gold.' Did I have things I needed to do? Yes. Was it worth it? Absolutely. I always say, you make time when things are important.

Low sickness – high retention and recruitment

The Preston way of life means we have no issues with recruitment or retention. We have very low rates of staff sickness and, if we begin to see signs of Burnout, we jump on it quickly. As in all jobs, we have peaks and troughs in terms of workload. At peak time, we make sure we give staff time to do things properly away from their responsibilities as a class teacher. I don't – and won't – have people filling in bits of paper for the sake of them. If what we do has no impact on the children, we don't do it! I told the staff via our WhatsApp group that I was writing this and asked if anyone would like to contribute their thoughts on what was important to wellbeing at Preston. Here are some of the answers:

'Support, solidarity and staff, including the headteacher, who have your back.'

'Your open office door.'

'Teachers need other teachers. This is not a job that can be done alone. Collaboration and friendship are vital in keeping teachers sane and happy.'

'Always having someone to talk to who you know will listen and help, guide you or hold you up if you need them to. The laughs we have and the banter we share … Without doubt, I laugh every single day at work! Friendship and being there for each other – it really is a second family' (this one was followed by the sick emoji!).

'Knowing however you feel and whatever type of day you are having, there is always someone you can laugh or cry with – [we are] not just colleagues at Preston [but] friends. Prestonites will always make time for each other.'

'Knowing there's a whole tree full of nuts (it is our school badge!) that don't judge.'

'It feels like you are working with an extended family and people who genuinely care about you as a person, a friend and a colleague. We get stronger and stronger in the face of crisis, sadness and happy moments of celebration together.'

'We have no cliques and we don't make comparisons between teachers – we all have things we can get better at. You can confide in anyone and folk are not looked down upon if they choose to participate in things or not. I don't know any other school that acknowledges everyone's birthday. But, more than anything, we all look out for each other and appreciate the different strengths, and don't all try to be the same. After all, a good team needs some good defenders, good attackers, some risk-takers and some "steady-as-you-goers". Our wellbeing is helped because we can be those people and we all play an important part in the team known as "Team Preston".'

I should also add that the staff look after my wellbeing too. At the start of the Covid crisis I walked into work at 6:30 a.m. to find four staff outside of my office door. It fell silent as I walked into the corridor, and one of them said, 'I would hate to be you right now, but you know we are here to do anything you want.' I promptly burst into tears and couldn't reply.

The long term

Thinking about the next steps for the school in the long term is pretty difficult right now. I have visions but I know they will not become realities for some time, due to Covid-19. So next steps for our wellbeing are to learn from the good we did during Covid-19 part one, recreate this in Covid-19 part two, ensuring wellbeing for all again, and then try to readjust when the time comes for normality. I am currently working on plans to try to keep the feeling of connectivity when lunches and breaks are staggered and social distancing means staff have to stay apart physically. I don't have all the answers yet. I do know that wellbeing at Preston Primary School will continue to be about being valued, safe, listened to and, above all else, respected. The page shown in Figure 17.2, from the lockdown scrap book the staff made me, sums it up.

Figure 17.2

Key strategies

- Wellbeing – the lifeblood of the school, not a policy document.
- Creating a large staff room where everyone could meet and share.
- Restructuring working patterns to bring staff together for weekly staff meeting.
- Acknowledging mistakes, learning from them and moving on – without judgement.
- WhatsApp group to communicate across teams and job roles.
- Praise publicly. Criticise privately.
- Say 'thanks' for the normal stuff.
- Lead by example: Don't ask someone to do something you wouldn't do yourself.
- Treat and respect people the way you would like to be treated and respected.
- Listening, listening, listening.
- Being open so that staff can bring their concerns to me.
- Individualised wellbeing for each member of staff.
- Take action as soon as a member of staff shows signs of Burnout.

18 Pentland Primary School, Billingham, Stockton-on-Tees, County Durham

New beginnings

Dawn Dacombe, Headteacher

'*Wellbeing is not about what we **do** for staff but how we **are** with staff.*'

Overview

Headteacher Dawn Dacombe takes us on her school's journey to improve staff wellbeing and mental health and to build it into the ethos of Pentland Primary School. By creating a 'we' culture, rather than an 'us and them' split, Dawn explains how the school created a family from a fractured staff who formerly collected in small, separate groups.

Context

Pentland Primary School is in Billingham, Stockton-on-Tees, in the North-East of England. The chemical industry, in particular ICI until it closed in 2006, has played an important role in the growth of Billingham. There are 320 children on roll between the ages of 3 and 11, including the Nursery, which has 30-hour provision. Breakfast and after-school care are provided. There is an equal number of girls and boys. Fifty-seven per cent of the children are designated as Pupil Premium (PP), and 43% are on free school meals. Twenty-seven per cent of our children are identified as requiring Special Educational Needs and Disability (SEND) support, and 12% are on an Education, Health and Care Plan (EHCP) – twice the national average. We have an over-subscribed autistic spectrum disorder base with 21 pupils. Children generally enter Pentland Primary School at lower than age-related expectations but the school is at the national average at Key Stage 2. Progress is good.

There are 23 teachers, five of whom are part-time, 20 teaching assistants, one parent support advisor and two administrative staff.

The school was built in the 1930s and retains many of its original features.

I took up post as headteacher in September 2019, having moved to the school from another within the 1 Excellence Multi-Academy Trust. My main focus was to develop a 'family' ethos in the school so that we are one community. The senior leadership team (SLT) were already in post; they openly welcomed, encouraged and cooperated in creating the 'family' ethos. My intention was not a conscious decision – it was more part of my philosophy of how a school should be run. I offered the school and the staff a fresh start, where openness and willingness to try new approaches would be supported. My core messages were that everyone is equal, and that teamwork builds a successful school. I wanted the school to be happy and welcoming, creating a positive working environment. I believe that a happy staff equals happy children and a happy community, and vice versa. We needed to move with the times and recognise that, with over 80% of the workforce being female, staff have to balance family and work, and that both are important to them.

Key staff wellbeing strategies

- Openness: staff know that my door is open, and I am there to support, listen and, at times, challenge. Staff are aware that, if they are challenged, it is because it comes from a determination to include everyone in our school community.
- When I arrived, there were several 'staff rooms'. These rooms were converted to teaching rooms, rather than simply applying a rule that the space couldn't be used for staff to meet. All staff, pre-Covid-19, sat together as one in the main staffroom.
- Building courage to be brave — trying new things, approaches and roles. Two staff applied for a Trust role which would have been unheard of previously. I also offered chances to develop leadership. One of the senior leaders thought that no-one would apply: four members of staff did so.
- Creating the Pentland brand that we are the 'Pentland Family'.
- Creating respect for all.

The impact of these strategies was that there was less staff sickness and a collaborative ethos was created, with a shared vision. Staff began to accept that they should take care of their own wellbeing and mental health and, as a result, were more able to support others – children, parents and colleagues. Staff confidence developed. Some members of staff had been criticised in unconstructive ways in the past and were affected by the school's previous tendency towards a fear culture. Not my style.

Introducing a wellbeing culture

A wellbeing culture was never officially 'launched', but I made clear during my opening address to staff that this underpinned my aims and intentions. I talked about myself, my family, my background and own mental health issues. My aim was to reassure staff that I was human and open, transparent, honest, modelling what I wanted to encourage in others.

I asked staff to 'rag-rate' the school (Red, Orange, Green). I acted immediately on some red issues and addressed how important I felt the greens were – showing that I listened and appreciated staff ideas. This gave staff ownership and confirmed the changes that I had in mind. Where appropriate, I discussed some of the decisions that involved change. Not all staff agreed with my changes but understood my reasons, which were to improve the school and raise standards of education. This was fundamental to good practice and staff knew that I would support them to achieve it – it was part of our school's ethos.

Creating a 'we' culture

I aimed to create a 'we' culture, not an 'us and them' structure. In the first half-term, I had a one-to-one with staff and sent everyone, at different points, a thank-you card to acknowledge their hard work. The timing and individual messages made it specific to each member of staff, not generic. I tried to say 'thank you' as much as possible and personal to the member of staff. I listened to staff and made time to listen. I learned the names of members of their families and important facts about them.

During Covid-19, I listened to staff and their worries. Staff who were anxious, or had family issues, worked from home. When they came back, their return was gentle and gradual with regular check-ins. I sent thank-you notes home and provided chocolate in the staffroom at pressure points. I arranged flexible working and called staff regularly who were not in school. Staff meetings were held on Zoom. This enabled staff to collaborate, even if they were isolating at home. Staff continued to be involved in decisions.

Five key factors in creating a culture of wellbeing

1. **Trust.** Staff know they can trust me and the SLT. That we are here for them and that we are open. Developing trust was an imperative part of the process of change. This took time and is still developing.

2. **Change.** Accepting change and being open to change, professionally and personally. This could only happen when trust was established. This will evolve and develop, as the level of challenge for change increases.

3. **Openness.** Nothing is hidden. There is clear, translucent leadership where aims and objectives are shared and, wherever possible, decisions are collaborative. It took time to develop a positive structure and framework. In the beginning, some staff challenged every decision, often negatively. This was a carry-over from the unhelpful criticism they had experienced in the past.

Sometimes, frank conversations needed to happen and for staff to be aware that openness is a two-way street.

4. **Appreciation.** Staff knowing they are appreciated – this, in turn, developed trust. This will continue to develop and will never change. Appreciation needs to be ongoing and part of the cultural norm.

5. **The Pentland Family: Creating the family ethos.** This continues to develop and will become more established. Staff, parents and children comment on being part of the Pentland Family and that they feel part of one community.

The impact of the wellbeing culture on staff and the school

Until Covid-19 became a national emergency in February and March of 2020, the supply budget was not used for staff absences. No teaching staff have left, except for two expected retirements. Supply staff or maternity covers want to stay and always ask to be contacted for permanent positions. Staff are willing to go the extra mile. They never ask, 'What do I get out of it?' We all pull together. Staff are happy and state they are. There is laughter, happiness and a willingness to work.

In June 2020, I successfully nominated Pentland Primary for the Teach Well Alliance Teach Well School Award: Covid-19 Pandemic. Staff supported the nomination with testimonials of how the school was looking after them during Covid-19. Their words might help you to get a sense of the impact of our wellbeing ethos.

'I've felt very supported through all the uncertainty of COVID. You and the SLT have provided a personalised plan for our school that eliminates risk and doesn't put pressure on staff. Staff wellbeing has been mentioned throughout and kept as a focus. It really has been so lovely to see the school team come together through a time of segregation and distancing. We have proven we make a great team, even when we work with different staff than we might normally. I think the positivity from the top filters down, and you and SLT have always been around to help and support with a big smile' (newly qualified teacher).

'I have felt a lot of support from you as a headteacher! You have been considerate on an individual basis with me. I had a lot of anxiety at the beginning of lockdown and was worried sick about XXXXX being in school with his condition. You allowed me to stay at home to protect him, because if I had had to work, he would have had to come into school! I am very much grateful for this, as is my husband. You have been supportive throughout this, constantly keeping staff up to date and managing staff fairly! It must have been a mammoth task to plan but you have done a great job! As a parent too, now that XXXXX is back at school, I have felt that he has been safe due to all that has been put in place. You have done a great job and I feel that I could come to you and talk if there was anything bothering me. Your openness about mental wellbeing is great and makes a massive difference to know there is someone there if you need to talk! X' (teaching assistant who is also a parent).

'Hi Dawn, can't thank you and SLT enough. Even before lockdown, you made sure I was protected because of my vulnerability. During my shielding, I felt sad I could not be in school, but felt very supported and informed about everything that was happening within school and felt very proud of the way our children and families were supported during this crisis. On my return to work, I received the most amazing support from you and other members of staff to make me feel safe. Pentland is one hell of a school and led by an amazing team and I'm sure all our families would agree with me' (Nursery teaching assistant).

'This Covid-19 has taken everyone by surprise. It has made a lot of people feel very anxious. As a teaching assistant, I feel my school has been very supportive to all pupils, parents and staff with their wellbeing and mental health. The wellbeing of all has been a priority. The head has communicated with staff every day. Keeping us all safe, following the government guidelines, social distancing and team bubbles. Clear communication is very important. Since lockdown, school has remained open to vulnerable pupils and pupils who have key workers as parents. Staff, parents and pupils have been given websites and lots of information about mental health, as we know this affects people in different ways. When working in our bubble, staff talk to each other and it helps to listen to how others are feeling. Our head has just joined our school in September, so this is on top of that. It's a big challenge but the support parents, pupils and staff get is excellent. Personally, I know the door is always open if I need to talk about my wellbeing. This has not just come about since the Covid-19 – she's always checking that parents, pupils and staff are okay. So, I do feel we are all well-looked after at our school. Thank you' (teaching assistant).

'I know you've already applied [Ed: for the Teach Well Alliance Teach Well School Gold Award: Covid-19 Pandemic] but I would like to say that throughout this year, before and during the pandemic, I have felt extremely supported in my new role. Supported by our amazing SLT, teachers, teaching assistants, parents and also the children themselves. I've only been at Pentland for 5 years which isn't long compared to some members of staff and, although the pandemic has meant we have had to distance ourselves, I've ironically never felt so close to the Pentland Family. The positive spirit that is seen in school is due to you, Dawn. You have created this, which has been just what we all needed, even if it did have to be brought out through strange circumstances. A huge thank you to our amazing Pentland Family as on a personal level it really has helped me' (member of SLT).

'I feel staff at Pentland are really friendly and welcoming. They are always happy to help you out. Staff always take the time to ask me how I am doing. They support and help me through things I am unsure about, especially XXXXX, XXXXX, XXXXX and XXXXX, who have made sure I am okay within my new job role. They always have time to listen and answer my queries and I know where they are, should I need them. This has helped me so much over the past few weeks. I am really appreciative of all your support' (parent support advisor).

What next? Suggestions from staff voice

- Continue developing wellbeing and cementing the ethos and values we have worked on.
- Staff meetings: staff will only attend meetings that are specific to them. When they are unable to meet face-to-face, they will be able to access them from home on Microsoft Teams.
- PPA can be organised at home, allowing staff a little flexibility.
- Wellbeing is not about what we *do* for staff but how we *are* with staff. I don't believe in gimmicks, but ensuring wellbeing is part of our practice and ethos.

Key strategies

- Pentland Family ethos and one community, integral to the staff wellbeing culture of the school.
- Openness and the importance of listening.
- Creating one staffroom.
- Building courage to innovate and take risks.
- Creating respect for everyone.
- Staff asked to 'RAG rate' the school to identify issues affecting wellbeing.
- Building a 'we' culture, not 'us and them'.
- Personalised 'thank-you' cards, not generic, and sent at the same time.
- Support for staff isolating during Covid-19.
- Learning the names and personal circumstances of the families of staff.
- Transparency and authenticity: headteacher shared personal journey, including mental ill-health.

19 Wayfield Primary School, Chatham, Kent

Proud to achieve: Wellbeing and collaboration in the digital age

Matthew Tragheim, Apple Teacher and Wellbeing Champion

Headteacher: Tim Williams

'A common problem with wellbeing and mental health strategies – in organisations outside education as well as within it – is that they can appear disingenuous. Rather than implementing a deep culture of staff wellbeing and mental health, schools can create a tick list of every-so-often "engagements". Staff may be given the opportunity to engage in a strain-inducing yoga class, an after-school session on mindfulness with an over-enthusiastic external facilitator, or maybe even an end-of-term plate of biscuits. These tokenistic gestures belie the complexities of establishing a genuine culture that has deep roots across the whole school. This is perhaps because the needs of staff can be so various and disparate. A culture of wellbeing and mental health will fail if staff feel it lacks sincerity and integrity. It should be a constant – accessible, reliable and trusted at any time. However, it must also be malleable and dynamic so that it can meet the changing needs, circumstances, pressures and demands of busy lives. Our approach to wellbeing and mental health needed to reflect the unique ideas, attitudes, customs and social behaviours that characterised the culture of our school.'

Overview

Matthew Tragheim, Apple Teacher and Wellbeing Champion at Wayfield Primary School, reflects on how headteacher Tim Williams collaborated with the staff to address the shortcomings identified in the school's Ofsted report. A key strategy was Tim taking on a teaching commitment to lead from the front and to see the school as teachers and support staff perceived it. Matthew describes how improving communication and collaboration, by digitising the school and upgrading technology, was instrumental in developing a culture of staff wellbeing and mental health. It also promoted and developed teachers as leaders of their classrooms and beyond. Ofsted saw a very different school when they inspected again in 2019.

Context

Wayfield Primary School is located in Chatham, south-east Kent. The local authority is ranked 118th out of 326 in England for deeprivation (Department for Communities and Local Government, 2015) and a review of previous data indicates that, throughout the last decade, the area has become increasingly more deprived. Ofsted's Annual Report (2020) highlights the disproportionate number of 'stuck' schools in the region and the focus on children 'left behind' by economic turbulence, political uncertainty and changing social policy. There are 294 children on roll, with an equal gender split (147/147). Almost half the children (133) are designated Pupil Premium (PP); 35 children require Special Educational Needs and Disability (SEND) support; six children have an Education, Health and Care Plan (EHCP), and 24 children speak English as an additional language. In terms of staffing, six are members of the senior leadership team (SLT), 13 are teaching assistants, and three are facilities or administrative staff. There are eight qualified teachers.

The issues experienced by deprived communities are multi-faceted, inter-generational and complex (Gorard and Siddiqui, 2019). They directly contribute to apathy, poor attendance, lack of academic ambition and low attainment (Doyle and Keane, 2019; Leckie and Goldstein, 2019). Even before the impact of Covid-19, strategies adopted by the school had to be sensitive, thoughtful, transparent and ambitious. The SLT was aware that student motivation, engagement and progress are influenced by both individual and institutional factors. Real and enduring cultural change can only be achieved if the individual and institution genuinely connect in a meaningful way.

Following a highly critical Ofsted inspection in 2016, Wayfield Primary School was transferred to the Primary First Trust by the Department for Education (DfE). A new leadership team was established to oversee a significant and transformational redesign of priorities, practice, policy and pedagogy. Tim Williams was appointed as headteacher in 2018. Although the ability of new leadership teams to instigate genuine change can be limited by a number of factors (Evens et al., 2015; Chi-Kin Lee, 2017), evidence-based literature reviews and contextual action research can help extend influence, especially on immediate procedural or pedagogical limitations that are impacting children (Dhillon et al., 2019). Schratz (2020) further argues that schools which successfully complete a period of significant change often have improved collaboration, staff resilience and fidelity at all levels. Such indicators are present at Wayfield Primary School (Ofsted, 2019d) and have been key to successfully navigating the often unforeseen pressures of Covid-19 on teaching, learning and wellbeing across the school community.

Our journey to implementing a culture of wellbeing and mental health

Preceding the involvement of the Primary First Trust, Wayfield Primary School had experienced tumultuous years. A sustained period of negative experiences had given rise to pernicious feelings of distrust and animosity. There is much research to support the view that toxic atmospheres and relationships often stem from poor communication (Justis et al., 2020; Lester et al., 2020; Snell et al., 2020). Failing to address issues with communication can undermine the ambitions of any school improvement plan, as it directly impacts trust, apathy and wellbeing. Within a school context, developing clear, coherent and compassionate communication is imperative for establishing good relationships. Although this can often be seen between the tripartite relationship of parent, teacher and pupil, it is the way leaders and staff communicate that impacts on trust and respect. Effective communication is an often underrated skill. It requires empathy, emotional literacy and intelligence, an ability to navigate the vocabulary and experiences of context, evidence-informed decisions and active listening. If staff feel confident and comfortable in having conversations, it creates a continuous and open dialogue that negates feelings that they have no voice and that their opinions are not valued. Furthermore, it prompts a collective responsibility and understanding that good mental health is predicated on regular reflection and talking to one another.

After Wayfield Primary School joined the Primary First Trust, it was important to clearly understand both the explicit and underlying challenges that impacted learning. The Ofsted inspection in 2016 summarised and expressed many of the concerns held by staff about the quality of education, behaviour and wellbeing. It also illuminated an array of negative experiences from learners, parents, carers, practitioners and school staff.

A staged transition programme, expressed through the school development plan, began by promoting stability and consistency of expectation. It was clear from initial assessments and reviews by Sheena Hamilton, Director of the Primary First Trust, that high staff turnover; curriculum changes and inconsistency; off-rolling and exclusions; standardisation of student isolation processes; low academic progress; and widespread distrust amongst parents had created a toxic atmosphere of suspicion, scepticism and resentment. Children and practitioners did not feel safe, valued or purposeful. A period of permanence, reliability and steadiness was essential to nurture staff trust. Vitally, there was also a need for time to reflect – one of the most important factors for healthy and flourishing wellbeing at Wayfield.

Pedagogy and practice are now directly connected, led and informed by continuous reflection and research. During the initial stages of the transformation programme, it became evident that a radical solution was required to address many of the underlying issues. Tim Williams, headteacher, moved into the classroom, taking up full teaching responsibilities, lesson planning, behaviour management and progress reporting. Moving to the frontline in this way was pivotal. It became an important signal and rallying call to all staff and was emblematic of a whole-school unification process that stitched together reflections, innovative ideas and practice. From the vantage point of a classroom teacher, Tim was able to talk with insight and integrity when expressing his vision for change, as he was drawing on direct and personal experience.

As a school leader, Tim had made himself visible, approachable and well-informed about the day-to-day life of the school. He had an awareness of what it felt like to be both a practitioner and a pupil in a classroom at Wayfield. He could better comprehend and articulate the pressures faced within the specific context but also offer solutions which were measurable, specific, relevant and relatable.

Following a wider whole-school review and his first-hand experience in the classroom, which enabled him to dissect the teaching and learning experience, Tim proposed a transformational vision. The changes he described centred on the complete digitisation of the school. This included the updating of technology, but, crucially, it also involved comprehensive cultural reform. Digitisation and the use of new technologies would become invaluable tools, but a cultural shift would require a commitment to a new way of working, interacting, sharing and thinking. For healthy wellbeing and mental health to be a truly embedded everyday expectation – and not just a standalone innovation revisited during training days or featured in occasional newsletter features – positive education, instant visible feedback and blended learning were necessary to establish a new, ever-evolving culture of collaboration.

Our aim in implementing wellbeing and mental health strategies

A common problem with wellbeing and mental health strategies – in organisations outside education as well as within it – is that they can appear disingenuous. Rather than implementing a deep culture of staff wellbeing and mental health, schools can create a tick list of every-so-often 'engagements'. Staff may be given the opportunity to engage in a strain-inducing yoga class, an after-school session on mindfulness with an over-enthusiastic external facilitator, or maybe even an end-of-term plate of biscuits. These tokenistic gestures belie the complexities of establishing a genuine culture that has deep roots across the whole school. This is perhaps because the needs of staff can be so various and disparate. A culture of wellbeing and mental health will fail if staff feel it lacks sincerity and integrity. It should be a constant – accessible, reliable and trusted at any time. However, it must also be malleable and dynamic so that it can meet the changing needs, circumstances, pressures and demands of busy lives. Our approach to wellbeing and mental health needed to reflect the unique ideas, attitudes, customs and social behaviours that characterised the culture of our school.

Clarity of intention

It quickly became apparent that clarity of intention was key. In many ways, the school was at a crossroads in 2017 and so the guiding principles, tenets and aspirations for the school were all being systematically redefined. Staff well-being and mental health did not exist only as a compartmentalised addendum to school policy or an irregular agenda item. As a collective, it was vital that we shared core values that demonstrated our intentions on a daily basis. It was hoped that implementing and promoting a culture of collaboration, innovation and recognition would create a single belief in the value of all staff. It would also alleviate some of the issues associated with schools who follow a more autocratic approach in relation to staff recognition and contribution. By pursuing a more meritocratic model, staff would hopefully feel empowered to proactively lead change, returning to them some of the esteem many felt their profession had lost. By investing trust and confidence in staff, as well as instilling a sense of professional pride, staff felt that they were appreciated, purposeful and valued contributors to the whole community. They also created virtuous cycles that influenced and impacted other aspects of school life, such as the close relationship with children and parents. Tim Williams set about promoting a genuine culture of care and collaboration that was dynamic and responsive and evolved to meet the changing needs of staff and the school community.

Digital transformation born out of classroom experience

The digital transformation at Wayfield Primary School has allowed greater collaboration and communication than ever before. As previously described, however, the greatest single step towards launching a commitment to staff mental health and wellbeing was Tim Williams returning to the classroom. Despite simultaneously overseeing a complex and intricate school development plan, Tim knew that the future success of the school depended on his ability to communicate effectively with the entire school community, motivating them to invest in his vision and share in the journey of change and challenge. By shouldering the burden of everyday teaching, Tim gained first-hand experience of the pressures on teacher mental health. Furthermore, he was able to reach a detailed understanding of the emotional and institutional expectations on staff in relation to planning, progress, pedagogy, assessment and feedback. He strove to understand the procedures and practices that influence a teacher's ability to create the best learning and teaching experience possible.

As well as inviting staff to observe his teaching, Tim Williams used his time to craft approaches that would have a direct impact on reducing teacher workload: improving transparency and embedding instant visible feedback. Following his in-classroom evidence-gathering, he also created an open-access document portal; launched an iMessaging system so that teachers could instantly share ideas; developed an understanding of the software needed for teachers to review and deploy work instantaneously; assessed the significance of blended learning; determined the role of specialist teachers within a creative curriculum; and, finally, established protected time for targeted continuing professional development. In isolation, the effectiveness of these measures would have been limited. It was the concerted combination and deliberate interleaving of initiatives that created the trust and homogeny needed for sustainable progress, implementation and cultural evolution.

Five milestones

1. Replacement of all old technology. Establishing a new culture in a school requires the participation of the staff as a community in a shared experience. As communication played such an important role in improving staff wellbeing and mental health, it was vital that our methods of communication were reviewed and unified. Old technology promoted antiquated and fractured processes, making staff interaction sporadic and inconvenient. As with many schools, technology and infrastructure had been updated in an irregular way, often when budgets allowed, with new systems sitting on top of previous software. Investing in a single system meant that all staff could share, edit and collaborate, using the same files. They also only had to learn a single process, remember a single password and contribute to a single stream of shared communication.

2. Versatile values to replace rules. Wayfield Primary School has five core values: Joy, Adventure, Teamwork, Resilience and Lifelong Learning. These values were established after a consultation with the entire school community. All behaviours were directly linked to the school's values. Not only did this approach remove antiquated lists of rules for staff to regurgitate or implement inconsistently, it empowered children to be more autonomous and judicious. Children could consider the core values when making decisions, connecting the actions and consequences of their behaviours with greater clarity.

3. Continual atmosphere of collaboration. Collaboration is unlike teamwork in that roles are not pre-defined and tasks are often not linear. There is an open-source approach that, at its most effective, promotes a richness and fidelity of creative ideas and solutions. Collaboration encourages the development of criticality and higher-order thinking and problem-solving skills. An atmosphere of collaboration invites positive challenge, ensuring the development of meaningful, purposeful and evidence-informed teaching and learning. Collaboration ensures that we never settle for mindlessly re-treading or reliving the status quo. There is a sense of possibility that runs through both our ideas and actions.

4. Empowered to be leaders in the classroom. Esteem and integrity have been re-ignited in our teachers. It can be argued that there has been a gradual erosion of teachers' authority, with control both from the centre of government and by more powerful governance. Disempowerment can limit a teacher's ability to shape experiences that nurture a child's well-rounded development, undermining their role as both a pedagogical researcher and practitioner.

Consumed by the pressures, stresses and strains of teaching, it is often difficult to find the time for self-care, reflection, professional development and collaboration. Protecting dedicated time for these behaviours and practices each day, for each teacher, is important. It signals to staff and the wider community that honing the craft of teaching is a significant pursuit. Moreover, it acknowledges the crucial role of a teacher as an influential leader of learning.

5. Commitment to a split-setting, single-stream approach. Although Wayfield is pioneering, the level of research and trialling prior to implementation is not to be underestimated. We are confident in adopting new strategies and approaches because of the careful and conscientious contribution staff make to testing their contextual relevance. For example, Covid-19 undoubtedly prompted the acceleration of digitisation, but it also challenged staff to adapt existing systems to meet new needs. Whereas most approaches are embedded holistically, staff had to run a slightly differentiated split-setting system. In our context, split-setting refers specifically to the at-home and in-school learning environment. Thus, we endeavoured to deliver a single curriculum by adopting a split-setting pedagogy. A commitment was made to ensure that as few children were disadvantaged as possible. All children would receive the same year-specific, daily package of blended learning to their devices. However, feedback, interaction and engagement would be modified to meet the constraints of home learning. Children (and parents) at home could engage with their teacher in real-time and access guided support from peers during their lessons. Lockdown showed how the staff could collaborate and work together. Collectively, we committed to a split-setting, single-stream approach that ensured the doors of Wayfield never closed for any child. The learning never stopped.

Impact of strategies

As described earlier, staff at Wayfield were well-placed to respond to the global pandemic in 2020. Not only was the technology in place to ensure the uninterrupted continuation of learning, staff had the shared sense of determination, resilience, trust and collaboration required to adapt to the unpredictable nature of such a crisis. The way in which staff rose to the challenge, with ambition and possibility, shows why it is crucial that wellbeing and mental health are ongoing priorities. Staff were well-versed in debating, researching and responding to a dynamic problem. They proactively sought feedback from peers, observed changes across the sector, learnt from and leant on others, shared a variety of fears, worries and concerns in a trusted forum, practised self-care, reflected on emerging pedagogical practice and rigorously pursued swift adaptation.

Prior to the arrival of Covid-19, the impact of our approach to staff wellbeing and mental health could already be seen in a variety of measures. Our relationships with stakeholders had continued to grow in transparency, openness and trust. Our network of professional collaborators had similarly increased at pace, with an ever-growing number of practitioners sharing their experiences with us across our social media platforms. In 2019, Wayfield Primary School was also recognised by Ofsted as having outstanding features in the area of staff development and wellbeing. Furthermore, the academic progress and results of children have flourished, improving dramatically each year to make us one of the top primary schools for results in Medway. Our sector-leading combination of technology, collaboration, wellbeing and instant visible feedback was also recently validated by our induction into the exclusive Apple Distinguished School programme. This global initiative recognises excellence in learning and teaching practice and is something all staff are incredibly proud to celebrate.

What next?

The next few years will be a period of ongoing collaboration, innovation and consolidation at Wayfield. We will refine those pathfinder practices already embedded, ensuring that they remain relevant, impactful, sustainable and reflective of staff teaching and learning needs. We will continue to be ambitious by investing in people, property, resources and reputation.

In the coming year, we hope to increase the number of staff by 30% to meet the demands of a two-form entry provision. We hope to extend our influence and impact by empowering staff to share their knowledge outside the school as specialism leaders. By sharing our learning with others, we hope to foster an open dialogue with other leaders and practitioners about wellbeing and mental health, enrich the holistic experience of staff at other schools, grow our network of collaborators, contribute to sector articles, journals and conferences in the field, nurture the supportive culture we have developed across the community, and remain evidence-informed in our pioneering practices.

Key strategies

- Transfer of Wayfield Primary School to Primary First Trust.
- Creating time for professional reflection.
- Headteacher moved into classroom role to gain understanding from both a teacher's and a pupil's perspective.
- Complete digitisation of the school, creating one unified system, led to a cultural shift of collaboration and effective communication which impacted on wellbeing and mental health.
- Removal of old technology.
- Wellbeing and mental health a culture, not tokenism.
- Clarity of intention in implementing strategies.
- Replacing outdated rules with values.
- Teachers become classroom leaders.
- Time created for self-care, professional development and collaboration.
- Commitment to a split-setting, single-stream approach enabling blended learning.

20 St. Joseph and St. Bede RC Primary School, Bury, Greater Manchester

Our SJSB family

Amy Chadwick, Year ¾ Class Teacher

Headteacher: Jane Myerscough

'Our aspiration was that each member of staff would feel loved, valued and respected.'

Overview

In her account of how staff wellbeing and mental health were the focal point for school improvement, Amy Chadwick emphasises that each member of staff is part of the St. Joseph and St. Bede family. This theme runs throughout Amy's description of how staff support and take care of one another and share in events which promote teamwork, laughter and celebration.

Context

St. Joseph and St. Bede is a primary school situated in Bury, Greater Manchester. There are approximately 340 pupils on roll, with a range of abilities and an average number of Special Educational Needs and Disability (SEND) pupils at 12.3%. The school has a growing number of pupils with social-emotional needs who receive support from a pupil support advisor and external counselling services. The school has slightly more boys than girls, although this varies across year groups and classes. The majority of pupils are White British and there are a lower than the national average number of pupils for whom English is an additional language at 12.9%. There is a higher than average proportion of children entitled to Pupil Premium funding at 32.8% and free school meals at 29.6%.

St. Joseph and St. Bede has 14 teaching staff, including two newly qualified teachers. Each classroom has a dedicated teaching assistant (14 in total), including two higher-level teaching assistants, one who covers Key Stage 1 (KS1) and the other Key Stage 2 (KS2). There are also eight special support assistants providing tailored provision for SEND pupils, and a pupil support advisor providing individual and group support. There is a range of non-teaching staff, including two office managers and a senior business manager, a site manager, five lunchtime supervisors, three cleaning staff and a catering team.

For many years now, issues of teacher workload and staff retention in the education sector have been of great importance. Although these issues have contributed to our implementation of a culture of staff wellbeing and mental health, the decision to sharpen our focus stemmed mainly from our Catholic ethos and our desire to provide the most supportive and enabling environment for our staff.

Interactive planning

Due to the number of pupils on roll at our school, planning is organised in 'unit teams' or Key Stage groups. KS1 teachers share the planning load between them, as do lower KS2 teachers and upper KS2 teachers. The workload is shared equally between three members of staff in each unit. This way of working enables a culture of staff wellbeing by reducing planning demands, and allows staff to communicate and collaborate more often to share ideas, creating a supportive working environment. In 2017, we changed our format from paper planning to 'interactive planning', using PowerPoint to create lesson presentations. This made the sequence of the lessons easier to follow, making planning more accessible and helped to reduce workload further, especially when staff plan lessons for each other. This had a positive impact on how staff approached planning and was a very positive starting point for our journey towards a culture of staff wellbeing and mental health.

Appointment of a new headteacher

At the start of the 2018/19 academic year, Spiritual, Moral, Social and Cultural Development (SMSC) became even more of a focus, following the creation of a SMSC leader role. As our journey to the Gold SMSC Quality Mark began, it became apparent that staff wellbeing was an area for improvement in our school. This prompted regular staff wellbeing questionnaires to help us identify what improvements were needed to raise morale.

A staff wellbeing culture would not have been embedded if it were not for the leadership of our current headteacher, Jane Myerscough. Jane took over the role fully in January 2019, following many years as the deputy headteacher, and a brief period of co-headship with the previous headteacher. Jane has contributed to the appointment of most of our staff and understands our school thoroughly. Staff wellbeing is at the heart of everything that she does and, since her appointment as headteacher, the school has moved rapidly forward in this area.

Fewer demands from marking and assessment and wellbeing packages

Academic year 2019/20 was Jane's first whole year within the role and, although there have been a number of unexpected challenges, our school has also welcomed a number of changes which have helped to raise staff morale even further and develop a family-like atmosphere. These changes range from policy amendments, resulting in fewer demands on marking and assessment, to simple touches such as staff 'wellbeing packages' to welcome us at the start of the academic year. The combination of these strategies has helped to bring staff together and has given us more time to focus, not only on individual children, but also on our own personal development and our relationships with one another.

Staff wellbeing and mental health: Intended outcomes

Improving the environment

The main outcome we hoped to achieve by implementing a culture of staff wellbeing and mental health was to ensure that our environment was one in which people loved to work. Our primary focus was on staff enjoying their teaching and feeling supported each day. It was important that staff felt exactly as we want the children to feel, as they walk through our doors.

Sharing ideas

One aim was that staff would feel safe in the knowledge that they have an important and valued place at our school. We hoped that all would feel so comfortable with their colleagues that they would be able to share ideas and strategies, as well as their unique personalities and talents.

Reducing anxiety

We also intended to help staff lower their levels of anxiety, whether the cause was within school or had an external cause. We hoped to provide each other with support and encouragement and for our staff to never feel alone in their struggles. We wanted them to know that there are always people who can lend a helping hand or offer a listening ear and that we are all in this together.

Increasing joy and laughter

Another main goal for implementing this culture was to bring more joy and laughter to our working day. We wanted to provide staff with meaningful professional relationships and friendships which gave them encouragement and fulfilment. We aimed to bring about a strong sense of unity, improve morale, develop their understanding of one another and bring them closer together

Our aspiration was that each member of staff would feel loved, valued and respected. We wanted everyone to feel united in the mission that we all have as a working 'family'. We also aimed to ensure that each member of staff knew how grateful we are for the incredible work that they do and for the daily contributions they make to improve the lives of our children and one another. We hoped that everyone would have more time to value themselves and what they bring to the world and to appreciate all that they have achieved. We also aimed to ensure that our staff would realise how much we valued their contribution to our school and how significant they are in our educational journey.

Our staff wellbeing and mental health journey

The first action that we took to launch the staff wellbeing and mental health initiative was to change our marking and feedback policy in January 2019, in order to reduce the pressure on staff of marking and assessment. Prior to this, staff had told us about whole-class feedback as an alternative to pen marking. During a staff meeting, we discussed the success of this approach in other schools and the various formats that this might take within our setting.

Verbal feedback instead of pen marking

The outcome of the consultation was that staff were no longer required to write extensive comments on individual pieces of work. Most teachers found that writing comments in children's exercise books was time-consuming and did not have as much impact on our children's learning as the 'in the moment' verbal feedback they received during lessons. Feedback would now be given to the class, and children were to respond accordingly. Staff could keep whole-class records of this feedback in a staff planner, where they would make minimal key notes of children who needed support, as well as high-attaining pupils, and general comments could be recorded about next steps for the class as a whole.

As we wanted staff to maximise the impact of feedback and reduce their workload, we began to use the whole-class feedback approach and trained the children on how to respond to it.

Across classes, the use of whole-class feedback enabled the children to make the necessary changes and improvements to their work and answer questions to extend their thinking, without the need for individual written comments.

The children enjoyed whole-class discussion to reflect on previous learning at the start of each lesson and found that it enabled them to take ownership of their work and make improvements more independently. From a teaching point of view, this approach not only reduced marking time but also summarised the impact of a lesson more concisely and enabled teachers to build a picture of the progress of the class as a whole.

The challenges we faced when implementing this initial change stemmed mainly from teachers' marking habits. Although staff agreed that writing individual comments was time-consuming, some found it difficult to adapt to the changes, given the fact that they had provided feedback in this way for some years. This led to some minor inconsistencies in approaches across classes, as each teacher adapted to this new way of working. Gradually, as mindsets changed, we became more accustomed to using whole-class feedback and it continues to be a great asset to both the children's learning and staff wellbeing.

Milestone 1: Increasing staff events

The first significant milestone we achieved on our journey to implement a culture of staff wellbeing and mental health was running more staff events. Towards the end of January 2019, a number of staff embarked on a fitness journey, as our sports coach ran weekly after-school bootcamp sessions. The group has continued to run ever since and, in the summer of 2019, the focus changed to train for the 'Race for Life Pretty Muddy' and raise money for Cancer Research UK, resulting in a donation of £1753. [Ed: 'Race for Life Pretty Muddy' is a charity event organised by Cancer Research where women climb over and crawl under an obstacle course.] Although all staff were welcome to attend the group, some with other commitments struggled to attend. However, this initiative brought staff closer together and it prompted us to plan more opportunities to spend time together as a staff, including an end-of-year staff celebration.

Milestone 2: Email policy

The next milestone we reached was the changes we made to staff communication. In the spring of 2019, expectations were clearly laid out which reduced demands for staff to reply to emails outside of working hours. This was a response to feedback from staff wellbeing questionnaires, which indicated that some staff felt that lines were sometimes blurred between home and school and more clarification was needed. A number of staff said that receiving emails in the evening made them feel obliged to reply and reduced time spent with their families. Making this simple change and clarifying expectations regarding communication enabled staff to take comfort that they were not obliged to check work emails once they had left the school building. The main challenge we faced was during the initial stage when staff were still taking time to adapt to this change. This is now, however, a fully embedded practice.

Milestone 3: Wellbeing package at beginning of the year

A further milestone was the gift of a 'wellbeing package' for all staff on the return to school in September 2019. Amongst other delights was a voucher entitling each member of staff to a 'wellbeing day', which they were allowed to take during the academic year. This was the first time staff had received such a gift and many used it to take an extra day away on holiday or to celebrate important family events. As staff arranged cover between themselves, we managed to provide each other with the opportunity to have a well-deserved break. Many staff agreed that it was a special feeling to be rewarded for their hard work and commitment to the school.

Milestone 4: Response to Covid-19

Our most recent accomplishment was our response to the Covid-19 outbreak in March 2020. Our school remained open for the following four months, providing childcare for the children of key worker families. In order to meet the needs of the personal circumstances and mental health of our own staff, several steps were taken. High-risk individuals were not required to attend work, and remaining staff were placed on a three-week rota, alternating between working in school, working at home and having a rest week. For those attending school, staggered start times were used to limit working hours, and time was organised between staff so that they had the opportunity to organise resources, as well as to provide activities for the children in their care. There were sufficient staff in each team to provide social interaction between adults, with the ability to socially distance. For those working online at home, this was at teachers' discretion, given each individual's personal circumstances. The system worked brilliantly throughout these testing times; challenges only arose as changes in staff circumstances caused some reduction in staff, while the number of key worker children continued to grow. Although the months between March and July 2020 presented staff with new challenges, we found that our response to the situation brought us closer than we had been before. In our Covid teams, we had the opportunity to develop working relationships, and the time we were apart from those in other teams made us truly value their presence in our usual working lives.

Impact of staff wellbeing and mental health strategies

Overall, the implementation of a culture of staff wellbeing and mental health has had a very positive impact on our school. Staff frequently say how much they enjoy their job and how they relish coming to work. Many of those who have been unfortunately absent over the past few months, due to personal circumstances, have commented on how much they have missed other members of staff and how eager they are to return to work in September. Even those who continued to attend school during the lockdown have voiced their enthusiasm about returning to the classroom and being united once more. Generally, the changes we have made have helped to raise morale and have resulted in minimal staff absence and greater staff retention. We have recruited two newly qualified teachers ahead of the new academic year and staff are feeling refreshed and prepared for the year ahead.

We can confidently say that staff feel more comfortable around each other and are pleased to engage in discussions with a range of different colleagues, both within the staffroom and around the school. The Covid working groups enabled newer staff to mix with those who they did not know as well, giving them the opportunity to learn more about their colleagues. This made staff feel more relaxed and confident around each other.

Staff now have a greater understanding that there are people who can provide support at times of challenge; closer relationships enable staff to ask one another for guidance or to seek company after a particularly demanding day. Newly qualified teachers who started at the beginning of the present academic year (2020/21) have commented on how supported they feel going into this new academic year and how staff have responded to their queries. This has helped to put their minds at ease, as they prepare for new challenges ahead. They have also felt a great sense of reassurance in the level of freedom that they have been given when preparing their classroom, enabling them to bring their creativity and flare to the environment and giving them a sense of ownership.

Due to the implementation of the Covid-19 rota, we have had fewer opportunities to participate in whole-staff events and have had more time apart than usual. Surprisingly, being apart has helped to bring staff closer together. Within our Covid teams, staff were able to mix with those whom they may not have had much opportunity to work with before and to get to know one another on a deeper level. This has helped some relationships to become stronger, and staff are now looking forward to a time when we have more opportunities to spend time as a whole staff, once restrictions are lifted.

Staff feel like part of a family, not just employees. The most recent challenges that we have faced together have made us understand how important we are, both in the lives of our children and each other. The measures that have been put in place to implement a culture of staff wellbeing and mental health have resulted in a realisation of how very privileged we are to work at St. Joseph and St. Bede RC Primary School.

Next steps

Moving forward into the next academic year, we will foster the culture of staff wellbeing and mental health by continuing to implement the changes we have put in place since the beginning of our journey. We also aim to focus more on making smaller improvements to the working life of our staff, as we have come to realise that even the smallest of gestures can make a huge difference. We will continue to provide staff with cover to attend their children's school events and we will strive to continue scheduling meetings during assembly times where possible, so that lesson times can be maximised, and staff breaks and lunchtimes are not reduced. We now take extra care when planning our diary of events, ensuring that events are spread appropriately in order to reduce pressure on staff across the year. We are aiming to continue to provide staff with the opportunity to have their car valeted on site each month during the school day to save them spending time doing so at evenings and weekends. We also hope to introduce another little touch in the form of 'wellbeing boxes' in staff bathrooms to provide toiletries and self-care items should staff require them during the working day. Hopefully, these small tokens of appreciation will continue to make staff feel valued and appreciated for all that they do at St. Joseph and St. Bede RC Primary School and make a difference to their day.

Key strategies

- Working in unit teams fosters relationships.
- Interactive planning.
- Staff questionnaires.
- Verbal feedback instead of pen marking.
- Wellbeing packages at the start of the school year.
- Staff support one another to reduce anxiety.
- Increasing joy and laughter.
- Cultivating a sense of unity.
- Each member of staff to feel loved, valued and respected.
- Increasing the number of staff events, including running for charity.
- Emails: removing the obligation to answer emails beyond the school day.
- Rota response to Covid-19 and support for staff shielding at home.
- Staff have got to know more colleagues during the Covid-19 rota system.
- Newly qualified teachers given freedom to decorate their own classrooms.
- Cover for staff to attend their own children's events.
- Meetings arranged during assembly time to ensure staff have breaks and lunchtimes.
- Yearly calendar planned to avoid clashes of events.
- Opportunity for staff to have their cars valeted on site every month.
- Wellbeing boxes containing toiletries and self-care products in staff toilets.

21 Harrowgate Hill Primary School, Darlington, County Durham

Staff wellbeing is not a tick-box exercise

Amanda Abbott, Headteacher

'It doesn't matter how big or how small – say "thank you". It costs nothing and it means everything.'

Overview

Amanda Abbott, headteacher, takes us on her journey to put staff wellbeing and mental health at the heart of Harrowgate Hill Primary School. Her moving and inspiring account of how staff were emotionally overwhelmed by being appreciated for their work when she first took up post at the school was the start of an ongoing process which is restoring staff belief in themselves and one another. Each member of staff is seen as a vital part of a larger family which can only take care of the children when the wellbeing and mental health of each adult are nurtured and supported.

Context

Harrowgate Hill Primary School has 618 pupils, with more boys than girls in every year group, apart from Year 1 in September 2020. Our pupils are low ability on entry to Nursery. We have 29.5% Pupil Premium pupils, with increasing levels of poverty or families who are just about managing. We operate the Fare Share programme to support families with food. [Ed: Fair Share is a UK charity which fights hunger and food waste. The charity saves good food from going to waste by redistributing it to frontline charities.] We employ a full-time emotional literacy support assistant (ELSA) lead to support the social, emotional and mental health needs of our pupils.

While we have a predominately White British cohort, we have increasing numbers of pupils from ethnic groups, many with English as an additional language joining each year. We now have eight languages spoken in school. We have a large group of young parents, many of whom attended the school themselves as pupils. Many of the children in the area continue to make their lives in Darlington after leaving school, as they are not widely travelled and, apart from school trips, do not venture beyond Darlington.

We are a Private Financial Initiative school, so we do not employ our own cleaning, site staff or caterers. We have 26 teaching staff, two dedicated welfare team staff (the ELSA lead and an inclusion manager), five admin team members, six Level 3 teaching assistants, 11 teaching assistants, two sports coaches (both part-time), 11 lunchtime supervisors and one apprentice teaching assistant. We have a breakfast club and an after-school club run by the same ladies who do lunch cover.

Staff wellbeing and mental health is a priority

Staff wellbeing and mental health have always been a priority for me as a school leader. It is not something you decide needs to be addressed; it should be part of the culture of the school and of your own leadership. We should never forget how precious and fundamental everyone who works or volunteers in the school is to its success. Every staff member is a gem – a vital cog 'in the machine'. If even one of those gems, those cogs, is not operating well because of poor physical or mental health, this can affect the entire school family.

The focus on staff wellbeing began at Harrowgate Hill the minute I received the phone call from the chair of governors offering me the job. After 22 years, I had a range of experience in a number of schools and had worked in many different environments – some positive, some negative and some verging on toxic. I was already an experienced headteacher, having worked as head of a junior school in Buckinghamshire, with approximately 250 pupils on roll, and a large primary Academy in Slough, with approximately 710 pupils.

Improving staff wellbeing and mental health

Whatever the status of staff wellbeing, when I took up post in a new school, I immediately set about maintaining, improving or making changes in terms of the workplace attitude to wellbeing and mental health. Harrowgate Hill had a staff team who needed a lot of TLC and, in the time between being offered the post in Spring 2018 to starting the role in Autumn, I had frequent conversations with the deputy head. The first in-service training (INSET) day in September 2018 focused on recognition, appreciation and learning how to be not just a team but a family. Staff wellbeing is not a project or tick off on a to-do list – it is all day, every day.

Harrowgate Hill staff needed a lot of care and team-building. They needed to feel valued and appreciated. There was a culture of distrust and a lack of appreciation for the huge amount of time and effort they put into their work.

For many reasons which do not belong in this article, Harrowgate Hill was not always a happy place in which to work. I remember being asked to lead a senior leadership team meeting as part of the interview process for my headship, and I asked the assistant headteachers about their management of time and well-being. Blank looks and then eyes that welled up when I stated that ensuring they had management time and wellbeing would be a focus if I was appointed, told me everything I needed to know – or so I thought! As an experienced teacher and headteacher, you think you have seen and heard it all. When I was through the door and I began to be trusted by the staff sufficiently for them to tell me what working there was like, I realised that I had not heard it all. What was clear was that we needed to strip everything back and begin again. Trust needs to be earned and I needed to do that from day one and to show staff through my actions that I meant what I said, and things were going to change.

Valuing and repairing 'broken' staff

That first INSET day was so quiet – no-one spoke. There were looks of disbelief on faces when I went through my expectations of them, not because it was too much but because I was suggesting 'radical' policies like 4 o'clock Fridays – no-one out the door later than 4:00 pm every Friday. I suggested we put Golden Time and celebration assemblies on Friday afternoon, so that staff didn't have any marking and didn't have to take books home. These are not new things in schools and are the surface of a very deep wellbeing well that can be drawn from but were almost alien to teachers for whom wellbeing was an unimaginable concept.

I remember talking to my chair of governors and using the phrase 'the most broken staff I've even worked with'. Not to put too fine a point on it, I had staff crying on an almost daily basis because I had been nice to them! My most poignant memory was of one of my teachers – such a lovely committed young lady – bursting into tears because I gave her a sticker for being so brilliant. In short, wellbeing and staff mental health were not a part of Harrowgate Hill. These truly amazing people deserved so much more.

I knew that achieving a culture of staff wellbeing and mental health was never going to be a quick fix at Harrowgate Hill. Two years on and we are much further down the line than we were but there is still a way to go. It's not as simple as 'just add water' – or, in this case, 'wellbeing practices' – and all will be well. People are not plants. People need long-term affirmative action. Trust needs to be built and this takes time.

Identifying what I hoped to achieve was the simple part. First as a school, we needed to be doing our very best for the children day in and day out, raising standards and giving the children the best possible life chances. Alongside this came the support we give to their families. To support children and families who have varying levels of need, you need staff who are both physically and mentally healthy to cope with what is the most demanding job in the world – working in a school. I wanted a staff team who felt they had the physical and emotional capacity and, most importantly of all, the support to do this demanding job day in and day out. Ultimately, I wanted what I felt we had achieved in my previous schools, a school family. Yes, families fall out and there are ups and downs, but ultimately, you've all got each other's backs and there is nothing you wouldn't do for one another.

Giving staff permission to take care of themselves

My gran used to say, 'You can't look after someone else if you don't look after yourself.' Self-care is not something Harrowgate Hill staff were very good at. This was not through any fault of their own; they almost needed permission to see themselves as important. They needed to look after themselves and this had to be modelled by someone who was going to look after them too.

A successful and sustainable school is one where everyone works together for a common goal – the best for the children – and one where the team grows and develops. I needed a team that wanted to stay with us, not complete their NQT (newly qualified teacher) year and move on at the earliest opportunity. I wanted to create a workplace where everyone felt valued, appreciated, recognised, where they had opportunities for progression and development and, above all, that they were seen as valued individuals – all vital to our school's journey. I wanted every member of staff to know and believe that, at Harrowgate Hill, they were trusted and their contribution to the school, including their workload, wellbeing and mental health, was recognised.

Recognition and appreciation

In the first phase of implementing a culture of wellbeing and mental health, I began with simultaneous recognition and appreciation, together with workload reduction. Recognising and appreciating staff may seem an obvious and relatively small step to take but at Harrowgate Hill it was vital. One of my key phrases has always been, 'It only takes a second to say, "Thank you".' This is how it began. I always try and make a point of thanking people for what they do, large or small. Walking round, I notice a gorgeous display; I say, 'Thank you'. I notice a class walking nicely to assembly – you don't just acknowledge the children; you thank the teacher because they are the reason the class is behaving that way. The children tell me about a lesson they enjoyed. In the lunch hall, I make a point of finding the teacher and thanking them. You see lovely work in books during book monitoring; you make a point of thanking the teacher for their hard work organising such wonderful learning opportunities for the children. You get the idea. It doesn't matter how big or how small – say 'thank you'. It costs nothing and it means everything.

Staff and children 'shout-outs'

I then added the 'shout-out'. I would send whole-school emails entitled 'Shout-Out', saying thanks to an individual or year group or everyone for whatever it was that was being recognised: 'Shout-Out to Koala Class for the most amazing assembly', 'Shout-Out to Mrs XXXXX for an amazing Halloween display on the piano'. This grew and grew and now everyone sends shout-outs and amongst the boring admin emails, one entitled 'Shout-Out' brightens your day.

Anyone who knows staffrooms knows that the arrival of sweet treats is greeted with much delight. For the first year every Friday I would buy cakes, biscuits and chocolates for the staffroom for no other reason than to show my appreciation at the end of the week for everything they had done.

Workload reduction

In terms of workload reduction, we began small and grew. This wasn't just about doing less – it was about working smarter and remembering that no-one is superhuman. It is not a lack of commitment that means tasks are not completed by the end of the day – that's just how life is. Anyone who works in a school knows that the 'best laid plans' are rarely executed. You think you have time to do x, y and z and then there is a fire alarm; the broadband goes down; someone is absent; child A comes in upset and you spend time supporting them; you don't feel well; or, the most common, you had three things on your list and, by the end of the day, emails have added another three!

Email sending and receipt policy

Tired staff are not productive staff. I've lost count of the times I've not slept because I read a work email before bed and worried about it all night. Solution? Time restrictions on emails. No emails before 7:00 am or after 7:00 pm on weekdays, and no emails at all on weekends and holidays, unless urgent. Yes, we have had to do work on what 'urgent' means, but the system works. Four o'clock Fridays: initially I would round staff up and usher them out of the door as they trundled out with cases of books. Now most – but not all – people are out the door by 4:00 pm without piles of books to mark because *it's just how we do it now*.

There is a whole list of things we did in Year 1 and more in Year 2: marking reduction; changes to assessment to reduce duplication of tasks; review – and removal – of admin tasks; restructuring of the office to suit work needs; time given to staff to lead subjects or phases (you can't do more unless you're given more time); the creation of a wellbeing team and a wellbeing room; a report writing day and changes to INSET days; no planning; revamping of the appraisal process – I could go on and on.

Milestone 1: Spring 2019 onwards: Wellbeing door sheets

I had used wellbeing door sheets in previous schools. Once we were a term in and staff were starting to accept that their wellbeing and mental health really were important, we introduced the wellbeing sheets in a staff meeting. They are literally a laminated A4 sheet that has wellbeing written on it and two boxes. One says, 'Come in and see what we are doing'; the other box says, 'I would rather you left us alone today'. These were used on all classroom doors and staff could tick whichever box they preferred, and it was to be respected. No-one asks why the 'Leave us alone' box is ticked unless it remains ticked for a while, in which case I do a welfare check on the teacher to see if there is anything I can help with. Everyone has a bad day or a lesson that's gone wrong and you just want to be left alone – if this happens, tick the box. There were a million and one questions like, 'What if you were coming to do a drop in?' Simple – 'I will come another day!' The feedback from using the wellbeing door sheets has been very positive. Staff were beginning to trust that their feelings were valued.

Milestone 2: September 2018: Getting rid of formal planning

I introduced getting rid of formal planning during my first INSET and it was met with disbelief. I'm not saying people should turn up and just wing it; what I am saying is that spending hours writing down in detail what you plan to do is a waste of time. Planning should work for you. What we want is well-prepared lessons, with quality resources for the children. I would much rather the team spent time preparing the quality resources than writing stuff down. Staff create resources for the interactive whiteboard and activities for the children (which can all be saved and used again or adapted next year or by colleagues). They would be creating these resources anyway for their lesson – beyond this nothing else is needed. Every teacher knows that, however detailed a lesson plan you create, you are constantly changing and adapting it in a lesson, so it's pointless spending time writing it all down. Who are you doing it for? If you want key questions – put them on your slides! If you want to differentiate tasks, just do it – you don't need to write down that you're doing it! Do what is useful for you as a practitioner and best supports the children. Yes, I have staff who do still plan but it's personal preference, not a requirement. The feedback from staff on this has been very much that they feel trusted as professionals now to plan and organise their lessons without having to justify it by writing lesson plans.

Milestone 3: Spring/Summer 2019 onwards: Staff wellbeing group and the wellbeing room

Staff wellbeing group

Following the staff survey, which was presented to the governing body in December 2018, it was decided that a staff wellbeing group would be set up and that staff wellbeing would be a termly item on the agenda of governing body meetings. This was well-received; the wonderful people who work in our schools are our most valuable resource and we want them to be happy and fulfilled in the workplace. The wellbeing group was set up with representatives from across the different roles in school and feedback was gathered about tackling issues that would make a difference to them. The initial basics that everyone should feel appreciated and safe in the workplace were in place but there is more to staff wellbeing than the basics. Maslow's (1943) entire hierarchy needs to be fulfilled. Having a group of people to approach about wellbeing issues was great, as people don't always want to come directly to the head or deputy head.

Wellbeing room

One suggestion was for a 'space'. You may think there is lots of space in schools but that is not true. Apart from the toilet (and not even there sometimes!), there is no quiet place to have five minutes to yourself. The wellbeing room plan was hatched. Yes, it was a financial investment, but the governors were completely on board, as we set about turning what used to be a large stock cupboard into a wellbeing room. It is now a lovely place with a rug, sofa, cushions, music centre, coffee and hot chocolate machine, telephone, computer and a lava lamp. You can go in here and chill, make a private call to your doctor or even just book some concert tickets on the computer. You can go into the wellbeing room for a cry, to calm down or for whatever you like. It's not used as much as we would like it to be but that is part of the journey we are on to persuade staff that that they don't just address their wellbeing after the children have gone home. Recognising that wellbeing and mental health require a greater investment than just time was a very important truth for all of us.

Stability – good and bad

Some say a stable staff are a happy staff, but I don't buy into that. It can be both a good and bad thing. Yes, staff turnaround can be high because people don't like the working environment, but equally people can stay in a school because they don't have the confidence to apply elsewhere or feel they will not get a reference that reflects their skills. This is not just my personal opinion; it has been formed after conversations with colleagues over the years who have been in this position. Context is everything and, when I joined the school, Harrowgate Hill was one of those schools where stability was both good and bad. There was a large turnover of newly qualified teachers but there were also groups of staff who believed 'better the devil you know'. As resignation date approached towards the end of my first year at the school, I kept waiting for a reference request to pop up in my email or someone to tell me they were leaving but resignation day came and went. The only staff we were losing were those who had been covering maternity, as their counterparts had returned or were about to return. There had been SO MUCH change in my first year as head – I hoped all of it for the better. They ALL stayed. I remember the faces of the governing body when they realised no-one was leaving that first year – this was very unusual for Harrowgate Hill. Earlier in the year, I had shared with them the summary of the confidential staff survey we had completed, and they had been horrified to have so many unhappy staff. Now – and I am not saying everything was perfect because it wasn't – they were staying, and the staff governor was feeding back to the governing body the positive journey of change we were on.

I remember the first time we recruited for a teacher due to an internal promotion and we got 60 applications. The reputation of Harrowgate Hill was not just changing inside the building but outside too. The second time we recruited, following another maternity leave, we received 80+ applications. Recruitment was no longer a challenge.

Open-door: 'Can I have five?'

I remember when I first started, I talked about having an open-door policy. No-one came to see me. I walked around school to check on everyone. I might have seen red teary eyes as staff walked in, or overheard a conversation about a fall-out, or a bad day, or just because I wanted to say hello. Over time this changed, and now staff 'Can I have five (minutes)?' is a huge part of the day. My open door began with issues that I was delighted they were sharing with me and slowly became more of a pop-in for a chat. We have 'welfare meetings' which staff can request at any time or I may invite a colleague for a meeting if I think they need one. After the first few meetings, I began to receive requests for them which was wonderful! Those who had had a welfare meeting said they felt they had been 'listened to, helped and supported', so others came. We always tell staff that no matter if the door is closed or there is a meeting sign on the door, always knock if it's a safeguarding issue, as it takes priority. This should also apply to staff mental health and wellbeing. Worries, concerns, issues do not conveniently occur before and at the end of the working day. If staff need support or need to talk, the door, closed or not, is genuinely always open. Just because you can't see mental health in the same way as you can see a gushing wound or a broken leg, doesn't mean it doesn't need immediate attention. Stress is real and can be damaging to your body and mind. I can honestly say I have completed more stress risk assessments with staff at Harrowgate Hill than I have done in any other school I've worked in and I don't see this as a negative at all. I see this as a hugely positive step that things are continuing to change for the better. They are confident to tell me there is a problem and together we make a plan to address it. Yes, some things can be solved with a chat and a coffee, but other matters require more formal action and there is nothing wrong with that. People get ill and leave the profession because of stress and Burnout. But there is always something that can be done. Staff are now more confident to come and ask for help if they need it.

I'm not saying we have solved all our problems. I am not saying everything is rosy at Harrowgate Hill because it's not, but we are so much further down the line than we were two years ago. As I said at the beginning of the chapter, supporting wellbeing and the mental health of staff is not a one-off event that you tick off, it needs to be an embedded part of the whole-school ethos. We have gone from a school where people kept their heads down and their mouths shut, to one where we are beginning to be a work family. Yes, we are still a dysfunctional family in some ways (what family doesn't have some dysfunctional aspects?), but the vast majority of staff are on board and strive every day to work with us to make Harrowgate Hill an even more amazing place to work than it already is.

What's next?

So, what's next? Next is to continue to revamp processes to make everything as streamlined and purposeful as we can. We started a piece of work before lockdown on 'What we do and why we do it' and it is fascinating how many procedures there are in schools because, 'That's the way it's always been'. Time is precious and workloads have to be manageable. We are going to continue to address workload and issues raised by staff which increase it. We've done a lot already like changing our marking policy and timetable, but there are other suggestions of processes which staff find don't work well or are time-consuming that we will continue to address. As an example, we introduced a 'Trips and Visits Leader' role to one of our very experienced teaching assistants who has designated time to complete this. This took away a lot of admin for teaching staff. If it isn't working for them, we need to ask, 'What can we do to make it work?' Keep asking the questions. Don't ever feel that one survey reveals every issue. As your school changes, everything else is changing, including staff priorities. What staff may have felt was important two years ago has been addressed but that doesn't mean there are no more issues! Keep the lines of communication open.

We introduced release time for everyone who has an additional area of responsibility and we want to spend more time working with them on how to develop their skills of leadership, rather than them wading through management tasks. Nothing adversely affects wellbeing more than being asked to do something you have never done before or do not have the skills to do. Continuing professional development for all will continue to be a key part of our journey forward.

Holding to account and modelling positive behaviours have been a significant part of our work. The next step is to continue to support leaders in school to approach challenging conversations with staff, without resorting to the former climate of the school where people feel got at, under-appreciated or unsuccessful. There are ways to deliver messages and we will be completing work with leaders on developing their confidence in leading such conversations.

Supporting wellbeing and mental health is not and never should be an 'add on' – it is the backbone of what we should be doing day in and day out. At Harrowgate Hill, staff wellbeing has its own policy, its own committee, its own place on governing body agendas, and even its own room. It will remain a key section on the school's annual school development plan for as long as I remain headteacher and hopefully beyond.

Key strategies

- Staff wellbeing integral to the culture of the school.
- A new beginning.
- The building of trust.
- The importance of team building.
- Looking after the staff as a family.
- Giving staff permission to take care of themselves.
- 4 o'clock Fridays.
- Golden Time and assemblies on Friday afternoon so staff didn't have to take books home to mark.
- Shout-outs to staff and children.
- A range of measures to reduce workload.
- Email sending and receipt policy.
- Wellbeing door sheets.
- Getting rid of formal planning.
- Staff wellbeing group and the staff wellbeing room.
- Wellbeing a standing termly item on governing body agendas.
- Open-door policy: 'Can I have five (minutes)?'
- Welfare meetings for staff.
- Wellbeing a key section on the school development plan.

Part **3**

Secondary School Case Studies

22 Dartford Science and Technology College, Dartford, Kent

Happy staff, happy students

Mrs Debbie Ellis, Vice-Principal and Pastoral/Designated Safeguarding Lead

'... *the leadership team firmly believe that, if staff are mentally happy and physically healthy, they will be able to support students more effectively. If students see staff taking care of themselves, they will use adults as positive role models for their own self-care.*'

Overview

As the quotation from Debbie Ellis, vice-principal, emphasises, students' well-being and happiness at Dartford Science and Technology College (DSTC) depend on the mental and physical health of the staff. She emphasises that it is not only essential for staff to be physically and mentally well; they must be *seen* to be well by the students. Role-modelling wellbeing involves being open and honest and building trust with learners and colleagues. Support and collaboration are at the centre of the ongoing development of a wellbeing and mental health culture at DSTC.

Context

Dartford Science and Technology College is an 11–18 secondary school in Dartford, Kent. It is an all-girls school with the full range of ability. Its mixed post-16 provision is situated in an area with a number of grammar schools, reducing the number of more able students in its intake. The number of students requiring Special Educational Needs and Disability (SEND) support is broadly in line with the national average, with autistic spectrum condition and attention deficit hyperactivity disorder predominant. Mental health needs are increasing and, over the past two years, we have noticed an increase in students needing wider support in this area.

Culture of staff wellbeing and mental health

A culture of staff wellbeing and mental health is critical to the work we do. First, the senior leadership team (SLT) firmly believe that, if staff are mentally happy and physically healthy, they will be able to support students more effectively. If students see staff taking care of themselves, they will use adults as positive role models for their own self-care. Second, there are wider benefits for the school, such as a reduction in staff absence and therefore a decrease in the cost of using supply staff. Students also benefit from continuity in their teaching and learning.

Staff wellbeing coordination group

When appointed as vice-principal in 2018, I was asked to coordinate staff wellbeing and mental health, as the principal fully believed in the value of taking care of the staff. This was my passion too. I set up a staff wellbeing coordination group and asked if staff wanted to be involved. A number of key staff volunteered, namely, the assistant vice-principal, the deputy safeguarding lead, a mathematics newly qualified teacher, a member of the SEND team, the raising standards leader for Years 7 and 8, the SEND coordinator (SENCO), and two other teachers. The group meets informally as needed.

Overall responsibility for staff and student wellbeing

As vice-principal responsible for pastoral care, I have overall responsibility for staff and student wellbeing. I oversee a wellbeing team of staff volunteers that organises events and creates opportunities for staff to support one another. This includes events such as: 'Make your own Pizza and Prosecco', 'Christmas Yule Logs and Mulled Wine' and 'Curry & Cava', after school on different days of the week to maximise attendance. Events are voluntary, as some staff prefer to manage their work–life balance differently. Sometimes there is a small cost to cover ingredients.

Previously, DSTC had started to work on elements of staff wellbeing and mental health, but there was not an overall structure or strategic action plan. This is now being implemented over a three-year period.

Staff nominations

A staff 'shout-out' system allows every member of staff to nominate other members of DSTC, whether office-based or teaching-based for a staff 'shout out'. This is coordinated by the vice-principal and logged on the staff wellbeing noticeboard in the staffroom. A congratulations email is sent to the nominated member of staff. Staff have praised this system.

Staff mentions in bulletin and suggestion box

The weekly *Staff Bulletin* has a staff special mention section and a weekly quiz which has a chocolate prize each week. Staff participation in this has been excellent. In addition, there is a section for staff suggestions where we feedback from the staff suggestion box that is kept on reception for anyone to post ideas/comments anonymously if they wish.

Teaching, learning and feedback policy

A large aspect of workload for teaching staff is marking. DSTC consulted staff and a subsequent teaching, learning and feedback policy was written. The focus became effective feedback, not only to promote student progression, but also to create a manageable system for staff, where one detailed piece of marking is completed once or twice per term for individual students and whole-class feedback is given at other times. This has impacted significantly on improving staff work–life balance. The assistant vice-principal responsible for teaching and learning quality ensures this.

Staff consultation

Staff consultation is an integral part of the way in which DSTC works. When staff feel valued, the community is strengthened. Staff are actively consulted on a very wide range of aspects of DSTC life, including new and reviewed policies, procedures, data drops and reports (Table 22.1). After consultation and amendments are made, a morning briefing is only called if needed. All members of the SLT are responsible for this. It has been crucial that staff feel that their feedback has been used to make a difference. In our annual staff survey conducted by the assistant vice-principal responsible for engagement, staff stated that they feel consultation has improved year on year.

Timetabling: consultative process

The vice-principal responsible for curriculum coordinates the assessment, recording and reporting schedule and consults extensively on aspects of timetabling and curriculum development. Data drops were reviewed and were reduced from five/six to three per year group as a result of staff consultation and use of government guidelines. Staff have said they appreciate this, as there is less data to enter, and the focus on accuracy has increased. The vice-principal for curriculum also works with directors of learning when constructing the timetable, allowing them a greater voice in ownership of the timetable in their faculties. This creates a sense of collegiality and leads to a sense of teamwork and wellbeing.

Cover for absences

Two cover supervisors are employed at DSTC to take the pressure off teachers covering colleagues due to sickness and planned absence. This allows teachers

Table 22.1   DSTC wellbeing survey results, May 2020 (Increase: % difference from 2018)

	Agree	Disagree	Increase (%)
Staff Wellbeing			
I know what is expected of me when I am at school	98	1.7	3
I have the resources and equipment I need to do my job effectively	82	17.0	15
I feel safe in school	93	6.8	2
There is someone at work who seems to care about me as a person	98	1.7	4
Staff behave positively at school	96	3.4	18
There is someone at school who encourages my professional development	82	17.0	10
I have opportunities to express myself in school	88	11.9	9
I generally enjoy my work at DSTC	98	1.7	3
I am doing well at my work	98	1.7	7
I can manage my workload	86	13.6	4
I know what to do if I feel anxious or stressed at school	84	15.3	4
I feel like my achievements are acknowledged	81	18.8	16
I feel like I have a responsibility in helping the school achieve its aims (Vision/College Development)	96	3.4	13
I have a chance to use my strengths and abilities at work	89	10.2	4

to plan the use of their non-contact times with the 'rarely used to cover' initiative. Staff have appreciated this as it allows a focus on teaching and learning, feedback and planning.

Professional development

Continuing professional development (CPD), led by the assistant vice-principal responsible for teaching and learning, is a vital part of the staff wellbeing strategy at DSTC. Staff feel valued if they are invested in, impacting positively on students. CPD can be either internal or external to DSTC, often with current staff sharing their expertise. During the recent Covid-19 pandemic, staff completed a range of online courses, ranging from prevent and safeguarding to mental health, SEND, autism awareness, direct instruction, and thinking hard strategies – to name but a few. The assistant vice-principal reviews the impact of CPD on staff annually with the SLT. She also leads a thorough new staff induction programme, together with the site manager and myself.

INSET linked to development plan

The principal ensures that in-service training (INSET) days link directly to the college development plan, but elements of choice are given to staff. This aids staff ownership and buy-in. Three days are dedicated to staff training at the start of the academic year, prior to students arriving. Faculty time is also built in so that directors of learning and raising standards leaders are able to train their teams effectively. Giving staff time to improve is important. DSTC has supported staff in gaining the SENCO qualification, National Professional Qualification for Senior Leadership (NPQSL) and masters degrees. Staff development is crucial at every stage of a member of staff's career. Two days' worth of INSET time are given to staff to improve teaching and learning. These sessions are directed by the directors of learning. This gives staff the time to complete interventions or subject-specific CPD. Staff morale is raised when we break up two days before most schools in the area in July!

Initial teacher training and newly qualified teachers

Staff undertaking initial teacher training and newly qualified teachers are ably supported by the assistant vice-principal responsible for teaching and learning and a thorough programme of development is in place (also opened up to other teachers who feel they would benefit). Feedback regarding the assistant vice-principal's support has been incredibly positive.

Mental health training

DSTC has invested in a number of staff being 'mental health'-trained and a member of staff holds a teaching and learning responsibility post for this area of development. This has raised the profile of mental health and wellbeing in recent years, as opposed to just physical health. Through a positive mental health culture, staff attitudes towards some students that suffer in this area have changed for the better.

Health and safety

Health and safety at DSTC are fundamental to ensuring an effective working environment. The business manager has strategic responsibility for this, and both teaching and non-teaching staff are part of the Health and Safety Committee, together with governors.

Open-door policy

The SLT operates an 'open-door' policy which enables staff to speak to someone if they need to. This could be linked to a minor issue or something they feel strongly about. This enables every member of staff to feel a valued member of the DSTC community. It also gives the SLT an opportunity to deal with issues that are causing staff to be concerned at an earlier stage. Staff are also aware that DSTC has invested in counselling if they feel they need it either through the charity Education Support or the Kent County Council Support Line. This information is published in the staffroom and then I share it with staff during their safeguarding/induction training.

Work–life balance

Modelling an effective 'work–life balance' is key to supporting staff mental wellbeing. It is not frowned upon by the SLT if staff leave immediately after school. Staff complete their work to the best of their ability in the setting that suits them. This could be at home or at school. DSTC is open late due to lettings until 10:00 p.m. every night. Staff are welcome to stay, but few do. The SLT endeavours to model a positive and healthy work–life balance themselves.

Covid-19 pandemic and whole-school collegiality

During the current Covid-19 pandemic, staff wellbeing has been at the forefront of the SLT's thinking. Every member of staff received a wellbeing phone call from a member of the SLT. This was welcomed by staff: one member of staff successfully nominated DSTC for the Teach Well Alliance Teach Well School Gold Award: Covid-19 Pandemic for looking after the mental health of staff and students during the pandemic. A successful virtual afternoon tea was led by the assistant vice-principal responsible for engagement via Google Meet with no set agenda. This allowed staff to offload and speak to each other. Both teaching and non-teaching staff attended. All virtual meetings have staff wellbeing as standing 'Item 1' on the agenda. Staff can see and feel that they are cared for.

During the pandemic, whole-staff collegiality was seen when a member of staff asked to organise a wellbeing message for students. An animation was published (https://animoto.com/play/ovPCafPoWe6y12b3PsDgXw) and was incredibly well received by parents and students:

'Lovely video! XXXX really misses school, she can't wait to go back. Thank you, DSTC staff, for thinking of us. Stay safe. SA (XXX's mum)'

'This is brilliant! Thank you so much! KN'

Staff wellbeing pack

Led by the assistant vice-principal responsible for teaching and learning during Mental Health Awareness Week (18–24 May 2020), all staff – teaching, support and office staff – were posted a wellbeing pack from the senior leadership team. Staff responses included:

'It was so lovely to know you were thinking of us. I thought the staff wellbeing phone call was a great idea, but this was so different …'

'It arrived yesterday – I thought it was something I'd ordered on Amazon … I cried when I opened the envelope …'

As a result of investing in staff wellbeing, DSTC is a fantastic place to work with ever-increasing retention rates. In fact, members of staff have left and then returned!

The DSTC culture is still evolving, with staff and student wellbeing at its heart.

Key strategies

- Culture of staff wellbeing and mental health.
- Staff wellbeing coordination group.
- Vice-principal responsible for pastoral care oversees staff and student wellbeing.
- Staff nominations.
- Teaching, learning and feedback policy.
- Staff consultation.
- Timetabling a consultative process.
- Absence cover.
- Continuing professional development.
- INSET linked to development plan.
- Support for initial teacher training trainees and newly qualified teachers.
- Mental health training.
- Health and safety includes mental health.
- Open-door policy.
- Work–life balance.
- Covid-19 pandemic support.

23 Queen Mary's Grammar School, Walsall, West Midlands

Mental health is everyone's concern

Sophie McPhee, Wellbeing PSHE Coordinator and Change Your Mind Programme Director

Headteacher: Richard Langton

'Measures introduced to help student wellbeing have had an inevitably positive effect on staff too ...'

Overview

Sophie McPhee, PSHE Coordinator, summarises how Queen Mary's Grammar School's approach to whole-school wellbeing ensures that staff and student wellbeing are interlinked.

Context

Queen Mary's Grammar School (QMGS) is an Ofsted-outstanding selective boys' school which is co-educational in the sixth form and has 1089 pupils on roll. It is in Walsall, an industrial town, eight miles north-west of Birmingham. In 2018, QMGS became a founder member of the Mercian Multi-Academy Trust, along with four other Walsall schools, following single academy conversion in 2011. The four pillars of QMGS are 'Academic in Purpose', 'International in Outlook', 'Generous in Approach' and 'Enterprising in Spirit', and life at the school reflects these characteristics equally, along with adherence to the QMGS Pastoral Charter. Some pupils travel to the school from as far afield as Derby, which is 36 miles away. The school motto is *Quas dederis solas semper habebis opes*: 'It is what you give that you will keep as eternal riches'.

The then deputy head, Richard Langton, made it a whole-school priority in 2016 to address the issue of rising mental health problems. The issue was being reported more and more nationally, and our school was no exception, putting additional pressure on our hard-working pastoral team. Initially, Mr Langton formed a staff working party, which discussed ideas and visited other schools to see the work they were doing. Some of us had had experience of mental health problems within our own families and this drove us to action. Mr Langton also initiated a school-wide mental health survey to assess the level of need. Since 2016 we have done a lot to implement a culture of student wellbeing:

Key strategies

- Held an annual **Mental Health Week** with a range of events, to coincide with Children's Mental Health Week in February. In 2019, these events spanned a full fortnight.
- **Incorporated lessons on mental health into the Key Stages 3 and 4 PSHE Scheme of Work** on such topics as 'the anti-depressant lifestyle', neuroplasticity and thinking patterns, mindfulness and gratitude, mental health problems, bereavement, anger and stress management. We held workshops on Key Stage 4 PHSE 'drop-down days' and ran school-wide year assemblies and form periods on themes such as happiness. We are also starting to introduce mental health lessons into Year 12.
- Set up our **Change Your Mind programme**, a year-long programme whereby Year 12 plan and deliver mental health and wellbeing workshops to Year 6 classes in Walsall on themes such as 'Transition' and 'Digital Detoxing'. Over the past four years, this project has grown considerably, and is now being set up in secondary schools across the country. Please visit https://qmgschangeyourmind.wordpress.com/ to find out more.
- **Appointed additional staff to the pastoral team**: two pastoral assistants, an assistant head with responsibility for pupil wellbeing, an additional Key Stage 4 head of year, a safeguarding and welfare officer, and an additional social, emotional and mental health mentor. We are also converting part of our school into a 'Welfare Hub'.
- Established a **QMGS Wellbeing Group**, which organises various projects and events, such as a mindful colouring club and a tea-tasting club. We also visit a local care home on a monthly basis.
- Established '**Rainbow Soc**', our school's LGBT group.
- **Removed end-of-year examinations** for Years 7 and 8.
- Established a **Year 7 Nurture Group** for those struggling with the transition to secondary school.
- Introduced a **Key Stage 3 optional extension work booklet and removed rigid homework timetables**.
- **Invited to school mental health organisations such as Child Adolescent and Mental Health Services (CAMHS) and Time to Change** to train pupils on how to support friends with mental health problems, or to preserve their own mental health.

Mental health is for everyone

One of our challenges is making sure pupils realise that mental health education isn't just for those who already have a mental health issue – it is designed to give guidance not only on how to support others, but also on how to achieve optimum wellbeing in order to live 'life to the full', another of our school's mottos, and to prevent mental ill-health developing. No-one can say with certainty they will never suffer from mental ill-health.

There is no doubt that, during the four years since our work started, mental health awareness has been embedded as part of our school's culture. Pupils are being given far more ideas now on how to look after their mental health – that is, a preventative approach, rather than a reactive one. There have been many ways in which staff wellbeing has also been supported, from reducing the length of meetings and word counts for subject reports, to training from Time to Change and a mindfulness teacher.

Student wellbeing and staff wellbeing: Two sides of the same coin

Measures introduced to help student wellbeing have had an inevitably positive effect on staff too, from an increased number of pastoral staff spreading workload, to a reduced number of end-of-year exams easing the amount of marking. As a school, we have had local and national attention for our work, which features in the book *Just Great Teaching* by Ross Morrison-McGill, published in September 2019.

If you are considering implementing a culture of student wellbeing in your school, my advice is not to be under the impression that mental health education can be adequately covered by assemblies, or by non-specialist PSHE teachers. It needs curriculum time, and staff – notably, the headteacher – passionate about the cause.

24 Sir Frederick Gibberd College, Harlow, Essex

Looking after school wellbeing

Dee Conlon, Headteacher

'Students need role models; they need to be inspired and encouraged, recognised and celebrated for their achievements and successes, both in and out of school. How can we hope to achieve this without the staff who stand in front of them feeling the same way? Our Gibberdians cannot thrive without the support of all staff at SFG, and we cannot expect our staff to provide that support if we don't look after their own wellbeing and mental health.'

Overview

Dee Conlon, headteacher at Sir Frederick Gibberd, explains the importance of ensuring a culture of staff wellbeing and mental health for both staff and students is at the core of her new school.

Context

Sir Frederick Gibberd College (SFG) is a brand-new secondary school in Harlow, Essex and is part of the Burnt Mill Academy Trust (BMAT). We currently have 120 Year 7 students and 120 Year 8 pupils. We will grow year on year, eventually having a full cohort of 1700. We are dedicated to the welfare of our students, with a specific focus on academic excellence. As a comprehensive school, the ability range of our students varies. Our Special Educational Needs and Disability (SEND) cohort includes students with physical, social and emotional needs and we have a mixed intake of boys and girls.

The school is located within a large town with a significant proportion of social housing. At present, we have 20% of children on free school meals, 29% of children designated as Pupil Premium, and 12.5% of students with English as an additional language. In our first year of opening, we had 13 staff employed at SFG: ten teaching staff, two support staff and one administrative employee. This year (2020/21) we employ a total of 24 staff.

Academic excellence is at the heart of everything that we do at SFG and we know that, for our students to be academically successful, we have to look after their mental health and wellbeing. We work hard to keep our children both physically and mentally healthy.

Culture of staff wellbeing

However, we know that we cannot do this successfully without providing the same culture for our staff. In the early developmental stages of our wonderful new school, a member of staff was appointed to oversee the welfare of our staff – someone from within the Trust who understands how to support and develop adults in our organisation. This has enabled us to promote a positive ethos in our school where our staff are confident in approaching us with their concerns, both school-related and personal. Within the first term, we were able to organise continuing professional development (CPD) for staff, arrange coffee mornings with the head for every member of staff, and regularly provide praise and thanks for the endless hard work of our committed SFG family. This is evident in all aspects of school life: from timetabling, to marking policies, to behaviour policies. Staff feel safe and well-supported in our school community.

Creating a caring community

As headteacher, I knew that I didn't want SFG to be just another school; I wanted to create a community. Our staff, students and parents/carers understand this vision and help to make this a reality every day. Students need role models; they need to be inspired and encouraged, recognised and celebrated for their achievements and successes, both in and out of school. How can we hope to achieve this without the staff who stand in front of them feeling the same way? Our Gibberdians cannot thrive without the support of all staff at SFG, and we cannot expect our staff to provide that support if we don't look after their own wellbeing and mental health.

Staff development

In order to launch the concept of staff wellbeing and mental health as a holistic overview, we first focused on completing more detailed CPD where we continued to encourage staff to use the resources and support on offer whenever they needed. We focused on removing the negative connotations associated with mental health and encouraged staff to think of it as we think of our physical health. We also completed workshops with the students in school and a workshop with parents, to ensure that staff knew how to access support for themselves, for their colleagues and also for our wonderful Gibberdians. We regularly send emails to staff with links to support networks as well as offering support in-house – this is both from SFG and the Academy Trust. We celebrate staff successes and achievements on behalf of our young people, but we also encourage staff to leave early when they can and take time to look after their own wellbeing.

Every Wednesday afternoon is devoted to whole-staff development. Our students leave early, so this is offered to staff during school time. By developing staff, we are empowering and equipping them with the tools to refine their skills and improve their teaching practice. This ensures confidence and greater subject knowledge, as well as wider professional knowledge.

The specific professional development that staff complete in relation to wellbeing and mental health focuses on recognising signs and supporting students but is largely related to supporting their own mental health. We ensure that tools are provided to equip staff to focus on and look after their own mental health, whilst also ensuring that the support network that SFG provides takes care of our staff. Following this CPD, staff have been more open with us about their concerns and wellbeing, and it has also created a more supportive network for colleagues to look after each other.

Every member of staff has been allocated a mentor and has fortnightly time-tabled meetings to focus on their professional development and wellbeing. This also provides opportunities for staff to contribute to the school development plan, ensuring that all staff take ownership of the vision of the school and feel part of the SFG community.

Staff workload

Prior to opening, care and attention were given to staff workload to ensure that a healthy work–life balance could be maintained in order to support staff wellbeing and mental health. This has been in place since opening in September 2019. We have ensured that staff allocations include duties to avoid additional pressure on staff. We have also worked tirelessly on the curriculum to ensure live marking is effective. We only mark assessments; no other marking is required, so that it does not impinge on personal time. Our behaviour policy ensures that senior leaders support staff as much as possible. All detentions are carried out by the pastoral team. Staff are not expected to organise and run their own detentions, reducing their workload.

Teach Well Alliance Teach Well School Gold Award: Covid-19 Pandemic

Throughout the Covid-19 pandemic, we have ensured that staff wellbeing and mental health are at the forefront of our working lives. We were awarded the Teach Well School Gold Award from the Teach Well Alliance in April 2020 for the support we provided to our staff throughout the Covid-19 lockdown. We called staff every week to check in on them, offering help; whether talking on the phone, sending care packages or collecting shopping for those who are isolating. We held team virtual chats to keep in touch and started a weekly staff quiz with prizes for winners.

Staff morale

There has been a significant impact on staff morale as a result of the measures we have put in place and the work we continue to do on staff wellbeing. We have a collective mindset where we are all willing to help and support one another. On occasions where we have staff off-site for the day, everyone is willing to help out, including offering to cover lessons and duties before even being asked. Even non-teaching members of the team step in to support both staff and students. The positive staff network that we have created is evident to the students and parents of our community and helps to create a positive environment for all stakeholders.

Recruitment has been very successful, with prospective new staff excited to be involved in such a wonderful school environment. Governors, Trust staff, external agencies and prospective new students have also commented on the feeling of community when visiting SFG. The happiness of our staff and students is evident for everyone to see. We are a warm and welcoming school because of the positive wellbeing felt by all those who are a part of it.

During a monitoring visit in term one, the 'close knit group of staff' was acknowledged, as well as the positive relationships built between staff and students and parents/carers. In order for the school to be effective, and for students to thrive and succeed, everyone must be happy, respected and be able to develop both personally and professionally. We are role models as well as educators, and we all contribute to developing our students into young adults who are successful and prepared for the constantly changing modern world. We are ambitious and hard-working, but we respect, appreciate and value all of our staff and their input into our young people's lives.

Staff morale at SFG is high. In our surveys, staff state how happy they are to be working at SFG and how much they are enjoying being part of the team:

'We have a great leadership within our school and [they] understand individual teachers' needs' (teacher, November 2019).

'All staff are respected and valued no matter what their job title is and students know this, so they respect all adults. I know who to go to if I have a problem and I really feel I am being listened to' (member of non-teaching staff, November 2019).

The rate of absence among staff is very low, none of our permanent staff are leaving us at the end of the academic year 2019/20, and we have a full complement of staff recruited for 2020/21.

Full reopening and addressing the impact of Covid-19 on the school community

Our next step during Covid-19 was to ensure that, when staff returned in September 2020, it was safe for them to do so and that they were supported. We know the pandemic is having an impact on all our lives and our mental wellbeing. We did not go straight back to teaching but organised and ran workshops to address the impact of living and teaching during the outbreak. This was crucial for all staff and students so that they could readjust and settle back into a routine.

Senior leaders received training on how to deal with trauma, loss and grief so that they could better support the children and the adults in our school. We also arranged de-escalation training for all staff. This was to ensure our staff slow down, create space, and use communication techniques to defuse potentially risky situations. The impact of this on staff wellbeing was to lower stress and anxiety levels in their lives both within and outside of school. In order to reduce teacher workload, we will continue to implement online assessments, live marking strategies, collaborate with other schools and share resources.

Reading is a great way of escaping and relaxing. I am an advocate of reading for pleasure and regularly share good reads and gift books or book tokens with staff. We plan to establish a mini-library in the staffroom for everyone to share their favourite novels or recommendations when we move to our permanent site. In my September welcome packs, I gifted everyone a book and, prior to staff returning, sent them Amazon vouchers which many used to purchase books. We also know the positive effect exercise has on individuals both physically and mentally. We intend to organise weekly classes for our staff and encourage them to exercise regularly, as soon as DfE guidance and risk assessments allow us to do so.

Finally, and most importantly, we constantly review all of our practices and ensure we only implement initiatives that are worthwhile and meaningful. This means our teachers have the time to plan and deliver outstanding lessons, enjoy teaching, and develop into exceptional professionals. Similarly, our non-teaching staff are able to provide the best support possible so we can all work as a team and make a difference to the lives of the young people in our care. #TeamSFG #DreamSFG

[Ed: In July 2019, Dee Conlon was awarded joint first place in the Teach Well Alliance 'Headteacher's Award for Outstanding Contribution to Staff Wellbeing and Mental Health 2019/20'. She was nominated for the Award without her knowledge by the staff at Sir Frederick Gibberd College.]

Key strategies

- Developing a culture of staff wellbeing.
- Creating a caring, supportive school community.
- Staff development, including mental health.
- Teach Well Alliance Teach Well School Gold Award: Covid-19 Pandemic.

- Tackling workload.
- Maintaining high morale.
- Amazon vouchers sent to staff in August 2020.
- Welcome gift pack for staff on returning to school in September 2020.
- Full re-opening – addressed the impact of Covid-19 on the school community and provided training on how to deal with trauma, loss and grief.

25 John Taylor Free School, Tattenhill, Burton-on-Trent

Succeed and thrive

Sue Plant, Headteacher

'Coaching is for everyone, not only for those who need support. I firmly believe that a coaching approach develops everyone and at every level. It creates a climate where people ask better questions, listen more effectively and are far more reflective in their work. Coaching leads to staff being open and honest when they make mistakes (and we all make them) or when they don't succeed. It prevents staff trying to cover up an error or misjudgement; they know that they will be supported to move forward and learn in the process. This cannot be achieved in a climate of fear and distrust. We are an open group of people who are prepared to share with each other, celebrate success and help each other when it is needed.'

Overview

Headteacher Sue Plant describes how the values, vision and culture of John Taylor Free School are integrated with the wellbeing of both staff and students. Education and personal development for students are mirrored in the way staff are nurtured, encouraged and supported to develop themselves both personally and professionally.

Context

John Taylor Free School (JTFS) is a new school which opened in September 2018 to 210 Year 7 students. It has been part of long-term place planning for Burton-on-Trent, Staffordshire, as a result of the changing demographic and increase in house building at Branston Locks, near Tatenhill. It is a partner school in the John Taylor Multi-Academy Trust, a family of 14 schools in the West Midlands. The vision statement for the Trust is:

'We believe in the power of education to change lives – and the world.'

The school did not have a catchment for the first two years. As the housing developments were late in starting, the school's first intake came from a wide geographical area, including 47 primary schools. In 2019, JTFS welcomed a further 240 students; it will grow year-on-year until it reaches its capacity of 1550 students, including provision for Pupil Premium students. It have been over-subscribed for the first three years of opening.

As a new school, we are in the fortunate position of being able to create systems and structures which support the culture of the school and which are based on our values to 'succeed and thrive'. We aim to achieve academic success for each student and to ensure that they become confident learners. We also strive to ensure that staff develop their professional expertise and reach the highest possible standards they can. We want everyone in our community to thrive as people: to develop kindness, respect and trust, and to contribute to a happy and healthy environment.

Staff recruitment

Without the right staff in place, we would not achieve our aims. I learned much from reading about the work of headteacher Hannah Wilson as she set up Aureus School in Didcot a year earlier. After speaking to Hannah and following her on social media, I knew that a values-led recruitment process, with flexible working front and centre, would enable me to secure high-quality staff who support the educational principles we are committed to developing at John Taylor Free School.

The first step in the process is an open recruitment event where I describe our culture, ethos and key operational features to attract applicants who agree with our ethos. I regularly write a blog and the school has a news feed which includes articles about what life is like in our school. I strongly encourage prospective applicants to read as much as they can about me and the school. I want them to understand how we work, to know what is important to us, and to buy into the expectations of all staff. I also make it clear that applications are welcome from people who want to work flexibly. This offer is open and up front – applicants are clear that they can raise flexible working in their applications and at interview. In their application, they can explain how flexible working will support them as professionals and contribute to the life of the school. This is discussed during the day, not as part of the assessment process, but so that we can understand how we might make it work for the right candidate. It supports future conversations if a candidate is successful.

Interview process

The interview process is also values-led. We explore values throughout the day and triangulate across different activities. We also ask about whether the day is a fair process. Our aim in encouraging feedback is to ensure that we create an interview process that allows colleagues to show what they can do, rather than what they can't.

Our interview process ensures that we appoint people who are not only talented in their field but also aligned to our vision and values. Values alignment is critical to ensure that our staff are happy and to avoid discordance between individual members of staff. When vision and values are aligned, staff are more likely to feel happy at work and that they can discuss an issue before it turns into a problem.

So far, we have had a great response to recruitment. In the first year, we had 400 people attend the open day and 160+ applications for 12 jobs across all subjects. In the second and third years of recruitment, we have had similar numbers for our recruitment event, and this has transferred to 200+ applications for teaching and support roles. We receive multiple applications for all subjects, including those typically hard to recruit, such as maths and science. In year two, we had similar numbers at the event and 200 applications for teaching and support roles. Feedback from the interview process is that colleagues have found it a great source of continuing professional development – there is always a vibrant atmosphere in the 'green room' with lively discussion and debate between candidates.

Professional learning

'Succeed and thrive' is for adults too. We want our staff to be able to continue learning and develop as professionals. For teachers and leaders to do this effectively, they need time. I decided very soon after I was appointed that I would create time for staff to read, learn, research and coach each other to success. Teachers have two hours each week to plan collaboratively, use the latest research pieces to inform their practice, and take part in coaching conversations. We have found that this supports a positive approach to wellbeing because of the investment we are making in each and every member of staff.

Coaching

Coaching is for everyone, not only for those who need support. I firmly believe that a coaching approach develops everyone and at every level. It creates a climate where people ask better questions, listen more effectively and are far more reflective in their work. Coaching leads to staff being open and honest when they make mistakes (and we all make them) or when they don't succeed. It prevents staff trying to cover up an error or misjudgement; they know that they will be supported to move forward and learn in the process. This cannot be achieved in a climate of fear and distrust. We are an open group of people who are prepared to share with each other, celebrate success and help each other when it is needed.

Professional review, not performance management

Other schools call it 'performance management'. For me, that is a very negative phrase. 'Professional review' describes exactly what we do: we review ourselves as professionals participating in a trusting and respectful dialogue, supported by evidence we collect ourselves which we believe showcases our very best practice. The questions/areas for discussion are shared in advance so that people can prepare their responses. Nothing is hidden or 'done to' someone. The review process is owned and driven by the reviewee. Targets are not data driven; they are related to professional growth, whether you are a newly qualified teacher, middle leader or teacher with 20+ years' experience. Professional review is used throughout the year to frame conversations and develop individuals. The process promotes positive mental health at work by giving teachers control and trusting them as professionals. We assume that every teacher wants to be a great teacher and we put support in place to enable this to happen.

Subject self-evaluation

I was asked at one of the open days, 'How often do you do book scrutinies?' My response was very simple: 'Isn't book scrutiny your job as the class teacher?' If we trust our teachers to do their jobs properly, we don't need to check up on them. Subject evaluations involve teachers being critically reflective of their own practice, by looking at themselves and others to see what works and what doesn't. Exploring what makes good practice in their subject specialism means that each member of the team aims to provide the best possible learning experience for young people in their care. Teachers are specialists in their field – they should be able to use research to inform their practice and apply it to our context at JTFS. Outcomes from school self-evaluation are shared between colleagues, enabling teachers to learn not only from other practitioners in their own subject but also from colleagues across the school.

Collaborative practice

We have created subject-based workspaces. Each subject team has a set of desks to work around to promote collaboration. Schemes of learning are planned together and saved on Microsoft SharePoint, which is available for everyone to access. No-one plans in isolation and no-one has to recreate the proverbial wheel. We aim to share and learn from each other, both within and between teams. Our curriculum is mapped on the wall so that everyone can see what others are teaching. 'Driving' questions frame the learning each half-term, which pull together the students' learning. Examples of 'driving' questions include 'How do we conquer terrain?', where students study landscape formation in geography, design an all-terrain vehicle in design and technology, and calculate dimensions in maths. We also investigate 'Does money make you rich?' and 'Who creates my image?' This means that staff talk to each other: geography teacher to maths teacher about grid references and coordinates; history teacher to English teacher about the Second World War; design technology teacher to PE teacher about movement. Talking is good: no-one is on their own, no-one is working in their classroom in isolation, and everyone can support each other to overcome challenges.

At lunchtime, everyone is expected to eat together in the restaurant with the students. This is partly to ensure that staff get away from their desks and have a proper meal, rather than sandwich in one hand and red pen in the other. It is also about role modelling for students how to sit, eat and talk together. It is about building relationships, enabling staff to have conversations with each other and the students in a less formal environment than the classroom. Staff tend to sit together, although some do sit with students, but you will see them talking and laughing together over a packed lunch, salad or school meal. This creates a wonderful family environment at mealtimes.

Relationships matter

We have a relationships-focused approach to school life. People matter, relationships matter. We invest in students and staff to have positive working relationships at all levels. When relationships are tested, we support people to move forward. We trust staff to do their jobs to the best of their ability. When mistakes happen, we rally round, roll our sleeves up and sort it out together. We don't have a 'wellbeing programme'. Having to do yoga with colleagues is not everyone's cup of tea! However, there is a staff walking netball team, a group who go to the pub on a Friday, a foodie group who road-test local restaurants, and a member of staff who is available for confidential 'off-loading' conversations. These initiatives have sprung up due to staff volunteering to run them and are supported by those who want to be involved, rather than because staff feel they have to participate. When staff who are parents have a nativity or special assembly they want to attend, we try and make sure they can. We use Office365 software to ensure that communication is freely available and at a time that is convenient for them. Some staff choose to be in work at 7:00 a.m. and leave at 4:00 p.m., others arrive at 8:30 a.m. after dropping children at nursery and leave at 4:30 p.m. for pick up and work again, once their little people are in bed.

What matters is that people are able to work effectively and can have a life, as well as work in a school.

Key strategies

- Recruitment: open days and value-led interviews.
- Professional learning.

- Coaching.
- Performance review, not performance management.
- Subject self-evaluation.
- Collaborative practice.
- Relationships matter.

26 Desborough College, Maidenhead, Berkshire

Wellbeing at Desborough College

Daniel Clawson, Assistant Principal and Wellbeing Lead

Headteacher: Maggie Callaghan

'During the last 12 months, following the appointment of our new principal in 2019, we have worked hard to begin to create a culture of wellbeing. Something more than a calendar of activities or words on a website, but an enduring commitment to all our staff – that we care deeply about how they feel about their work, their mental health, safety and ability to achieve a work–life balance.'

Overview

Daniel Clawson, wellbeing lead at Desborough College, describes how staff wellbeing sits within a framework agreed by the trustees and ratified in the 'Staff Wellbeing Charter' as an ongoing commitment to developing a whole-school culture of wellbeing and mental health.

Context

Desborough College is an all-boys secondary school, with a mixed sixth form, serving the communities of Maidenhead and surrounding areas. We operate as a single Academy Trust and currently have almost 1000 students on roll and over 100 staff. We have an established partnership with Radley College and are part of a sixth-form consortium with four local secondary schools.

Wellbeing – a standing item

The wellbeing and mental health of staff at Desborough College have never been in sharper focus than during the Covid-19 lockdown, and while planning for and looking ahead to full school re-opening. We have kept the welfare of our staff as a standing item on our agendas and risk assessments throughout the pandemic. It has been a golden thread throughout our strategy and our college's approach to working in unprecedented times. We were, therefore, delighted to achieve the Teach Well School Gold Award: Covid-19 Pandemic from the Teach Well Alliance for looking after the wellbeing of our staff.

A culture of wellbeing

The level of attention to staff wellbeing was an instinctive response. During the last 12 months, following the appointment of our new principal in 2019, we have worked hard to begin to create a culture of wellbeing. Something more than a calendar of activities or words on a website, but an enduring commitment to all our staff – that we care deeply about how they feel about their work, their mental health, safety and ability to achieve a work–life balance. We are acutely aware of the impact supporting their wellbeing can have, not only on our colleagues, but how it also affects our students' experiences of school, and the quality of learning they receive.

Staff wellbeing policy

Our work in this area started with a staff wellbeing policy, ratified by our trustees, ensuring we had a framework for our commitment, accountability and oversight, and a document which clearly set out leaders' roles and responsibilities. This was followed by our Staff Wellbeing Charter, which provides a more succinct overview of our promise to staff, whilst also outlining the practical steps taken to achieve our goal in this area (Figure 26.1).

We consider engagement with staff crucial in creating a wellbeing culture, and during the year we consult staff regularly via online surveys or working parties, to help us better understand wellbeing issues, and to plan our response and support. Our staff truly have a voice at Desborough, and their views matter, and so a great deal of time is spent surveying staff and analysing these results. Going further, we have recently engaged with a third party to provide a completely anonymous platform to gather staff feedback, where staff can tell us how they're feeling or ask questions, when it suits them; they no longer need to wait for the next wellbeing survey.

We have also made a number of successful attempts to support staff to achieve a better work–life balance, a mission critical issue identified by staff early in our journey, including: an email embargo in the evening; a going home checklist; termly 'out the door by 4' afternoons, which include an opportunity to take part in yoga; and more opportunities to socialise with staff, including staff breakfasts. During lockdown, we augmented our efforts with a weekly virtual happy hour and quiz, as well as a book club. Our yoga class also continued from home.

We believe it is important at this point to note that you can't force wellbeing on staff, and particularly with our 'out the door by 4' afternoons, the premise

Figure 26.1 Desborough College Staff Wellbeing Charter

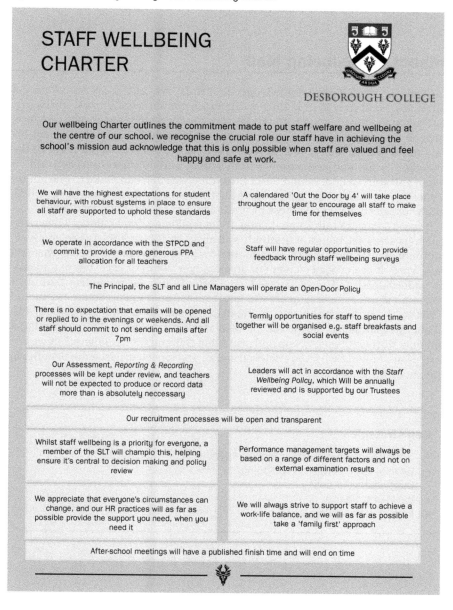

STAFF WELLBEING CHARTER

DESBOROUGH COLLEGE

Our wellbeing Charter outlines the commitment made to put staff welfare and wellbeing at the centre of our school. we recognise the crucial role our staff have in achieving the school's mission aud acknowledge that this is only possible when staff are valued and feel happy and safe at work.

We will have the highest expectations for student behaviour, with robust systems in place to ensure all staff are supported to uphold these standards

A calendared 'Out the Door by 4' will take place throughout the year to encourage all staff to make time for themselves

We operate in accordance with the STPCD and commit to provide a more generous PPA allocation for all teachers

Staff will have regular opportunities to provide feedback through staff wellbeing surveys

The Principal, the SLT and all Line Managers will operate an Open-Door Policy

There is no expectation that emails will be opened or replied to in the evenings or weekends. And all staff should commit to not sending emails after 7pm

Termly opportunities for staff to spend time together will be organised e.g. staff breakfasts and social events

Our Assessment, *Reporting & Recording* processes will be kept under review, and teachers will not be expected to produce or record data more than is absolutely neccessary

Leaders will act in accordance with the *Staff Wellbeing Policy*, which Will be annually reviewed and is supported by our Trustees

Our recruitment processes will be open and transparent

Whilst staff wellbeing is a priority for everyone, a member of the SLT will champio this, helping ensure it's central to decision making and policy review

Performance management targets will always be based on a range of different factors and not on external examination results

We appreciate that everyone's circumstances can change, and our HR practices will as far as possible provide the support you need, when you need it

We will always strive to support staff to achieve a work-life balance, and we will as far as possible take a 'family first' approach

After-school meetings will have a published finish time and will end on time

has always been promoting the opportunity to reclaim the time for yourself, and take part in self-care, rather than mandating a blanket early finish that might not suit everyone's situation or way of working. We recognise that no number of activities or initiatives will change a culture on their own, but the feedback from staff has been reassuring, and confirms that they feel more comfortable prioritising their wellbeing.

Impact of wellbeing lead

Early in our journey, we acknowledged that staff, over and above activities and initiatives, want to *believe* in their workplace's commitment to their wellbeing, and so having a wellbeing lead on the senior leadership team ensures we look through a consistent wellbeing lens when making decisions and planning for the future. The wellbeing lead, however, should not be the sole purveyor of the school's mission and commitment in this area, and an important step will be helping all staff to understand the contribution we each can make to one another's wellbeing. At Desborough, leaders at all levels operate an open-door policy, with transparency and openness promoted and exemplified by leadership.

It is very easy to talk romantically about wellbeing, particularly when tranquil yoga sessions, boxes of gratitude and an all-staff secret Santa are involved, but fundamentally we are talking about how people feel about themselves and their work. It is a crucial element of an employer's duty of care, but one so easily undervalued and unrecognised. At Desborough, we recognise that staff wellbeing is never simply 'achieved' but is rather an ongoing commitment and effort by the organisation, and an important layer of scrutiny to be applied to all actions and decisions. We have lots of work still to do, including forming a dynamic staff wellbeing group and providing training for managers, but we are very proud of what we have achieved so far, and can clearly see the benefits in and out of the classroom.

> **Key strategies**
> - Staff wellbeing on every meeting agenda.
> - Developing a culture of wellbeing.
> - Staff wellbeing policy.
> - Wellbeing Charter.
> - Impact of wellbeing lead.

27 The James Hornsby School, Basildon, Essex

Everybody matters, investment in staff is key – welcome to our family!

Daniel Steel, Headteacher

'*From my time working in a number of schools ranging from outstanding to those in serious weaknesses, the one thing I learnt very quickly is, for the students to get the best outcomes and experience, investment in staff development, well-being and mental health is absolutely essential. I believe it is imperative that teams of people need mechanisms of support before they hit breaking point and think about leaving our rewarding profession. On appointment at James Hornsby, there was a real opportunity to build on the foundations already in place.*'

Overview

Daniel Steel explains how he was able to build on the solid foundations of wellbeing that already existed at The James Hornsby School when he became headteacher. He cultivated a sense of openness and teamwork, encouraging staff to seek support when necessary. A survey was carried out to identify key issues, resulting in a focus on reducing workload and further development of the staff development programme. Staff socials became more frequent. A counselling service was provided, and staff were 'buddied' to provide support to one another. There are plans to introduce a Level 1 mental health qualification to increase staff awareness of the signs of mental ill-health.

Context

The James Hornsby School is an academy and is smaller than the average-sized 11–16 secondary school in Basildon, Essex. The school is situated approximately an hour from London and in the middle of a small council estate. We are a popular, oversubscribed school, with 930 students on roll from September 2020. There will be an increased intake in Year 7 from September

2020. The school is currently part of the Zenith Multi-Academy Trust which has been influential in turning the school round from being 'Requires Improvement' in 2014. The school is currently rated as 'Good' by Ofsted.

The proportion of pupils for whom the school receives the Pupil Premium is significantly above the national average. The proportion of pupils with a statement of Special Educational Needs (SEN) or an Education, Health and Care Plan (EHCP) is above average. There is equal parity of girls and boys currently on roll.

The school is built around a very strong family ethos. Our ultimate purpose as a school is to ignite hope, drive ambition and advance the life chances of everyone who is part of our family. We want our young people to gain the qualifications needed that will open the door of opportunity and develop the character to get them through.

The school currently consists of 160 committed employees; 90 are teachers and 70 are support staff.

I was appointed as headteacher at the school in September 2019. I spent much time researching my next career move having worked in a number of successful and challenging schools across London. Having visited the school as an external candidate prior to interview, what stood out for me was the 'family ethos' and the togetherness of the staff, which is a real credit to the Trust and my predecessor.

From my time working in a number of schools, ranging from outstanding to those in serious weaknesses, the one thing I learnt very quickly is, for the students to get the best outcomes and experience, investment in staff development, wellbeing and mental health is absolutely essential. I believe it is imperative that teams of people need mechanisms of support before they hit breaking point and think about leaving our rewarding profession.

On appointment at James Hornsby, there was a real opportunity to build on the foundations already in place. The school had a very good wellbeing and mental health strategy in place for the students. For example, the school has a very effective virtual tutoring system, through four colleges. In terms of staff wellbeing, I felt that there were pockets of good practice in the school such as 'Project Me', which was in place as part of staff directed time. At the end of every half-term, staff were encouraged to undertake wellbeing activities in small groups. Emails were discouraged after 6:00 pm daily. As the new headteacher, I wanted to build on this and make it stronger, for the reasons outlined above.

The number one priority of any school is to ensure the students gain good qualifications and improve their life chances. I am really keen that our school's core values are 'lived and breathed' and linked to our vision. It is imperative as the headteacher that the staff within the school are supported to be committed, work hard, have high expectations, and to be relentless and resilient for the students. I want a culture where staff are motivated and happy and will be able to go above and beyond for the students. As part of staff briefings, I often talk to the staff about being open and sharing their work. I want staff to feel comfortable talking to one another about areas of good practice or aspects of their teaching where they feel they need more guidance. I often talked to the staff in some of the early briefings about being together and working as a team. I discouraged the sending of numerous emails unless it was absolutely necessary. Where possible, it is really important that staff do not go home consuming their work and worry about the following day.

In my first few months as headteacher, I interviewed every member of staff – both teaching and support staff. I asked them three things: (1) what they thought was good about the school; (2) what they would improve; and (3) how well supported they felt in terms of professional development and their wellbeing. The reason for the last question was to ascertain what the levels of staff workload were like at the school.

One thing that was common amongst them all was a desire to make the school successful for the students. There was also a desire to make the 'family ethos' even stronger at the school by working together more as a school community, sharing good practice and supporting one another. Working alongside the leadership and human resources team we spent time unpicking, analysing and discussing the feedback. We undertook an exercise shortly after these interviews, whereby all members of the school were asked to re-visit the school values. Having the staff on the same page was extremely important to me.

This detailed feedback was used by the school leadership team to formulate a short-term development plan that would allow me, not only to get to know the school, but also support the staff to understand what the key priorities were. Staff wellbeing was a key part of this. I wanted from the outset an open culture, encouraging staff to work together in teams across the school to make an impact and real difference to the life chances of our students, but making this achievable in terms of work–life balance. I also really believed in the staff I inherited and wanted to increase their desire and motivation even more.

I also wanted to ensure that the plan was focused on not only outcomes for students but was considerate of staff wellbeing and their mental health, with this being part of the family ethos of the school. This has been achieved by implementing the following strategies:

1. An open-door culture from all members of the school leadership team including urgent out of hours. I wanted the staff to know that no matter how big or small an issue they were having, it could be discussed with a senior member of staff. This eradicated a number of emails being sent between staff and improved face-to-face professional discussions. To support this culture, all staff across the school are assigned to one of our colleges and encouraged to play a role in supporting and developing key aspects of the school. There are regular meetings within colleges to discuss any key issues that may arise within the school and community. This encourages staff to meet with colleagues outside of their faculty areas. The impact of this was clearly seen through the unfortunate time of Covid-19 when weekly competitions put together for students were also opened up to staff. Initiatives such as running, walking targeted distances, baking and quizzes were all designed to support wellbeing. We talk about what it means to be part of the 'James Hornsby family'. This is not tokenistic. The leadership team sit together weekly. We not only celebrate together but also solve problems together.

2. An overhaul and re-write of the staff development programme and creating more opportunities internally for career development. As part of this strategy, we were keen to run not only a whole-school development programme linked to our key priorities but a personal development plan for all staff. Although it is still in its early stages, staff feedback reassures us that our continuing professional development (CPD) offer has improved considerably over the past twelve months. The CPD offer is personalised and is open to all members of staff, not just teachers. We have also opened up staff research groups, where staff at all levels in the school can be involved in a particular school improvement initiative. This is totally optional. They are very well attended, and the feedback has been very good.

3. Where we could, we would create opportunities for internal promotion linked to the initial priorities in the school development plan. To date, over the past twelve months we have internally promoted 20 members of staff. A staff survey, conducted at Easter 2020, clearly highlights that staff feel they have more opportunities and are keen to apply for internal roles, not only to support the school but to enhance their careers. This, in turn, leads to better motivation and greater self-esteem.

4. A review and reduction of unnecessary workload, including numerous data deadlines. As a leadership team, we have reduced the number of unnecessary deadlines that have had no impact on student learning. We also regularly check the times staff sign in and out of school, not for accountability purposes but to check their work patterns. We now ensure all members of staff are off-site by 5:30 p.m., promoting work–life balance. Staff are consulted when needed about workload. A comment in a staff survey indicated that the school is led by all school leaders in a transparent way and that staff feel supported with these arrangements. As a senior leadership team, we look at the key pinch points of the school calendar. This is done to support staff workload by either rearranging or cancelling meetings, looking for opportunities to give staff extra personalised time to complete things such as planning and feedback.

5. With the support of the Trust, the introduction of a new counselling service. Our staff are entitled to counselling support through our private health care provider, Benedon. This was put in place to support the staff in not only dealing with professional matters, but also personal issues that may have happened outside of school that could impact on their attendance and workload.

6. Staff socials. We have also strategically placed staff socials at times in the school year when we felt they would contribute to wellbeing, such as at end of January. This has helped staff wellbeing during some of the more difficult times in the school year.

There has been noticeable impact as a result of implementing these strategies, as follows:

- A significant reduction in staff absence. This is tracked monthly and compared to previous years.
- For the first time in many years, the school is fully staffed in all significant areas.
- The number of staff leaving compared to the previous year is down significantly.
- Much better feedback from staff regarding the quality of professional development within the school.

Where next ...?

A lot of time has been spent on the school development plan for the next two academic years. Staff wellbeing and mental health play a significant part in future planning. Our induction programme is now fully based around our family ethos and we invite staff to be part of our family. Every new member of staff has a 'buddy' to support them, irrespective of their role. Like every other school it is a non-negotiable that every member of staff completes a Level 1 safeguarding qualification once a year. To go one step further, alongside this for September 2020, we will be asking all members of staff to complete a Level 1 mental health qualification. This is important so that staff understand the signs of mental ill-health for both students and adults.

Key strategies

- High standards, high support.
- Living and breathing core values, linked to vision.
- Sharing good practice and seeking advice.
- Open-door leadership team culture.
- Improving staff development, including more opportunities for internal promotion.
- Incorporating wellbeing and mental health in CPD.
- Review and reduction of workload.
- Introduction of counselling service.
- Staff socials.
- Looking ahead: buddy system, induction, Level 1 mental health qualification.

28 Rivermead Inclusive Trust, Gillingham, Kent

A whole-Trust approach to staff wellbeing and mental health

Paul Dadson, Strategic Lead for Teaching and Learning and Trust Wellbeing Lead

CEO of Rivermead Inclusive Trust:
Tina Lovey

'*My belief was that the relationship between pupil wellbeing and attainment is only part of the picture; if staff wellbeing and mental health are also taken care of, they will be able to teach at their very best and produce high-quality teaching and learning experiences for their pupils. Having been the headteacher of one of the schools within the Trust before my current role, one of the key strategies that I had used to move the school forward on its journey was to look after the wellbeing of staff. By putting staff wellbeing at the heart of the school, staff morale and commitment had noticeably improved.*'

Overview

Paul Dadson, the wellbeing lead of Rivermead Inclusive Trust, focuses on the importance of having a consistent culture of staff wellbeing across the Trust as well as in each individual school. The creation of a staff wellbeing group was a key strategy in achieving this goal, leading to improvements in the quality of teaching and learning across all the Trust's schools.

Context

The schools in the Rivermead Inclusive Trust include Hoo St. Werburgh Primary School, Walderslade Primary School, The Marlborough Centre, Rivermead Special Secondary School, Rivermead Routes for Reintegration (Triple R) and the Sixth Form Partnership.

The Rivermead Inclusive Trust comprises a range of diverse, yet highly inclusive schools, based across the Medway towns. Although we have six quite distinct provisions, they fall under three DfE numbers. We have two mainstream primary schools: Walderslade Primary and Hoo St. Werburgh Primary. Both of these schools have a fairly equal number of boys and girls and a mixed-ability intake. Walderslade is a one-form entry primary school (237 pupils) and Hoo is two-form entry (461 pupils) Attached to Hoo St. Werburgh Primary is The Marlborough Centre (64 pupils), which is an autistic provision catering for primary age pupils. We have one special secondary provision, Rivermead School (107 pupils), which caters for young people aged 11 to 19 years with a range of complex needs. Our specialism is in autistic spectrum disorders. Under the Rivermead umbrella is also our unique sixth-form partnership (58 pupils), which is run in conjunction with Mid Kent College and prepares pupils for the next step in their education and/or the workplace. We also have Rivermead Routes to Reintegration (Triple R – 39 pupils). Triple R is a social, emotional and mental health specialist school, a holistic and educational wraparound provision, with an experienced team, supporting secondary age learners in accessing education and finding their way back into a learning environment. Across all of our provisions, we have 966 pupils and 227 members of staff.

Pupil wellbeing, staff wellbeing, teaching and learning and attainment

On taking on the role of Trust wellbeing lead, as part of my wider responsibilities as strategic lead for teaching and learning, I was interested in exploring the links between the quality of teaching and learning within our schools and that of wellbeing. I began by reading a collaborative research report conducted in 2014 by the National Association for Headteachers and Public Health England: 'The link between pupil health and wellbeing and attainment: A briefing for head teachers, governors and staff in education settings'. I was struck by the potential for raising attainment by improving pupil wellbeing:

> 'Research evidence shows that education and health are closely linked; so, promoting the health and wellbeing of pupils and students within schools and colleges has the potential to improve their educational outcomes and their health and wellbeing outcomes.'

My belief was that the relationship between pupil wellbeing and attainment is only part of the picture; if staff wellbeing and mental health are also taken care of, they will be able to teach at their very best and produce high-quality teaching and learning experiences for their pupils. Having been the headteacher of one of the schools within the Trust before my current role, one of the key strategies that I had used to move the school forward on its journey was to look after the wellbeing of staff. By putting staff wellbeing at the heart of the school, staff morale and commitment had noticeably improved.

All of the schools within the Rivermead Inclusive Trust were implementing wellbeing initiatives and there were pockets of very good practice. However, the experiences and opportunities between schools were inconsistent, with some colleagues getting a 'better deal' than others. Although the Trust ethos supports school autonomy and promotes individuality, it was also important that staff experienced consistency of opportunity and personal and professional development. This became the starting point for the wellbeing group I established and the beginning of a Trust-wide journey to develop a 'wellbeing offer and charter' across all of our schools.

It was really important that we harnessed all of the effective staff wellbeing strategies that were taking place within our individual schools, refined them and enhanced what was already happening, rather than starting from scratch. This was key to ensure 'buy in' and ownership, rather than staff seeing it as a top-down initiative. It was also important that the wellbeing initiative was a collaboration of existing and new ideas. I was careful to avoid the impression that staff wellbeing comprised the initiatives I had promoted when headteacher of one of the Trust's schools.

As an inclusive Trust, we have a duty of care to each and every member of our school community. By implementing a culture of staff wellbeing and mental health, we aimed to promote a culture which matched our ethos. As our website explains:

> 'The idea behind forming a MAT [Multi-Academy Trust] was to allow us to build on our existing partnerships, work collaboratively and support schools to improve achievement, efficiency and the overall wellbeing of our learners, staff and wider communities.'

We recognised that, as recruiting teachers is a challenge, the best way to secure the highest quality staff at all levels, both now and in the future, was through 'growing our own' staff and that a culture of staff wellbeing and mental health was part of this growth. This was especially important because one of our Trust schools, Triple R, provides mental health services. We were clear that it would be incompatible with Trust values to support the mental health of some of the most vulnerable learners within our schools if we were not also safeguarding the mental health of staff across the Trust.

As well as growing our own staff through, for example, developing our teaching assistants to become teachers, and our teachers to become leaders of the future, we wanted to improve staff retention. By having our Trust Wellbeing Charter (Trust 30) clearly displayed on our website as our commitment to all staff, we were making a public commitment that this would be the minimum expectation of care that they would receive while working for the Trust (Figure 28.1).

We are driven by the belief that a happy and valued staff will produce the best results for our pupils and also support our schools and Trust to grow and develop. It is also most important that staff at every level are supported to perform to their maximum potential, whether they work directly with pupils (i.e. teachers and teaching assistants), or indirectly through roles such as reception staff or site staff. Our commitment reinforces the value and importance of all staff, not just our teaching staff. We also aimed to reduce staff Burnout.

Figure 28.1 Rivermead Inclusive Trust Wellbeing Charter: Trust 30

We also felt that in relation to future recruitment, a strong wellbeing commitment across our schools would mean that we would be recruiting staff who bought into our ethos of supporting their own wellbeing and mental wellbeing, as well as the wellbeing and mental health of their colleagues. It is very important to us that we recruit staff across the Trust who share our values.

The Wellbeing Group

The first step we took was to form a group of wellbeing champions across our schools who would take the lead. Our champions needed to be both passionate about the wellbeing of staff within their school and have the vision and capacity to influence whole-school and whole-Trust change. I aimed for a mix of experience and roles in the membership of the Wellbeing Group so that it was not senior leadership-driven and therefore a 'top heavy' group in relation to the demographic of each school. We deliberately ensured that the group comprised a range of members, including senior leaders, teachers and teaching assistants. I saw my role in supporting the group to influence change across the Trust. As the key Trust lead for wellbeing and a member of the core Trust team, I was able to influence the Trust's headteachers to ensure that they would implement what their wellbeing leads brought back into each school from the strategies decided by the Wellbeing Group. Having this buy-in from our headteachers allowed for maximum impact within each of our schools.

As chair of the Wellbeing Group, I was also acutely aware of the need to avoid the group just being a voice for Trust-wide strategies. For this reason, we made sure that, from the first of our six wellbeing group meetings each year, every member of the group had equal importance by giving them the opportunity to formulate the agenda and chair a meeting in rotation. This prevented a hierarchical structure, as well as reinforcing the message that members of the group were of equal stature.

The first action which the group took was to plan a wellbeing week as a high-profile event across the Trust. The event was to include, amongst many ideas: thank-you messages from the CEO, gifts delivered to staff, early finishing at the end of one school day and 'No Pen Day'. On No Pen Day, staff and pupils are not allowed to use pens of any sort. This means all activities are very practical and hands-on, and evaluation of work is carried out in imaginative ways. This could include, for example, oral feedback from peers, recording something visually with a camera or sound recording. Other activities undertaken during our wellbeing week included:

- Having fresh cut flowers in the staffroom and school reception areas.
- Giving staff the opportunity to get a head massage from the trainees at the local college – staff sign up on a rota and pay a donation.
- Encouraging staff to put positive comments on the staff shout-out boards which all of our schools display.
- Cakes and drinks delivered by the senior leadership team to staff on a set day.
- All after-school meetings cancelled for the week.

Wellbeing week enabled quick high-profile wins and allowed the group to see the immediate impact on staff of promoting their wellbeing. Using the success of the staff wellbeing week as a launch pad, we then began to work on longer-term projects that the group had identified:

1. Our wellbeing timeline: Getting everyone on board – September 2018. It was really important that we had everyone within our schools on board with what we were trying to achieve. The Wellbeing Group gave us buy-in from each of our schools and also facilitated influence and impact from each of our locations, as well as reinforcing Trust-wide consistency.

2. Achieving short-term wins: September 18 onwards. The Wellbeing Group felt that it was important to achieve short-term wins which would demonstrate the immediate impact of the group and quickly show tangible results. We decided to organise two wellbeing weeks during the year in which a number of wellbeing initiatives took place, such as providing cakes, thank-you notes, massages, wellbeing days and speakers delivering supportive wellbeing strategies. This gave staff instant rewards for their work. We also introduced initiatives such as 'You've got mail', where staff are paired up across sites and three times a year purchase a gift for their partner, based on their interests. This gave an immediate lift to staff and encouraged friendships to develop across different sites.

3. Achieving long-term wins: January 2019 onwards. Despite the immediate reward of our wellbeing achievements, we felt it was key that we also implemented long-term meaningful and systemic changes to go beyond the immediate thank you for staff. The long-term plans we put into place included rewriting our marking policies to allow for more focused marking. This reduced the time staff spend on marking, without diminishing the quality of feedback. We also looked at lesson planning within each of our schools to make it focused and manageable. We also committed as a Trust and as individual schools to buy into an outside support resource, Care First, which includes access to counselling, a 24-hour support line, and free and impartial advice on issues linked to school, as well as personal support for issues beyond school, such as debt management and relationship support.

4. Providing longevity: January 2020 onwards. Despite the progress we were making, it was important that the core of our wellbeing work was current and ongoing. We regularly changed the composition of the Wellbeing Group by adding members rather than removing them. This allowed new ideas to be considered, while maintaining the core values of the group. Wellbeing newsletters were crucial in keeping staff informed across the Trust.

5. A structured approach to measure progress and impact: September 2019 onwards. We decided that it was really important to benchmark our progress. The Medway Wellbeing Award gave us the opportunity to do this, as it not only provided external verification of our progress to date but also gave us targets and strategies to work towards. It was also beneficial to be involved in the free Teach Well Alliance Teach Well School Gold Award: Covid-19 Pandemic, as it allowed us to compare how we were doing in relation to other organisations. However, we ensured that we did not just use these awards as compliance 'tick lists'; we wanted to make wellbeing within our schools meaningful and embedded rather than a paper exercise to meet external criteria. It was key that any award was earned, rather than opting for an award that we paid to achieve. Our structure has also allowed staff in our Trust schools to see what we are working towards and how wellbeing has developed through practical and impactful strategies.

Impact of wellbeing actions

A major impact of wellbeing actions has been a noticeable drop in staff absence rate across our schools. Feedback from staff has told us that they now feel that they have somebody to speak to or know where to get support. Our newsletters regularly signpost the external wellbeing service Care First, and feedback from staff shows that they feel that their wellbeing is considered. Retention of staff has been strong and, at the time of writing (August 2020), we do not have any vacancies across all our schools in the Trust. Exit interviews from staff who have left our schools show that they felt supported during their time with us and, in the majority of cases, are only leaving due to relocation or promotion elsewhere. Where possible, we have grown many of our own leaders, with four of our senior leaders gaining promotion from within during the last 18 months. Two of our current headteachers have been grown internally and promoted to their current roles. Our commitment to promoting our teaching assistants to teaching roles can be seen in that, in 2019/20, we had three members of staff following the School Direct programme as internal candidates from within our schools.

Recently, wellbeing initiatives have centred around finding ways to reduce workload and support mental wellbeing. Our last survey, undertaken in June 2020, shows that the vast majority of our staff feel that their workload is manageable (Table 28.1).

Feedback from staff also tells us that they have a much better work–life balance (see Table 28.2). Key strategies which have been put into place have included restructuring our approach to marking, adapting lesson planning commitments, reducing data drop expectations, as well as putting in place initiatives such as 'Friends and Family Friday', where staff are encouraged to leave work at a reasonable time on a Friday evening to spend the weekend with their family and friends.

Table 28.1 Rivermead Inclusive Trust: Staff survey results – 'My workload is manageable'

Answer choices	Responses	(%)
Strongly agree	48	34.04
Agree	75	53.19
Neither agree nor disagree	11	7.80
Disagree	4	2.84
Strongly disagree	0	0.00
Not applicable	3	2.13
TOTAL	141	

Table 28.2 Rivermead Inclusive Trust: Staff survey results – 'I have a good work–life balance'

Answer choices	Responses	(%)
Strongly agree	42	29.79
Agree	74	52.48
Neither agree nor disagree	21	14.89
Disagree	2	1.42
Strongly disagree	1	0.71
Not applicable	1	0.71
TOTAL	141	

Much of our work as a wellbeing group has been about thanking staff for their work through our wellbeing weeks and wellbeing days, raising awareness of mental health and reducing the stigma of mental ill-health (Table 28.3). Supporting staff and signposting them to mental health services have also been important. Our recent survey suggests that staff have a much greater awareness of mental health and wellbeing. Our newsletters have been very effective in developing this understanding, as well as providing support to staff, as they are packed with support, advice and articles. All our resources and newsletters are downloadable from the Rivermead Inclusive Trust website: https://www.rivermeadinclusivetrust.co.uk/about-rit/health-and-wellbeing

Whilst we fully appreciate that we still have aspects of staff wellbeing to work on, it is reassuring, as outlined in the survey results in Table 28.4, that staff feel confident to be able to access, or at least find, the support available to them.

Table 28.3 Rivermead Inclusive Trust: Staff survey results – 'The school/Trust demonstrates positive awareness about mental health and wellbeing'

Answer choices	Responses	(%)
Strongly agree	79	55.63
Agree	57	40.14
Neither agree nor disagree	5	3.52
Disagree	1	0.70
Strongly disagree	0	0.00
Not applicable	0	0.00
TOTAL	142	

Table 28.4 Rivermead Inclusive Trust: Staff survey results – 'I am aware of the support available to me if I need it'

Answer choices	Responses	(%)
Strongly agree	55	38.73
Agree	78	54.93
Neither agree nor disagree	7	4.93
Disagree	0	0.00
Strongly disagree	0	0.00
Not applicable	2	1.41
TOTAL	142	

Society's attitude to mental health has changed over the last 10 years. It is crucial to support, rather than judge, those suffering from mental ill-health. The work on mental health within our schools has underlined why wellbeing is so important, both on an individual and organisational level, and how the education system has an obligation to reduce the negativity around mental ill-health.

During the Covid-19 partial opening period between March and July 2020, there was a huge focus on the mental wellbeing of our staff. As Covid-19 is still with us as we re-open our schools in September 2020, we will maintain this focus as we move into academic year 2020/21. We will continue to signpost mental wellbeing resources through our fortnightly newsletters and also ensure that some of our continuing professional development throughout the year is focused on wellbeing, with particular emphasis on the mental, emotional and social wellbeing of staff.

There are also plans to focus more on wellbeing issues which affect staff outside of the workplace. This will include making links with outside agencies and obtaining literature to display in our school reception areas about issues such as health screening and support groups for cancer sufferers and similar long-term illnesses. By raising awareness of different illnesses and having a clear commitment to arranging diagnoses and testing within work time, we can make a significant contribution to the physical and mental health of staff. We also hope that displaying resources in a public area will enable us to reach out to our local communities. We believe that each of our schools in the Trust is at the heart and hub of their community. Our existing commitment to wellbeing will continue to develop and build in all of our schools and Trust-wide during the coming academic year and beyond.

Key strategies

- Connection between pupil wellbeing, staff wellbeing, teaching and learning and attainment.
- Cross-school strategies and development of professional relationships.
- Formation of staff wellbeing group.
- Developing and 'growing' staff internally, within the Trust.
- Trust 30: Wellbeing Charter.
- Recruiting staff across the Trust who share its values.
- Wellbeing week across the Trust, with additional 'treats' and wellbeing services, such as a head massage from trainees at a local college.
- 'You've got mail' – staff paired across schools mail each other a gift.
- Marking and lesson planning reviewed and streamlined.
- 'Care First' company membership: counselling and financial advice.
- Trust newsletter.
- Staff surveys, providing feedback on staff wellbeing.

29 Ladybridge High School, Bolton, Greater Manchester

Leading as you wish to be led

Paddy Russell, Headteacher

'There is often a misconception about whether young people or staff come first in schools. I don't accept that this competition exists. Although a ruthless, relentless push to work teachers harder may appear to be in the best interests of children, the reverse is often true. If, as headteacher, I put unreasonable pressure and stress on the senior team, they will in turn apply this to the heads of department, who 'pass the pain' to the classroom teachers, who finally 'pass the pain' to the young people, negatively impacting their wellbeing and diminishing their intrinsic motivation to learn. Young people recognise that they are working for the survival of their teachers rather than for their own future success in life. In summary: unhappy, demotivated staff = unhappy, demotivated and low-achieving learners.'

Overview

Headteacher Paddy Russell describes his priorities on taking up post at Ladybridge High School, shortly before Year 11 sat GCSE exams which led to poor results. At the core of his leadership is an unerring belief that staff wellbeing is essential to bring about improvement and to ensure that the pupils are motivated and taken care of. Paddy speaks of the need to see failure as an opportunity for learning, not judgement. He encourages staff to voice their concerns and to be authentic by modelling this approach himself. He also considers personal and professional development when creating learning opportunities for staff. The ethos and values of the school were co-constructed with staff to create a school community committed to the same goals.

Context

Ladybridge High School is a local authority maintained secondary school in Bolton, currently serving 991 learners, with numbers rising to meet local demand. One of the main strengths of Ladybridge is its diversity. It's a wonderful mix of families that make up Ladybridge! We have learners from all backgrounds in terms of academic starting points, ethnicity and socio-economic status. Over 30 languages are spoken, and around 50% of the learners are from Black and Minority Ethnic (BAME) backgrounds. The number of learners with Education, Health and Care Plans (EHCP) is not high compared with national figures, but many of our learners with an EHCP have emotional, social and behaviour difficulties, along with mental health issues. We have slightly more boys than girls at Ladybridge, with 54% boys and 46% girls.

It would be difficult to find a more genuinely comprehensive school than Ladybridge. A large proportion of our learners live on one estate of predominately social housing. There are extreme issues with drugs, antisocial behaviour and criminal exploitation of young people in the community. Over 40% of our families live in areas which are in the 10% most deprived areas nationally. However, a significant proportion are also from relatively advantaged backgrounds. We have approximately 120 staff in total, split almost evenly between teaching, support, admin and site staff.

I took up post as headteacher at Ladybridge in the summer of 2019, having previously worked as deputy headteacher at Matthew Moss High School in Rochdale. I think it would be inaccurate to state that I made a fully conscious decision to focus on implementing a culture of staff wellbeing – I don't think I had much choice in the matter! Let me try and explain why …

Building on core beliefs

People tend to lead in a way that fits with their core beliefs. Most of us would struggle to lead in any other way. I firmly believe in treating people in the way that I wish to be treated: respectfully, kindly, and with permission to think and have agency. It is the only authentic way for me to lead. I have no choice. I am not stating this in a smug manner to appear saintly! It is just a simple truth that I would not be capable of leading in a different way. I would be rubbish at leading in an authoritarian and brutal manner. I simply would not be very good at it. I lead in a way that aligns with core beliefs, including:

- Staff want to do a good job and care about young people; most are not in teaching just for the money.
- Staff perform better and work harder when they are happy.
- Staff are happiest when they are learning, when they are treated well, when they have the autonomy to think, and can see the positive impact of their actions.

If you keep these core beliefs in your mind, you won't go far wrong when seeking to develop a culture of staff wellbeing. Our job as school leaders is about creating the climate and environment where staff and learners thrive. It's like being a gardener ... you are creating the conditions for the plants to thrive, but you're not actually doing the photosynthesis for them.

Staff are more likely to thrive if they are treated respectfully and encouraged to learn and be curious. It also helps if we are encouraged to reflect on the positive impact we have on others. Recognising the positive impact we have as teachers can be easier said than done, as amongst the positives there are daily failures. We need a different relationship with this failure. Reaching a point of acceptance of the imperfections of classroom life, whilst maintaining high expectations, is the sweet spot that we must aim for. Our curiosity needs to extend learning from as many of these daily failures as possible.

Although I did not make a conscious decision to focus on staff wellbeing, there is no doubt in my mind that looking after staff makes strategic sense. As my core beliefs suggest, happy staff put in more discretionary effort.

Clarity of vision and purpose – the 'WHY'

I also believe that staff are likely to be more committed and happier in their work if there is a clear sense of mission and an openly communicated rationale behind decisions that are made by school leaders. Asking ourselves 'WHY' when making decisions and communicating the 'WHY' to others tend to create a more harmonious culture where the underlying purpose, and 'big picture', of our work as teachers and as a school are clear.

Our Ladybridge mission was co-constructed with staff when I joined the school:

'The mission of Ladybridge High School is to ensure all of our learners develop the knowledge, sense of direction and moral purpose to thrive in the future. The success learners experience at Ladybridge will instil the self-belief and resilience required to overcome challenges in life. Our young people will leave Ladybridge as good citizens who are ready to make a positive contribution to their communities.'

There is often a misconception about whether young people or staff come first in schools. I don't accept that this competition exists. Although a ruthless, relentless push to work teachers harder may appear to be in the best interests of children, the reverse is often true. If, as headteacher, I put unreasonable pressure and stress on the senior team, they will in turn apply this to the heads of department, who 'pass the pain' to the classroom teachers, who finally 'pass the pain' to the young people, negatively impacting their wellbeing and diminishing their intrinsic motivation to learn. Young people recognise that they are working for the survival of their teachers rather than for their own future success in life. In summary: unhappy, demotivated staff = unhappy, demotivated and low-achieving learners.

As a biology specialist, I liken this to pollutants building up in a food chain within the ecosystem. The toxins get passed down the chain and build up over time, leading to a cumulative negative impact that lasts for years. In contrast, if the staff team are energised and optimistic, this is passed onto the learners and has a positive impact on their wellbeing and academic progress.

Teaching is a wonderful profession. The enjoyment and satisfaction I have gained from teaching have been life-changing for me personally, and I hope to have influenced the life chances of a few young people along the way! But teaching is also hard and demands far more working hours than those that are paid through 'directed time' [1265 hours per annum in the UK]. The profession functions around discretionary effort. I think we need to remember this as school leaders.

Schools have real impact on the development of children, particularly schools in disadvantaged areas. It really does take a village to raise a child. Pupils all need positive affirmation from different people in our lives, even those who are brilliantly supported from home. Many of these positive affirmations come from staff in schools – all staff, not just teaching staff. When we recognise and reflect upon this positive impact, there is not only a boost to the wellbeing of staff, but also an increase in staff agency and the inner belief that their actions make a difference.

There was no grand staff wellbeing and mental health initiative when I started at Ladybridge. The first step was to co-construct our beliefs, mission and the qualities we wished to develop in our learners with the staff team. This involved sending a Microsoft Office form to all staff who were asked the following questions:

1 Why did you decide to work at Ladybridge High School? Why did you choose to take on your current role?
2 State three key beliefs that you hold about education.
3 Describe what you believe the mission of Ladybridge High School should be.
4 Select three qualities that you believe are the most important to help us to thrive and be happy in our lives (there was a choice of around 30 qualities).
5 Can you name any other important qualities that I may have missed?

After carefully reading the responses from staff, we created various iterations of our mission and beliefs before settling on the mission statement described earlier, and the three key beliefs that are below. Co-constructing the mission statement was important to give us all a clear sense of direction. We tend to be energised and make better decisions in life when we are clear where we are headed and when we can see the purpose behind our work. Even better if we have helped to shape this direction.

In my view, the three beliefs we co-constructed were particularly influential from a staff wellbeing perspective. Our three beliefs are:

• Learning is for all.
• Learning changes lives.
• Honesty promotes learning.

'Learning is for all' helps to promote staff wellbeing, as it encourages all staff to see themselves as learners. Lifelong learning makes us realise we are not stuck; we have the capacity to change and learn throughout our lives. Learning also makes us happy!

'Learning changes lives' – staff are happier when they recognise the impact of their hard work on their pupils.

'Honesty promotes learning' is particularly significant in influencing school culture. I passionately want a culture at our school where people know that it is okay to make mistakes. It was clear from the feedback from staff on the Microsoft Office form that they agree with this. An aspect of this belief is the link between honesty and responsibility. We all mess up sometimes. As I indicated earlier, teaching involves daily failure. If we are honest with ourselves and others when we mess up, we learn from the experience. If we look to shift the blame and responsibility onto others when we make mistakes, we stop ourselves from learning. As a school community we have committed to being open and honest about the mistakes we make. This applies to all of us, me included!

The key milestones on our journey to implement a culture of staff wellbeing are outlined below.

1. Co-construction of our beliefs, mission and the qualities we wish to develop in our learners (April and May 2019). As described above, this stage was crucial to help to implement a culture of staff wellbeing. This culminated in the creation of 'The Ladybridge Way', which gives us all a clarity of purpose. Figure 29.1 is the teachers' version, Figure 29.2 the learners' version

2. September training day presentation to staff (September 2019). I started at the school at the start of the summer term in 2019, just a few weeks before the GCSE exams began. Despite the successes of many learners that summer, there is no doubt that the results overall were extremely disappointing. There were a number of factors that contributed to this that I will not expand on here. The question was what we did about it, and how we talked about and learned from the disappointment. As anyone who has worked in schools will know, the headteacher's presentation on the first training day in September always reflects on the summer's results and sets the scene for the rest of the academic year. From what staff have since fed back to me, they were expecting public naming and shaming during my presentation. It was with great relief for the staff team that this did not happen. Let me be clear, I did not shy away from the fact that the results were not good enough. This was clear for all to see. But what would have been gained from publicly humiliating individual departments on the details of the results? Instead, we looked at what we could learn from the experience with this cohort and explored strategies to improve the learning and life chances of our young people in the future. It was clear that we were choosing hope over fear.

3. Changes to the monitoring of teaching and learning (Autumn 2019 and beyond). Far too often, monitoring activities in schools focus on teacher compliance rather than the learning of young people. You end up with a box

Figure 29.1 The Ladybridge Way: Teachers

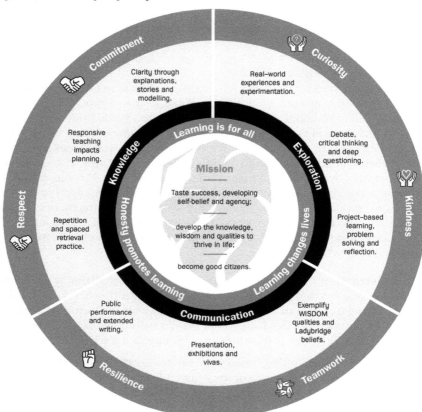

ticking process of, for example, how many feedback stickers you can see in each pupil's book. When we started our subject reviews at Ladybridge, teachers quickly realised that our approach to monitoring was going to be different to this. It comes back to that word 'curiosity'. If we are curious about what is happening in classrooms, not to judge the teacher on a crude metric, but to learn what is going well and what we can improve, then we are on track towards a learning culture. Teachers need feedback in order to improve. A healthy culture of embracing feedback and challenge helps us all to learn and grow. I also noticed that our learning directors (posh words for heads of department!) also seemed to enjoy the process. It felt like we were collaboratively solving a puzzle, rather than deciding which member of staff to whack with a big stick!

4. Focus on professional learning (Summer 2019 and beyond). As summarised by our belief that 'Learning is for all', we are determined to provide the very best opportunities for our staff to continue their professional learning

Figure 29.2 The Ladybridge Way: Learners

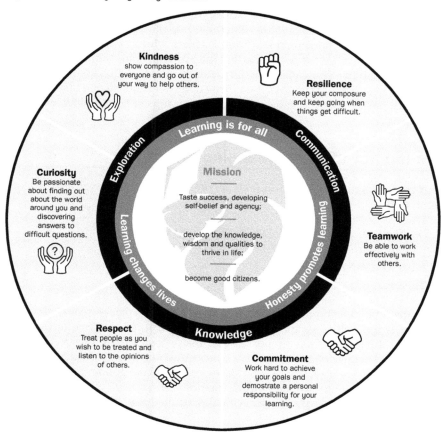

journey. Too often in schools the appraisal process is judgemental rather than developmental. We have changed the language to 'professional learning and performance' rather than appraisal. This is not simply about the semantics; it is a totally different process. Staff are encouraged to read, think, reflect and consider their growth both personally and professionally. Teaching and associate staff have had the opportunity to experience courses in mindfulness and transactional analysis (TA), as part of this broad and distinctive professional learning offer.

5. Decision regarding partial school closure during the Covid-19 pandemic (March 2020). In March 2020 schools were instructed to remain open for vulnerable children and the children of key workers. The decision we took prior to this instruction led to a member of our staff contacting the Teach Well Alliance to successfully recommend us for a Teach Well School Gold Award: Covid-19 Pandemic. I'll keep this brief and try and not to get too political! I was concerned for the safety and welfare of our learners, staff and families. A large proportion of our learners and staff were either in named vulnerable groups or lived with people who had greater vulnerability to the Covid-19 virus. I decided that we would send home any staff and learners who met these criteria. This was a bold decision. At the point of attempting to send home hundreds of young people and staff, we were informed that a family member of one of our learners had tested positive for the virus. It confirmed the decision we had taken. It was unsafe for the school to remain open for these groups of staff and learners.

The impact of staff wellbeing strategies

Staff morale is high at Ladybridge. In a recent staff survey, over 90% of staff reported that:

- 'Leaders and managers are considerate of my wellbeing.'
- 'I am proud to work at this school.'
- 'I feel well supported working at this school.'
- 'This school is well-led and -managed.'

The impact of implementing a culture of staff wellbeing can be seen on recruitment. It is difficult to quantify this, but the majority of staff we have interviewed and appointed have reported that they specifically chose to apply to Ladybridge because of our distinctive culture and our strong focus on treating staff well. We have been delighted with the calibre of the appointments, including for shortage subjects such as mathematics and science.

Below, I have summarised evidence that each milestone has made a difference.

Co-construction of our beliefs, mission and the qualities we wish to develop in our learners (April–May 2019). Staff have a clear sense of direction. This has not been imposed upon them; they have been able to shape and influence where we are headed. Staff are united by a compassionate ethos which is based around the future learning and life chances of young people, rather than a short-term focus on numerical outcomes.

September training day presentation to staff (September 2019). Staff are driven by hope and not fear.

Changes to the monitoring of teaching and learning (Autumn 2019 and beyond). Curiosity drives our monitoring work, not fear of Ofsted or other accountability measures.

Focus on professional learning (Summer 2019 and beyond). We have a staff team who are learning, which helps them to be both happier and more successful in their roles. Mindfulness and TA theory are helping our staff to be more self-aware, more composed, more empathetic to others and more open to challenge.

Decision regarding partial school closure during the Covid-19 pandemic (March 2020). Our staff were already highly self-motivated prior to the Covid-19 pandemic. However, I believe that, since the decision to send home vulnerable staff, we have seen even greater levels of staff commitment and motivation. I must stress that I did not make the closure decision to manipulate the work ethic of staff. I was simply trying to keep people safe.

Our staff have been incredible during the school closure, finding endlessly creative ways to engage learners and support families. They have been immense. I am grateful to lead such a remarkable staff team.

Comments from staff include:

'The level of support and understanding given to staff has been fantastic, as well as continuing to provide a quality education for key worker families and those staying at home.'

'It has been a challenging time for all staff and students but, from my point of view, staff have all pulled together, been sharing practices and resources, and there is a general feeling of family.'

'The decision to close the school early showed the gravity of the situation. Knowing what we know now and how the spread of the virus was rife in the community, if we had waited until the Friday it could have spread further to students, staff and their families and there could have been very serious health implications of this. There is no script for our current situation, erring on the side of caution is the right thing to do.'

'I think that the reaction to the crisis was exceptional.'

'The way the school as a team have been supporting the pupils and indeed each other is outstanding.'

'I think the way the decision to close the school before government acted was the right one. It showed that the headteacher was aware of staff's concerns and it was handled without judgement and with sensitivity. I think that it demonstrated clear leadership in a marked contrast to what has gone previously. The head seemed in tune with how staff were feeling and was keen to put their safety at the forefront whilst recognising that students' education should not be compromised.'

'The way staff have been looked after is amazing. I know not all school heads would have done that. Expectations have been well balanced and staff having other commitments, for example, children at home, has been taken into account. The bigger picture has been looked at. It's a win from me!'

'I feel that the leadership team have genuinely been looking after our health and wellbeing and making informed decisions that are in staff's and learners' best interests.'

Staff work hard at Ladybridge. It is not a free-for-all where everyone does what they want. There is challenge – in fact, open, honest, respectful challenge – and disagreement is encouraged. Indeed, one of our most forthright members of staff successfully nominated us for the Teach Well School Gold Award!

Staff are encouraged to:

- Challenge others.
- Support others.
- Voice vulnerability.

This is different to:

- Persecuting others.
- Rescuing others.
- Adopting a victim mentality.

Clarity is also important. Staff are clear about their roles, including their limit. This clarity reduces the unhealthy game-playing that corrodes the effectiveness of any organisation.

I wrote this chapter during the summer break of 2020. Due to the lockdown and partial school closure caused by the Covid-19 pandemic, the return to school in September 2020 was like no other return to school we have experienced. There were greater restrictions on learners, with expectations around social distancing, hygiene and limited routes around the school site. Staff were expected to move classrooms more than ever before to prevent the mixing of year group bubbles. This was not the time for a shift to a more authoritarian 'command and control' style of leadership. I believed there was a need for compassionate leadership, more so than ever before. To this end, we decided to communicate a very clear and public priority to the school community:

> **Priority:** Re-connect learners and staff with the school post-lockdown, strengthening a sense of belonging to Ladybridge and provide the school community with a clear direction for the future. Be ready to respond and be flexible to whatever we face in September 2020 and beyond. Take every practical step to keep learners, staff and their families safe. Focus on the wellbeing of all.

Our plans for the re-opening of the school reflected this priority. Staff and learners jointly engaged with psychological theory, encouraging us all to adopt an 'I'm OK, You're OK' perspective. Learners also engaged in courses in mindfulness. Staff were encouraged to voice their own vulnerability to learners on return to the school. Many of us, myself included, felt some mental turbulence. This is always the case in September. But, after close to six months without facing a full school and the intensity of a 'normal' school day of teaching, this mental turbulence was stronger than ever. Many of us were full of doubt and uncertainty. The more we acknowledge that it is okay to not feel okay, the more we can have a healthy relationship with the everyday ups and downs of our mental state. An acceptance and openness to the rapidly changing state of our mind are good for our mental health and wellbeing.

Now is not the time for us to be fearful. There is so much negative publicity about schools and education. I fully understand the reasons for these concerns. During 2020, young people across the world lost months of face-to-face teaching. But we will not resolve this through a narrative of fearfulness about a lost generation of children. I believe we must continue to look to the future with hope and optimism and consider how we can help some of our learners to re-engage, whilst unleashing those who have discovered new levels of agency and independence during lockdown. We will be working collaboratively as a staff team to do just that over the coming weeks. I'm looking forward to the challenge.

Key strategies

- Core beliefs at the centre of the culture of the school.
- Protecting the most vulnerable during Covid-19 partial closure.
- Learning staff are happy staff.
- Mistakes not regarded as failure.
- Create conditions in which staff will thrive.
- Vision co-constructed with the staff.
- Feedback and challenge, not judgement.
- Re-connecting pupils and staff when schools re-opened in September 2020.

30 Baines School, Poulton-le-Fylde, Lancashire

Rapidly improving a school while developing staff wellbeing

Alison Chapman, Headteacher, with Clare Doherty, Deputy Headteacher

'Wellbeing is about helping staff to achieve great things in their role in school but that must not come at the cost of their health and wellbeing.'

Overview

Headteacher Alison Chapman and deputy headteacher Clare Doherty describe how, by implementing a culture of staff and student wellbeing over the last three years, results have risen, and staff morale has improved. Staff absence through illness has reduced, relieving pressure on the school supply budget, and motivation of both learners and adults has increased. Alison and Clare explain how actively listening to staff views and celebrating their success have played an important role in developing their wellbeing and mental health.

Context

Baines School is a stand-alone non-denominational voluntary aided 11–16 secondary school located in Poulton-le-Fylde in Lancashire, close to Blackpool. There are approximately 850 students in the school, with a fully comprehensive intake. There are roughly equal numbers of girls and boys, with 51% boys. There has been an increase in the number of students registered as Pupil Premium (PP), rising from 16% in 2017 to 24% in 2020. The number of students receiving Special Educational Needs and Disability (SEND) support is below the national average at 12%, while 7.7% of students have medical conditions. Baines School has a very low intake of students who speak English as an additional language at 2.4%. The school has representations from the broadest range of deprivation indices, with students from the affluent Poulton-le-Fylde area having an Income Deprivation Affecting Children Index (IDACI) score of 0.094, while the children from Blackpool (over half of the school) have a much higher IDACI deprivation score of 0.307. There are almost 100 members of staff, comprising teachers, student-facing non-teaching support staff, and the administration, catering, cleaning and site teams.

I became the headteacher in September 2017, following the worst summer results the school had ever received. The school was well below the government's 'floor measure', on the lowest quartile for all main measures, and in the bottom 250 schools for progress in England. The school also had a deficit budget and the sixth form was not financially viable. The demographic of the school had changed during recent years, with an increase in the number of students classed as 'disadvantaged'.

Three years later, the school is almost unrecognisable. It is now an 11–16 school; a major curriculum change has taken place to offer a full range of subjects; teaching and learning have improved; and there is a rising trend in Progress 8, well above the old floor measure

Developing the whole child is very important to us. When students leave Baines School, we want them to be well-rounded individuals with strong examination results for their ability. They will know how to keep themselves safe and healthy and can develop respectful relationships with others, appreciating that everyone is different. Most of all, there is a pride about our school across our community where staff, students, parents/carers and former pupils all recognise the improvements and are working together to continue the improvement journey.

The start of a new era

The long-standing deputy headteacher retired; for over twenty years she had been the trusted 'go to' person for staff wellbeing. With the start of a new era and many challenges for the school in raising standards, it was time to overtly focus on the culture of staff wellbeing. As headteacher, I try to lead from the front so that everyone knows that it is my expectation (even though to be honest I do not always practise what I preach!). I attended external training that focused on wellbeing, but the approach was not for me. We were treated to a presentation about healthy eating, a mini-massage, and a walk in the fresh air, but these were not things that would be sustainable in the workplace. There were also the challenges of changing the way staff worked, raising expectations in the classroom, managing a deficit budget, and balancing all of these changes with staff wellbeing.

The principles of wellbeing

The principles that are important to me when considering wellbeing across the school are:

- Wellbeing is not an add-on or special events that happen once.
- Wellbeing is about helping staff to achieve great things in their role in school but that must not come at the cost of their health and wellbeing.
- Wellbeing is considered with regards to workload and how we can improve systems so that work is not duplicated.

- Wellbeing is linked to how a member of staff feels supported, trusted, respected, consulted and thanked when they have gone the extra mile and their success is celebrated.
- It is also important that staff know that, if they need help, they have a place to go and we will support them.
- Baines School cares about the wellbeing of both our student and adult community.

Until writing this chapter, I hadn't realised that the first phase of supporting wellbeing and mental health started as I took up post as headteacher because it is so inextricably linked to the culture of the school. I had actually started to create the culture from the first day, and only later have wellbeing policies and strategies become more formalised.

When establishing yourself as a new headteacher, it is important to take people on the journey with you. Given where Baines School was in 2017, moving the school forward was always going to be difficult, especially with a lack of resources and a very tight contact ratio. I promised that I would listen to staff and to be open and honest about the things we needed to do. I made it clear that they could discuss their concerns with me. Every member of staff is important to me, irrespective of their position. I personally know everyone by name and recognise the contribution they make to the smooth running of our school.

The school was at such a low point in its history that it could have been easy to have missed the positives. If that had happened, I don't believe the staff would have had the energy to improve our school so quickly. I believe that there are crucial strategies that helped the staff to believe and to stay positive in my first year in post:

Celebrating success

Celebrating success includes recognising what we do well and acknowledging and being proud of the achievements of our community. It is vital that success is communicated to staff and that they are thanked for their contribution. We can draw many likenesses to the children we teach. We have all heard of 'invisible' children in the classroom (Pye 1989, cited in Cowley 2019). It is equally important that staff are not invisible, and their achievements do not go by unnoticed. As with our students, staff respond to praise in different ways: some like to be publicly acknowledged, while others prefer a private acknowledgement. While I do both, it is also important that there is a culture of success and staff should not be embarrassed by their achievements or contributions. Every Friday. our staff briefing celebrates the student and staff successes from that week. We award 'Staff and Student Stars of the Week' and a fortnightly newsletter goes to all stakeholders to share their success. We have a 'Staff of the Half-Term' raffle, open to all staff in the school, not just teachers. Staff nominate colleagues who have gone above and beyond during the half-term. Each person nominated receives a letter explaining who nominated them and what it was for, and we hold a raffle on the last day of each half-term. The person drawn from the box is allowed to leave at lunchtime on one day the following half-term. If they are teaching in the afternoon, I cover their class. It is a small token of my appreciation for their extra effort.

Building trust through openness, honesty and consultation

It is widely recognised that feeling trusted contributes significantly to staff wellbeing (Cowley 2019; Humphries 2019; Paterson 2013). When staff feel trusted, it instils self-confidence, encourages innovation and allows them to express their opinions without being afraid of repercussions. This contributes to a positive culture in school, and staff will go the extra mile because they aren't fearful of making mistakes or being blamed.

During the early stages of headship, there have been some difficult decisions and changes at Baines School, many stemming from historical financial difficulties. I know that the staff were not always happy with the situation, but they appreciated my honesty and they knew that I would always inform them about change, such as the decision to close the sixth form, and ask their views when implementing major change (e.g. moving from a vertical to a horizontal pastoral year group system).

The staff would have liked an increase in the number of non-teaching lessons and leadership time, smaller class sizes and improved teaching resources, but they understood the financial constraints we were working under.

Investing in CPD to develop staff as professionals

Professional development is an entitlement for every member of staff. According to Tiplady (2019), continuing professional development (CPD) can be a quick win as long as it is appropriate, relevant to the individual and does not add unnecessarily to workload. A key part of my educational philosophy is to ensure that all staff have the opportunity to develop themselves and to develop an aspect of their role where they are 'specialists'. While many in the profession view the appraisal process as a negative experience, I view it as an opportunity to be proud of all the things you have achieved and to positively contribute to the planning of your future professional development, empowering staff to take ownership for developing skills and leadership potential.

The Leadership Matrix

Since taking up the headship, the school has invested in increasing the professional development of all staff at all levels. For most, it has been subject-specific or linked to pedagogy or leadership. It is important that CPD is relevant and not seen as a waste of time. I developed a Leadership Matrix which includes all levels of leadership, from newly qualified teacher status through to executive headship. It outlines the types of skills, activities and experiences that are needed at the various levels so that staff can identify the aspects they wish to develop in order to prepare for the next leadership step. The range of learning has been tremendous. Staff now receive an annual professional development certificate. This contributes to staff feeling appreciated and valued, which, in turn, contributes to positive emotional wellbeing. The Human Resources (HR) section is reproduced in Table 30.1 to illustrate how the matrix works.

Through the implementation of a positive wellbeing culture, sickness and staff absence has been reduced. In addition, if staff feel well and are happy, they are more successful in their role. This positivity also rubs off on the students; lessons are highly educational but also fun, and there is a positive sense of a community working together to achieve the best for our students and school.

Emails

The school already had some basic health systems in place, such as free flu vaccinations and bi-annual health checks for staff. The members of the senior leadership team (SLT) were also mindful about the stress caused by workload, especially during holidays, so we developed some loose expectations around email etiquette. We felt that, if we had a strict rule about the sending and receipt of emails, it would cause undue worry for those whose work pattern fell outside of those times. Instead, we have a system where staff can send emails when they wish. Staff ask themselves whether the email could be drafted and sent the following morning. We have no expectation that the recipient will check their emails or respond out of hours. I appreciate that communication from the headteacher can make a member of staff feel obliged to respond, so I have also tried to reduce the emails and communications I send at night, weekends and during school holidays.

Supervision and training

I attended a three-day training course on implementing supervision in school. The course made me think about all the difficult circumstances staff have to cope with, especially the safeguarding and pastoral team. Working with the deputy headteacher, we developed and implemented a supervision policy, approved by the governors. While the timeframe for regular supervision meetings has not gone to plan, the staff have the opportunity to access supervision in school. The deputy head has developed a very strong safeguarding team which meets weekly.

The deputy head attended a 'Leading a Mentally Healthy School' programme with the Ripley Teaching School Alliance. This helped to shape an action plan and develop our staff wellbeing policy. While I am at the forefront as the lead and role-model, the deputy head leads the strategy and has expanded the number of staff involved. I know we are now ready to move our staff wellbeing strategy to the next level, which involves staff far more in the development of provision.

Table 30.1 Baines School: Extract from Leadership Matrix: Human Resources

Area	MPS Basic	UPS Emerging	M Leader Developing	Lead Practitioner/ SLE	SLT/Embedding	HT Leading
Leadership						
Human Resources	Awareness of school policies and ensure you are compliant with policies.	Contribution to school policies. Have an understanding of how HR issues can impact on a school. Contribute to the improvement and development of school policies through consultation. Contribute to the development of departmental policies.	Development and production of departmental policies in line with whole-school policies. Ensure that other staff fulfil the requirements as set out in school policies.	Share research from best practice in other schools or from research to support the improvement and development of new school policies.	Development and production of whole-school policies. Ensure that school policies are consistently applied to a high standard across groups of staff in the school. Have an understanding of workload, staff absence, appraisal, capability, disciplinary policies and processes.	Lead and implement whole-school policies for all HR aspects. Liaison with governors, local authority and unions to ensure policies are adhered to, especially during times of change. Restructuring, disciplinary, staff reduction processes.

Following our involvement in the Leading a Mentally Healthy School programme, Baines School based the promotion of whole-school positive mental health and wellbeing on the 5 steps promoted by the NHS (2019):

1 Connect to others.
2 Be active.
3 Keep learning.
4 Give to others.
5 Take notice (being mindful).

The 5 steps were first introduced to staff in November 2018, along with our staff wellbeing policy. A 'Staff and Student Wellbeing Continuum' was developed in conjunction with colleagues (Figure 30.1). Staff are now much more aware of where and how they can get support for their mental health and wellbeing.

1. Connect to others. For consistency, we have set agendas for all SLT/ departmental line management meetings. The first item on the agenda is to discuss wellbeing, not only of the subject lead, but also the staff within their departments. This proved to be supportive during lockdown. We continued with our meetings remotely and wanted to ensure our staff were keeping well, especially those with challenging personal circumstances. Staff we were concerned about were contacted regularly with wellbeing calls and offered support where appropriate. Staff very much appreciated this additional level of support.

When new staff are appointed, we run an induction programme which lasts one term. It is an opportunity for new staff to bond together and also to allow them to develop confidence with new systems. We spend some time discussing issues like behaviour and how to use our electronic systems. One member of staff who was involved in the induction programme from September 2019 felt it was such a useful and valuable process that she asked to help to lead the programme this academic year (2020/21) – a fantastic example of empowerment and personal development.

Another member of staff has recently become a 'menopause mentor'. There has been little recognition of how the menopause impacts both personally and at work. The mentor provides staff with information on how the menopause can affect staff and offers mentoring and support.

2. Be active. Baines School offers a large number of enrichment clubs and encourages staff to run clubs in areas that are different to their normal subject specialism; for example, a biology teacher runs an after school ballet class, a history teacher runs a metal detector club, and one of the maths teachers has offered to run a golf master class. Staff have increased student opportunities to join extracurricular clubs and trips. We now have a special trip for every year group.

We trialled yoga mornings for staff to reduce stress and depression during our Random Act of Kindness Week in January 2020. Staff involved felt really

Figure 30.1 Baines School Mental Health Wellbeing Continuum, designed by colleagues on the Leading a Mentally Healthy School programme at the Ripley Teaching School Alliance (2018)

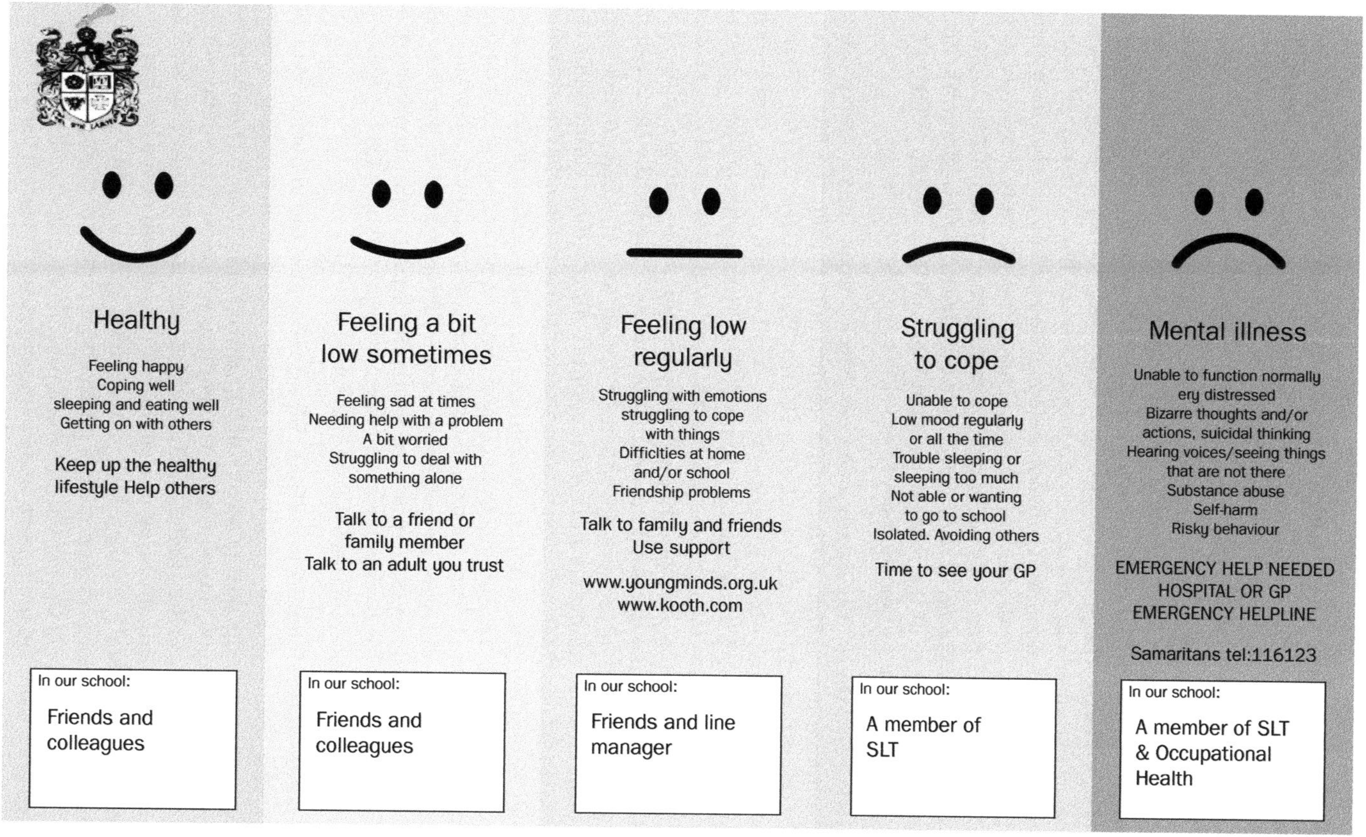

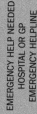

Healthy

Feeling happy
Coping well
sleeping and eating well
Getting on with others

Keep up the healthy
lifestyle Help others

In our school:

Friends and
colleagues

Feeling a bit low sometimes

Feeling sad at times
Needing help with a problem
A bit worried
Struggling to deal with
something alone

Talk to a friend or
family member
Talk to an adult you trust

In our school:

Friends and
colleagues

Feeling low regularly

Struggling with emotions
struggling to cope
with things
Difficulties at home
and/or school
Friendship problems

Talk to family and friends
Use support

www.youngminds.org.uk
www.kooth.com

In our school:

Friends and line
manager

Struggling to cope

Unable to cope
Low mood regularly
or all the time
Trouble sleeping or
sleeping too much
Not able or wanting
to go to school
Isolated. Avoiding others

Time to see your GP

In our school:

A member of
SLT

Mental illness

Unable to function normally
eg distressed
Bizarre thoughts and/or
actions, suicidal thinking
Hearing voices/seeing things
that are not there
Substance abuse
Self-harm
Risky behaviour

EMERGENCY HELP NEEDED
HOSPITAL OR GP
EMERGENCY HELPLINE

Samaritans tel:116123

In our school:

A member of SLT
& Occupational
Health

focused and energised for the day ahead. We intended to offer it on a weekly basis prior to lockdown and will hopefully pick it up again when restrictions in schools are eased. There is also a suggestion of starting a 'Couch to 5km' club to support staff in regaining their fitness after lockdown.

3. Staff wellbeing: Keep learning. One of the subject teams had a mixture of staff within it in terms of experience and opportunities. In September 2018, the deputy head clarified each person's role, identified their strengths and needs, and considered where further training was needed. Staff who were lacking confidence in their ability are now much more aware of how to carry out their role, and more experienced staff are more adept at delegation. This has improved the mental health of staff who were stressed because they were uncertain of their role and lacked the skills to complete tasks associated with it. It has also improved the wellbeing of staff who previously had an unhealthy work–life balance. One member of the team in June 2019 thanked the deputy head for giving her a purpose and supporting her to develop her self-confidence.

4. Give to others. The deputy head has developed an active Student Council, which involves staff in all aspects of their plans. During the past 12 months they have organised events such as a Charity Week, collections for a homeless shelter, a Random Act of Kindness Week, two Lip-Sync Battles, and a Reverse Advent Calendar for our families in need. This is as well as being involved in national charity events such as Children in Need and Sports Relief, and international projects like the Samaritan's Purse (Operation Christmas Child). At first, staff were shy about joining in events like the Lip-Sync Battle. However, more staff became involved the second time round and the self-confidence and morale of both staff and students increased, as positive relationships developed. Staff now look forward to such events, some saying that they could not remember having such fun previously. The majority of staff get involved in the charity work of the Student Council and there is a real sense of community spirit within school. This became clear during the lockdown, when one of the first things we did was to collect donations from staff for families whom we knew would struggle financially. Each Christmas a member of staff coordinates the Christmas Pixie, where staff buy small gifts for the member of staff they have been allocated during the month of December.

5. Take notice (being mindful). We all recognise the importance of being mindful (being fully aware of the present moment, without thinking about what has happened in the past or what will happen in the future). When a member of staff speaks to you, no matter how busy you are, turn from your work, put down your pen and give them your undivided attention. If a meeting is planned, going to the colleague's room instead of using your own office can have a positive effect on staff, as they feel more comfortable in their own classroom. Being mindful does not necessarily mean about nature and your environment; it can also be about the people you work with. When you are mindful of others, both your own and their mental wellbeing improve. They feel listened to and it can often help resolve concerns, leading to a more positive staff experience of school.

As we are in the early stages of implementing our wellbeing policy, we do not yet have long-term quantitative data to demonstrate improvements. However, staff retention remains positive and there is a lower level of short-term unplanned staff absence.

Given the challenging journey to rapidly improve our school, staff are positive and buoyant. Working in a school and being on top form every day for the students is energy-sapping, but our staff really do work as a team.

The number of staff nominations for Star of the Half-Term has rapidly increased. In the second half-term of summer term 2020, there were 76 nominations! Staff look forward to 'Stars of the Week' and 'Stars of the Half-Term' and are proud to accept their rewards in the full staff briefing. Applications for jobs have increased, with over 70 applicants for a recent pastoral officer role compared with eight only a year earlier. This demonstrates that more people now want to work at Baines School. Our reputation has improved substantially.

The staff surveys during our most recent Ofsted inspection were positive about the changes made to the school and the considerations made for staff wellbeing and workload:

'Staff are highly positive about the improvements that senior leaders have made. They say that leaders consider their wellbeing' (Ofsted, 2019e).

Next steps

In preparation for taking our staff wellbeing provision to the next stage, I completed a Level 2 Certificate in Understanding Mental Health, First Aid and Mental Health Advocacy in the Workplace. The knowledge gained on this course will help to support the staff and develop resources further, including a guide for line managers – and all staff – to look out for the potential signs that someone requires support for their mental health.

During the next academic year (2020/21), the deputy head is planning to form a Staff Wellbeing and Social Committee. This will help staff to take a leading role in supporting the adults in school. The committee will also help with future school improvement initiatives and run events aimed at raising awareness about wellbeing and leading a healthy life.

The menopause mentor has developed a mini action plan and is delivering an introductory session to all staff during the first half-term, to raise awareness of the 'symptoms' of menopause and its impact on work and home life, and to ensure that staff know how to get support.

We must recognise the impact that Covid-19 has had on our community and that many families, both staff and students, have suffered loss and have faced difficult challenges. All staff are receiving training entitled: 'Covid-19 – Recognising the Impact' to support staff personally and their work with our young people and their families.

The final development is to continue the empowerment of staff in developing their roles in school by encouraging them to carry out a mini project of practitioner research. Every member of staff makes a positive contribution to school and this will enable them to share their professionalism more widely, as well as contributing to their wellbeing and personal development.

Key strategies

- Wellbeing integral to students and staff wellbeing, not an add-on.
- Listening to staff and being open and honest.
- Celebrating staff and student success.
- Praising staff publicly.
- Staff and student 'Stars of the Week' announced in staff briefing each Friday.
- 'Stars of the Half-Term' – names of staff nominated go into a raffle for a half-day off.
- Fortnightly newsletter announcing staff and student success.
- Investing in professional development.
- The Baines 'Leadership Matrix'.
- Email policy.
- Developing supervision.
- Using the NHS 5 steps to support staff wellbeing and mental health.
- Baines School 'Staff and Student Wellbeing Continuum'.
- Clarifying roles and responsibilities.
- Giving to others outside the school: 'Random Acts of Kindness Week'.
- Student Council.
- Exercise classes/groups.
- Wellbeing a standing first item on meeting agendas.
- Comprehensive induction programme for new staff.
- Menopause mentor.
- Mindfulness and mindful attention during conversations.
- Headteacher completed Level 2 Certificate in Understanding Mental Health, First Aid and Mental Health Advocacy in the Workplace.
- Staff Wellbeing and Social Committee.
- All staff to receive training: 'Covid-19 – Recognising the Impact'.
- Staff offered opportunity to carry out a mini research project.

31 Holy Family RC and CE College, Heywood Greater Manchester

Together, we can do great things

Karen Ames, Headteacher

'*I can do things you cannot,*
You can do things I cannot;
Together we can do great things.'
(St. Mother Teresa)

Overview

The quote from Mother Teresa captures the vision of collaboration and team-work, underpinned by a spiritual ethos, that headteacher Karen Ames has pro-moted at Holy Family RC & CE College. Karen's long-serving commitment to the college ensured that, when she became headteacher in 2019, she was able to draw on her experience to develop the positive strategies that had been taken to support staff wellbeing and to change aspects which were not developing as they should. By giving staff a voice to identify issues that should be tackled and involving them in the process, Karen transformed a 'coasting' staff well-being and mental health strategy into a proactive driver for school improvement.

Context

Holy Family RC & CE College (HFC) is an 11–16 mixed voluntary aided sec-ondary college in the north-west of England. The college serves Roman Cath-olic and Church of England students of the township of Heywood and the locality of Rochdale. It is supported by the diocese of Salford and the diocese of Manchester. The college became a joint faith college in September 2007 at the request of Rochdale Local Authority and both dioceses. The college was previously known as St. Joseph's RC High School.

Holy Family RC and CE College is on a five-year journey to increase in size from 600 to 750 students, due to demand for student places. There are currently 713 students on roll, with an almost equal split between boys and girls. The college has a stable population, taking students from a variety of socio-economic backgrounds. Heywood is classed demographically as a deprived area with Pupil Premium (PP) at 23%. The college population is approximately 90 per cent White British, with 10% comprised of other ethnicities. There is a range of abilities in each year group, with Special Educational Needs and Disability (SEND) pupils making up approximately 3.5% of the college population.

There are 46 teachers, 17 teaching assistants and 47 support staff (comprising site, admin, finance, catering and cleaning staff). Staff are employed directly by the college. Reducing staff absence and retaining staff are essential to decreasing pressure on the college budget.

I have been a member of staff at Holy Family College for 18 years. I joined the college when it was St. Joseph's RC High School as an assistant head from inner city Manchester, before gaining promotion to deputy head and then becoming acting headteacher in January 2019. I was appointed to the substantive post of headteacher in September 2019. During this time, I have seen a lot of change. Some good and some bad decisions have been taken with regard to staff wellbeing.

My personal belief is that if we look after each other and support one another as a team, we are capable of providing the best opportunities for our students. Prior to taking up the post of headteacher, I was responsible for staff development. I have used the quote from St. Mother Teresa frequently with staff to lead sessions and to develop the ethos that 'we are all in this together' and no-one is better than anyone else.

Staff wellbeing was generally positive when I stepped up to headship, but we were not explicit in giving our staff a voice to say what it was that they wanted to improve or the means to do it. Leadership believed staff were content because no issues were being raised.

Staff Spiritual Day

Ten years ago, in 2010, I was given the opportunity to develop a staff Spiritual Day at the end of the autumn term. It was the first time we gave staff time and space to focus on their wellbeing. The Spiritual Day has become a welcome chance for staff to recharge their batteries during an extremely long term, providing a focus on spiritual development for part of the day, as well as allowing time for staff to take some 'me time' – offering a yoga session, a walk in a local beauty spot, a chance to participate in staff sport, to name but a few of the workshops that we have run. It also allows us to come together as a whole staff and share an early Christmas dinner, with members of the senior leadership team serving. It is difficult to identify why this is important but being able to bring everyone together in this way is something we have worked hard to retain over the years because of the value it provides.

It was really important to our staff to take stock each year of where they were personally and professionally, and what it meant to work in a faith college. It also helped us to develop a real sense of camaraderie – out of it has emerged our staff choir, which performs at least twice a year. This led to an online choir during lockdown, open to all, building towards a song recording for our HFC community. Not only did it raise a few smiles, it also provided a lifeline for people who had little contact with other members of staff due to shielding. As someone who loves singing, it was a real joy to be involved and gave a really positive wellbeing boost.

The importance of trust and working together

When you look to improve the wellbeing and mental health of staff, you are hoping to develop a culture where staff feel valued, that they are listened to and to cultivate a real sense of working together to do the best for our students. It is also my belief that you need to be honest and transparent as a leader so that trust is built up between the leadership team and staff.

From judgement to development

You can become too driven by data and staff achieving 'the right outcome' in observations. When I was the deputy headteacher with responsibility for teaching and learning, I looked to develop an open-door policy that allowed staff to engage in their own professional development without having a checklist marked off against them or a surprise observation. Moving away from a blame culture has been key to developing openness with staff. It has allowed staff to be honest in return about how they feel as well as where they would like support to improve their own practice.

We invest heavily in supporting students, offering advice and care when needed. The question we asked ourselves was, 'Why do we not do that for staff as a matter of course?'. As Tomsett and Uttley write in *Putting Staff First* (2020), looking after your staff so that they can do their job well will help improve staff wellbeing; managing workload and prioritising effective continuing professional development (CPD) opportunities are key to this. This has a knock-on effect for our students in that they get the best of the best: staff who want to be here, enjoy working, are highly motivated and able to develop their own classroom practice (Tomsett and Uttley, 2020: 21). Most importantly, staff work hard because they want our students to achieve.

Staff wellbeing group and survey

My first action was to launch a staff wellbeing group in the September of my first year as headteacher. My initial thought had been to set this up myself and lead it, but I don't think I quite realised the extent of the 'other things' that would take over my life as a new headteacher.

Having read lots of articles about the importance of wellbeing for staff, I became aware that wellbeing had been allowed to tick along in the background and this really bothered me. After speaking to staff and launching the group at the end of a week in the middle of September, I found that I just didn't have the time to give it my full attention.

I was fortunate to have many members of staff who wanted to get involved in staff wellbeing. Very quickly, a member of staff came forward to run the staff wellbeing group meetings. Their first action was to undertake a staff wellbeing survey.

This was an important first step, as wellbeing needed to have a starting point that took into account the views of all staff, not just teachers. We are a small staff in comparison to other secondary colleges where everything is delivered in-house. Staff needed to know that collecting everyone's views would give them the opportunity to say how they felt about our college, as well as identifying areas that we could develop to improve our culture and ethos.

There were two outcomes from the survey. The first of these was offering staff the opportunity to be honest about how they were feeling and to enable them to identify improvements that could be made to the culture of Holy Family. The second outcome was that I realised as headteacher that staff had lots of ideas about how our environment could be improved and were willing to get involved to make it happen.

Milestone 1: Weekly newsletter

My first important milestone was introducing a weekly newsletter to staff. The aim was to develop a sense of team, to review the previous week and to highlight events in the week to come. The newsletter has also allowed me to thank staff as a whole, as individuals or groups, for specific events or strategies that they have been involved in or taken responsibility for. It is really easy in a college not to notice things, especially when life is so busy but, when it is pointed out to you, it also allows others to comment and people to engage with each other. My weekly message goes out on Sunday afternoons – called 'Sunday Thoughts'. It is something I have done since taking on the role as acting head. I also include a final reflection in keeping with the ethos of our college and a short prayer for anyone who would like to use it. During our weeks of lockdown this was something that I kept doing, as I felt it kept the staff together as a team and, for those people at home due to underlying health conditions, it continued to give them a link to work and colleagues. The response from staff started as a trickle and slowly grew. Often, staff will respond to a comment made or something that has been highlighted to them and are pleased that they knew it was happening. Similarly, staff respond to the final reflection, offering their own thoughts or suggesting a prayer for the following week.

Milestone 2: Staff survey

The next milestone was our staff wellbeing survey. We felt it was important to find out what issues the staff thought should be addressed. We started to develop our 20 questions in November 2019. We found that asking the right questions was more complicated than we first thought. We wanted to avoid individual responses which were not representative of the staff and the college as a whole. I also realised that a particular question could lead me to second-guess why it had been included and whether it was a criticism of my leadership.

Once we had agreed the questions, our next challenge was getting staff to respond to it. That should be a milestone in itself. However, doggedness and perseverance won through and the wellbeing team were able to get information back from staff that they could review and consider the next steps for. This was really important in planning where we would go in order to improve staff wellbeing at every level. We made the decision to make the survey anonymous, as we felt this would encourage staff to be as honest as possible.

Thanking and acknowledging staff

Some issues that emerged from the wellbeing survey responses were easy to tackle and didn't provide too many challenges. We run a weekly 'kudos corner' with 'shout-outs' for hard work for students. This is something we extended to staff, acknowledging the small things that staff do with a 'Thank You' postcard from me as headteacher. There is always a small token gift for one member of staff nominated by another member of staff for something they have done. This is done without fuss and fanfare. Another simple change for us was to introduce a care basket in staff bathroom areas that is regularly topped up by the wellbeing team. It was a really easy change to make and caused us to think – why didn't we do this before?

Our journey during lockdown: Email and WhatsApp

During lockdown it has been difficult to continue our journey. However, at the start of lockdown on 23 March 2020, we made a number of decisions that we felt would have a positive impact on staff mental health. We made it clear to staff that work emails should not be sent or received outside the hours of 9:00 a.m. to 3:00 p.m. If staff had to send an email outside these times, due to their home circumstances, a response was not expected. For some staff, this was a real challenge. I quietly reminded staff of the new email policy if it wasn't followed. I don't think any of us realised what a weight of expectation this places on colleagues when others are responding to messages at 9:00 and 10:00 p.m. and you are not doing so. When someone is sending emails in the early hours, we also need to check that they are okay.

We also introduced a staff WhatsApp group. I posted short messages to staff to keep them up to date. This reduced anxiety for some of our staff who were worried that they were missing important events. Staff do not reply to the messages. It wasn't all smooth sailing and I had to remind staff at the beginning how the system was intended to work. WhatsApp is now quick and efficient, pre-empting some of the communication issues we might otherwise face.

Talking about wellbeing

The greatest impact of our wellbeing work has been that staff talk about it. Prior to launching the Staff Wellbeing Team, it was often the case that people might talk in the background about a niggle they had or 'why don't we do …'. By encouraging staff to ask questions and make suggestions, 'Why don't we do it a different way?' now became a discussion rather than a criticism or negative comment.

Innovation as well as performance appraisal

Since starting our wellbeing journey, I have questioned whether we are focusing too much on performance in appraisals and not giving staff, at all levels, opportunities to take on new challenges and to innovate. Providing staff with opportunities to develop themselves professionally demonstrates my belief that, as a leader, I am interested in them and have confidence that this is an area they can take on and develop. Staff at Holy Family College are encouraged to discuss their CPD needs and how it will be of mutual benefit for them as individual professionals and for the college. We are really fortunate that staff take the opportunity to put back what they have learned into the college community for the benefit of both staff and students.

The impact of wellbeing changes

When I consider the impact of changes we have made, I believe they have had a really positive impact on staff morale. As staff respond so positively to the weekly newsletter, it confirms that it is worth doing. I am reminded if I forget anything or, on the odd occasion it goes out later than expected (due to family commitments on a Sunday afternoon), I usually get a reminder text to email the newsletter from a member of staff. I feel it gives HFC a sense of community. Staff will regularly ask me to include something so that everyone in college is aware of it. It is not just a list of what happened that week, but a real reflection of life at Holy Family College.

The impact of our wellbeing survey got staff talking about how they support each other and how they feel supported. Yes, there were lots of ideas about coffee mornings and book clubs. These are important because we spend a lot of time in college. Building strong relationships is vital, as is being able to let off steam with each other. The idea of having a staff handball game after work doesn't just generate an opportunity for sport – it gives people a chance to speak to each other, allows individuals to offload worries and helps with staying healthy, as well as spending an enjoyable hour of exercise with friends.

The wellbeing survey also provided an opening to discuss workload with staff and areas of work that staff felt needed to be fairer. We had already started work on reviewing marking and feedback, and how we could use 'marking in the moment' to reduce staff daily workload. The survey also made us consider whether meetings needed to take place so often. What was the point of the meeting? Was it a meeting for meeting's sake? By reviewing our workload in this way, we were looking to reduce stress on staff.

Work–life balance

We have become increasingly more specific about what staff should not be doing outside of work and stressing the importance of a work–life balance. Communication has been key for this to be successful. Where there are concerns about expectations and deadlines, this comes back to the leadership team via line management meetings but also from the wellbeing team who meet regularly with me to feed back any concerns that have been raised. The nature of Holy Family College is that we listen to staff and look to find a solution that meets everyone's needs. To be told by my staff that they feel valued and supported, that we listen to their needs and that they feel lucky to work in such an environment, reassures me that we are getting something right.

Where next?

Where next for us as a college? First and foremost, after the last six months when college was partially open, is to get staff back in college, happy to be here, feeling supported and all of us working together. We have begun to look at how we can use the behaviour and wellbeing mentor, who works with students on their wellbeing, also to provide support for staff, with a focus on positive mental health. She was employed initially as part of a two-year project, but the college is finding that her role is also important in supporting the wellbeing and mental health of staff.

We are still on our journey to ensure that we get the culture and ethos of our college right. The strategies that we have implemented during lockdown and in moving towards getting back to college haven't been undertaken as part of any gimmick. There is a real sense of togetherness at Holy Family College. The words of St. Mother Teresa are not just a passing comment.

I believe very strongly that when you get things right and staff are happy in their environment, feel valued by leaders and are part of a team moving in the same direction, they want to contribute to that positive culture. It is really important that we don't just give ourselves a pat on the back and roll out the bacon sandwiches every half term. For our staff to continue to be at their best for our students, they need to be given the chance to develop themselves, to have the right work–life balance and know that, when things are tough and they are struggling, it is okay to say so. It is also having the knowledge that, because you are being looked after, you are able to make a difference and have an impact on the students that we are privileged to teach. This enables staff to bounce back when they encounter challenges.

Our next step? To ensure that, at Holy Family College, we can continue to do great things together.

Key strategies

- Stronger in collaboration.
- Staff Spiritual Day: leadership serve meal; choir performs; wellbeing activities.
- The importance of trust.
- Moving away from blame and judgement culture to a culture of staff development.
- Staff wellbeing group.
- Staff wellbeing survey.
- Weekly newsletter.
- Thanking and acknowledging staff.
- Email policy and use of WhatsApp.
- Staff nominated for a gift.
- Staff 'shout-outs'.
- 'Care' basket in staff bathroom areas.
- Constructive suggestions or questions, rather than expressing individual frustrations.
- Marking strategy revised.
- Work–life balance.
- Spirit of togetherness as a staff team.

32 Tamworth Enterprise College, Tamworth, Staffordshire

Whatever it takes to be remarkable

Jon Spears, Vice-Principal

Principal: Gemma Simon

'If we truly believed in wanting our students to lead "remarkable lives", then we knew we needed to enable staff to be the remarkable teachers we knew they were.'

Overview

In this account of how Tamworth Enterprise College addressed a 'Requires Improvement' judgement in June 2018 and a monitoring judgement in May 2019, Jon Spears focuses on how the appointment of the new principal, Gemma Simon, focused the college's attention on raising staff morale by addressing staff wellbeing. He describes the role played by the Academies Enterprise Trust (AET), the review of the curriculum, the development of trust and credibility, and professional development in the rebirth of the academy. As well as enabling staff to be 'remarkable' teachers, the process of developing a whole-school culture of staff wellbeing and mental health enabled the academy to respond flexibly and successfully to the demands of the Covid-19 pandemic.

Context

Despite its name, Tamworth Enterprise College – known locally as TEC – is an 11–16 academy within the Academies Enterprise Trust (AET). The academy is nestled in the Belgrave area of Tamworth, a once-thriving market town on the fringes of Birmingham. Tamworth is a predominantly White, working-class town. In the Social Mobility Commission's report, 'State of the Nation 2017', it is listed as a 'cold spot', an area that performs badly on both educational measures and adult outcomes, giving young people from deprived backgrounds limited opportunities to succeed. The Belgrave estate is one of the most deprived in the town with low aspiration and high levels of passivity.

Tamworth Enterprise College has around 600 students, 37% of whom are Pupil Premium (PP) and 24% of whom have a Special Educational Need or Disability (SEND). There are more boys on roll at 54%. The academy has 64 members of staff, including 34 teachers, five teaching assistants and four support staff. There are four staff on the leadership team, plus four on the extended leadership team.

It's a well-worn cliché to say, 'We've been on a journey,' but there is no cliché more appropriate to describe academic year 2019/20 at Tamworth Enterprise College. The challenges facing TEC have not just been due to our locale; annual redundancies pre-2019 and issues at leadership level, culminating in three principals in 12 months, left staff wellbeing, morale and motivation at rock bottom. Something had to be done – and fast – if there was any hope of the academy getting itself to a place that would allow our young people to thrive and for us to survive our next Ofsted inspection.

Drawing on my experience as a former student at the college

I am in the unusual position of having once been a student at my school, giving me a unique insight into the community we serve and the contextual problems we face. I had been an assistant principal at the academy since 2016 and could fully understand why staff felt dejected and disheartened. It is one thing for a 'Requires Improvement' school to battle the ever-changing scrutiny of the twenty-first-century educational landscape, but a challenge on a different level to change the culture of an organisation that has lost its way. Fortunately, June 2019 brought a glimmer of hope in the shape of new principal, Gemma Simon.

Our new principal

Gemma is an experienced school leader with a record of successfully transforming struggling schools. She had to draw on her experience to quickly pinpoint the problems at TEC, find solutions and put them in place; this was a journey that needed to move at break-neck speed. Gemma immediately identified that the morale of staff needed to be raised if we were going to improve the fortunes of the academy. Staff absence and feedback from surveys indicated that wellbeing and mental health were not only an issue for our students but were also a key factor in how the adults in the building felt about the academy.

Strengthening links with the Academies Enterprise Trust (AET)

The first action that Gemma took was to develop the academy's links with the AET. She recognised that the level of training and continuing professional development (CPD) had stalled during the tumultuous last few years and that, by utilising the extensive support on offer from the AET, staff would begin to feel part of a network and recalibrate their own feelings about the teaching profession. I too benefited from this approach. Meeting other senior leaders and talking about the difficult experiences I had been through helped me to see that a whole-school approach to wellbeing was sorely needed. This wasn't something that would just happen: it needed careful planning and had to start with reflection.

AET has very clear values and a vision for all students to lead 'a remarkable life'. Whilst we wholeheartedly subscribed to this sentiment, we didn't know what this should look like in our academy. Our own values and vision had become lost.

Evaluating our vision, values and the curriculum

With the help of the AET, we sat down as a leadership team and talked about our academy. We evaluated our context, our curriculum, our key drivers and what we wanted for our stakeholders. It was clear that we had a shared moral purpose when it came to improving the lives of those in our community, as well as a shared desire to confound the bleak picture presented by the Social Mobility Commission. The work around vision and values coincided beautifully with our reshaping of the school curriculum. When the outcomes of our discussions were shared with staff, the conclusions were the same: we had reached rock bottom but were totally united in our shared vision. This culminated in the following curriculum statement:

> 'At Tamworth Enterprise College we believe that *every* child should gain the knowledge, skills and character to live a remarkable life: that includes positive relationships, resilience and financial independence.'

Building trust and credibility

I knew that, in order to improve morale, we first needed to build trust and credibility. I reflected on my own experiences growing up in the area and the challenges I faced and relayed these as honestly as I could to staff. I presented the reality for many of our young people and tried to use this as an impetus for staff to find something to fight for. It worked. Each middle leader developed a vision for their own subject which reflected that of the academy and, collectively, we rediscovered our purpose. We had found a common starting point from which to grow. The next step was to ensure that staff felt sufficient belief in themselves to bring the vision to fruition. Staff wellbeing needed attention, and we knew it would require a multi-faceted approach to be both timely and successful.

We mapped out our plan for 2020: create a shared vision; secure our curriculum; develop CPD opportunities for staff; revisit the behaviour policy to ensure staff feel supported; and introduce rewards and recognition to boost morale.

Christmas 2019 was our first milestone. At this point, we had been able to implement some strategies from our plan and achieve some success. Our vision-building and curriculum work were on the way to becoming embedded and had successfully been through external scrutiny from both members of the wider trust and a DfE partner assigned to work with us.

CPD plan

The CPD plan was also well under way, with more staff attending external courses/opportunities than ever before. We had several staff undertaking National Professional Qualifications (NPQs), and the feedback following in-house CPD was increasingly positive. I listened to staff comments and made changes accordingly. For instance, I split after-school sessions to offer middle leaders more bespoke training, as some felt being in a whole-staff session wasn't always useful for their role. Middle leaders worked with me on materials provided by Leadership Matters, and it was refreshing to share ideas and strategies about leadership. I relayed my own experiences as a former head of English and ensured everybody shared their thoughts in a safe, non-judgemental environment. This was particularly helpful in encouraging staff to begin to feel more valued and supported, as shown by the comments below:

> 'Today's meeting was exactly what I needed. No data, no pressure, not another to do list but just a sincere chat. For the first time this year I felt part of a team; I felt that I don't face the challenges alone. I am privileged to work with such a wonderful group of people.'

> 'Hi Jon, I was just about to message you to say I think, for the first time in a while, I've got some motivation back. Both meetings, yesterday and today, have made me want to step up and take back control :) I have some ideas for a middle leaders' programme that will offer support, systems and strategies to pull us all together.'

Role of leadership team in reducing staff stress and removing barriers to effective teaching

Gemma Simon looked at all aspects of school life and implemented many changes that helped to make things easier for staff. She impressed on all of us at leadership level the need to do what we could to enable staff to teach free from stress and interference. As a result, the senior leadership team (SLT) took on more duties and played an increased role in the implementation of the behaviour system. Processes and procedures were examined, and staff included in their scrutiny and reorganisation. If we truly believed in wanting our students to lead 'remarkable lives', then we knew we needed to enable staff to be the remarkable teachers we knew they were.

Staff camaraderie and collaboration

Systemic changes certainly seemed to impact positively on staff and, despite it being a tough start to the year, there was a real sense of camaraderie building. Staff were volunteering to take on more responsibility and were becoming more visible during non-teaching times, instead of hiding away, frantic to keep up with the demands of the job.

Praise and recognition for staff

The icing on the cake was the personal touch Gemma brought to whole-school change. Having a successful principal join our academy who was full of praise for what we were doing made a huge difference in quickly developing relationships in the first half-term. She made us feel valued and trusted to lead on the shared vision, rather than sitting meekly back waiting to be told what to do. It certainly made me realise that empowering others can have a huge impact on mental health and wellbeing, and I tried to mirror this approach with the colleagues I worked with. Gemma made sure that staff meetings, briefings and emails that came from SLT were always clear in their contribution to our shared moral purpose. There was to be no blame, no personal digs or fear-inducing rants, just fair professional discussions aimed to get the best from everyone. Gemma made sure she was accessible to everyone – her open-door policy and inclusive way of dealing with staff were supported by personal recognition such as birthday cards and a willingness to 'work around' personal issues that affect us all, such as parenthood.

By February we were firing on all cylinders and things were looking more positive than they had been in years. Student data was looking positive and was set to result in an upward swing. We felt that, if we could keep the momentum going, we were headed for a positive summer inspection. And then the world came to a halt. We found ourselves prematurely saying goodbye to our Year 11 students and locking the school gate without any idea when we would be able to unlock it again. Our journey had seemingly come to an abrupt end. How could we hope to continue to develop staff wellbeing when we were no longer in the building and in the grip of a pandemic?

Facing the pandemic with common purpose

The work we had done to build a positive, wellbeing-rich culture at Tamworth Enterprise College was unexpectedly put to the test in ways we couldn't have imagined during the period of 'lockdown' due to Covid-19. However, the overwhelming evidence was that the staff wellbeing culture had indeed been created, was strong and could withstand even the demands of a global crisis.

Our collective aim for all of our students to thrive and find their own 'remarkable' meant that in the days prior to school closure we worked collaboratively, as a full body of staff, to ensure every parent had been called, all IT needs assessed, and any vulnerable students identified for a package of support. Staff rose to meet the challenges and, looking back now, we are extremely proud of how quickly we pulled together to support our community. I know that some schools focused on completion of work, with sanctions for students not following their school timetable online at home. Our approach was different. We put our emphasis on student wellbeing and mental health. We promoted schoolwork as a way for students to maintain some sense of normality. We needed our students to feel that they still belonged to TEC, that we cared about them and would be there for them (albeit virtually). This approach also had a beneficial impact on staff wellbeing.

Some staff had to self-isolate before lockdown and it is a testament to the sense of belonging and buy-in that all of them (including two on supply) joined us virtually via Google Meet for the daily staff meetings we held during the final week of school. Our approach during virtual schooling has been to focus on staff health and wellbeing rather than to identify what they are or are not doing. We went back to our starting principles in September 2019: staff needed to know that they were working together towards a clear vision; they needed to feel supported, equipped and enabled to do their jobs; they needed access to quality CPD; and they needed to feel valued as people.

'Teaching and Learning' weekly video briefing

On the first Monday – and subsequently every Monday – of lockdown, I filmed a short briefing and shared it with staff. Whilst officially called our 'Teaching and Learning Briefing', it was more a chance to connect with staff with some humour, share reflections on the ever-changing news, offer staff reassurance and to reiterate how our virtual school approach still adhered to the collective vision that had bought us together and had driven us since September. I regularly received emails and texts from staff thanking me for the videos and, more importantly, offering suggestions and support to make our student offer better. The teaching and learning briefing was followed on Fridays with whole-staff briefing. Not only did these give Gemma the chance to relay Trust-wide messages or government advice, but they became a heart-warming opportunity for staff to share, to 'meet' each other and to connect. There was 100% attendance to the Friday briefings and staff feedback confirmed how much they helped them cope with the uncertainty of the pandemic.

Achieving high engagement of students in online learning through staff commitment

We pulled together and launched an online school that bucked the trend in terms of student engagement. We tracked that 70–80% of our students were engaging with us online. Assemblies were streamed live and focused solely on rewarding students. They were watched weekly by 80–90% of students. This was only achieved by the hard work and collegiate response of our staff. We had a rota for staff to be in school with vulnerable students, a rolling rota of staff calling home to make wellbeing checks and a timetable of teaching each day.

When faced with the challenge of moving from face-to-face teaching to online learning, we had succeeded beyond expectation. The culture of staff wellbeing had enabled us to work as a team, to collaborate and support one another. It is hard to think that, 18 months earlier, we had struggled as a school to get full staff attendance at parents' evening. Now, here we were with staff engaging every day and offering to do more. There was no edict that staff had to log on and off at set times, only that lessons had to be uploaded for students to access by 9:00 a.m. There was no expectation that every teacher had to deliver live lessons or had to attend the academy if they didn't feel able to do so. The only expectations were that staff would switch off their email alerts after 5:00 p.m. and would feed back to us in regular staff surveys. We had set out to staff in September that we trusted their professional integrity to do what was right by the students and during lockdown we demonstrated that the trust was genuine and well-deserved.

Praising and recognising staff

This is not to say that we got our approach to staff wellbeing perfect. We were learning and reacting to how to cope during lockdown. On one occasion a member of staff commented that we were doing great things for student well-being – including postcards home, rewards assemblies and competitions – but that it would be nice to remember staff needed these signs of appreciation too. It was a helpful interjection and a reminder we could do more. It also confirmed that we had successfully promoted the openness that allowed such discussion to take place. As a result, we made staff rewards a key element of our Friday briefings. Throughout the week, staff could nominate each other for recognition. Nominations were then shared during the briefing with all staff via PowerPoint, accompanied by inspirational music.

Through weeks of virtual meetings, telephone conversations, emails, texts and videos we got to the end of the summer term knowing we had done our best. We had risen to a challenge unlike any other and our collaborative approach to fulfilling our academy's vision had been a success.

As we look ahead, we have many more challenges. But we know that we can now weather any storm and meet adversity with confidence. Our journey is still very much in progress, but we have already learned so much to continue to take us forward. Staff need to be listened to; to be treated and trusted as professionals; to have a strong, shared moral purpose; and to be free of constraints and barriers that stop them from doing their job. As leaders, we have to do whatever it takes to enable staff to be remarkable.

Key strategies

- Appointment of new principal.
- Drawing on author's experience when a student at the school.
- Raising morale of staff identified as priority by increasing trust in leadership.
- Improving links with Academy Trust to offer comprehensive professional development and support.
- Middle leaders offered customised professional development.
- Creating a vision and values integrated with the development of the curriculum.
- Review of behaviour policy.
- Review of rewards and recognition for staff as well as students.
- Leadership team played a greater role in reducing staff stress and enabling them to teach with minimal interference.
- No-blame culture.
- Open-door policy.
- Staff family commitments taken into account.
- Collaborative, whole-staff response to school lockdown during Covid-19.
- Weekly 'Teaching and Learning' video briefing when school was partially open during pandemic.

33 Firth Park Academy, Sheffield, Yorkshire

Staff, student and family wellbeing: An integrated whole

Frankie Arundel, Associate Assistant Principal, Deputy Director of Humanities and Mental Health & Wellbeing Lead, with Stephen Waters

Principal: Dean Jones

'*Be big-hearted: treating each other with kindness, warmth and care, believing that everyone matters, and believing in one another.*'

Overview

Frankie Arundel, associate assistant principal, subject lead for personal, social, health and economic (PSHE) education, and mental health & wellbeing lead, reviews the integrated approach to wellbeing and mental health at Firth Park Academy. She presents extracts from a range of documents from 2019/20 to show the work that the staff and students have done to promote whole-school wellbeing, including the Academy action plan, references to the relationships, sex and health education (RSHE) curriculum, and addresses staff wellbeing in the Leadership and Management section of the May 2019 Office for Standards in Education (Ofsted) Framework, effective from September 2019. Frankie Arundel wrote this case study before the outbreak of the Covid-19 pandemic.

Context

Firth Park Academy (FPA) is a larger than average 11–16 secondary school in Sheffield and is part of the Academies Enterprise Trust. There are 1170 pupils on roll. The proportion of disadvantaged students supported through the

Pupil Premium (PP) is over twice the national average at 60%. The proportion of students whose first language is not English is high and over twice the national average at 35%. The proportion of students with Special Educational Needs and Disability (SEND) is 12%. A number of students join or leave the Academy at times other than that normally expected, and this figure is much higher than the national average. The Academy has its own additional provision unit, called 'The Workplace', where students are offered vocational education as well as employability and life skills. In addition, an inclusion centre called 'Think for the Future' provides mentoring and alternative provision. It is an exciting new approach to education at Firth Park Academy, designed to make sure that all students have a successful journey at school with a clear focus on qualifications and careers.

Firth Park Academy integrates mental health strategies for staff, students, carers, parents and families in its planning and delivery, viewing each stakeholder as essential to its whole-school approach. The Academy's commitment to wellbeing and mental health underpins its educational vision:

'Our vision is for each and every child at Firth Park Academy to be inspired to choose a remarkable life. We wish to instil in our children a set of values that will positively shape their characters to lead truly remarkable lives.
   These values are to:

- **Be unusually brave:** we challenge wrongs and do what is right, no matter how difficult.
- **Discover what's possible:** we step forward to explore a world of possibilities and opportunity.
- **Push the limits:** as we never settle for less than excellent and intend to overcome any barrier to our achievement.
- **Be big-hearted:** treating each other with kindness, warmth and care, believing that everyone matters and believing in one another.'

The Academy also drew on the 'definition' of mental health from the Anna Freud Centre for National Centre for Children and Families:

'A mentally healthy school sees positive mental health and wellbeing as fundamental to its values, mission and culture ... child, staff and parent/carer mental health and wellbeing are seen as "everybody's business" ... It needs partnership working between senior leaders, teachers and all school staff, as well as parents, carers and the wider community.'

This is one reason why the school has dedicated a senior leader to the role of mental health lead, as it will be statutory by 2025.

The Academy is in the process of applying for the Edupod Innovating Minds Whole School Mental Health Award, which informed the direction and focus of the Academy's wellbeing strategy. [Ed: EduPod is a platform for mental health leads to enable them to plan, manage and evaluate their journey to creating happy and mentally healthy environments for the whole school community and to implement best practice. It includes professional mental health resources and action plans.]

The award criteria are based on implementing five principles within a self-assessment audit tool. The self-assessment audit tool brings together recommendations from Public Health England (now the National Institute for Health Protection), the Department for Education and the expertise within EduPod. The five principles are:

- Readiness and Motivation.
- Leadership and Strategy.
- Working Together.
- Staff Support and Development.
- Student Support.

Action plan

Objectives

In June 2020, the Academy drew up an action plan for student, staff and family wellbeing. The objectives of the action plan were to:

1 Facilitate a whole-school approach to positively impact mental health and wellbeing at Firth Park Academy.
2 Provide all of our pupils with the confidence and ability to embrace the challenges of creating a happy and successful adult life, by equipping them with the knowledge that will enable them to make informed decisions about their wellbeing, health and relationships and to build their self-efficacy.
3 Engage with, and increase participation of, parents/carers to be representative of the school community as part of the Firth Park Parent and Carer Advisory Board (PCAB).

Success criteria

(a) Edupod self-audit assessment for caregivers, staff, students and governors to achieve 10 key indicators for each area. The goal was to move 80% of responses from 'disagree' to 'agree' in the audit tool by the end of spring term 2020. The key indicators include:

Caregivers, e.g.

1 I feel that the school is aware of their responsibility to support my child's mental health.
2 The senior leaders within the school are committed to supporting my child's learning and mental health.
3 I have seen information from the school about how they are creating a mentally healthy environment.

Staff, e.g.

1 I am committed to integrating strategies that will support students and educational staff's mental health.
2 Our school is motivated to implement the whole-school approach to mental health.
3 The school's vision relating to the whole-school approach to mental health has been communicated to me.

Students, e.g.

1 My school is committed to helping students' mental health.
2 The staff at my school are motivated to help everyone's mental health.
3 I know what my school is planning to do to help everyone's mental health.

Governors, e.g.

1 The governing board is committed to supporting the senior leadership team with the implementation of a whole-school approach by reviewing current systems and implementing actions to influence change.
2 The governing board is willing to allocate resources (staff time and/or money) to support the implementation of the whole-school approach.
3 The vision for the whole-school approach to mental health was communicated to me.

(b) 80% of the 10 key indicators to be completed by the end of spring term 2020.
(c) A wellbeing and RSHE policy completed and available online by September 2020.
(d) One PCAB meeting per half-term throughout the year of at least eight parents/carers, with representation of members in line with the school community.

Tables 33.1–33.7 present the details of the action plans implemented by Firth Park.

Table 33.1 Firth Park Action Plan: Provisional strategies for impact (to be finalised after completion of EduPod audit tool)

Objective	Actions	When	Outcome
1	Up-to-date wellbeing policy and addendum Self-audit tool for caregivers, staff, students and governors Self-audit tool for whole-school strategy	Audit tools: September and November 2020	Identifying gaps based on results and implementing changes
2	Mental health and wellbeing staff and student ambassadors (including line-managing the chair of Wellbeing Steering Group)	Staff and student meetings at least once a half-term	A review of the last half-term's actions A clear plan of 2–3 actions to implement as a group in the next half-term (e.g. Mental Health Awareness Week plans)
3	RSHE policy and curriculum complete	September 2020	RSHE policy and curriculum available for anyone to see
4	Implement RSHE audit tool	July and November 2020 (review)	Identifying gaps based on results and implementing changes
5	Liaise with XXXXX, XXXXX and XXXXX to calendar dates for PCAB and delegate recruitment strategies	Once every half-term Additional PCABs if needed	Operating PCAB of no less than 3 members and no more than 10 members, meeting once every half-term

Table 33.2 Firth Park Action Plan: Provisional strategies for impact – Students

Official Wellbeing launch: September 2020	Made aware of wellbeing opportunities at FPA
Student voice	Surveys. Students will be trained to support their peers with matters of wellbeing, similar to mental health first-aiders, e.g. bullying or other friendship-related matters. A button will be added to the website to report abuse
Safe spaces	Creation of wellbeing zones: specified areas of the school that are designated for a calm atmosphere and mindfulness activities during breaks and lunchtime
Raising awareness/ wellbeing messages	Weekly social media uploads, national wellbeing celebrations, website space and equality walks. Equality walks are where we encourage the school community to go out for a walk or some form of exercise and discuss equality topics such as the Black Lives Matter campaign, Pride month, disability awareness, etc.
Education	PSHE lessons, Samaritans talks, links with PE initiatives

Table 33.3 Firth Park Action Plan: Provisional strategies for impact – Staff

Official Wellbeing launch: September 2020	Made aware of wellbeing opportunities at FPA
Training	Wellbeing launch, mental health first-aider, Samaritans active listening, Innovative Minds webinars, safeguarding
Staff voice	Clear outline of this system, surveys, wellbeing ambassadors, button on the website to report abuse
Raising awareness/ wellbeing messages	Official Wellbeing launch: Wellbeing Wednesday blog – written by a staff member (normally anonymous) on a mental health topic, usually describing their own experience. Weekly social media upload, weekly wellbeing tip, website space and Helping Hands Facebook, a Facebook group to support wellbeing, where staff can share experiences, access support
Safe spaces	Weekly discussion/safe space forum, guardian angel system – staff are buddied up with each other outside their specialism and can support one another if needed. Google communities page – a social networking page specifically linked to our Google account. Signposting and support can be posted here
Governors	Named governor for RSHE

Table 33.4 Firth Park Action Plan: Provisional strategies for impact – Parents and Carers

Eco shop	Food available to purchase at a cut price from a 'shop' by XXXXX to be built by XXXXX (September 2020)
Raising awareness/ wellbeing messages	Official Wellbeing launch, weekly social media upload, button on the website to report abuse, parent section of the website, equality walks
Training	Mental health first-aider, Samaritans active listening, Innovative Minds webinars, safeguarding, parent workshop, e.g. how to talk to my child about their emotions, how to support my child with a mental health condition

Table 33.5 Firth Park Action Plan: Provisional strategies for impact – Student Leadership

Training	Diana Award, Mental Health Student first aiders, LGBTQ+ Ambassadors, Sports Leaders.
Pride identification	Different coloured ties.
Supporting staff	With enrichment, with duties.
Raising the profile	Assemblies delivered by students.

Relationships, sex and health education

Changes to the curriculum and Ofsted's inspection framework mean that supporting children's mental health and wellbeing will become more of a focus for schools, including Firth Park. From September 2020, we will teach relationship, sex and health education (RSHE). We have planned our strategy for developing healthy and respectful relationships, including families and friends, addressing both physical and online relationships. We encourage our students to understand how to be healthy, with a particular focus on mental wellbeing and including learning how to take care of themselves, and knowing how and when to ask for support, if problems arise.

Table 33.6 Firth Park Academy Action Plan: Provisional strategies for impact – RSHE

Training	Staff who are delivering RSHE fully trained, in-house if necessary
Consultation	PCAB (phase 1 complete, phase 2 to include an example lesson), governor consultation
Named governor	XXXXX

Table 33.7 Firth Park Academy Action Plan: Provisional strategies for impact – PCAB

Recruitment parents	Write to all parents of Gold Learner status students, reflective of outstanding attendance, attitude and aspiration. Gold learners are students who display excellent attendance and punctuality as well as attitude to learning through data collection from their teachers
Recruitment community members	Head-hunt individuals with skills and connections that will benefit our school (positive recruitment of BAME individuals)
Training	Safeguarding, Exclusion Panel training, school system and processes refresher
Activities	Academy learning walk allows for openness and transparency, which builds trust
Alumni	To continue a connection with our successful past students through social media (Academy Twitter and Facebook) in order to benefit from their skills and celebrate their success
Award-winning	To nominate the students, staff and parents at our school for local and national awards, securing funding for any awards and opportunities
Fundraising	Running and encouraging fundraising events which benefit our students and bring our whole community together
Listening and learning	Gathering parent, student and community voice on the reputation of the Academy
Networking	Establishing connections to city-wide stakeholders for work experience, careers talks
Parental awareness	Promoting initiatives and campaigns relating to personal development, behaviour and welfare
Participating on panels	Participating on complaint, exclusion or staff disciplinary panels as required
Responding to community concerns	Creating proactive responses 'you said …, so we did …'
Line management responsibilities	Restorative practitioner, chair of Wellbeing Steering Group

Links to Ofsted

From September 2019, both staff and children's mental health and wellbeing will take a more prominent place in Ofsted's new inspection framework. Schools will be assessed on how well they support children's personal development through some of the following ways:

- Teaching pupils how to build their confidence and resilience so that they can keep themselves mentally healthy.
- Promoting equality and making sure all pupils can thrive together; children should understand that being different is positive, not negative.

Table 33.8 shows an example of the topics discussed at a meeting of the Staff Mental Health and Wellbeing Steering Group.

Table 33.8 Firth Park Academy: Minutes of meeting of Staff Mental Health and Wellbeing Steering Group

Agenda item	Points raised	Action
1. Social calendar for staff	Currently doesn't exist Once/twice a year – staff night/day Event: examples – staff curry night in school. End of term – department meals/activity/department buddy Staff family day – outdoors Used to do Super Friday – shared lunches cooked by a different person each week Charity event – brings people together Dedicate a morning per year for a wellbeing hour: NHS health check-ups, mindful colouring, beauty – outsourced Afternoon – motivational speaker/comedy: highlight the importance of this to staff – how it positively affects you; happiness, getting to know each other, enjoyment Reduced-cost yoga, etc. Volleyball club – Staff VS Equality 4:00 pm Singing/staff choir Staff wild swimming/walks Workload – affecting people's engagement in wellbeing activities	Google form – if we did put on something like a wellbeing morning, what would you want, and would you want to be involved? What would you choose to do? Would a specific group e.g. for anxiety be useful? Complete by Friday 10 July 2020 CPD: 'How to' video for Google XXXXX by Wednesday 4:00 pm. Create communities that you need to ask to join Collate blogs somewhere – XXXXX Wednesday Calendar in 'Staff VS' where staff challenge students to various sports such as badminton for different sports – XXXXX for September 2020

(Continued)

Table 33.8 (continued)

Agenda item	Points raised	Action
2	Student leaders – SSH ideas Student mental health Ambassadors/Champions (XXXXX could train?) Mental health safe space/ wellbeing zone/nurture group (XXXXX has done this with Year 8) Anxiety gremlins – XXXXX Self-harm support group – XXXXX	All research – September
3	Teaching pupils how to be safe online and the impact social media and the internet can have on their wellbeing	
4	Developing pupils' understanding of healthy relationships.	
5	AOB	Next meeting **Wednesday 4:00 pm –** 15 minutes to look at Google form and XXXXX's CPD video

Wellbeing – supporting our students, staff and communities

We provide information for students, staff, parents and families on how to access wellbeing and mental health support.

Signposting support for students

Figure 33.1 shows examples of wellbeing review questions for in-school or online meetings following lockdown and returning to school (September 2020).

Mental health support websites

- 'Clear Fear' is a free app to tackle anxiety. It helps to reduce the physical responses to threat as well as changing thoughts and behaviours and releasing emotions [https://www.clearfear.co.uk/]
- 'Calm Harm' is an app developed for teenage mental health charity stem4. Calm Harm provides tasks to help you resist or manage the urge to self-harm [https://calmharm.co.uk/]

Figure 33.1 Firth Park Academy: Wellbeing review questions

Question	☺	☹	😐	Comments
"I am excited about getting back to school, although I might struggle to get up early and it might be strange to be with lots of other people. I wonder how you feel about coming back - you might feel excited too, or worried, shy, happy or a bit strange"				
"I've had some up and down days during lockdown, how have you been feeling?"				
"Is there anything you've enjoyed doing during lockdown?"				
"Have you had any difficult times during lockdown?" (may link to bereavement)				

- Papyrus is a suicide prevention charity for young people [https://papyrus-uk.org/]
- IMALIVE is a non-profit organisation dedicated to suicide intervention, prevention, awareness and education. It provides an online crisis chat service [www.imalive.org]
- The Mix is a support service which supports young people with any challenge they may be facing – from mental ill-health to finances, from homelessness to finding a job, from relationship problems to drugs. Access is via social media, an online community, a confidential helpline or counselling [https://www.themix.org.uk/]

Tap into local charities and services

The Samaritans are known for their support if you are feeling suicidal. However, they also provide help for a range of other mental health issues. There is an all-year round, 24-hour helpline: 116 123 [https://www.samaritans.org/]

Signposting support for families

- Sheffield Carers Centre aims to enable carers to access as many opportunities, services and support as possible [https://sheffieldcarers.org.uk/health-wellbeing/]
- Carers UK supports the 6000 people who start looking after someone each day, including online meetups [https://www.carersuk.org/help-and-advice/get-support/online-meetups]
- Combined Minds: when a child or young person has a diagnosed mental health condition, families and friends want to support them in the best way they can but they also want to step back to allow them to help themselves. The Combined Minds app is designed for this [https://combinedminds.co.uk/]

Signposting support for staff

- Action for Happiness support website [www.actionforhappiness.org]
- Education Support: the UK's only charity providing mental health and well-being support services to all education staff and organisations. There is an all-year-round 24-hour helpline [https://www.educationsupport.org.uk/]
- Child Bereavement UK: support after the death of a child. Video [https://www.youtube.com/watch?v=OID-Ea68idY&feature=emb_logo]
- Every Mind Matters: NHS site offering support for a range of mental health issues and challenges [https://www.nhs.uk/oneyou/every-mind-matters/]
- For Flourishing Sake: a 5-minute podcast to boost and inspire wellbeing in teachers and school leaders [https://www.forflourishingssake.com/]
- DfE modules on Teaching Mental Health and Wellbeing [https://www.gov.uk/guidance/teaching-about-mental-wellbeing]
- Mental Health and Behaviour in Schools, DfE pdf (November 2018) [https://assets.publishing.service.gov.uk/government/uploads/system/uploads/attachment_data/file/755135/Mental_health_and_behaviour_in_schools__.pdf]
- Online support: our staff wellbeing Facebook group. Our weekly wellbeing tips. Lunchtime Google Meets 'staffroom' with themed topics for discussion, e.g. balancing work and looking after pre-school children.

Students

- **Mentoring: Think for the Future** mentors teach character education every day of the week to targeted groups and hold one-to-one meetings to support wellbeing, using Google Classroom and videos to extend their reach. Academic 'Achieve' mentors support study skills and help students balance aspiration and exam anxieties. [Ed: Think for the Future is a social enterprise offering education with a difference. Their educators are inspiring mentors, using their personal experiences to challenge negative attitudes and misconceptions of young people. Think for the Future has singers and entrepreneurs, rappers and poets using their stories and skills to make a positive difference. Think for the Future inspires young people to build resilience and self-esteem to overcome challenges and barriers in their lives. Their progress benefits their school or community both holistically as well as financially.]
- **Counselling: Forge Youth workers** invest two days each week in counselling and coaching sessions to support students in managing the challenges and traumas life can bring. [Ed: Forge Youth is a Christian organisation, providing youth services in the communities of Sheffield.]
- **Monitoring: AS Steer** is an online screening tool to identify hidden vulnerabilities which we can then support students to overcome. Student voice 'pulse surveys' allow identification of pressures.
- **Pastoral care:** assemblies and form times on wellbeing themes (in-school and online).

- **Enrichment:** an extended school day, broadening opportunities for mental and physical enrichment. Wellbeing-focused clubs such as Young Carers, including home cooking skills. Fun staff videos, video challenges and treasure hunts of wellbeing messages.
- **Social media:** feel-good content and hidden educational signposting.
- **Online support:** our student wellbeing webpages and signposting.
- **Academic and wellbeing reviews:** in-school and online reviews for students and their families, on returning to school following lockdown in September 2020.
- **Curriculum:** PSHE curriculum and post-Covid recovery curriculum.

Families

- **Food bank:** having raised £3000 to fund our food bank during lockdown, this enterprise has grown sufficient networks with regular supplies to allow us to create a weekly eco-shop, providing low-cost shopping for Firth Park Families.
- **Bereavement support:** cards sent to all families who have lost someone, on behalf of our Firth Park Family.
- **Doorstep culture:** a culture of 'support to the doorstep' with pairs of staff regularly visiting home for advice, intervention and celebration. Also delivering food, clothes and books to families in need.

Firth Park Academy has always naturally been a caring and supportive environment for its students, their families and staff. In 2020, we recognised the need to support our community even more, due to the tragic and challenging circumstances of the Covid-19 pandemic. In addition to a national increase in the need for mental health and wellbeing support, we knew a clear vision for the school was a priority. There is uncertainty of what the future may bring. A quote from Maya Angelou sums up our response to tackling this uncertainty and building upon our strong foundations:

'Continue to be who and how you are, to astonish a mean world with your acts of kindness.'

FPA has the kindest staff I have ever known, and I have no doubt we will continue to support one another as we face future challenges together.

Key strategies

- Integrated approach to wellbeing and mental health, involving students, staff, parents and families.
- Working towards the EduPod Innovating Minds Whole School Mental Health Award.

- Wellbeing and mental health action plan with clear objectives, timed actions, intended outcomes, success criteria and impact.
- Preparing to teach RSHE.
- Parent and Carer Advisory Board (PCAB).
- 'Signposts' to support for staff, students, carers and families.
- Organising Firth Park Food Bank for struggling families.

34 The Sheikh Zayed Private Academy for Girls, Abu Dhabi, United Arab Emirates

Isolated, but never alone – we're in this together

Ashley D. Johnson, School Counsellor

Principal: Carolyn Bailey

'In implementing a culture of staff wellbeing, I wanted staff to know that we were in this together and that, even if they were isolated, they were never alone.'

Overview

School counsellor Ashley Johnson describes how the appointment of a new principal, and support for staff isolated during Covid-19 lockdown interconnected to raise morale and create a greater sense of community.

Context

The Sheikh Zayed Private Academy for Girls (SZPAG) is a private school located in Abu Dhabi, United Arab Emirates (UAE). Our school consists of three academic buildings on one campus, serving approximately 1700 students in grades KG1–12. New students are required to complete an entrance exam prior to enrolling into our school and our intake has the full range of ability, including students who receive Special Educational Needs and Disability (SEND) support. Our student body is approximately 30% male and 70% female in grades 1–3, and 100% female in grades 4–12. The majority of our students are Emirati, UAE natives (91.21%), but we also have a very small percentage of students of various nationalities, which include: Jordan (2.63%); United States of America (1.59%); Egypt (0.55%); Syria (0.55%); Oman (0.49%); Sudan (0.37%); Pakistan (0.37%); India (0.31%); Yemen (0.31%);

Saudi Arabia (0.24%); South Africa (0.18%); Morocco (0.18%); Kenya (0.18%); Libya (0.18%); Palestine (0.12%); Canada (0.12%); Australia (0.06%); Algeria (0.06%); Iraq (0.06%); Kuwait (0.06%); the Philippines (0.06%); Qatar (0.06%); and Lebanon (0.06%). Our staff consists of 139 teachers, 32 teaching assistants, four SEND teachers, four SEND learning support assistants and 25 support staff.

I began working at SZPAG in August 2017 as one of three school counsellors. During my first year, I supported the secondary school, but I am now supporting children in the early childhood and primary sectors. I have also had the pleasure of getting to know the majority of our staff members, as I have worked in all three academic buildings. I offer support to both students and staff. When I joined the school, staff morale was quite low. Many teachers spoke of feeling weighed down by their heavy workload and, at times, felt unsupported by the administration. With a recent change in leadership, things have improved tremendously, as staff now report being more supported and feeling more appreciated.

Supporting staff wellbeing during lockdown and tackling isolation

When we were informed that we would be leaving school for a month in early 2020 due to the Covid-19 pandemic, none of us could have predicted what was coming. As many things began to rapidly change, affecting all schools in the UAE, including nurseries and day-care provision, many teachers, especially those with small or school-age children, worried about how they would manage care/schooling for their children and be able to continue to work. I began to realise that this 'new normal' would present many challenges. Staff could feel isolated and alone, especially those who are single and live on their own. Some staff caring for small children while working from home reported feeling helpless, as they were unable to have a break. Others who had family members and friends in far locations reported feeling sad and disappointed that they would not be able to visit them for some time.

In my personal life, wellbeing is a priority. I have seen first-hand the benefits of being intentional in giving the same priority and energy to my mental health as my physical health. I believe that this has helped me to become more resilient and capable of adapting to life's challenges and unexpected situations such as the one which we are currently facing with Covid-19. It also helps me to maintain a positive outlook on life, elevates my mood, and ultimately gives me a positivity that I can share with others. I understand, however, that this way of being is not something that comes naturally to others and needs to be taught and practised daily. I have learned that many people want to improve their wellbeing and to feel better about themselves, but simply don't know where to start or don't realise that a shift in mindset can make a difference. In both my counselling role and outside it, I aimed to provide them with practical tools, encouragement and support which would benefit themselves and, in turn, would have a positive impact on their interaction with students, parents, and their own family and friends. In implementing a culture of staff wellbeing, I wanted staff to know that we were in this together and that, even if they were isolated, they were never alone.

Assigning staff to houses: August 2019

Prior to Covid-19, we implemented several initiatives focusing on staff morale and wellbeing, including a house system which was developed between 2018 and 2020. The house system was fairly new to our school and I inherited responsibility for it as coordinator during my first year. I made a number of changes to the way the inter-house programme was run, and I believe that it has begun to gain momentum with our students in creating a culture of inclusion, camaraderie and friendly competition. Initially, our house system was student-focused, creating smaller inclusive fun-based communities within the larger school community. Staff and students in the secondary school were formerly the only people assigned to houses. However, at the beginning of the 2019/20 school year, we decided to assign every staff member in the school to a house. We continued to assign only students in the secondary building to houses, not pupils in the primary and early years phases. By placing staff in one of four houses and including them in inter-house activities, the sense of inclusion has increased across the three campuses. This has encouraged staff to get to know colleagues who work in another building or who teach another subject.

Sustaining staff commitment to the house system

The new house system began with enthusiasm and lots of positive energy, but some staff were slow to warm up to engaging in the activities. Although activities were optional, we strongly encouraged everyone to participate. The biggest challenge that I faced was organising activities when everyone was available. Some staff were sceptical of participating because mixing with staff they didn't know was new and out of their comfort zone. Other challenges included keeping the momentum and spirit of competition going outside of organised activities. As it is the first year that we have offered this, I am still learning about managing an effective house system. I have also found it challenging to create strategies to keep the idea of inter-house competition relevant and in the forefront of everyone's mind.

Pairing new staff with a mentor

In addition to house activities, our school has a wellbeing department in the secondary building to ensure student wellbeing and mental health are cared for and prioritised. We also pair any new staff members with a mentor to ensure their induction is smooth and to provide support and guidance as they settle into the school. A teacher acts as lead mentor to organise activities for new staff and their mentors, with the goal of building relationships both inside and outside of the school. Mentors and mentees also have whole-group meetings each month to support their wellbeing.

Post-lockdown: Greater focus on staff wellbeing and mental health

Prior to lockdown because of Covid-19 in March 2020, my primary focus was on student activities and engagement. After we began virtual learning in April 2020, I began to focus more on ensuring our staff were being provided with resources and wellbeing/mental health support. My desire to create a strong culture of wellbeing and mental health increased during lockdown. I teamed up with one of our secondary school counsellors to offer sessions on a range of topics to anyone who was looking for support. We asked staff members to fill out a survey indicating what support they needed. They were able to say if they felt comfortable participating in a group session with others or if they preferred to have a one-on-one session with myself or the secondary school counsellor. We also directed staff to virtual resources that were being offered within the school community.

Weekly videos offering support and celebrating staff birthdays

I asked the principal for permission to create and email a video to inform staff that I was available if staff needed someone to talk to. This led to creating two videos each week, containing words of encouragement and positivity, and acknowledging staff who were celebrating their birthday during the week. I have several friends on the staff who had birthdays during the first couple of weeks of lockdown and I saw how upsetting it was for them not being able to celebrate with anyone. I knew it was especially hard for those of us who lived alone. When I first began to share birthday celebrations, I wasn't sure how impactful it would be. I started getting feedback from many staff members of how appreciative they were of my efforts and how the videos were really lifting their spirits. This motivated me to continue.

Transparency from the principal

The principal also sent out a weekly staff briefing to keep everyone up to date, which helped people feel more informed about changes that were taking place. I believe that transparency from the principal helped to set people's mind at ease, knowing that she was always doing as much as she could to keep everyone's best interests in mind. Knowing that our principal cares, values and respects every person on the staff has helped to reduce stress and boost morale.

The Shukran Award

We have a weekly draw called the Shukran Award ('shukran' means 'thank you' in Arabic) where we submit the names of staff members who others would like to thank for an act of kindness or for being supportive, or another act which has helped a member of our staff community. Each name goes into a weekly draw and a winner is selected at the end of the week. During the pandemic lockdown, more names were submitted for a weekly Shukran Award than ever before. Although only one winner is selected each week, everyone who has been nominated receives all of their nominations, including a short write-up of why they were nominated. This has truly boosted morale, as staff reported feeling appreciated by their colleagues.

Weekly quiz night

A member of the senior leadership team asked if I would be interested in hosting a weekly quiz night on Thursday nights for anyone who wanted to connect virtually with other staff members towards the end of the working week. This became a fun event that many people looked forward to, as we would have lots of laughs, while engaging in friendly competition.

Staff survey

A few months into student distance learning, we asked staff to complete a survey to gather data about the virtual learning experience: 99% of staff indicated that the school supported and cared about their mental health and wellbeing. A larger number of staff wanted to continue to teach at SZAPG than in the last three years. I attribute this increase to the change in leadership and better support for teachers.

The future – next steps

The 2019/20 school year undoubtedly had its challenges, with staff having to adjust to virtual learning and balancing their personal and work lives, but the efforts that the school has put in place this year have made what could have been a rough journey a lot smoother. This school year has taught me that taking the time to implement strategies to ensure everyone is feeling cared for and supported is important. I believe that continuing our mentoring programme for new staff and maintaining house activities will make an important contribution to sustaining morale. I have learned that feeling heard and validated and having someone to check in on you when you're going through a difficult time, are essential to a positive working environment and the school community. As we entered a new school year in 2020/21, I resolved to include mental health and wellbeing topics into our weekly professional development schedule. There are many community organisations that we could partner with to provide more resources. I also want to be sure that our staff knows that their mental health and wellbeing are a priority and that they will be supported. I am committed to continuing to ensure our staff know that isolation does not mean that you are alone. We are truly in this together!

Key strategies

- Supporting staff during lockdown, especially those who lived alone and staff who had family and friends in far locations.
- Providing staff with the practical and emotional tools to take greater care of their mental health.
- Changing the house system, including assigning staff to houses.
- Pairing new staff with a mentor.
- Greater commitment to staff wellbeing and mental health during Covid-19 lockdown.
- Weekly videos offering support and celebrating staff birthdays.
- Transparency from the principal.
- The Shukran Award.
- Staff quiz night.
- Staff surveys.

Part **4**

Alternative Provision

35 Bishopton Pupil Referral Unit (PRU), Billingham, Stockton-on-Tees

Investing in staff

Emily Carr, Headteacher

'As a school leader, I firmly believe that it is our moral duty to ensure that our workforce, students and their families are safe, valued, loved and cared for; this must take priority over everything else. If staff are happy and achieving success, I believe that students will also be happy and achieve their full potential and go on to lead successful lives. A positive ethos is essential.'

Overview

Since Emily Carr took up post as headteacher at Bishopton Pupil Referral Unit in 2017, she has increased support for staff in their work with often challenging young people. Although the unit's latest Ofsted report was 'Good', staff wellbeing continued to be an area where focus and development were needed. Work–life balance, clarity of systems, procedures and policies, acknowledgement for staff achievements and a customised approach to professional development have led to increased motivation, a collaborative approach and an increase in morale.

Context

Bishopton is a Pupil Referral Unit (PRU) within Stockton-on-Tees Local Authority, commissioned by the local authority to support permanently excluded children from Key Stage 3 (KS3) and Key Stage 4 (KS4). The PRU is based on one site in the north of Stockton and has two buildings – one for KS3 and the other for KS4. The PRU takes referrals from 13 secondary schools. There are currently 60 students on roll.

Bishopton takes permanently excluded students, as well as students who come into the area via the Fair Access Protocol. The purpose of Fair Access Protocols is to:

'... ensure that – outside the normal admissions round – unplaced children, especially the most vulnerable, are found and offered a place quickly, so that the amount of time any child is out of school is kept to the minimum. This is why every local authority is required to have in place a Fair Access Protocol, developed in partnership with local schools ... the School Admissions Code 2012 gives local authorities and schools, including Academies, the freedom to develop and agree Protocols which best serve the needs of children in their area ... the Code [does not attempt] to prescribe the structure or detailed content of Protocols. It is for participating schools to ensure that the local Protocol works for them and is reviewed as required with the local authority' (DfE November 2012, updated 2014).

Some students come to Bishopton on a partnership arrangement with their home school, which is time-limited, with specific outcomes identified by their school. The main focus for these students is to re-integrate them into mainstream schools or to support them through an Education, Health and Care Plan assessment in order to enable them to move into specialist provision. In KS4, Bishopton mainly supports students who are permanently excluded or have been admitted through the Fair Access Protocol. However, there are occasions when short-term partnership places are successfully used to re-engage students with their mainstream school.

Bishopton's ethos and aims

Bishopton is committed to providing a safe, caring and stimulating environment for all our students. Our key aim is to prevent further exclusion, and the adverse consequences that such labelling and experiences create, and to enable students to succeed in education. The placement process for students is rigorous. Students that are referred to Bishopton often exhibit disruptive and challenging behaviours and have underlying social, emotional and mental health issues.

The intense intervention that Bishopton offers creates an environment where often ingrained behaviours and attitudes can be managed effectively. This allows students to re-engage with education and to experience success. In turn, this fosters their confidence and self-belief and makes it possible for them to change their educational trajectory. As a result of the calm, focused and supportive setting, students experience academic progress and begin to attain academic levels that are more closely aligned to those of their peers.

At KS3, Bishopton's aim is to re-engage students and enable them to successfully return to mainstream schooling. This can be done via a 'managed move', with transition support, as well as re-integration with outreach support to their home school. Managed moves between schools are used as an intervention to reduce the risk of a student being permanently excluded and are arranged with the consent of parents.

If an individual student is not able to cope in a mainstream setting, guidance from Bishopton will help to inform the school so that appropriate educational provision can be obtained to meet their educational needs. At KS4, the main aim is to ensure our young people can access a broad and balanced curriculum and achieve qualifications and success, allowing them to move on successfully to the next stage of their educational journey.

Students access an academically challenging curriculum, including GCSEs, with core subjects taught on site, whilst more vocational subjects are offered at quality assured alternative provisions across Teesside. Alternative provision outside Bishopton is closely monitored to ensure high standards of safeguarding, quality assurance and outcomes for students. A member of the senior leadership team (SLT) leads on alternative provision and careers, and a member of staff visits providers each week.

Bishopton also offers a bespoke and engaging outdoor programme of education (known as COPE) to support students. The outdoor education curriculum has been developed to complement the core educational curriculum offered on-site. Bishopton believes that exposure to a range of outdoor activities helps to support the development of the whole child: emotionally, physically and academically. There are many important benefits of providing students with an outdoor curriculum. These include improving:

- Creativity.
- Health.
- Social skills (managing conflicts, cooperation and teamwork).
- Wellbeing (good mental health).
- Independence and leadership skills.

The outdoor curriculum that has been carefully developed is highly inclusive and fully aligns with the ethos of the school. Students that access this curriculum can also achieve nationally recognised qualifications which can support them in later life.

Some of the exciting, adrenaline-packed activities that students can experience include: power-boating, archery, kayaking, climbing, abseiling, archery and mountain biking. These activities encourage the development of key life skills such as tolerance, resilience, self-belief and aspiration.

Bishopton staff are proud to support the local communities as part of the school outdoor curriculum by being actively involved in activities such as beach cleans, improving the local area and positively engaging with the community.

By providing students with stretching academic opportunities alongside the outdoor curriculum, we aspire that Bishopton students achieve the following outcomes:

- A healthy and happy body and mind.
- A sociable, confident person.
- A self-directed and creative learner.
- An effective contributor.
- An active global citizen.

COPE is now striving to deliver key qualifications to some Year 11 students that would not normally be available to them until they are aged 18. These nationally recognised qualifications include skills such as employability, with an aim to allow for a smooth transition into either work or further education when Year 11 leaves the school.

Sharing good practice

The last Ofsted inspection, in June 2017, judged the school's provision to be good in all areas. This judgement reflected the improvements that had been made since the previous inspection and verified the leadership team's self-evaluation judgements. Bishopton has also started to look at ways it can support other PRUs and organisations to improve their support for young people. As a result of this work, Bishopton leaders have developed a 'Menu of Services' to offer to local schools. The headteacher and deputy headteacher are now specialist leaders of education. The headteacher has formed a local PRU network, as well as subject specialist groups for the network (e.g. English). Bishopton also held a conference in October 2019 in which colleagues from Stockton and across the country took part in workshops hosted by Bishopton staff.

Awards and recognition

Bishopton's vision for high-quality, inclusive education is highlighted through the achievements made during external inspections. For example, in September 2019, the school was proud to be awarded the Inclusive Quality Mark (IQM) Centre of Excellence. The report stated:

'Pupils follow the high expectations of the new National Curriculum and it is creatively and imaginatively planned to engage the disaffected.'

The school was also awarded the Quality in Careers Standard for high-quality careers guidance in December 2017, and achieved the 'Gold' Spiritual, Moral,

Social and Cultural (SMSC) quality mark in April 2019. The SMSC inspector recommended that the school became a 'beacon school' for SMSC to share good practice. (Reports can be found on the Bishopton school website.)

Staff physical and mental health

It is well-researched that poor mental health is one of the biggest causes of staff sickness in the UK. The 'Thriving at Work' report (Stevenson and Farmer 2017) estimated that poor mental health costs employers in the UK between £33 billion and £42 billion a year. It is also no secret that working in the education sector can have a significant negative impact on employees' mental health, as it is considered to be amongst the most stressful of professions. Excessive workload, poor pupil behaviour, lack of communication and conflict at work are contributory factors to the poor mental health of staff.

At Bishopton, all staff and leaders subscribe to the belief that good levels of staff wellbeing, both physical and emotional, are essential for fostering a mentally well school. Staff need to feel in control of their workloads, which results in them being motivated and engaged and having more resilience to cope with unexpected challenges. Good staff wellbeing is understood by all Bishopton leaders to result in improved staff retention, lower levels of sickness absence and improved recruitment. Investing in staff emotional and physical wellbeing has been a high priority over the last three years and is identified in the strategic vision and school development plan (SDP).

A new focus on staff wellbeing

On appointment in September 2017, I recognised that staff wellbeing was not identified formally in the SDP. There was an acknowledgement by the SLT of the importance of staff wellbeing and they were exploring ways to improve it, but nobody had formally taken a lead on staff wellbeing and mental health, resulting in a lack of cohesive and comprehensive action in this area.

I put vision and values at the top of my priority list for the school. I reflect on our journey throughout the remainder of the chapter, outlining the key features of our approach.

It was vitally important to cultivate a culture of wellbeing throughout the whole school. As a school leader, I firmly believe that it is our moral duty to ensure that our workforce, students and their families are safe, valued, loved and cared for; this must take priority over everything else. If staff are happy and achieving success, I believe that students will also be happy and achieve. A positive ethos is essential.

I wanted staff to feel empowered and supported in implementing changes to the daily running of the school, which would have a positive impact on pupil behaviour, engagement, attendance and attainment. I was also keen to create a more equal, and less hierarchical, culture where staff felt safe to make decisions, suggestions or comments without fear of criticism or recrimination.

I also wanted to ensure that staff felt a sense of balance between work and life, that they felt well and motivated to come to work, committed and productive. Staff have personal lives and families – the most important aspect of anyone's life. With immediate effect, I stated that I would honour any leave of absence requests made for family/life events within reason and with adequate notice. I aimed to ensure that we were sensitive to staff work–life balance and celebrated it, and that key life events like birthdays and other milestones were acknowledged by all staff and supported by leaders.

I also considered it crucial to develop clarity in our school's vision, values and practice. With clarity of roles and responsibilities comes improved accountability.

The journey

1. Clarity of vision and values. I commenced my tenure on the first day of a new academic year. It was an ideal opportunity to use the Professional Development Day to look at our vision and values, and to begin to survey staff for their mental health and wellbeing as well as to identify some short-, medium- and long-term plans relating to mental health and wellbeing for the whole school community. I took the time to find out about staff and their interests and skills. I wanted to find out how they saw their professional development and progression, and to utilise their strengths in order to improve the school and support students in the best way possible.

2. Staff wellbeing. The mental health and wellbeing lead conducted staff wellbeing surveys which fed into a staff wellbeing policy and worked with me to tailor it to our current workforce. Staff were supported to assume accountability for their own workload and were advised where to seek support outside of the traditional human resources signposted routes. One source of support was QWELL, an online service designed for people experiencing issues with their emotional wellbeing, such as anxiety, low mood or stress. The website has a range of self-help tools, including friendly online discussion boards to connect with people having similar experiences, journals and goal trackers, and self-help articles. Another source of support was 'Brain hAPPy', an app that digitises therapies proven to reduce stress, improve mood and improve health.

Staff surveys found that our current workforce valued time with their family and friends above all else. We therefore introduced staff appreciation sessions. On these afternoons, groups of staff have the opportunity to spend time together away from the school building to build relationships and relax and get home early to spend quality time with family and on self-care. Staff reported improved morale and a reduction in work-related stress.

In order to further support staff wellbeing, and their health, staff also attended fitness classes and circuit training together at the end of the school day. This is another way of supporting the physical and mental health of staff – enabling them to balance their work life with their personal wellbeing, by providing them with opportunities to exercise at the end of the working day. It has also allowed staff to develop relationships and a team ethos.

3. Celebrating staff success. In order to support staff and acknowledge staff work and achievements, I introduced a 'Celebrating Staff Success' initiative. I believe that staff recognition is important because it:

- Communicates to staff that their work is valued and appreciated.
- Gives staff a sense of ownership and belonging in their place of work.
- Improves morale.
- Enhances loyalty.
- Helps build a supportive work environment.
- Increases staff motivation.
- Improves staff retention.

The aim of the initiative and accompanying policy is a recognition and celebration scheme that will demonstrate and deliver on Bishopton's ethos and meet a number of key objectives. The scheme recognises and values staff achievements and contributions that make a positive impact on school outcomes, for both staff and the young people we work with.

The celebrating staff scheme aims to:

- Encourage staff to develop their talents, skills, abilities and knowledge and in doing so, become fully engaged in whole-school life.
- Support and develop effective teaching and learning.
- Maintain a positive learning community and school ethos.
- Promote a culture of fairness and equality for all.
- Contribute to the maintenance of good order and discipline.
- Promote best practice.
- Improve productivity and staff engagement.
- Support and promote Bishopton values and a culture of recognition.

As a school, we recognise the importance of seeking opportunities to acknowledge and reward the achievement of staff as well as students. A culture of praise seeks frequent and consistent opportunities to celebrate successes and achievements. We use staff briefings/meetings to announce successes of a professional or personal nature and more formal opportunities will be used to acknowledge staff achievements.

The Celebrating Success initiative promotes and supports a culture where new ideas are shared and good practice and innovation are recognised throughout the organisation, thereby exemplifying Bishopton values. The Celebrating Success initiative runs throughout the school year, with an award assembly and winner revealed at the end of each half-term. All staff who work at Bishopton take part. Nominations are made via the nomination forms that are collated at the end of each half-term where all staff will attend a celebration assembly. Staff read out examples of the positive comments and nominations. A winner is revealed and is able to have a day at home during the following half-term, as a thank you. Staff report that they enjoy these assemblies and listening to the nominations.

4. Continuing professional development (CPD). Staff report that our bespoke CPD offer is supportive of staff wellbeing and workload because they are able to 'pick and mix' CPD which suits their career path. They are thus more empowered and motivated because they are in control of their own personal development journey. Feedback surveys reported positive engagement and outcomes from sessions attended, as training met their needs, rather than attending a whole-school session which may not necessarily be applicable to their role.

5. Clarity of procedures, systems and policies. In order to ensure staff were able to confidently prepare for their time in school and be confident that they understand key priorities, systems and procedures, a number of strategies were put in place:

- A robust induction programme for new staff.
- A staff handbook to provide clarity of important areas.
- A Teaching and Learning Calendar that outlines key dates, such as when learning walks are taking place, so that staff are prepared and aware of when things are happening.
- Clear whole-school policies that all follow the same format, to allow for clarity and consistency.

The next steps

Bishopton PRU has identified, through staff surveys, increased productivity and feedback from students and parents, that a focus on positive mental health is a key priority and reaps rewards.

As with all schools, there are daily challenges, strategic challenges, including unforeseen hurdles such as the global pandemic. However, through these challenges and opportunities for growth and change, the staff and leaders support each other to maintain a positive mindset and continue to be mindful and caring of each other's needs. Bishopton is currently working towards the Gold Mental Health award from Leeds Beckett University, to become nationally recognised as a mentally healthy school for both staff and student wellbeing; staff are very proud of the progress made since 2017. As a further commitment to supporting staff family life, the local authority, chair and governors of the PRU have approved a co-headship structure, providing progression and development for a senior leader to join the current head in leading the school. Whilst challenging, this is further evidence of the commitment at Bishopton PRU to support a positive work–life balance and to recognise the important of staff and their wellbeing.

Key strategies

- A clear long-term vision.
- Staff wellbeing.
- Work–life balance and importance of family.
- Developing clarity of vision and practice.
- Staff wellbeing policy and Celebration of Success initiative and policy.
- Staff appreciation days.
- Choice of CPD.
- Opportunities for staff growth and development.

36 Coal Clough Academy, Burnley, Lancashire

Back from the brink

Nathanial Eatwell,
Designated Safeguarding Lead

Headteacher: Holly Clarke

'*The Trust took great care to talk to staff at every opportunity. They consulted with staff, governors and representatives from the trade unions and worked hard to reassure staff through this difficult process. They began by creating a welcoming in-service training day and discussed the importance of staff well-being, mental health and togetherness.*'

Overview

Nathanial Eatwell, designated safeguarding lead at Coal Clough Academy, describes how the school climbed from two consecutive Ofsted judgements of 'Requires Improvement'. Nathanial explains that this was as a result of support from the Education Partnership Trust, which became responsible for oversight of the running of the school, and the appointment of Holly Clarke as headteacher. Staff wellbeing, mental and physical health became the focus of school improvement, including better information sharing, workload reduction, relevant professional development and creating a social spirit amongst the staff. Acknowledgement and appreciation of the work of staff became the core of the school's ethos.

Context

Coal Clough Academy is an Alternative Provision school in Burnley, East Lancashire. We have 142 commissioned places and a further 60 for respite pupils. Respite pupils are pupils who have been referred to us directly and are struggling with the mainstream environment or are close to permanent exclusion. We also have commissioned place pupils for whom the local authority is responsible and are referred to us for a range of reasons, mainly:

1 Medical provision – pupils are unable to access mainstream education, due to physical and/or mental ill-health and are referred to Coal Clough by a consultant.

2 They have been permanently excluded from a mainstream school.
3 Pupils who have recently moved into the area but who have not been offered a place in mainstream education or are unable to find one themselves.

We also take referrals from schools who are in need of respite provision for pupils deemed to be close to exclusion or who are in need of and EHCP application on our Gold Package. Pupils who are referred to us come with an array of needs, generally in relation to social and emotional factors, but can also include a high number of undiagnosed or not investigated Special Educational Needs and Disabilities (SEND) such as dyslexia, dyspraxia and autistic spectrum conditions.

Our school is predominantly made up of White male pupils, with a small proportion of Black, Asian and Minority Ethnic (BAME) pupils. Our male-to-female ratio is 82:28. We have 47 classroom staff, including specialist subject teachers and teaching assistants, supported by dedicated pastoral, safeguarding and SEND teams to address pupils' specific needs. The school also has a small admin, catering and site supervision team.

Coal Clough Academy was established after the Education Partnership Trust (EPT) was approached by the Department for Education (DfE), following two consecutive poor Office for Standards in Education (Ofsted) inspections of the former Coal Clough High School. At the time of the first inspection, the former school had only recently been established, following decisions from the local authority to amalgamate three previously centrally run services: a Key Stage 4 Pupil Referral Unit (KS4 PRU), a Key Stage 3 Pupil Referral Unit (KS3 PRU) and a medical provision service for both KS3 and KS4. The staff who were employed by the local authority PRU had only been working together for a short time and, at the time of the Trust takeover, had been subjected to two Ofsted inspections in quick succession. The school was found to 'Require Improvement' in all areas, ratified by subsequent Her Majesty's Inspector monitoring visits, during which very little improvement was seen. Staff were bewildered by the sense of failure, and staff absences due to illness were at an all-time high. Staff wellbeing had been neglected and it was the priority of the newly established senior leadership team (SLT), led first by a seconded headteacher and then our current headteacher, Holly Clarke, to ensure that staff felt that their wellbeing and mental health were being supported.

When Holly Clarke took up post, staff turnover within school had increased, staff absences due to sickness were at their highest level, and the school was spending an exorbitant amount on supply staff. The lack of consistency in teaching staff led to instability for pupils and undermined attempts to promote positive behaviour and deliver high-quality, engaging lessons. The ultimate goal for the SLT was then – and still is today – to provide a supportive and empathetic learning environment for the most vulnerable pupils in our community and to enable them to achieve their potential. This meant that the SLT needed to get staff on their side and improve their wellbeing and sense of belonging, whilst making sure that we were able to show consistency of behaviour and teaching and learning across the school.

Collaboration with the Education Partnership Trust

The first step in improving staff wellbeing was taken during the transition process between being a local authority school, whose staff had experienced failure, and being given a fresh start under the EPT. The Trust took great care to talk to staff at every opportunity. They consulted with staff governors and representatives from the trade unions and worked hard to reassure staff through this difficult process. They began by creating a welcoming in-service training day and discussed the importance of staff wellbeing, mental health and togetherness. As the first term as an academy came to an end, difficulties were still emerging on a range of issues, including the wellbeing of staff. The Trust put the welfare of staff and pupils first and made some tough decisions regarding the existing SLT to turn things around. A new headteacher was brought into the school who had worked in another Alternative Provision school within the Trust. He restructured SLT, developing existing staff who showed leadership potential and also recruited externally to bring in fresh ideas and approaches.

The Trust introduced a package of physical and mental health support through an external private health care provider, Simply Health, that gave staff access to a 24-hour helpline and assessment of their mental health and counselling, if needed. The package is promoted in school, and staff are encouraged to use it as often as required. A range of other initiatives was implemented to support staff wellbeing.

EPT's support for staff wellbeing

Information sharing

Information sharing had been highlighted as requiring improvement. Numerous staff had cited this problem as a cause for stress during the transitional phase between local authority oversight and becoming an academy. The Trust improved communication so that staff were kept up to date with student behaviour, sanctions, safeguarding and changes to the school day. This was a major focus for developing staff wellbeing and an 'easy win' for the SLT, as it led to more effective management. Staff felt better equipped to deal with the problems pupils brought to school and became more aware of potential behaviour issues. This means that 'surprises' in class reduced and staff were more prepared to mitigate situations that have led to negative behaviour or concerns.

Reduced workload

The Trust reduced staff workload by simplifying planning, requiring less onerous schemes of work and cutting down on admin. Marking has been streamlined and lesson observations focus on the positive and are ungraded. The SLT are present in school at crucial times to ensure the smooth running of the school and that classes start promptly. The members of the SLT also provide advice and are ready to discuss problems as they arise in school.

Staff feel supported in making decisions and managing behaviour and pupil anxiety in class and around school. Staff now feel less pressure throughout the school week and are therefore more able to concentrate on delivering outstanding lessons to pupils.

Continuing professional development

The following strategies have made continuing professional development (CPD) more relevant and engaging, with staff feeling it is beneficial, rather than doing it because it is in the calendar:

- Staff wellbeing is part of the CPD calendar and topics are designed to support staff in their role.
- Food is provided during training.
- CPD is about delivering solutions to problems.
- A coaching programme is in place, designed to support teachers and their development.
- There is a focus on good practice and working across subjects. Staff feel listened to and supported by peers.
- A team ethos has been created – staff support one another.
- Staff are regularly praised and encouraged by the SLT, both face-to-face and in emails. Staff feel supported in their efforts.
- Briefings and meetings are focused on acknowledging and sharing positive achievement.
- A feeling of togetherness. Although there are safeguarding briefings on Friday afternoons, there is a raffle where every winner is cheered, and staff leave on a happy note.
- On World Mental Health Day in October, the Trust arranged for a health and wellbeing coach to run drop-in sessions for staff.

Formation of a wellbeing team

In September 2018, a wellbeing team was formed, led by staff. The wellbeing team implemented a number of ideas and events to promote staff wellbeing and mental health of staff, such as an end-of-year celebration and BBQ. More opportunities have been created to celebrate success in social situations. A staff fitness class was formed and staff were encouraged to take care of themselves.

A staff 'Welcome Back' kit was provided in September, a selection of items to welcome staff back to school after the summer break. This included a message which explained the relevance of each of the items in the kit; for example, a chocolate bar to 'reward your hard work, care and attention', or a small packet of mints to 'reward all of your accomplish-mints'!

Guardian Angel scheme

Staff are given a name of a colleague to 'look after' over the course of a half-term. Guardian Angels step up to care for, help out or give a small gift to the person they have been allocated. This creates an opportunity to acknowledge each other's roles and the valuable part each person plays in the running of the school.

Shout-out board

The shout-out board is a space where staff can add someone's name to show appreciation publicly for acts of kindness or to acknowledge a job well done.

Consultation and asking staff to contribute ideas

Staff have been asked for their opinions through staff forums and questionnaires on what wellbeing and mental health strategies would generate impact. Consultation has led to:

- Behaviour and pastoral support throughout the day and beyond.
- Mental health first-aiders – several staff have this qualification.
- Friday – early finish encouraged.
- Breakfast and break time food/drink, plus Friday lunch, are provided free. Staff are encouraged by the SLT to take a full half-hour for lunch to ensure they give themselves adequate 'down time'. Staff lead lunchtime duties but those on duty are volunteers and are provided with free lunch and extra pay.
- Social time between staff and students is encouraged.
- Book swap.
- Xmas and Halloween quizzes.
- Xmas party.

The impact of these wellbeing and mental health initiatives has been significant:

- **Staff absence:** The number of staff who have been signed off for stress-related illness or poor mental health has declined steadily since the Trust took over the school.
- **Staff turnover:** Staff retention is at its best-ever level. After an initial period of adjustment where staff left due to changes or out of choice, the changes implemented have led to staff wanting to stay as part of the team.
- **Recruitment:** The headteacher is constantly contacted by people seeking employment at our school. Requests come from colleagues who are members of external agencies and from schools in the local area who have seen or heard about the positive atmosphere and team approach at Coal Clough. When posts become available, we receive a large number of applications and our shortlists are drawn up from a pool of highly qualified and well-motivated staff.

- **Staff wellbeing surveys:** 98% of our staff report a high level of wellbeing and support. There is a culture of staff helping one another to do the best job possible.
- **Staff attendance at events:** As the team ethos has developed, staff have engaged socially with each other outside of school and attendance at events organised by members of staff or the school to celebrate success has grown and grown. This highlights togetherness and shared values.
- **Recognition from others:** Visitors to Coal Clough Academy often comment on the atmosphere in school. These visitors include Ofsted inspectors and external quality assurance consultants. Their comments extend to how staff interact with each other in corridors and support each other when needed. This can be seen in the relationships between pupils and staff, as they are modelled on how staff themselves work together and collaborate.

Joint leadership training with the Education Partnership Trust

The key to future wellbeing and mental health is sustainability. This includes encouraging attendance and engagement at existing events and continued involvement in staff professional development at all levels. Joint emerging leadership training with the EPT is also a key component of the school's core values.

Social, emotional and mental health for pupils and staff

As awareness of the importance of social, emotional and mental health (SEMH) for pupils grows, so it does for staff. A newly formed internal SEMH team ensures that their approach is interconnected with staff CPD so that they recognise the importance of taking care of their own mental health in working in what can be an extremely challenging environment.

Key strategies

- Collaboration with the Education Partnership Trust.
- Relevant continuing professional development, including staff wellbeing.
- Joint leadership training with the EPT.
- EPT support for staff wellbeing.
- Workload reduction.
- Formation of a wellbeing team.
- Staff consultation, including invitation to propose wellbeing strategies.
- Joint leadership training with the EPT.
- Social, emotional and mental health team for staff, as well as pupils.

Gretton School, Girton, Cambridgeshire

Acknowledging and supporting the management of transactional stress

Beth Elkins, Headteacher Primary and Secondary

Executive Principal: Ian Thorsteinsson

'*Staff wellbeing is essential to the learners' development, security, consistency of provision and welfare; all that we do is based on the success of supportive relationships with the adults that work here. If the staff are not OK, the students cannot be OK.*'

Overview

Beth Elkins, headteacher of Gretton School, describes how staff wellbeing is inextricably linked with pupil wellbeing. She emphasises the vital importance of relationships between learners and staff, and between staff themselves, in facilitating their rewarding but challenging work to support the emotional, physical, mental and educational development of the children and young people in her school. Gretton School is a striking example of how staff and pupil wellbeing are two sides of the same coin.

Context

Gretton is an autism spectrum condition specialist school in Girton, Cambridge for students aged 5–19 years. Class sizes are small, with high staff-to-student ratios. There are 130 pupils on roll, with more boys than girls. The number of girls is increasing, as society improves its diagnosis of girls on the autistic spectrum. All learners have a diagnosis of autism and an Education, Health and Care Plan. Pupils come from 12 local authorities and from a range of school and family backgrounds. The school has a team of wonderful staff, from subject specialist teachers to support staff. The senior leadership team (SLT) is comprised of the executive principal, deputy head, head of safeguarding and quality, head of boarding, the admin manager and me – the headteacher. New additions for academic year 2020/21 are an assistant head primary and Key Stage 3, and assistant head Key Stage 4 and sixth form. We have approximately 25 teachers and many more teaching assistants, residential support workers – whose role is to offer support to learners who struggle to manage independently – and form tutors. Complementing this structure, we have a range of teams to support our learners:

- Residential team.
- Referrals and admissions team.
- Behaviour and welfare team.
- Multidisciplinary team, including a range of therapists and psychology professionals.
- Administration team.

In total, we have about 130 members of staff who are wrapped around the children and young people and who support their academic, social and emotional development.

The learners who come to Gretton School are unique and wonderful and we have a team of equally unique and wonderful staff to support them. The staff are resilient, resourceful, remarkable and ready for anything, but working at Gretton can be enormously challenging. Staff wellbeing is essential to the learners' development, security, consistency of provision and welfare; all that we do is based on the success of learners' supportive relationships with the adults that work here. *If the staff are not OK, the students cannot be OK.* When we recruit, we are looking for 'that certain something', in addition to the other skills that teachers and staff require. When we find that right person, we want to keep hold of them; this is a large part of the reason why we decided to focus on implementing a culture of staff wellbeing. Our vision of wellbeing goes far beyond peaceful meditation and token temple massages. We are driven to embed a sense of responsibility in staff for wellbeing through the lens of personal agency, tight support networks of informed people, a celebration of success – no matter how small – and a true sense of job satisfaction through the identification and acknowledgement of the tremendous impact our school has on the children and young people we educate.

I joined the school two and a half years ago as assistant head and was promoted to the post of headteacher in 2020. During the last two years, the school has been through significant changes, including both systemic change and the establishment of a variety of different systems. When I started at the school, there was a real sense of 'staff' and 'management' as separate entities; the former felt the latter were responsible for everything and the latter was a small group of people trying to do too much. We did not have a structured approach to staff wellbeing, and staff were seeking support from one another, resulting in small, tight groups of staff not all working collaboratively within a fractured social environment. The learners, desperately in need of consistency and structure, were, as a consequence, struggling.

Their behaviour reflected these struggles and staff, in turn, were managing this in small groups, rather than implementing a whole-school approach. Staff wellbeing was poor, and many staff expressed their frustrations, often in inappropriate ways. The environment was tricky and the staff – empathic beings with big hearts – were trying hard to keep it all together and support the students.

Morale was low and needed urgent attention.

Transactional stress

We sought opinions from staff to identify why staff wellbeing was low. Their feedback convinced me that transactional stress was a major cause of lack of morale.

'The transactional model of stress and coping argues that ... We can either adopt *problem-focused* or *emotion-focused* coping styles. Problem-focused approaches involve attempting to deal with the situation itself ... an emotion-focused approach ... reduces the stress it causes. This can involve denial, avoidance or cognitively re-framing the meaning of the event' (Lazarus and Folkman, 1984).

Lazarus and Folkman suggest these strategies are an attempt to engage in a reappraisal to try to find a positive approach to the situation. Emotion-based coping may be particularly suitable to circumstances which cannot actually be influenced in a meaningful way because they are beyond the control of the person who is in the situation.

'Coping strategies can be classed as *adaptive* if they help us manage our stress responses in the long term (for instance, changing the problem, or focusing on the good in a situation). In contrast, *maladaptive* coping behaviours reduce our experience of stress (the arousal, or the symptoms) in the short term, but don't help, or actually exacerbate the problem in the longer term' (Frings, 2017).

It was the maladaptive staff coping strategies that we sought to change, as they were causing staff significant and harmful stress.

Mitigating the impact of transactional stress

Once we acknowledged the significant impact of transactional stress on staff, it was important that we took action to mitigate its impact – to consider how we could 'top up' staff who were flagging, and to identify how we could turn challenges into positive opportunities for change and growth. It was so important to invest in our staff, but also to role-model this resilience to our learners. We understand the correlation between autism and mental health difficulties, so we sought to create a culture in which mental health was discussed openly and that recognition and acknowledgement of mental ill-health were followed by positive action. Our main goal for implementing a culture of staff wellbeing was learner-centred. We are here to support the growth and development of the children and young people in our community. However, the staff are what makes the school work, so investing in them – finding time to talk about things they were finding difficult; thinking of different ways to keep staff 'in touch'; identifying actions teams could take to relieve stress or to work more effectively together – were all essential areas of focus in the development of the staff wellbeing culture.

Scottish Autism: Autism Practice-Informed Improvement Project

We also worked with Scottish Autism to identify areas of practice where improvements could and should be made. Scottish Autism is an organisation which accredits schools and other organisations by creating focused Autism Practice-Informed Improvement Projects (APIPs). The team that volunteered to work with Scottish Autism on the APIP identified the need to reflect on how we manage the impact of transactional stress.

Transactional stress seeps unbidden from troubled and complex young people and is absorbed by the sensitive, kind and patient staff. The APIP team also evaluated the ongoing impact of transactional stress, because, beyond the original transaction of stress from learner to staff, we were also seeing the retreat of affected members of staff to the staffroom, where it was transacted to another four people, and so on. The exponential growth of stress levels needed to be considered very seriously in order to identify ways in which we could counteract its impact.

Wellbeing team

One of the outcomes of the APIP was to establish a wellbeing team which would collaborate with the SLT to identify ways of supporting and improving staff wellbeing and to offer a point of contact for staff at times of need. Importantly, this team also now organises staff social events and plans different ways to relieve stress at the end of term.

We started with a small group of staff from every area of the school – teachers, therapists, admin and support staff – who came together as part of the APIP with the aim of supporting the development of the school *from the perspective of the staff*. The group was keen to think about transactional stress within the school environment and identify strategies to alleviate it. Shortly after the wellbeing team emerged from the project, a questionnaire was sent to staff to gain an understanding of the stress levels within school and to pinpoint the main issues that were creating difficulties. Four main areas of development were identified:

- **Student reflections:** the opportunity to work reflectively with a learner after an incident occurs to enable them to think about how this might have been different and what would have helped to create a different outcome.
- **Staff reflections:** an opportunity post-incident to think through what happened in a protective and supportive way and to consider how things might have turned out differently.
- **Restorative practice:** when relationships have gone wrong and communication is not as positive as it could or should have been, to provide the opportunity to have a mediated conversation with the learner, with repair and restoration as the goal.
- **Relational practice:** the opportunity to bring to professional supervision topics and issues which need careful thought and an effective solution. Relational practice invites both students and teachers to enter into a dialogue about learning. In supervision sessions, teachers reflect on both their own and the learners' views about learning.

Relational practice was considered to be the most important strategy for some staff. It provided space and time with a supervisor to think about the learners, the environment, the challenges and the opportunities, and to reflect on how to achieve the best possible outcomes for learners and for themselves when things became challenging. With support from the school's clinical and educational psychologists, we are now *well* on the way to implementing these strategies and providing staff with regular opportunities to reflect and take stock of where they are *personally* within their *professional* environment – and to work out where one starts and the other ends. Relational practice has played a crucial role in improving staff wellbeing.

Milestone 1: Appointment of principal Ian Thorsteinsson in September 2018

The most significant milestone in this journey of change was the appointment of a new principal, Ian Thorsteinsson, in September 2018. Ian had had previous experience of turning around specialist schools for young people with autism and getting all the 'ducks in line'. Under Ian's guidance, systems, expectations, policies, procedures and approaches were all clearly defined, and staff were given some clear training and time to implement new processes and strategies. This has inevitably taken time, but it gave the SLT clear parameters within which to work and we were delighted to get stuck in!

There had previously been significant staff turnover, and this didn't improve in the first year, as a number of staff reflected on whether the environment and the changes that were in the offing were for them. This was one of our biggest challenges initially, as I suspect it is in any organisation undergoing a shift in culture. However, from September 2019 onwards we saw a significant steadying and consolidation of the staff team. Those who are here now want to be here. They want to be part of the change. They value the culture shift and they recognise the positive impact on the atmosphere and on the students. The school is calmer. So are the students.

Milestone 2: Staff consultation

The next step was to identify and get feedback from staff about what they wanted for their school, what their struggles and successes were, what strategies would provide support, and how the leadership team could support them. In school year 2018/19, we consulted with staff on how their wellbeing could be improved through staff meetings (sometimes very challenging!), curriculum team meetings, student focus meetings, individual feedback and via the supervision process. Supervision sessions took place every six weeks during the school year and this schedule came with its own challenges: finding the time and space to sit with staff; fitting sessions into busy school days; line managers who didn't feel equipped to manage the impact of transactional stress on staff; discussions that seemed to go nowhere. It was most important that we aimed to have regular supervision meetings, even if we did not always succeed. The outcome was that there was a significant increase in the number of supervision sessions, and information started to flow through the organisation as a result.

We still have some way to go as, in the present academic year (2020/21) we plan to start underpinning supervision sessions with training for line managers. Our aim is to support them to have difficult/courageous conversations; to be able to put a 'frame' around the conversation so that those participating understand its purpose; and to be able to hear difficult reflections and still feel positive about the school and our aims. We know that supervision sessions will also be a really important place to recognise all the valuable work being done and to encourage and validate staff.

Milestone 3: Collaboration with Scottish Autism

As explained earlier, an important step was to work closely with Scottish Autism, an organisation which accredits schools and organisations providing support for autistic learners through focused APIPs. In November 2019, we invited representatives from Scottish Autism to visit the school and meet the staff and students. In January 2020, a team was chosen from a cross-section of staff to work on identifying the areas for project development. The coming together of a group of staff who were keen to organise staff social events and a group of staff who had offered to analyse the impact of transactional stress through the APIP then formed our wellbeing team. One-to-one sessions were scheduled for staff who wanted to talk things through, quizzes/activities organised for those who felt socially isolated, and sessions set aside to talk in groups or just to cheer one another up. The wellbeing team came into its own during the period of lockdown from March 2020 because of Covid-19 and positively *shone* through their online/Google Hangouts presence to support and encourage staff who felt really isolated.

Embedding and consolidating wellbeing developments

This academic year, 2020/21, is a truly exciting time for me as a headteacher. This is the year that we embed all that has been established over the last two years – all that we have shared. We are developing a shared language, an understanding of relational practice, of restorative approaches, and of a reflective and adaptive culture. We have a staff team who are naturally empathic, who love working with our exceptional young people and who want to make it a positive place to work. Many staff have experienced the opposite and understand how important this change is. Our relational practice extends beyond staff–student relationships to all within the school, ensuring that communication is shared effectively, discussed supportively, and has a clear and purposeful outcome. It is so important that the school structures – timetables, meetings and workload – allow the necessary time for individual supervision, the time and space for reflection, and the repair and restoration of broken relationships or hurt feelings. It is essential that we continue to consult with staff about what works and what doesn't in relation to supporting their wellbeing and mental good health.

It can be difficult to encapsulate the impact of a culture change but, in this case, I am delighted to say that we have seen a *significant* reduction in the turnover of staff, and this is coupled – more importantly and probably unsurprisingly – with a significant reduction in the number of challenging incidents of behaviour from our students. The retention of staff has played a major part in stabilising the environment for the learners and has also allowed us to develop our leadership team, to develop and support their practice, to train staff to implement future school developments, and to see some real progress as a result. There has, for example, been a significant reduction in staff absence due to sickness and, most notably, due to stress. Whilst we still have challenging days, staff morale is much more positive, and teams work together to offer support to staff with greater consistency and openness. Staff have a better understanding of restorative practices and model this daily to the children and young people, which supports learners in adapting their own responses to conflict and challenge.

Ian, the principal, has developed a team of confident, competent staff who understand and promote the school's provision for learners. Everything we do is learner-centred and we are all now in the habit of ensuring that the learner is at the heart of our decision-making. A phrase that sits with me, and that I now use very regularly, is that we hold the learners in positive regard no matter what. When we talk about learners or decide on the most appropriate support mechanisms for them, I have an image of them sitting in the palm of my hand – truly precious.

The wellbeing team continues to meet regularly to consider staff wellbeing, to gather their views, to feed back to the leadership team, and to develop new ideas. The wellbeing team is a strong and positive group of staff and we are very lucky to have them at Gretton. The APIP is ongoing: meetings and progress related to staff wellbeing were disrupted by the lockdown but, while delayed, the wellbeing team nonetheless continues to focus on improvement projects to support staff development.

As for the establishment of a shared language and a coherent understanding of relational practice, 'watch this space!' This is very much a work in progress, but one that I and the rest of the SLT are passionate about and believe is the surest way to make the biggest difference for the precious pupils at Gretton School. We are very fortunate to work with these children and young people and the reward helps to 'top up' our sense of wellbeing!

What next?

- A continued clarity of purpose around a truly person-centred provision.
- A continued focus on our wonderful staff team and what they need from us and from one another.
- More training – on any topic that is likely to enhance and support best practice.
- Increased SLT presence across the school. The leadership team needs to know that they are not alone and that any one of us could and would step in to support when the going gets tough.
- Staff get-togethers, virtually if needs be until they can be in person again.
- A continued open-door policy and a real sense of being heard and listened to when needed ...
- ... and, of course, the continued opportunity to work every day with some of the most wonderful, life-enhancing, creative and intriguing children and young people you will ever meet. What a joy!

Key strategies

- Support for staff to practise self-care.
- Addressing the gap between staff and leadership/management.
- Bringing 'fractured' groups of staff together.
- Developing a whole-school approach to behaviour.
- Introducing a structured approach to staff wellbeing through the wellbeing team.
- Reducing the impact of transactional stress.

- Scottish Autism: Involvement in Autism Practice-Informed Improvement Project (APIP).
- Wellbeing team.
- Staff supervision sessions: student reflections, staff reflections, restorative practice and relational practice.
- Appointment of principal Ian Thoresteinsson.
- Staff consultation.
- Creating time to reflect.
- Effective communication.

38 King Edwin School, Norton, Stockton-on-Tees, Teeside

Implementing a culture of staff wellbeing helped us get from 'Requires Improvement' to 'Good'

The King Edwin School staff team

Headteacher: Lorna McLean

'Over the last four years, piece by piece, we have developed and joined communities and networks, many of which have been professionally mutually productive, allowing us to contribute to the educational community in our locality and more widely, and to benefit from their good practice. All staff are encouraged to develop peer relationships with other schools and establishments. We recognise that schools are different, but we can all bring a perspective on a shared issue or development.

'Developing external partnerships is not what some would consider to be a part of a staff wellbeing strategy. We believe, however, that it contributes to wellbeing, as our staff enjoy the opportunity to develop themselves and to contribute to the development of others. Staff from King Edwin represent themselves with a pride that is impressive to see, and they are always the best advocates of our school and students.'

Overview

Lorna McLean, headteacher at King Edwin Free School, describes how focusing on staff wellbeing enabled the school to move from 'Requires Improvement' to 'Good'. She describes how being 'outward' facing and creating supportive networks have been key in preventing staff feeling isolated, as well as influencing good practice in the school. By underpinning the school values and processes with 'kindness', staff and students alike were able to care for one another in practical personal and public acknowledgement of support received and given. At the core of staff wellbeing and mental health is the commitment of staff to one another as a 'work family'.

Context

Our school is a small, independent school in the Tees Valley. It provides education for children with social, emotional and mental health difficulties, and autism spectrum disorder. Within those broad definitions lie everything from anxiety and attachment to attention deficit hyperactivity disorder to pervasive demand avoidance, gaming addiction and beyond. Some of our students also have learning difficulties and other disabilities. The school is overseen by a larger geographically remote organisation, Spark of Genius, which works in partnership with the local council and is able to benefit from devolved accountability and a highly supportive budget setting and accountability process. The skills of the staff are valued and recognised, providing a strong foundation for developing our provision further, with the guidance and oversight of a number of well-chosen advisors.

Some of our students' families are financially comfortable, and some are not, in the same way most non-selective schools have differing demographics. Eighty-five per cent of our children are boys. Around 20% of our students are in the care system – this compares to about 1–2% in most schools.

Independent schools can differ greatly, and independent special schools offer education to some of the most challenged and challenging of young people, quite often after they have been unable to maintain placements in maintained mainstream or special schools. Children can present with aggression, oppositional behaviour, refusal and defiance, as well as outright fear, lack of trust, and lack of self-esteem and self-control. Staff are traditionally recruited from a diverse workforce; some have qualified teacher status but, as there is greater flexibility in the independent sector, others do not. Independent special schools are usually unique, offering provision that does not already exist in the community, and therefore are often not involved in existing networks and communities. They also frequently have to recruit staff from a wider geographic area in order to secure the appropriate specialisms and approaches they need.

When the current team first formed at the school, it was in a very different place to the one it is today in 2020/21. There were few students, a very small number of staff, and the general pervading atmosphere appeared almost to be one of survival. Staff were somewhat isolated and not really connected to the community. However, students loved their school and their staff, and had a massive respect for them and how they were trying to educate them. That is a starting point that many schools who are not at least 'Good' in Ofsted terms may not be lucky enough to have. Today we have more than 60 students and around 35 staff and are proud that Ofsted agreed at their last visit that we are 'Good'.

We have worked through our challenges from being 'Requires Improvement' to 'Good' as a team every step of the way. We all believe being part of the team has been the biggest contributor to staff wellbeing. Our Ofsted reports refer to a small part of our journey. The following information includes details of how we considered our approach to staff wellbeing alongside developing our provision to become 'Good'.

Conducting an effective scoping activity

Initially, the task was to scope who did what, what the staff strengths were and areas for development. We spent a lot of time in the early days talking to each other about every aspect of school life to gather a range of perspectives, including about the students and how staff felt about their interactions with them. We also explored each staff member's role and how our roles impacted on each other and on the students. In our early days, it appeared unclear to staff who was accountable for what, and it was an expectation that senior staff would be able to solve all of the emerging problems and have answers to any situation. Staff with more experience often do have another way of looking at a situation, but if a member of staff does not feel that they have played a significant part in the solution, they will be unable to deal with it in the future and to apply learning from it in a new context.

Conversations and meetings

Daily conversations allowed a developing picture of where staff were in their understanding of each other, the task at hand and their job roles, along with where broadly the school was aiming to be. However, this was only a short-term solution for us, as twice daily meetings are a big drain on resources and can result in more time being spent talking about issues than carrying out solutions and actions. It did allow staff to support each other, and to visibly receive support and backup from colleagues and to start to take ownership and accountability for their school and students in a new way. We also built a shared picture of each other's values and vision to a degree, as conversations and problem-solving were/are reciprocal and not top down. We also found time each day to raise morale amongst ourselves, with a section in each of our meeting slots of 'highs and lows' of the day before, or the day which had just gone, and 'what I could do differently'. We even encouraged students to have a similar approach to evaluating a large part of their learning during their weekly Duke of Edinburgh expedition.

A refreshed and restructured timetable

This was followed by providing a refreshed stable structure to the week for both staff and students. Due to low numbers of students and staff, there had been a reliance on flexibility to work with the resources on offer; instead, a refreshed structured timetable was put in place, with additional resources provided. Staff and students were able to look ahead to the routines of the day, then the routines of each week, and then each month and term. Ultimately, the shape of the year became predictable.

Alongside this, the 'steerers' of the school formed an informal extended leadership team, to ensure that there were clear and shared areas of responsibility, with actions that could be understood and shared and were completed.

It may seem that this scoping was counter-intuitive to the issue of staff wellbeing, as nothing had been written down as a staff wellbeing strategy, but in the first instance, routine, having a listening ear for one another and working towards a shared goal are, we at King Edwin believe, very important to both staff wellbeing and student wellbeing, particularly for students with the greatest challenges. Staff also need the support of an extended group of leaders. Forming a larger leadership team, even an informal one, allowed the staff team to know that they were part of a bigger picture, had access to support and guidance, and somewhere they could go for help and support where matters were more complex.

Connecting with the community

With staff travelling each day for a significant amount of time to get to work, the early school workforce was essentially an island, and the school was cut off from its community. Local groups and networks were in place but there were few natural links.

The benefits of being part of a community can range from shared problem-solving to joint learning and development of new approaches, as well as peer and leadership support and business expansion. Networking locally was not something the school staff had had much of an opportunity to take part in. For the most part we were an individual school with its counterpart schools further afield in the UK. We looked outside of the school, within and beyond the local area, for the best examples of practice and developed good links with experts, first at leadership level, then at all levels in the school.

Over the last four years, piece by piece, we have developed and joined communities and networks, many of which have been professionally mutually productive, allowing us to contribute to the educational community in our locality and more widely, and to benefit from their good practice. All staff are encouraged to develop peer relationships with other schools and establishments. We recognise that schools are different, but we can all bring a perspective on a shared issue or development.

Developing external partnerships is not what some would consider to be a part of a staff wellbeing strategy. We believe, however, that it contributes to wellbeing, as our staff enjoy the opportunity to develop themselves and to contribute to the development of others. Staff from King Edwin represent themselves with a pride that is impressive to see, and they are always the best advocates of our school and students.

The school vision at the heart of staff and student wellbeing

The next task to be carried out (and it probably should have been done first) was to develop a refreshed vision and an identity. This task drew together the team as a task force with an end goal in site. We identified, through research and our own visions for developing a provision we were proud to be associated with, four key values: kindness, a growth mindset, resilience, and personal responsibility. In the first instance, we explored what these shared values meant and why they were important to King Edwin. As our teaching and relationships were underpinned by these values, they enabled us to develop a shared language between staff and students.

Kindness champions

Kindness was our starting point, and being kind to our students, each other, visitors and our children's' families permeates everything we do. For example, staff chose a staff member to be a 'kindness champion' for a period of time. Staff would support the kindness champion by offering them acts of kindness. Our students were encouraged to recognise kindness in each other and in themselves, and to carry out acts of kindness, speaking kindly to each other at all times, treating our students' parents kindly and going the extra mile. We included 'kindness' in our staff appraisals (along with our other values) and asked staff to reflect on when and where they could evidence kindness in their work. We have had some inspirational answers when taking part in staff appraisals.

Growth mindset

As a team, as we developed our shared vision, one of the areas that stood out was the students' unwillingness to make a mistake, and a fear of failure which was extremely debilitating. An example was a student refusing to write in a thank-you card for his personal tutor – just to thank her for the hard work she had done for him. He was unable to do it and lost his temper pretty quickly, as he did not want to 'mess up' the card with his writing. We recognised that a growth mindset approach for students who had not yet achieved their potential could be a powerful thing, and it could also help staff to overcome their fears of failing their students or worries about trying something new.

Developing resilience

We also recognised that resilience was a massive issue for many students, and that both staff and students needed to develop resilience together to work through the challenges of supporting and receiving an education within our sector. Our staff are expected to be resilient, and to 'keep going' when things get tough, and to know they can deal with challenges and overcome them. We generally believe that as humans, this trait is a useful one, and at King Edwin we continue to promote it and hopefully foster it, using opportunities for self-reflection and supported reflection as part of our everyday practice. We also take the opportunity to tell each other and our students if we recognise resilience in ourselves or others. Most recently, we have begun a whole-school resilience mapping activity which staff are leading. The potential is that we will arrive at a range of effective interventions to improve and foster resilience in our students, and in ourselves too. We believe that resilience is a significant factor in enhancing staff wellbeing.

Developing personal responsibility

Our other key focus was personal responsibility. For there to be leadership at all levels of the school, we identified there must also be devolved decision-making, accountability and autonomy within clear frameworks. The leadership team developed a 'school within school' system of personal tutors, linked with teaching support staff. Tutors were made accountable for their student group and its members, in all areas of their progress and development. Initially staff struggled with this. They gradually gained confidence when they knew that leaders had confidence in them and their decision-making and were on hand when shared approaches needed to be redeveloped. The benefits to staff wellbeing were considerable. We believe that staff were able to gain a rounded view of pupils' academic progress and also see more clearly the small steps of progress their students were making socially. They were better informed to advise subject teachers of new ways to adjust and adapt their approaches to match the students' developing needs. We also have staff at all levels of the organisation recognised as experts for their own specialism, assuming greater responsibility for it and taking pride in their work.

At the heart of our ethos, we uphold our four values; kindness, growth mindset, resilience and personal responsibility. We require all staff and students to sign up to these and to live them at work and school, modelling them for others. We believe our values are a significant contributor to staff wellbeing in our school. When potential candidates are interviewed for positions in our school, we pride ourselves on saying this should be 'the best job they ever have' and we really do mean it.

Training and development, progression and succession for wellbeing

We believe that, as members of a leadership team, we should only be doing the things that others cannot yet do because we have not trained them, or they have a specialism that we have not planned for regarding succession, or we do not have the resources, or it is inappropriate that someone else does it. We started our planning for succession with this in mind and have worked over the last four years to support staff to lead the way in their own areas, whilst also ensuring that we have provided the right training and climate for doing so first.

We have invested significantly in staff development and have done so every year, providing opportunities for staff to train for the role in school they aspire to, as well as for the role they have, and work with them to provide a pathway to the next steps in their career where appropriate. We believe that helping our staff to receive the best training, coaching and support, and encouraging ambition, supports our staff wellbeing. This might look different for some staff than it does for others. We are also determined that staff do not 'walk into' roles just because they already work for the organisation and might be on a pathway to progression. We challenge rigorously as part of the recruitment process, and for staff to be successful in joining or progressing within the organisation, they have to be very special and have something special to bring. As a result, we are starting to see some highly skilled practitioners with the best approaches to young people and their needs coming through our ranks and taking our message out to other members of the community. Being proud of your workplace and being proud of yourself and your progress is certainly something our staff exemplify.

Systems and processes

One of the significant factors to being able to self-assess as a 'Good' school, and having this ratified during our Ofsted inspection, was being very 'boring' when it came to systems and processes. 'Things happen by themselves' – because someone else's name is on it and that is their job and they did not need any prompting to do it – was a mantra regularly used in our first two years. We unpicked systems to find potential for errors, and hopefully put them all back together in a more streamlined way.

Some staff, in moving from a flexible, responsive system to a more rigid and standardised one, required support to understand the requirements for a 'relentlessly boring systematic approach' to things. They discovered that if they were unable to take part, they would be helped, but if they were unwilling to take part, they would be challenged and they ultimately decided to work within the structured guidance offered.

This is probably the opposite to what some would consider a contributor to staff wellbeing. However, we were in a position where staff could suffer as a result of others not fulfilling their accountabilities, and this was a significant detractor from staff wellbeing. Additionally, introducing any element of chaos into a work environment is detrimental, and staff not working within systems impacts other staff (as well as students). Orderly, effective systems that require rigid compliance have supported our approach to staff wellbeing, as well as our journey from 'Requires Improvement' to 'Good'.

Our staff wellbeing approach

We have an explicit focus on staff wellbeing. We have tried a range of approaches (staff awards, staff thank you, staff member of the month, staff activities, staff wellbeing committee) and continue to do so. We thank staff/each other regularly. Some of the best successes have been staff nominating each other for staff awards: 'she cares so much about our kids – and did you know also builds wells for children in Africa?'; 'he keeps his classroom so tidy and it makes my job (as a cleaner) easier'; 'she is just a great influence on her students' – such nominations are received on a regular basis in our school.

We also keep an eye on what other schools are doing. One local school is very flexible with staff start and finish times; for example, we are trying to adopt some aspects of flexibility, within a framework that will not detract from staff or student productivity or needs. We already offer an occasional 'thank you' day off to staff for a job well done.

We also provide for the big picture: training on attachment, trauma, autism, expert input into children's solutions if things are not working or where they are working well, and provide options for in-school offloading with line managers, counsellors and the school educational psychologist. We understand that, unlike 'secondary trauma' (trauma/psychological distress that can be experienced by a practitioner and is associated with supporting young people with trauma impacts), there is unlikely to be 'secondary wellbeing', where everyone is supported, and therefore we need to take deliberate action to care for our staff and help them to take care of themselves.

We have 'go have a moan and a [well-known chocolate bar] Monday' with our operations manager, who is often the bearer of the brunt of 'I am having a bad day' outbursts, and staff meals out to say, 'we appreciate you'. Unfortunately, that idea didn't work on the last occasion, as the staff were too competitive with another group who they thought were getting a better offer of a Go Karting trip! We make a deliberate effort to 'do' things that staff would view as being 'about their wellbeing'.

We are well supported by our parent organisation, Spark of Genius, which enables us to use our budget innovatively to support staff and student wellbeing. We have goats, a horse, alpacas, chickens, rabbits and a puppy among our current workforce, all contributing to the general good spirit and wellbeing of staff. Anyone who has ever taken part in training with two frolicking goats in their eye-line or cleaned up puppy pooh while trying to answer a reception phone will understand the rewards – and challenges – of looking after animals! We offer our students, and therefore our staff, regular opportunities to experience nature and the outdoors, using the Duke of Edinburgh programme as a framework for engagement and achievement.

Our salary for each staff member's role is competitive for the sector. Along with a healthy training budget and appropriate resources, the right levels of staffing well-matched to our student needs, a supportive parent organisation, and the range of wellbeing strategies we have described, our school operates in a climate conducive to a happy workforce.

Our staff: Our work family

Our staff are an inspiration in the way that they approach their roles and consider each other and our students. For example, our school nutritionist caters for our staff as 35 individuals and our 60+ children individually too. Our facilities manager will support a team member with a group of students if we have a staff member down and he will do it with pleasure. He also offers work experience and 'restorative' opportunities for students to repair any damage they cause when in crisis. Our office staff are commended as 'so welcoming' when visitors come to the school, and our leadership team see only potential in our children and staff – and solutions rather than problems. Each staff member takes a delight in our students and appreciates the opportunity to work with them. Our cleaning staff and kitchen staff offer work experience to our students, some over an extended period of time. We have had staff move on to new and rewarding careers and continue to come back to talk to our students – giving them an insight into the careers and opportunities beyond and after our school. Some of our former students return regularly to talk to their peers about their experiences of post-16 education.

We are currently working together with Spark of Genius to look at how we can further develop our provision to allow even greater progression and succession opportunities, and a renewed challenge for those ready to tackle it at work. We describe our provision and our school as 'a bit like a weird family' – our parents have regularly used this phrase to describe how our staff and students work together and care for each other. We also appreciate that we all come to work and school to put in a 'good day' and so any time that does not happen exactly as we planned, we may need to be supported, treated with kindness and given the opportunity to learn from it. For all of our staff, we respect, appreciate and consider their home lives and their needs, but we are also unapologetic in putting forward our view that our children/pupils come first, and that it is an honour to do our jobs.

Our 'King Edwin work family' really are inspirational and have that absolute commitment to each other, the school and our students. As a result, they are all significant contributors to our staff wellbeing approach.

Key strategies

- Conducting an effective scoping activity.
- Conversations and meetings.
- Restructuring the timetable.
- Connecting with the community.
- The school vision at the heart of staff and student wellbeing.
- Kindness champions.
- Growth mindset.
- Developing resilience.
- Developing personal responsibility.
- Training and development, progression and succession for wellbeing.
- System and processes.
- A whole-staff wellbeing approach.
- Our staff: Our work family.

Part 5

Reflections

39 Reflections

Stephen Waters

The outbreak of Covid-19 in early 2020 challenged schools in ways that could neither have been foreseen nor planned. National lockdown in March 2020 meant that schools were open only for vulnerable children and children of key workers, while in a matter of days, schools moved to face-to-face lessons for the majority of pupils at home. Schools have had to respond with immediacy and flexibility to a range of issues, including:

- Restructuring the school day and timetable to teach vulnerable children and the children of key workers who attended school throughout the lockdown from March to July.
- Reopening fully in September 2020, to confusing and contradictory DfE guidance, often released on a Friday evening and following closely previous guidance.
- Teaching students remotely through live streaming, often using unfamiliar technology or overcoming the limitations of their school's hardware and software, which was often not designed or configured for distance learning.
- Preparing pre-recorded lessons for students to watch at home.
- Supporting disadvantaged communities by running food banks and delivering food parcels to families, some of whom had lost their jobs or had little chance of finding employment as firms closed during lockdown, some never to re-open.
- While teachers were facing their own anxieties about catching Covid-19, they were supporting children who were also worried about catching the virus or members of their families becoming infected.
- Staff coping with their own bereavements and/or supporting the children of families who had been bereaved.
- Allowing staff with health conditions or who had family members who were vulnerable to remain at home, while contributing to teaching online.
- Trying to maintain 2 metres social distance in classrooms of 30 children or more and ensuring surfaces were cleaned regularly in their classrooms, corridors and communal areas.
- Allocating children to 'bubbles' whose members had to isolate at home if anyone in their bubble had a positive test for Covid-19. In secondary schools, this could mean a whole year group. In the largest secondary schools, 250+ pupils were being sent home to isolate.

- When schools opened fully in September 2020, organising further social distancing measures, increasing the cleaning regime, making arrangements for parents to drop off and pick up children that minimised social contact between the adults, including one-way systems in the playground, and attempting to enable parents to social distance outside the school gates.
- Maintaining a hot meals service while reducing the risk of spreading the virus.
- Following up pupil absence, especially where children were at risk because of their home circumstances.
- When staff had to isolate, additional costs were incurred to cover their classes with supply teachers.
- As there was no additional funding, schools were spending their already stretched budgets on additional and intensive cleaning of their schools.

Such challenges were compounded by what many headteachers and teachers saw was government failure to support schools adequately. Schools were concerned that:

- The advice about social distancing and the use of masks was contradictory and confusing. For example, by law, from 8 August, 2020, young people aged 11 and over had to wear a mask in indoor settings such as museums, galleries, cinemas and places of worship, but not in classrooms, despite pupils sitting next to one another at distances of 1 metre or less.
- On 21 August 2020, the World Health Organization (WHO) advised that, 'children aged 12 and over should wear a mask under the same conditions as adults, in particular when they cannot guarantee at least a 1-metre distance from others and there is widespread transmission in the area.' On 25 August, the UK government then gave schools the discretion to require face coverings in communal areas if they believed that was right in their particular circumstances. The government also advised that additional measures were put in place in areas where the transmission of the virus was likely to be high, stating that face coverings should be worn by adults and pupils in secondary schools when moving around the school, such as in corridors and communal areas, where social distancing is difficult to maintain (DfE, 2020). Face coverings, the government concluded, should not be used in the classroom, where 'protective measures already mean the risks are lower, and where they can inhibit learning'.
- Only 10 test kits were provided to schools to use if a pupil or adult had Covid-19 symptoms.
- A scheme announced in April by the then Secretary of Education, Gavin Williamson, to provide free laptops to vulnerable children to enable them to learn at home failed to deliver on its promise. Some schools did not receive laptops, others received an allocation which did not meet their needs, and there were problems with passcodes.
- The focus on keeping children safe was not accompanied by advice – and some would say – concern about keeping staff safe.

- There was a relentless negative message from the Department for Education about how far behind children were and the divide between advantaged and disadvantaged families and that teachers should focus on enabling pupils to 'catch up'.
- There was controversy over the algorithm Ofqual used to produce GCSE and A Level results when exams were unable to go ahead in Summer 2020.

Covid-19: Was there a positive?

The disruption that Covid-19 caused to education prompted a renewed focus on the purpose of education and on the high-stakes accountability strategies that are used to monitor teachers and results. This was seen on social media and in educational journals. Some schools welcomed children's return by delivering a 'Recovery Curriculum', designed to address pupil anxiety caused by the pandemic and focusing on pupils' feelings and responses in readjusting to full-time education. Other schools preferred to regard the return to school in September 2020 as 'business as usual', and that returning to a routine and as much normality as possible was the best way to reassure the children.

Schools understandably focused on the pupils and their emotional response to being back in the classroom and the physical protection, such as could be managed, of children and staff. Less attention was paid to the mental health needs of staff. The schools featured as case studies in this book have a culture in which staff wellbeing and mental health are a priority and therefore staff will continue to be supported and valued during the extraordinary circumstances of the Covid-19 pandemic. The concept of school as a family that looks after its members featured in several of the case studies, emphasising the importance of looking after staff as a community which also looked after its members.

Leadership: Looking after others

In Chapter 6, the concept of 'buffer leadership' was discussed. We considered the impact on school leaders of taking on the role of a buffer – placing themselves between external demands and internal staff wellbeing. We noted the risk of Burnout if leaders attempted to protect their staff in this way without having support themselves. We also referred to the importance of developing a school community in which anyone in the school, leadership included, could ask for help. Authenticity and honesty are difficult to achieve if a leader is in the role of helping everyone else, to the exclusion of their own wellbeing. We concluded that, difficult as it is, being authentic is a way of communicating that every school should aim to achieve. Just as teachers are unable to take care of the children unless they first take care of themselves, leaders are unable to take care of their staff unless they first look after themselves. The first step to doing so is to admit to the staff that they need help and support. The second is to accept it.

Thread of common strategies

Dylan Wiliam's statement, 'Everything works somewhere; nothing works everywhere' (2018), which we met in the Introduction, is apt when considering strategies the case-study schools used to develop a culture of staff wellbeing and mental health. Every school is unique, with its own demographic and ethos. What works in one school might not work in another. However, the case studies provide an opportunity to take a look inside each school to see how it supports staff wellbeing, enabling you to consider if the strategies a school uses might work in your own school. Having said this, there are strategies that seem to be more frequently used than others:

- Reducing workload.
- Decreasing or removing high-stakes accountability measures, including moving away from judgemental, hierarchical and one-way lesson observations to peer-to-peer lesson study; reducing pen marking by using verbal feedback.
- Creating one family/community.
- Transparency and authenticity from the school leader, including asking for help and support.
- Drawing up a staff wellbeing and mental health policy and/or action plan.
- Gifts of appreciation to staff (where culture of wellbeing is recognised, to avoid token gestures).
- Appointing a wellbeing lead.
- Creating a staff wellbeing group.
- Surveying staff anonymously to identify wellbeing concerns.
- Providing choice in professional development with a range of options.
- Including teaching assistants, support staff, admin, ancillary and site staff in decision-making and professional development.
- Flexible working, including part-time contracts and job shares. Co-headship arrangements.
- Effective communication, including restricting when emails can be sent and received.
- Distributed leadership.
- Work–life balance and appreciation of the importance of teachers' family life.
- 'Shout-outs' to show appreciation for the work staff do.
- Creating a welcoming space for staff to relax.
- 'An open-door' policy, to provide openness and support.

- Providing a counselling service.
- Organising staff events, including having fun.
- Early closure on Fridays.
- Including staff wellbeing in the school development/improvement plan (SDP/SIP).

Where next?

The future of education and of schooling is uncertain, given the impact that Covid-19 has had on society in general and schools in particular. What is certain is that the case-study schools, and schools like them, have built into their culture a mutual support system and a resilience that afford them the ability to withstand challenges and difficulties, whatever the future may bring.

If your school is yet to start out on your journey to develop a culture of staff wellbeing and mental health or wishes to develop it further, I hope that, in reflecting on the schools featured in this book, you will find strategies of good practice that you can introduce in your own school. We need to take care of the wellbeing and mental health of our teachers so that they can teach with energy and take care of the children and young people in their care. After all, that's why they went into teaching in the first place, not to join the alarming numbers of teachers leaving education, never to return.

Glossary

Academy. Academies have more freedom than other state schools over their finances, the curriculum, and teachers' pay and conditions. A key difference is that they are funded directly by central government, instead of receiving their funds via a local authority (*see* Local authority).

Age-related expectation (ARE). A set of skills and knowledge for each curriculum area, tested by Standard Assessment Tests (SATs) that a child should have mastered by the end of Key Stages 1 and 2.

Alternative provision. Education in specialist schools or units, arranged by local authorities or schools for pupils who do not attend a mainstream school for reasons such as school exclusion, behaviour issues, school refusal, or short- or long-term illness.

Assistant headteacher. An assistant headteacher is a member of the senior leadership team (SLT) who is responsible to the deputy headteacher and headteacher.

Assistant principal. An assistant principal is a member of the senior leadership team (SLT) who is responsible to the vice-principal and principal. An assistant principal is an alternative name for assistant headteacher.

Assistant vice-principal. A member of a school leadership team, responsible to the vice-principal.

Attention deficit hyperactivity disorder (ADHD). A behavioural disorder that includes symptoms such as inattentiveness, hyperactivity and impulsiveness. The symptoms of ADHD tend to be noticed at an early age and may become more noticeable when a child's circumstances change, such as when they start school.

Autism Practice-Informed Improvement Project (APIP). A joint pilot project between Gretton School (Chapter 37) in Cambridge and Scottish Autism to continuously develop good autism practice in the school.

Autism spectrum condition (ASC). A diagnosis of autism (*see* Autism spectrum disorder).

Autism spectrum disorder (ASD). A diagnosis of autism (*see* Autism spectrum condition).

Best Practice with Teaching Assistants Award (BPTAA). An award from 'Award Place' which provides a framework for the strategic management of teaching assistants, with clear systems of induction, appraisal and professional development.

Black, Asian and Minority Ethnic (BAME): People of mixed, Asian, Black and non-white ethnicities.

Chief executive officer (CEO). The most senior corporate, executive or administrative officer in charge of managing an organisation – especially an independent legal entity such as a company or non-profit institution. CEOs lead a range of organisations, including public and private corporations, non-profit organisations and some government organisations (notably Crown corporations). The CEO of a corporation or company typically reports to the board of directors

Child and Adolescent Mental Health Services (CAMHS). CAMHS is the name for the NHS services that assess and treat young people with emotional, behavioural or mental health difficulties. CAMHS support covers depression, problems with food, self-harm, abuse, violence/anger, bipolar disorder, schizophrenia and anxiety, among other mental ill-health conditions. There are local NHS CAMHS services around the UK, with teams made up of nurses, therapists, psychiatrists, support workers and social workers, as well as other professionals.

Church of England (C of E) school. The purpose of a Church of England school is to offer education within a framework of Christian beliefs and values, within the traditions of the Church of England. Twenty-five per cent of primary schools in England have a Church foundation. Before secular state schools were introduced, the Church of England and the Roman Catholic Church provided education until the nineteenth century.

Continuing professional development (CPD). CPD (or simply PD) is the term used to describe the learning and training activities which school staff engage in to develop and enhance their skills and qualifications. The CPD process usually involves keeping a training record and reflecting on its impact.

Covid-19. Covid-19 is an infectious disease caused by a newly discovered coronavirus which became a pandemic in early 2020. Most people infected with the Covid-19 virus experienced mild-to-moderate respiratory illness and recovered without requiring special treatment. Older people, and those with underlying medical problems like cardiovascular disease, diabetes, chronic respiratory disease, and cancer were more likely to develop serious illness. The Covid-19 virus was spread primarily through droplets of saliva or discharge from the nose when an infected person coughed or sneezed. People were asked to protect themselves by washing their hands frequently and keeping 2 metres apart from others. Masks had to be worn in certain places like shops. At the time this book was going to press, the first vaccines for Covid-19 had been approved. There are also many ongoing clinical trials evaluating potential treatments.

Department for Education (DfE). The Department for Education is responsible for children's services and education, including early years, schools, higher and further education policy, apprenticeships and wider skills in England.

Deputy headteacher. The deputy headteacher is a member of the senior leadership team/senior management team (SLT/SMT). The deputy headteacher assists the headteacher in leading and managing the school and represents the headteacher at meetings. The deputy headteacher leads the school if the headteacher is absent.

Designated safeguarding lead. The designated safeguarding lead is the person appointed to take lead responsibility for child protection issues in school. The person fulfilling this role must be a senior member of the school's leadership team, and the role must be set out in the post holder's job description.

Early Years Foundation Stage (EYFS). The EYFS sets standards for the learning, development and care of children from birth to 5 years of age. All schools and Ofsted-registered early years providers must follow the EYFS, including childminders, preschools, nurseries and school reception classes.

Education, Health and Care Plan (EHCP). A plan for children and young people aged up to 25 who need more support than is available through special educational needs support. An EHCP identifies educational, health and social needs and sets out the additional support required to meet those needs.

Education Inspection Framework (EIF). The Education Inspection Framework sets out how Ofsted will inspect state schools, further education and skills providers, non-association independent schools and registered early years settings in England.

EduPod. A commercial software platform which helps mental health leads to plan, manage and evaluate mental health activities for the school community. It provides mental health resources and action plans.

Emotional literacy support assistant. A specialist teaching assistant who helps children to understand their emotions and respect the feelings of those around them.

English as an additional language (EAL). English as an additional language refers to learners whose first language is not English. The learner may already be fluent in several other languages or dialects.

Every Child a Reader (ECAR). Every Child a Reader is a whole-school programme of delivering a range of effective literacy interventions for children struggling to read and write across the school. It aims to ensure that every child achieves success in literacy through targeted support.

Every Child a Talker (ECAT). Every Child a Talker helps practitioners and parents to create a developmentally appropriate, supportive and stimulating environment in which children can enjoy experimenting with and learning language. ECAT encourages early language development, extending children's vocabulary so that before they start school, children are confident and skilled communicators.

Evidence leader in education. An outstanding teacher, who is a middle or senior leader, with the skills to support individuals or teams. They use a good practice, evidence-based approach to develop an understanding of what outstanding leadership looks like and support other leaders to achieve it in their own context.

Fischer Family Trust. The Trust is a non-profit organisation which provides data and analyses to all schools and local authorities in England and Wales.

Free school. Free schools are funded by the government but are not run by the local authority (*see* Local authority). They have more control over decision-making and can set their own pay and conditions for staff and change the length of school terms and the school day. They are 'all-ability' schools. Apart from general free schools, there are two types of specialist free school: *University technical colleges* specialise in subjects like engineering and construction, and teach these subjects along with business skills and using IT. Pupils study academic subjects as well as practical subjects leading to technical qualifications. The curriculum is designed by the university and employers, who also provide work experience for students. University technical colleges are sponsored by universities, employers and further education colleges. In contrast, *studio schools* are small schools (usually with around 300 pupils) teaching mainstream qualifications through project-based learning. This means working in real situations, as well as learning academic subjects. Students work with local employers and a personal coach, and follow a curriculum designed to give them the skills and qualifications they need in work, or to take up further education.

Free school meals. In England and Scotland, children in Reception, Year 1 or Year 2 and who go to a state school are entitled to free school meals regardless of household income. From Year 3 onwards, in any part of the UK, children could get free lunches, and sometimes milk, at school if the parents or carers are receiving a means-tested state benefit.

Full-time equivalent (FTE). The calculation of full-time equivalent is an employee's scheduled hours divided by the employer's hours for a full-time working week. When an employer has a 40-hour work week, employees who are scheduled to work 40 hours per week are 1.0.

General practitioner (GP). A general practitioner (commonly known as 'the doctor') treats all common medical conditions and refers patients to hospitals and other medical services for urgent and specialist treatment. GPs focus on the health of the whole person, combining physical, psychological and social aspects of care.

Greater depth. Primary children are considered to be working at 'greater depth' when they have mastered learning at KS1 and KS2 in a subject and are capable of exploring it in further detail.

Headteacher. A headteacher is the most senior teacher and leader of a school, responsible for the education of all pupils, leadership and management of staff, and for school policymaking. Headteachers lead, motivate and manage staff by delegating responsibility, setting expectations and targets, and evaluating staff performance against them.

Health and Safety at Work Act 1974. The Health and Safety at Work Act is the primary piece of legislation covering occupational health and safety in

Great Britain. It is sometimes referred to as HSWA, the HSW Act, the 1974 Act or HASAWA.

Her Majesty's Inspectorate (HMI). Her Majesty's Inspectors inspect education and care providers, challenge them to improve and help them get the support they need.

Higher-level teaching assistant. A higher-level teaching assistant does all the tasks that a teaching assistant does but has increased responsibilities. They teach classes on their own, cover planned absences, and give teachers time to plan and mark. They receive their designation by taking an additional qualification (*see* Teaching assistant).

Human Resources (HR). Human Resources handle recruitment, payroll, employment policies and benefits. They also often act as a go-between for employees and school leaders and can clarify basic company information such as maternity leave and sick pay. If HR is given a more proactive role, they can work with school leaders to help develop long-term strategies for growth and development, including training.

Improving Access to Psychological Therapies (IAPT). IAPT services provide evidence-based psychological therapies to people with anxiety disorders and depression (*see* QWELL).

Inclusion Quality Mark (IQM). Inclusive education – also called inclusion – is education that includes everyone learning together in mainstream schools. It is a process of change and improvement within schools so that all children can be valued equally, treated with respect and provided with real learning opportunities. The Inclusion Quality Mark is a standard for assessing schools against a nationally recognised framework on inclusion. It contains eight elements, all practical parts of the life of a school, which encompass inclusion in its widest sense and in all aspects of school life.

Income Deprivation Affecting Children Index (IDACI). This index measures the proportion of all children aged 0–15 living in income-deprived families. It is a subset of the Income Deprivation Domain, which measures the proportion of the population in an area experiencing deprivation relating to low income.

Information and communication technology (ICT). Information and communications technology (or technologies) is the infrastructure and components that enable modern computing. The term is generally accepted to mean all devices, networking components, applications and systems that combined allow people and organisations, including schools, to interact in the digital world. ICT encompasses both the internet-enabled sphere as well as the mobile one powered by wireless networks.

Initial teacher training. To teach in a state school in England, you must have a degree, and gain qualified teacher status (QTS) by following a programme of initial teacher training. You can teach in independent schools, academies and free schools in England without QTS.

In-service training (INSET) day. Schools have five statutory days per year when they are closed to students for staff training and professional development.

Inspection Data Summary Report (IDSR). The IDSR is a tool showing historical data for school inspectors to use when preparing for inspections. During inspections, inspectors will give most weight to the outcomes, attendance and behaviour of pupils currently in the school, taking account also of historical data. The IDSR is designed to show how well previous cohorts showed characteristics of good or better performance.

International Classification of Diseases (ICD). The International Classification of Diseases is a globally used diagnostic tool for epidemiology, health management and clinical purposes. The ICD is maintained by the World Health Organization (WHO), which is the directing and coordinating authority for health within the United Nations system.

Investors in People. Investors in People began in 1991 as a government project. It is now a not-for-profit community interest company. The Investors in People Standard is a business improvement tool designed to improve performance and realise objectives through the management and development of an organisation's employees.

Key Stages 1–5 (KS1–KS5). Schools in England are usually divided into the following key stages: Key Stage 1: Years 1–2 (5–7 years old); Key Stage 2: Years 3–6 (7–11 years old); Key Stage 3: Years 7–9 (11–14 years old); Key Stage 4: Years 10–11 (14–16 years old); Key Stage 5: more commonly referred to as college or sixth form, it covers Years 12–13 (16–18 years old). Subjects at this level are more tailored to each student's further education.

Leadership team. The leadership team in a school is usually made up of the headteacher / principal, deputy headteacher / deputy or vice-principal, and the assistant headteacher / assistant principal (*see* Senior leadership team).

Learning support assistant. Learning support assistants work with students in a pastoral role (e.g. children who have special needs, or whose first language is not English) to help them cope with the classroom environment, usually on a one-to-one basis. They support the student and share some of the responsibility for their progress with the teacher (*see* Teaching assistant and Special support assistant).

Local authority. A local authority is an organisation that is officially responsible for all the public services and facilities in a particular area.

Looked-after children. A 'looked-after' child is a child in the care of the local authority either through a Care Order made by a court or a voluntary arrangement with their parent(s) (*see* Local authority).

Lower Layer Super Output Area (LSOA). A Lower Layer Super Output Area is a geographic area. An LSOA is a geographic hierarchy designed to improve the reporting of small area statistics in England and Wales. There is an LSOA for each postcode in England and Wales.

Maslach Burnout Inventory (MBI). The Maslach Burnout Inventory, published in 1981, is a psychological inventory consisting of 22 items relating to occupational Burnout. The original form of the MBI was constructed by Christina Maslach and Susan E. Jackson, in order to assess an individual's experience of Burnout. The MBI measures three dimensions of Burnout: emotional exhaustion, depersonalisation and personal accomplishment. The MBI takes between 10 and 15 minutes to complete and can be administered to individuals or groups.

Maslach Burnout Inventory for Educators (MBI-ES). The Maslach Burnout Inventory for Educators is a version of the Maslach Burnout Inventory designed for teachers, administrators, other staff members, and volunteers working in an educational setting (*see* Maslach Burnout Inventory).

Multi-Academy Trust or Trust. A Multi-Academy Trust is a single organisation established to undertake a strategic collaboration to improve and maintain high educational standards across a number of schools. A group of schools form a single Trust, which has overarching responsibility for their governance.

National Association for Headteachers (NAHT). The NAHT is a union that represents school leaders working within a number of different areas of the education sector, including headteachers, deputy and assistant heads, school business leaders, special educational needs coordinators, virtual school heads and leaders of outdoor education centres.

National Curriculum. In England and Wales, the National Curriculum must be taught in all local authority maintained schools. Other schools, such as academies and free schools, are able to opt out of following the National Curriculum should they wish to, although academies must teach a broad and balanced curriculum and include English, mathematics and science. The National Curriculum sets out programmes of study and attainment targets for all subjects in all key stages, with the exceptions of English, mathematics and science. Some subjects are included in the curriculum for certain key stages – for example, English and mathematics, which are taught to Year 11 pupils and the science curriculum, which is taught to Year 10 and Year 11 students.

National Institute for Health Protection (NIHP). The National Institute for Health Protection was formed in 2020, bringing together Public Health England (PHE) and NHS Test and Trace, as well as the analytical capability of the Joint Biosecurity Centre (JBC), under a single leadership team to strengthen the response to the Covid-19 pandemic. It provides support to local directors of public health and local authorities. NIHP marked the end of the single body of Public Health England.

National leader in education. Successful headteachers who work alongside other school leaders to drive forward improvements and build capacity to ensure that improvements can be sustained. The role of the national leader in education is to work outside their own school to increase the leadership capacity of other schools to help raise standards (*see* National Support School).

National Professional Qualification for Headship (NPQH). The National Professional Qualification for Headship supports the professional development of aspiring and serving headteachers. It involves face-to-face training, online learning, a placement in a school different from the learner's own school, creating an action plan for that school and leading a whole-school change programme.

National Professional Qualification for Middle Leadership (NPQML). The National Professional Qualification for Middle Leadership supports the professional development of aspiring and serving middle leaders. It involves face-to-face training, online learning and the completion of a project.

National Professional Qualification for Senior Leadership (NPQSL). The National Professional Qualification for Senior Leadership supports the professional development of aspiring and serving senior leaders. It involves face-to-face training, online learning and the completion of a project.

National Support School. National leaders of education are outstanding headteachers who, together with the staff in their schools, which are known as designated National Support Schools, use their skills, expertise and experience to support other schools in challenging circumstances (*see* National leader in education).

Newly qualified teacher (NQT). Newly qualified teacher is a category of teacher in the UK. Newly qualified teachers are those who have gained qualified teacher status (QTS) but have not yet completed the statutory twelve-month programme known as the 'induction for newly qualified teachers'.

Office for National Statistics (ONS). The Office for National Statistics is the UK's largest independent producer of official statistics. It is responsible for collecting and publishing statistics related to the economy, population and society at national, regional and local levels. It also conducts the census in England and Wales every 10 years.

Office for Standards in Education (Ofsted). Ofsted inspects services providing education and skills for learners of all ages. They also inspect and regulate services that care for children and young people. Ofsted is a non-ministerial department.

Parent support advisor. The role of the parent support advisor is to assist in tackling underachievement by working in partnership with families, parents, carers and pupils in a school context to enable pupils, particularly the most disadvantaged, to have full access to educational opportunities and overcome barriers to learning and participation.

Pathological demand avoidance (PDA). Pathological demand avoidance describes someone with autism who avoids everyday demands and expectations to an extreme extent. This demand avoidance is often accompanied by high levels of anxiety. The 'diagnosis' of PDA is widely debated. The term 'extreme demand avoidance' is sometimes used instead, as some educators and practitioners feel that it is more acceptable and less medically judgemental.

Performance management. Teacher performance management is a continuous process for identifying, evaluating and developing the work performance of teachers, so that the goals and objectives of the school are achieved, while at the same time benefiting teachers in terms of recognition of performance and professional development. The term 'teacher appraisal' is sometimes used instead of 'performance management'. Performance-related progression is the basis for all school decisions on pay for classroom teachers and leaders.

Planning, preparation and assessment (PPA). Planning, preparation and assessment time is time set aside for teachers during their timetabled teaching day to allow them to carry out planning, preparations and assessment activities. Its purpose is to relieve some of the existing workload pressures on teachers.

Post-traumatic stress disorder (PTSD). Post-traumatic stress disorder is an anxiety disorder caused by very stressful, frightening or distressing events. Someone with PTSD often relives the traumatic event through nightmares and flashbacks, and may experience feelings of isolation, irritability and guilt. They may also have problems sleeping, such as insomnia, and find concentrating difficult. Symptoms are often severe and persistent enough to have a significant impact on the person's day-to-day life.

Private Finance Initiative (PFI). Private Finance Initiative schools are paid for by private companies, who then lease the buildings back to the government over a period of up to 40 years. Maintenance costs and interest are also added to the rates paid back.

Professional development (*see* Continuing professional development).

Public Health England (PHE). Until 2020, Public Health England was an executive agency of the Department of Health and Social Care, and a distinct organisation with operational autonomy. It provided government, local government, the NHS, Parliament, industry and the public with evidence-based professional, scientific expertise and support. It was subsumed by the National Institute for Health Protection (NIHP) in 2020, in response to the Covid-19 pandemic (*see* National Institute for Health Protection).

Pupil Premium (PP). Publicly funded schools in England get extra funding from the government to help them improve the attainment of their disadvantaged pupils. The Pupil Premium grant is designed to allow schools to help disadvantaged pupils by improving their progress and the exam results they achieve. Schools get Pupil Premium funding based on the number of pupils they have in January each year who are eligible for free school meals, looked-after and previously looked-after children. A looked-after child is a child in the care of the local authority either through a Care Order made by a court or a voluntary arrangement with their parent(s). In April 2020, the Pupil Premium rates were £1345 for primary-aged pupils and £995 for secondary-aged pupils (*see* Free school meals, Local authority, Looked-after children).

Pupil referral unit (PRU). Pupil referral units are a type of school that caters for children who are not able to attend a mainstream school. Pupils are often referred there if they need greater care and support than their school can provide. Children who attend a PRU might be: permanently excluded from their mainstream school for behaviour reasons, or at risk of permanent exclusion; experiencing emotional or behavioural difficulties, including problems with anger, mental health issues, and school phobia/refusal; experiencing severe bullying; diagnosed with Special Educational Needs (SEN), or in the process of getting a diagnosis; suffering from a short- or long-term illness that makes mainstream school unsuitable; a new starter who missed out on a school place; pregnant or young mothers. Some pupils will have all their lessons at a PRU, while others split their time between the mainstream school where they're registered and a PRU. PRUs are not special schools, and pupils who have more severe Special Educational Needs or Disabilities should not be sent to a PRU as a long-term solution.

Qualified teacher status (QTS). Qualified teacher status or qualified teacher learning and skills status (QTLS) is required in England and Wales to work as a teacher of children in state schools under local authority control and in special education schools. A similar status exists under a different name in Scotland and Northern Ireland.

QWELL. An online counselling and wellbeing service for adults. It is an extension to 'Improving Access to Psychological Therapies', with a strong focus on prevention, recovery and pre-assessment care (*see* Improving Access to Psychological Therapies).

Religious education (RE). Religious education is the term given to education concerned with religion. It may refer to education provided by a church or religious organisation, for instruction in doctrine and faith, or for education in various aspects of religion, but without explicitly religious or moral aims (e.g. in a school or college).

Religious, social and health education (RSHE). The Relationships Education, Relationships and Sex Education and Health Education (England) Regulations 2019 make relationships education compulsory for all pupils receiving primary education, and relationships and sex education (RSE) compulsory for all pupils receiving secondary education. They also make health education compulsory in all schools except independent schools. Personal, social, health and economic (PSHE) education continues to be compulsory in independent schools.

'Requires Improvement'. A school judged as 'Requires Improvement' at its last inspection is a school that is not yet 'Good' but overall provides an acceptable standard of education. The school is inspected again, under Section 5 of the Education Act, within a period of 30 months.

Residential support worker. Residential support workers look after the physical and mental wellbeing of children or vulnerable adults in care.

Roman Catholic (RC) school. A private primary or secondary religious school run by a church or parish.

School business manager. A school business manager is responsible for drawing up the budget, HR duties, including assisting with the recruitment process and premises management (*see* Human Resources).

School development plan (SDP). A school development plan is a strategic plan for improvement, a road map that sets out the changes a school needs to make to improve the level of student achievement, and shows how and when these changes will be made (*see* School improvement plan).

School improvement plan (SIP) (see School development plan).

School self-evaluation. School self-evaluation is a collaborative, reflective process of internal school review. It provides teachers with a means of systematically looking at how they teach and how pupils learn and helps schools and teachers to improve outcomes for learners.

School Workload Reduction Toolkit (SWRT). A practical resource for school leaders and teachers to help reduce workload, produced by school leaders and other educational experts, in conjunction with the DfE.

Senior leadership team (SLT). The senior leadership team is responsible for the daily planning and management of a school and includes the headteacher (or principal) as well as assistant and deputy heads (or assistant headteachers or vice-principals).

Senior management team (SMT) (*see* Senior leadership team).

Social, emotional and mental health (SEMH). Social, emotional and mental health needs are a type of special educational needs in which children/young people have severe difficulties in managing their emotions and behaviour. They often show inappropriate responses and feelings to situations.

Special Educational Needs and Disability (SEND). A child or young person is considered to have a Special Educational Need or Disability if they have a learning difficulty and/or a disability that means they need special health and education support.

Special educational needs coordinator (SENCO). A special educational needs coordinator is a teacher who coordinates the provision for children with special educational needs or disabilities in a school. Many are also class teachers and fulfil their SENCO duties on a part-time basis.

Special support assistant. Special support assistants have a similar role to learning support assistants but are usually given a role with a specific group of students with an educational need, e.g. students defined as SEND. The terms special support assistant and learning support assistant are often used interchangeably (*see* Learning support assistant, Teaching assistant).

Specialist leader of education. Specialist leaders of education are middle and senior leaders in positions below headteacher, including deputy and assistant headteachers, subject leaders, pastoral leaders and school business managers, with at least two years' experience in a particular field of expertise and a successful track record, supported by evidence of impact, of working effectively within their own school, and/or across a group of schools. They work to support individuals and teams in other schools by providing high-level coaching, mentoring and support, drawing on their knowledge and expertise in their specialist area.

Spiritual, moral, social and cultural (SMSC) development. All maintained schools must promote the spiritual, moral, social and cultural development of their pupils. Through ensuring pupils' SMSC development, schools can also demonstrate they are actively promoting fundamental British values. Meeting requirements for collective worship, establishing a strong school ethos supported by effective relationships throughout the school, and providing relevant activities beyond the classroom are all ways of ensuring pupils' SMSC development. Pupils must be encouraged to regard people of all faiths, races and cultures with respect and tolerance.

Statutory Inspection of Anglican and Methodist Schools (SIAMS). All Church of England dioceses and the Methodist Church use the Church of England Education Office's framework for the Statutory Inspection of Anglican and Methodist Schools (SIAMS) under Section 48 of the Education Act 2005. SIAMS inspection focuses on the impact of the Church school's Christian vision on pupils and adults.

Teacher research group (TRG). A teacher research group studies teaching and learning strategies, usually via lesson observation, to improve practice collaboratively by developing pedagogy for mastery. TRG originates from teaching observations and educational discussions in Shanghai.

Teaching assistant. A teaching assistant's main role is supporting pupils academically in small groups. By comparison, a learning support assistant is more likely to have a one-to-one role and to be focused on pastoral development (see Higher level teaching assistant, Learning support assistant, Special support assistant).

Teaching and Learning Responsibility (TLR) payment. TLR payments reward additional leadership and management responsibilities undertaken by classroom teachers. Governing bodies determine the overall number of TLR payments available in the school and the levels and values of those payments.

TES (formerly Times Educational Supplement). Weekly publication, with articles aimed at educators. It also has a section where universities, colleges, schools and private educational organisations can advertise job vacancies.

Transactional analysis. The transactional model of stress and coping proposes that stress is experienced as an appraisal or evaluation of the situation we find ourselves in. The transactional model suggests we go through two stages of appraisal before feeling and responding to stress.

Vice-principal. In larger school systems, a principal is the leader of a school who is often assisted by a vice-principal, deputy principal, or assistant/associate principal (*see* Deputy headteacher).

WhatsApp. WhatsApp is a free text and voice messaging service owned by Facebook. WhatsApp allows for messages and calls on both desktop and mobile devices. It is used in schools by teachers to form groups with a common interest, e.g. teachers who teach the same subject. The group's members can send a message to all members of the group at the same time.

World Health Organization (WHO). The World Health Organization is a specialised agency of the United Nations responsible for international public health. The WHO Constitution states its main objective as 'the attainment by all peoples of the highest possible level of health'. Its headquarters is in Geneva, Switzerland, with six semi-autonomous regional offices and 150 field offices worldwide

References

Aldridge, J.M. and McChesney, K. (2018) 'The relationships between school climate and adolescent mental health and wellbeing: A systematic literature review', *International Journal of Educational Research*, 88: 121–145.

Beck, A., Crain, A.L., Solberg, L.I., Unützer, J., Glasgow, R.E., Maciosek, M.V. et al. (2011) 'Severity of depression and magnitude of productivity loss', *Annals of Family Medicine*, 9 (4): 305–311.

Berry, W. (1994) 'Health is Membership'. Delivered as a speech at a conference, 'Spirituality and Healing', at Louisville, Kentucky, on October 17, 1994. Available online at: http://tipiglen.uk/berryhealth.html (accessed 20 September 2020).

Bishop, J. (2017) 'Jeremy Hannay – Three Bridges School, Southall', *A Head of Our Time*, 4 June. Available online at: https://aheadofourtime.co.uk/2017/06/04/jeremy-hannay/ (accessed 20 September 2020).

Chi-Kin Lee, J. (2017) 'Life and work of teachers: Interaction between the individual and the environment', *Teachers and Teaching: Theory and Practice*, 23 (7): 763–765.

Copping, D. (2016) *Eliminating Unnecessary Workload Around Marking: Report of the Independent Teacher Workload Review Group*. Available online at: https://assets.publishing.service.gov.uk/government/uploads/system/uploads/attachment_data/file/511256/Eliminating-unnecessary-workload-around-marking.pdf.

Cowley, A. (2019) *The Wellbeing Toolkit: Sustaining, Supporting and Enabling School Staff*, London: Bloomsbury Education.

Department for Communities and Local Government (DCLG) (2015) *The English Indices of Deprivation 2015*, London: DCLG. Available online at: https://www.gov.uk/government/statistics/english-indices-of-deprivation-2015.

Department for Education (DfE) (2014) *Schools Admissions Code*, London: DfE. Available online at: https://assets.publishing.service.gov.uk/government/uploads/system/uploads/attachment_data/file/389388/School_Admissions_Code_2014_-_19_Dec.pdf (accessed 20 September 2020).

Department for Education (DfE) (2018) *School Workload Reduction Toolkit*, London: DfE (updated 2019). Available online at: https://www.gov.uk/guidance/school-workload-reduction-toolkit (accessed 27 September 2020).

Department for Education (DfE) (2020) 'Update on face coverings in schools', 25 August, London: DfE. Available online at: https://www.gov.uk/government/news/update-on-face-coverings-in-schools.

Dhillon, J., Howard, C. and Holt, J. (2019) 'Outstanding leadership in primary education: Perceptions of school leaders in English primary schools', *Management in Education*, 34 (2): 61–68.

Doyle, G. and Keane, G. (2019) 'Education comes second to surviving: Parental perspectives on their children's early school leaving in an area challenged by marginalisation', *Irish Educational Studies*, 38 (1): 71–88.

EdCentral Team (undated) 'A beginner's guide to: Professor Barak Rosenshine', *EdBlog*. Available online at: https://edcentral.uk/edblog/expert-insight/a-beginners-guide-to-professor-barak-rosenshine (accessed 20 September 2020).

Education Support (2019) *Teacher Wellbeing Index 2019*, London: Education Support.

Evens, M., Elen, J. and Depaepe, F. (2015) 'Developing pedagogical content knowledge: Lessons learned from intervention studies', *Education Research International*, 2015: 790417. Available online at: https://doi.org/10.1155/2015/790417.

Freudenberger, H.J. (1974) 'Staff burnout', *Journal of Social Issues*, 30: 159–165.

Frings, D. (2017) 'The transactional model of stress and coping', *PiB blog post*, December. Available online at: http://psychologyitbetter.com/2017/12 (accessed 29 August 2020).

Glazzard, J. and Rose, A. (2019) 'The impact of teacher wellbeing and mental health on pupil progress in primary schools', Leeds: Carnegie School of Education, Leeds Beckett University. Available online at: https://www.leedsbeckett.ac.uk/carnegie-school-of-education/research/carnegie-centre-of-excellence-for-mental-health-in-schools/school-mental-health-network/-/media/253bcf64213a4a8582a2a0a2be6b1d49.ashx.

Gorard, S. and Siddiqui, N. (2019) 'How trajectories of disadvantage help explain school attainment', *SAGE Open*, 9: 1. Available online at: https://doi.org/10.1177/2158244018825171.

Gray, C., Wilcox, G. and Nordstokke, D. (2017) 'Teacher mental health, school climate, inclusive education and student learning: A review', *Canadian Psychology*, 58 (3): 203–210.

Grayson, J.L. and Alvarez, H.K. (2008) 'School climate factors relating to teacher burnout: A mediator model', *Teaching and Teacher Education*, 24 (5): 1349–1363.

Greenfield, B. (2015) 'How can teacher resilience be protected and promoted?', *Educational and Child Psychology*, 32 (4): 52–69.

Hannay, J. (2019) 'Teachers are miserable because they're being held at gunpoint for meaningless data', *The Guardian*, 30 April. Available online at: https://www.theguardian.com/education/2019/apr/30/why-teachers-miserable-held-gunpoint-meaningless-data (accessed 20 September 2020).

Harding, S., Morris, R., Gunnella, D., Ford, T., Hollingworth, W., Tilling, K. et al. (2019) 'Is teachers' mental health and wellbeing associated with students' mental health and wellbeing?', *Journal of Affective Disorders*, 242: 180–187.

Health and Safety Executive (HSE) (1974) *Health and Safety at Work Act 1974*, London: HSE. Available online at: https://www.hse.gov.uk/legislation/hswa.htm.

Humphries, Z. (2019) 'Why trust is more important than wellbeing', *theHRDIRECTOR*, 22 April. Available online at https://www.thehrdirector.com/features/employee-benefits-reward/trust-important-wellbeing2162019/ (accessed 13 August 2020).

Jain, G., Roy, A., Harikrishnan, V., Yu, S., Dabbous, O. and Lawrence, C. (2013) 'Patient-reported depression severity measured by the PHQ-9 and impact on work productivity: Results from a survey of full-time employees in the United States', *Journal of Occupational and Environmental Medicine*, 55 (3): 252–258.

Jamal, F., Fletcher, A., Harden, A., Wells, H., Thomas, J. and Bonell, C. (2013) 'The school environment and student health: A systematic review and meta-ethnography of qualitative research', *BMC Public Health*, 13: 798. Available online at: https://doi.org/10.1186/1471-2458-13-798.

Jennings, P.A. and Greenberg, M.T. (2009) 'The prosocial classroom: Teacher social and emotional competence in relation to student and classroom outcomes', *Review of Educational Research*, 79 (1): 491–525.

Jones, T. (2020) 'After coronavirus, the penny has dropped that wellbeing isn't individual but social', *The Guardian*, 12 April. Available online at: https://www.theguardian.com/world/2020/apr/12/after-coronavirus-the-penny-has-dropped-that-wellbeing-isnt-individual-but-social.

Justis, N., Litts, B., Reina, L. and Rhodes S. (2020) 'Cultivating staff culture online: How Edith Bowen Laboratory School responded to COVID-19', *Information and Learning Sciences*, 121 (5/6): 453–460.

Kidger, J., Araya, R., Donovan, J. and Gunnell, D. (2012) 'The effect of the school environment on the emotional health of adolescents: A systematic review', *Pediatrics*, 129 (5): 2011–2248.

Kidger, J., Brockman, R., Tilling, K., Campbell, R., Ford, T., Araya, R. et al. (2016) 'Teachers' wellbeing and depressive symptoms, and associated risk factors: A large cross sectional study in English secondary schools', *Journal of Affective Disorders*, 192: 76–82.

Kidger, J., Gunnell, D., Biddle, L., Campbell, R. and Donovan, J. (2010) 'Part and parcel of teaching? Secondary school staff's views on supporting student emotional health and well-being', *British Educational Research Journal*, 36 (6): 919–935.

Kraft, U. (2006) 'Burned out', *Scientific American Mind*, 17 (June/July): 28–33.

Lazarus, R.S. and Folkman, S. (1984) *Stress, Appraisal, and Coping*, New York: Springer.

Leckie, G. and Goldstein, H. (2019) 'The importance of adjusting for pupil background in school value-added models: A study of Progress 8 and school accountability in England', *British Educational Research Journal*, 45 (3): 36–43.

Leiter, M. and Maslach, C. (2005) *Banishing Burnout: Six Strategies for Improving Your Relationship with Work*, San Francisco, CA: Jossey-Bass.

Lester, L., Cefai, C., Cavioni, V., Barnes, A. and Cross D. (2020) 'A whole-school approach to promoting staff wellbeing', *Australian Journal of Teacher Education*, 45: 2. Available online at: https://doi.org/10.14221/ajte.2020v45n2.1.

MacNeil, A.J., Prater, D.L. and Busch, S. (2009) 'The effects of school culture and climate on student achievement', *International Journal of Leadership in Education*, 12 (1): 73–84.

Maslach, C. (1982) *The Cost of Caring*, Englewood Cliffs, NJ: Prentice-Hall.

Maslach, C., Jackson, S.E. and Schwab, R.L. (1986) *MBI: Educators Survey (MBI-ES)*, Menlo Park, CA: Mind Garden, Inc. Available online at: www.mindgarden.com/products/mbi.htm.

Maslach, C. and Leiter, M (2000) *The Truth About Burnout*, San Francisco, CA: Jossey-Bass.

Maslach, C., Schaufeli, W. and Leiter, M. (2001) 'Job burnout', *Annual Review of Psychology*, 52: 397–422.

Maslow, A.H. (1943) 'A theory of human motivation', *Psychological Review*, 50 (4): 370–396.

Michel, A. (2016) 'Burnout and the brain', *Observer*, 29, no. 2 (February), Washington, DC: Association for Psychological Science. Available online at: https://www.psychologicalscience.org/observer/Burnout-and-the-brain#.WS7wRhPytBw (accessed 20 September 2020).

Mind Garden (2019) 'A message from the Maslach Burnout Inventory Authors', *Blog post*, 19 March. Available online at: https://www.mindgarden.com/blog/post/44-a-message-from-the-maslach-Burnout-inventory-authors (accessed 3 September 2020).

Mind Tools (2020) 'Burnout self-test: Checking yourself for burnout', Edinburgh: Emerald Works. Available online at https://www.mindtools.com/pages/article/newTCS_08.htm (accessed 20 September 2020).

NHS (2019) *5 Steps to Mental Wellbeing*. Available online at: https://www.nhs.uk/conditions/stress-anxiety-depression/improve-mental-wellbeing/ (accessed 25 August 2020).

Ofsted (2019a) *Summary and Recommendations: Teacher Well-being Research Report*, July, Manchester: Ofsted. Available online at: https://www.gov.uk/government/publications/teacher-well-being-at-work-in-schools-and-further-education-providers/summary-and-recommendations-teacher-well-being-research-report (accessed 20 September 2020).

Ofsted (2019b) *Teacher Well-being at Work in Schools and Further Education Providers*, July, Manchester: Ofsted. Available online at: https://assets.publishing.service.gov.uk/government/uploads/system/uploads/attachment_data/file/819314/Teacher_well-being_report_110719F.pdf (accessed 27 September 2020).

Ofsted (2019c) *School Inspection Handbook*, Manchester: Ofsted.

Ofsted (2019d) *Ofsted Report for Wayfield Primary School*, Manchester: Ofsted. Available at: https://reports.ofsted.gov.uk/provider/21/143909 (accessed 21 August 2020).

Ofsted (2019e) *Inspection Report: Baines School, 26–27 November 2019*, Manchester: Ofsted. Availabkle online at: https://baines.lancs.sch.uk/wp-content/uploads/2019/12/10110903-Baines-School-119813-Final-PDF.pdf.

Ofsted (2020) *Ofsted Annual Report 2018/19*, Manchester: Ofsted. Available online at: https://www.gov.uk/government/collections/ofsted-annual-report-201819 (accessed 21 August 2020).

Paterson, J. (2013) 'Trust is key to wellbeing and performance in workplace', *Employee Benefits*, 1 July. Available online at: https://employeebenefits.co.uk/issues/july-online-2013/trust-is-key-to-wellbeing-and-performance-in-workplace/ (accessed 13 August 2020).

Plenty, S., Östberg, V., Almquist, Y.B., Augustine, L. and Modin, B. (2014) 'Psychosocial working conditions: An analysis of emotional symptoms and conduct problems amongst adolescent students', *Journal of Adolescence*, 37 (4): 407–417.

Public Health England (PHE) (2014) *The Link between Pupil Health and Wellbeing and Attainment: A Briefing for Head Teachers, Governors and Staff in Education Settings*, London: PHE. Available online at: https://assets.publishing.service.gov.uk/government/uploads/system/uploads/attachment_data/file/370686/HT_briefing_layoutvFINALvii.pdf (accessed 20 September 2020).

Public Health England (PHE) (2015) *Promoting Children and Young People's Emotional Health and Wellbeing: A Whole School and College Approach*, London: PHE.

Schools Week (2020) 'Headteacher Jeremy Hannay speaks to JL Dutaut about beating scepticism and building a culture of trust', *Schools Week*, 28 January. Available online at: https://schoolsweek.co.uk/profile-jeremy-hannay/ (accessed 20 September 2020).

Schratz, M. (2020) *Qualitative Voices in Education*, London: Routledge.

Snell, E., Hindman, A. and Wasik B. (2020) 'Exploring the use of texting to support family–school engagement in early childhood settings: Teacher and family perspectives', *Early Child Development and Care*, 190 (4): 447–460.

Social Mobility Commission (2017) *State of the Nation 2017: Social Mobility in Great Britain*, London: SMC. Available at https://www.gov.uk/government/publications/state-of-the-nation-2017.

Stansfeld, S.A., Rasul, F., Head, J. and Singleton, N. (2011) 'Occupation and mental health in a national UK survey', *Social Psychiatry and Psychiatric Epidemiology*, 46 (2): 101–110.

Stevenson, D. and Farmer, P. (2017) *Thriving at Work: A Review of Mental Health and Employers*, London: DWP/DHSC. Available at https://assets.publishing.service.gov.uk/government/uploads/system/uploads/attachment_data/file/658145/thriving-at-work-stevenson-farmer-review.pdf (accessed 20 September 2020).

Teach Primary (2019) 'How Three Bridges Primary School is taking a fresh approach to the teaching environment', *Teach Primary*, 20 June. Available online at: https://www.teachwire.net/news/how-three-bridges-primary-school-is-taking-a-fresh-approach-to-the-teaching-environment (accessed 20 September 2020).

Thapa, A., Cohen, J., Guffey, S. and Higgins-D'Alessandro, A. (2013) 'A review of school climate research', *Review of Educational Research*, 83 (3): 357–385.

Tiplady, J. (2019) 'Can CPD really tackle staff wellbeing? A wellbeing quick win or just another workload woe?', *TES Institute*, 19 September 2019. Available online at: https://www.tes.com/news/can-cpd-really-tackle-staff-wellbeing (accessed 14 August 2020).

Tomsett, J. and Uttley, J. (2020) *Putting Staff First: A Blueprint for Revitalising Our Schools*, Woodbridge: John Catt.

Van Vliet, V. (2010) 'Tom Peters', *Tools Hero*. Available online at: https://www.toolshero.com/toolsheroes/tom-peters/ (accessed 20 September 2020).

Waters, S. (2019a) 'Teacher Wellbeing Survey, 21st May, 2017 – 12th June, 2019: Key findings', unpublished report. Available online at: https://drive.google.com/file/d/1g_-Sbjwl38_Bv2QzbGicW3zKI1OXEuu-/view?usp=sharing.

Waters, S. (2019b) 'Teachers' Lack of Wellbeing and Mental Ill-Health in Schools: Research report based on a survey of teachers and support staff who experienced a lack of well-being and mental ill-health while working in a school', unpublished report. Available online at: https://drive.google.com/file/d/180qqKMDUC9DYxNk_WmPIdbNhF1BTwsqF/view?usp=sharing.

Wiliam, D. (2018) *Creating the Schools Our Children Need: Why What We're Doing Now Won't Help Much (and What We Can Do Instead)*, West Palm Beach, FL: Learning Sciences International.

World Health Organization (WHO) (2014) 'Mental health: A state of wellbeing', Geneva: WHO. Available online at: http://www.who.int/features/factfiles/mental_health/en/ (accessed 8 August 2019).

World Health Organization (WHO) (2019) 'Burn-out an "occupational phenomenon": International Classification of Diseases', 28 May, Geneva: WHO. Available online at: https://www.who.int/mental_health/evidence/burn-out/en/ (accessed 11 September 2020).

World Health Organization (WHO) (2020) 'Coronavirus disease (COVID-19): Children and masks', 21 August, Geneva: WHO. Available online at: https://www.who.int/news-room/q-a-detail/q-a-children-and-masks-related-to-covid-19.

Index